Language Policy

Volume 17

Series Editor
Joseph Lo Bianco, University of Melbourne, Australia
Terrence G. Wiley, Professor Emeritus, Arizona State University, USA

Editorial Board
Claire Kramsch, University of California at Berkeley, USA
Georges Lüdi, University of Basel, Switzerland
Normand Labrie, University of Toronto, Ontario, Canada
Anne Pakir, National University of Singapore, Singapore
John Trim, Former Fellow, Selwyn College, Cambridge, UK
Guadalupe Valdes, Stanford University, USA

The last half century has witnessed an explosive shift in language diversity not unlike the Biblical story of the Tower of Babel, but involving now a rapid spread of global languages and an associated threat to small languages. The diffusion of global languages, the stampede towards English, the counter-pressures in the form of ethnic efforts to reverse or slow the process, the continued determination of nation-states to assert national identity through language, and, in an opposite direction, the greater tolerance shown to multilingualism and the increasing concern for language rights, all these are working to make the study of the nature and possibilities of language policy and planning a field of swift growth.

The series will publish empirical studies of general language policy or of language education policy, or monographs dealing with the theory and general nature of the field. We welcome detailed accounts of language policy-making - who is involved, what is done, how it develops, why it is attempted. We will publish research dealing with the development of policy under different conditions and the effect of implementation. We will be interested in accounts of policy development by governments and governmental agencies, by large international companies, foundations, and organizations, as well as the efforts of groups attempting to resist or modify governmental policies. We will also consider empirical studies that are relevant to policy of a general nature, e.g. the local effects of the developing European policy of starting language teaching earlier, the numbers of hours of instruction needed to achieve competence, selection and training of language teachers, the language effects of the Internet. Other possible topics include the legal basis for language policy, the role of social identity in policy development, the influence of political ideology on language policy, the role of economic factors, policy as a reflection of social change.

The series is intended for scholars in the field of language policy and others interested in the topic, including sociolinguists, educational and applied linguists, language planners, language educators, sociologists, political scientists, and comparative educationalists.

More information about this series at http://www.springer.com/series/6209

Jennifer Joan Baldwin

Languages other than English in Australian Higher Education

Policies, Provision, and the National Interest

Jennifer Joan Baldwin
Faculty of Arts
University of Melbourne
Melbourne, VIC, Australia

ISSN 1571-5361 ISSN 2452-1027 (electronic)
Language Policy
ISBN 978-3-030-05794-7 ISBN 978-3-030-05795-4 (eBook)
https://doi.org/10.1007/978-3-030-05795-4

Library of Congress Control Number: 2019931022

© Springer Nature Switzerland AG 2019
This work is subject to copyright. All rights are reserved by the Publisher, whether the whole or part of the material is concerned, specifically the rights of translation, reprinting, reuse of illustrations, recitation, broadcasting, reproduction on microfilms or in any other physical way, and transmission or information storage and retrieval, electronic adaptation, computer software, or by similar or dissimilar methodology now known or hereafter developed.
The use of general descriptive names, registered names, trademarks, service marks, etc. in this publication does not imply, even in the absence of a specific statement, that such names are exempt from the relevant protective laws and regulations and therefore free for general use.
The publisher, the authors, and the editors are safe to assume that the advice and information in this book are believed to be true and accurate at the date of publication. Neither the publisher nor the authors or the editors give a warranty, express or implied, with respect to the material contained herein or for any errors or omissions that may have been made. The publisher remains neutral with regard to jurisdictional claims in published maps and institutional affiliations.

This Springer imprint is published by the registered company Springer Nature Switzerland AG.
The registered company address is: Gewerbestrasse 11, 6330 Cham, Switzerland

Dedicated to Amanda Marie Burritt

Contents

1 **Introduction** 1
   1.1 Australia: The British Colony 1
   1.2 Research Questions 3
   1.3 Themes 5
   1.4 Discussion of Literature and Other Sources 8
   1.5 Overview of the Book 13
   1.6 Conclusion 15

2 **The Founding of Australian Universities** 17
   2.1 The Foundation of Universities in the Colonies 18
   2.2 Two British Colonies: Canada and New Zealand 20
   2.3 A Second University in Melbourne, Australia 21
   2.4 A Third Colonial University in Adelaide 23
   2.5 The Later Colonial Universities 24
   2.6 The Language Offerings of the Universities 26
   2.7 The Importance of the Classical Languages 26
   2.8 Modern European Languages 29
   2.9 The Melbourne Solution for More Languages 36
   2.10 Asian Languages 38
   2.11 Conclusion 42

3 **Post-War Expansion** 45
   3.1 Post-World War II Australia 47
   3.2 The Mills Report: The First Reckoning 50
   3.3 Murray Report and More Commonwealth Control 52
   3.4 Martin Report: A New Framework for Higher Education 55
   3.5 The First Survey of Language Teaching 59
   3.6 Auchmuty Report: The First Asian Languages Report 60
   3.7 Concurrent Language Surveys: Kramer and the Academy
       of the Humanities 61
   3.8 The Galbally Report: Migrant Services and Programs 65
   3.9 National Policy on Languages 68

    3.10 The Dawkins Era: Reforms and More Reports 69
    3.11 Conclusion 73

4 Australia: Both Multicultural and Multilingual 75
    4.1 Migration to Australia 76
    4.2 Academic Interest in Migrant Languages 80
    4.3 Assimilation to Integration 82
    4.4 The End of the White Australia Policy and the White
        Zealand Policy 85
    4.5 Kramer Report: A Timely Report into Languages 88
    4.6 A New Government in a New Era 90
    4.7 Galbally Report: A Report for Migrant Services 91
    4.8 The Consequences for Community Languages 95
    4.9 The Fortunes of Ukrainian and Yiddish: Case Studies 98
    4.10 Conclusion 102

5 Three Trade Languages: Japanese, Chinese and Indonesian 105
    5.1 Australia/Japan Contact Begins with Trade 106
    5.2 Japanese Language 107
    5.3 Defence Needs Japanese Skills 110
    5.4 From Defence Needs to Trade Needs 111
    5.5 The Influence of Universities on Japanese in Schools 113
    5.6 Chinese Migration to Australia 115
    5.7 Trade and Diplomacy with China 117
    5.8 The Imperative for Chinese Language Teaching 118
    5.9 Oriental and Asian Studies Expand 120
    5.10 Official Recognition of China 123
    5.11 Indonesia: Trade First Then Security and Defence 125
    5.12 Government Commitment to Indonesian Language Teaching 127
    5.13 Auchmuty and Kramer Reports: Stocktakes for All Languages ... 129
    5.14 The Testing of Diplomatic Relations and Language Popularity ... 130
    5.15 Conclusion 134

6 Three Strategic Languages: Russian, Korean and Arabic 137
    6.1 Early Australian Relationships with Russia 139
    6.2 Russian Language Begins at University of Melbourne 141
    6.3 Collapse of Soviet Union 146
    6.4 Australia's Relationship with Korea 148
    6.5 Arabic: A Pluricentric and Religious Language 152
    6.6 Arabic as a Scholarly Language 152
    6.7 Arabic as a Migrant Language 154
    6.8 Arabic as a Trade Language 157
    6.9 Waning Support for Arabic in the Universities 158
    6.10 Conclusion 159

Contents

7 Languages in the 1990s: The Context and the Changes 161
    7.1   Comparison of University Languages Structures 162
    7.2   A Case Study of the University of Melbourne 164
    7.3   A Review of Languages 170
    7.4   The New School of Languages at the University of Melbourne 173
    7.5   Other Universities' Languages Structures in 1999 175
    7.6   Political Implications for Languages 178
    7.7   Reports from the Academic Sector 179
    7.8   Conclusion 182

8 The Asian or Global Century? 183
    8.1   Government Languages Policy from Mid 1990s to Early 2000s ... 184
    8.2   Internationalisation 187
    8.3   Differing Understanding of the Role of Languages 188
    8.4   Australia in the Asian Century 190
    8.5   The New Colombo Plan 191
    8.6   The Languages Component of the Australian Curriculum 193
    8.7   The Stakeholders for Languages 195
    8.8   Current Issues: Collaborative Arrangements 196
    8.9   New Models: University of Melbourne and UWA 198
    8.10 New Countries (and Languages) of National Interest? 200
    8.11 The Global Perspective: Languages Elsewhere
          in the English-Speaking World 201
    8.12 Conclusion 205

9 Conclusion 207

Appendices 213

Bibliography 225

Abbreviations

AACLAME	Australian Advisory Council on Languages and Multicultural Education
AAH	Australian Academy of the Humanities
ABC	Australian Broadcasting Commission
ACPEA	Australian Council on Population and Ethnic Affairs
AFMLTA	Australian Federation of Modern Language Teachers Associations
AHRC	Australian Humanities Research Council
AIMA	Australian Institute of Multicultural Affairs
ALLP	Australian Language and Literacy Policy
ALP	Australian Labor Party
ALTC	Australian Learning and Teaching Council
ANU	Australian National University
ASEAN	Association of Southeast Asian Nations
AUC	Australian Universities Commission
AVCC	Australian Vice-Chancellors' Committee
BHP	Broken Hill Proprietary Company Limited
BRITAC	British Academy for the Humanities and Social Sciences
CAAR	Council for Australian-Arab Relations
CAE	College of Advanced Education
CEDA	Committee for Economic Development of Australia
C of A	Commonwealth of Australia
CLOTE	Community Language Other Than English
COAG	Council of Australian Governments
ComDepEd	Commonwealth Department of Education
CSIRO	Commonwealth Scientific and Industrial Research Organisation
CTEC	Commonwealth Tertiary Education Commission
CUC	Canberra University College
CURA	Centre for Urban Research and Action
DEET	Department of Education, Employment and Training
DEETYA	Department of Employment, Education, Training and Youth Affairs
DEST	Department of Education, Science and Training

DFAT	Department of Foreign Affairs and Trade
DIMIA	Department of Immigration and Multicultural and Indigenous Affairs
EFTSL	Equivalent Fulltime Student Load
EFTSU	Equivalent Fulltime Student Unit
ECC	Ethnic Communities Council
FSU	Former Soviet Union
Go8	Group of Eight
HEFCE	Higher Education Funding Council for England
HEFPRCA	Higher Education Financing and Policy Review Committee (Australia)
JCP	Joint Committee on Policy
JSCFADT	Joint Standing Committee on Foreign Affairs, Defence and Trade
LC	Legislative Council
LOTE	Language Other Than English
MGHS	MacRobertson Girls' High School
MEA	Migrant Education Action
MIAESR	Melbourne Institute of Applied Economic and Social Research
NALCWG	National Asian Languages and Cultures Working Group
NALSAS	National Asian Languages and Studies in Australian Schools
NCEIS	National Centre for Excellence in Islamic Studies
NKSC	National Korean Studies Centre
NLA	National Library of Australia
NPL	National Policy on Languages
NSWUT	New South Wales University of Technology
NUC	Newcastle University College
SHAPS	School of Historical and Philosophical Studies, University of Melbourne
SIT	Swinburne Institute of Technology
TAFE	Technical and Further Education
TEC	Tertiary Education Commission
UMA	University of Melbourne Archives
UniMelb	University of Melbourne
UNSW	University of New South Wales
UniSyd	University of Sydney
UTas	University of Tasmania
VTAC	Victorian Tertiary Admissions Centre
VUAC	Victorian Universities Admissions Committee
VUSEB	Victorian Universities and Schools Examinations Board

List of Tables

Table 5.1 Matriculation Japanese candidates 1967–1974 114

Table 8.1 Enrolments on first beginners' language unit,
by language- UWA 199

Chapter 1
Introduction

> Languages are a vital part of a well-rounded education for all Australian students as citizens of a rapidly expanding world. (Lo Bianco, Nettelbeck, Hajek, & Woods, 2011)

This thought-provoking statement from the executive of the Languages and Cultures Network for Australian Universities reflected that lobby group's strong belief in the importance of languages other than English to Australian higher education, and society more generally, in the twenty-first century, as well as a need for urgent discussions about the importance of languages. However, the extent to which languages have been valued by governments and universities as an essential component of education has varied throughout Australia's history since colonial times. As part of the British Empire and subsequently, when Australia became a federated nation, its British traditions and the English language were at the heart of its burgeoning school and university education systems. That tradition included the classical languages, Latin and Ancient Greek. Thereafter the influences on language offerings widened as Australia as a nation became a distinct entity in the international scene.

In this chapter I introduce the topics of this book: the foundations of Australian tertiary teaching in languages, the policies which have framed developments in language offerings, the distinct multiculturalism which evolved in Australia, and the growth of Australia's strategic and economic involvement with Asia. I will discuss the context for investigating tertiary languages, how languages may be seen in the national interest of Australia and the themes on which this research is based, offering a clearer understanding for the contemporary issues for languages in Australia.

1.1 Australia: The British Colony

Notwithstanding British settlement of Australia, researchers have however, drawn attention to the fact that Australian colonial society was not solely English-speaking. Apart from English, the major languages in nineteenth century Australia were

German, Chinese, Scottish Gaelic, Irish Gaelic, French, Italian, Danish, Welsh and a multiplicity of indigenous languages (Clyne & Kipp, 2006, p. 8). When Australia became a federation, legislation was enacted to exclude migrants who did not fit the nation's sense of its British-based identity. As the twentieth century unfolded, that sense of identity and Australia's place in the international community changed, as did the size, cultural and ethnic mix of its population. It was the need for a larger population to facilitate economic development post-World War II which fuelled that cultural and ethnic change as Australia opened itself up to a greater diversity of ethnic peoples. By the latter years of the twentieth century, Australia had transformed itself from a geographically isolated outpost of the British Empire to an independent, multilingual and multicultural nation (Clyne, 2003, p. 17).

Australia's evolution into a multicultural nation was eventually reflected in Australia's first language policy, the *National Policy on Languages* (NPL), commissioned by the Hawke Labor government, published in 1987, with most of its budgetary recommendations accepted by the government (Lo Bianco, 1987). This policy, according to its author, Joseph Lo Bianco, was formulated to consider 'the linguistic diversity of Australia, the need for national unity, the external, economic and political needs of the nation and the wishes and needs of Australia's citizens' (Lo Bianco, 1987, p. 4). Such a policy with its clear public expectations would enable Australia 'to plan those aspects of its international, trade, economic and diplomatic relationships which relate to language in an objective and rational way'. Australia's recognition of its multiculturalism and multilingualism were drivers for a national coordinated policy (Senate Standing Committee on Education and the Arts, 1984, p. 2). This policy was intended to give recognition and support for Australia's diverse languages, to 'enrich Australia's cultural, artistic and intellectual life', to improve communication generally in society and enable migrants' voices to be heard (Lo Bianco, 1987, p. 4; Rickard, 1996, p. 230).

The NPL gave credence to Australia's multilingualism as an essential part of the nation's culture, which along with diverse traditions contributed to the national identity. There has been a lively scholarship on the development of Australian national identity and its development over time (Anderson, 1983; Curran & Ward, 2010; Inglis, 1991; Rickard, 1996; White, 1981), particularly from writers such as Richard White, Benedict Anderson and John Rickard. White contended that images of nation are constructed reflecting prevailing concerns over time. As he said, it is not which ideas about national identity are true or false but 'what their function is, whose creation they are, and whose interests they serve.' (White, R., 1991, pp. viii, ix). Anderson stressed the importance of language for generating imagined communities and as a core component of national identity (Anderson, 1983, pp. 122, 123). Rickard charted the evolution of cultural identity of Australia through changing relationships with Britain, the United States and the Asian region, and the post-World War II demographic changes (Rickard, 1996, pp. xiii, 217, 218, 226, 277).

This book builds on that scholarship by exploring the presence of languages other than English in Australia's university sector as an aspect of that national identity. The changing attitudes towards, and values attached to, the place of languages within national priorities and educational interests can be tracked not only through the multiplicity of reviews from the 1950s to the 2000s into both higher education and tertiary language offerings, but also in successive government iterations of 'the national interest' as this relates to language teaching and cultural literacy. Coupled with this constant reviewing of the higher education sector had been the increased scrutiny and auditing of the sector requiring 'tangible benefits' for the justification of federal funding (Forsyth, 2014, p. 59, 140, 141).

I have investigated the study of languages other than English,[1] and their place in the tertiary sector in Australia from the founding of the first universities in the 1850s up to the present day. Chronologically, languages are examined in the context of the histories of Australian universities, and the series of reports and surveys about languages across the second half of the twentieth century. The implications of the sector becoming a unified national and regulated system are explored. This study is couched in an historical context to illustrate current concerns about languages, reflecting on the influence of social and cultural change. Central to the broader national context for language policy are the demographic and cultural shifts in post-World War II Australia.

I demonstrate how changes in the ethnic mix of society are reflected in language offerings, and how policies on languages have changed as a result of societal influences. For example, Australian census data on languages other than English spoken at home illustrate the changing ethnic mix of the population. In the 1986 census the top five languages in order were Italian, Greek, Chinese, German, Arabic/Lebanese (Australian Bureau of Statistics (ABS), 1986, p. 17), whereas in the 1996 census the top five languages were Italian, Greek, Cantonese, Arabic (including Lebanese), and Vietnamese (ABS, 1996, p. 1). As a striking contrast, the top five languages other than English spoken at home in the most recent Australian census of 2011 were Mandarin, Italian, Arabic, Cantonese and Greek, showing the increasing number of Australians who spoke an Asian language at home (ABS, 2011b, p. 9). These different ethnic mixes at different times have influenced the teaching of various community languages, the ethnic composition of lobby groups and philanthropy from various ethnic groups. I also demonstrate how, as various aspects of the national interest, such as defence, geopolitical, economic and social have changed over time, the status and place of particular languages within university curricula have consequently been affected.

1.2 Research Questions

In identifying and examining a range of factors which influenced the teaching of languages in Australia from colonial times to the twenty-first century, several key questions are addressed. These include the extent to which influencing factors changed over time depending on social, cultural, political and economic contexts,

---

[1] Languages other than English here include foreign languages, but do not include the Indigenous languages of Australia.

and the extent to which governments prioritised the promotion and funding of languages because of their perceived contribution to the national interest.

Although there is significant scholarship on the history of universities in Australia and on higher education policy, such as that of Simon Marginson (1997, 2002, 2013), Allan Barcan (1980), Tony Coady (2000), and more recently Hannah Forsyth's *A History of the Modern Australian University* (2014), there has been no systematic documentation and analysis of the history of language teaching in the tertiary sector. Initially this book demonstrates that classical and modern European languages, as part of a nineteenth century liberal education, were seen by the early colonial leaders as an important contribution to the development of the future leadership of the nation. The main emphasis will be to document the situation of language teaching and show how it has changed as the nation's industrial, technological and scientific research capabilities developed throughout the twentieth century, with the post-World War II university expansion.

The numbers of people seeking tertiary education had begun to increase rapidly by the middle 1950s (Commonwealth of Australia (C of A), 1957, pp. 81–82; C of A, 1964, p. 1). Universities had moved from being places symbolic of the elite and high culture, to places whereby from the mid-1960s, students from much wider demographic backgrounds were enrolling (Forsyth, 2014, pp. 11, 68). The 1964 Martin Report quoted 17,066 university students enrolled in 1946 increasing to 69,074 in 1963 (C of A, 1964, p. 12). At this time with increasing regional interaction based on trade, government rhetoric was starting to suggest that Australians should become more Asia-literate, both in knowledge of culture and languages (Andrews, 1988, p. 144; C of A, 1970, p. 7). This book addresses the question of the relationship between this political and economic context and languages. In the framework of changing economic and social attitudes and values and the ethnic diversification of the population, an examination of the expansion of the tertiary sector in the 1960s, 1970s and 1980s is undertaken. A range of factors which led to institutional and educational priorities for language offerings in this context will be identified and their influences evaluated.

As the tertiary sector developed in the twentieth century, numerous reports and surveys both about higher education and language offerings, were produced. The question which is addressed is how, through the results of those reports and surveys, the higher education sector was shaped by government policies over the latter half of the twentieth century. The public university sector grew rapidly from eight universities in 1949 to 19 universities by 1975. Subsequent reviews and reports trace aspirations for the tertiary sector as a whole, as well as shifting priorities for, and concerns about, language offerings (C of A, 1970; Australian Universities Commission (AUC), 1975a; Lo Bianco, 1987; Department of Employment, Education and Training (DEET), 1991a; National Asian Languages & Cultures Working Group (NALCWG), 1994). The 1990s and 2000s are examined given large structural changes in the tertiary sector resulting from the formation of the Unified National System (DEET, 1988). A sense of crisis for university languages was signalled as academic surveys of the late 1990s reported on the costs of language teaching and significant losses in the number of language offerings nationally. As a

1998 Australian Academy of the Humanities (AAH) report pointed out: 'language teaching needs to be funded at a higher level than for many Humanities subjects because it is teaching-intensive' AAH, 1998, p. 68). These reports of the late 1990s and into the early 2000s are explored to see whether all languages were affected, or only those not deemed by government to need prioritisation for Australia's national interests (AAH, 2000; NALCWG, 1994; White, Baldauf, & Diller, 1997). Not all reports were negative or involved the higher education sector. The 1994 government-commissioned report into Asian languages (by the NALCWG, known as the Rudd Report) recommended substantial Asian languages funding for the school sector beginning at Year Three. Subsequent research findings showed a more than 50% increase in government primary and secondary school students studying an Asian language from 1994 to 1997 (Henderson, 2007, pp. 8, 15).

This research examines what the roles of business and trade, ethnic and migrant organisations, and philanthropy have been in relation to language offerings. This research will question also the influence that various waves of migration have had on attitudes to, and the increase in, the teaching of community languages, as well as the rise of teaching English as a second language.

The language plurality of Australia includes many indigenous languages variously estimated as somewhere between 200 and 250 distinct languages in 1788 at the time of white settlement. Linguists have contended that it is difficult to be precise because of numbers of dialects for these languages (Dixon, 1980, p. 18; Walsh, 1993, p. 1). Walsh cited a study which had estimated 'that 160 languages are extinct, 70 are under threat and only 20 are likely to survive' (Walsh, 1993, p. 2). Whilst indigenous languages have been taught in linguistics and anthropology departments in the past, a 2011 survey of university language offerings showed that three indigenous languages were taught at three separate universities, two of which were in specialised indigenous/aboriginal studies departments (Dunne & Pavlyshyn, 2011, pp. 18, 19). These are not part of the scope of this book which concentrates on foreign languages which have been brought to Australia as part of British language teaching traditions as well as those languages brought to Australia in various waves of migration.

1.3 Themes

The first of the key themes is that of the overriding issue of national interest. The term national interest is used as a thread throughout this study to track reasons for decisions about language offerings and to analyse how successive governments, educationalists and interest groups understood Australia's evolving identity and place in the world. As Joseph Frankel contended in his 1970 *National Interest*, the term is 'a singularly vague concept, which assumes a variety of meanings in the various ways it is used, meanings which often cannot be reconciled' (Frankel, 1970, p. 15). This definition meshes with the uses of national interest discussed, where the national interest refers to those actions, decisions and policies which governments, educationalists, and interest groups believe will further develop Australia as a nation. Throughout the twentieth century, the idea of national interest was often applied by governments to economic, strategic, defence, cultural and social priorities and programs in accordance with their political aims, objectives and ambitions. The Howard Coalition government highlighted national interest in their two White Papers, *In the National Interest,* in 1997 (C of A, 1997), and *Advancing the National Interest,* in 2003, which reiterated the Coalition's strategies encompassing both economic prosperity and the strengthening of security as important for Australia's national interest (C of A, 2003, p. vii). This book demonstrates that decisions about tertiary language offerings were rarely made on purely academic or cultural grounds but were more often decisions made for financial and budgetary reasons.

The second theme discussed is the changing demographics of the Australian population and the change to a policy of multiculturalism which is traced from the mass migration of the late 1940s up to the 1970s, which was called the decade of multiculturalism by the linguist, Suzanne Romaine (Romaine, 1991, p. 5). The many reports and reviews of government programs examined demonstrate that Federal governments were gradually coming to grips with the multicultural and multilingual nature of Australia (C of A, 1978; Department of Education, 1979; Australian Institute of Multicultural Affairs (AIMA), 1980; Australian Council on Population and Ethnic Affairs (ACPEA), 1982; Commonwealth Schools Commission, 1984). The population increased by 38% between 1947 (the year the mass migration program began) and 1961, and then by 68% between 1947 and 1971, with increasing numbers of migrants from non-English speaking backgrounds (Department of Immigration and Multicultural Affairs (DIMA), 2001, pp. 18, 19). The 2011 census reported that 76.8% of Australia's population spoke only English at home, whilst the most commonly spoken languages, other than English, included Mandarin (1.6%), Italian (1.4%), Arabic (1.3%), Cantonese (1.2%) and Greek (1.2%), showing the language diversity of Australia in the early twenty-first century (ABS, 2011a).

Issues on migration and multiculturalism are highlighted through an exploration of the work of key writers. Jean Martin contributed important seminal research in 1978 on migrants and non-migrants in Australian society (Martin, 1978). James Jupp and Jerzy Zubrzycki were also important commentators on multiculturalism and migration (Jupp, 1966, 1989, 1993, 1996, 2011; Zubrzycki, 1991). Zubrzycki, as early as 1968, wrote of the diversity of cultures and languages in Australia as 'a natural resource' which should not be wasted (Zubrzycki, 1968, p. 25). Together with these studies, the work of other commentators such as Lois Foster and David Stockley (Foster & Stockley, 1984), and Christine Inglis (2004), is analysed in the discussion on multiculturalism. Michael Clyne, a prominent linguist, summed up the connection between multiculturalism and languages when he wrote: 'Multiculturalism legitimizes all languages used in the Australia community (Clyne, 1991, p. 34). This significant policy shift to promote multiculturalism led to increased support for community languages, particularly through ethnic lobby groups and philanthropic support. However, one aspect of government policies at this time, as will be shown, was the increasing emphasis on English proficiency which came to have the greatest priority with significant funding by 1991.

1.3 Themes

Australia's changing regional trade and security policies with Asia and consequent Asian language prioritisation is the third theme explored. The changing attitudes to Asia are tracked from the restrictive immigration policy of White Australia and much anti-Asian sentiment in the late nineteenth and early twentieth centuries to an opening up of trade with the Asian region. As the proportion of migrants to Australia born in Asia increased, so did the importance of Australia's trade with Asia. Chinese-born migrants, for instance, had increased from 4766 in the years 1975–1980 to 16,000 in the years 1985–1990, and then 36,288 in the years 1995–2000 (ABS, 2011b, p. 27). By 2014, China was reported as Australia's largest trading partner for both imports and exports (Department of Foreign Affairs and Trade (DFAT), 2014, p. 1).

Several key reports are examined in this analysis – known popularly as, the 1970 Auchmuty Report, the 1994 Rudd Report, the 2012 Asian Century Report and the 2013 New Colombo Plan (C of A, 1970; NALCWG, 1994; Australian Government, 2011; DFAT, 2013b) – to show the changing emphases of governments towards engagement with Asia. The history of Australia's teaching of several Asian languages, Japanese, Chinese, Indonesian and Korean is investigated in depth to demonstrate the influence of Federal government policy on tertiary language offerings. As the more recent government reports showed, Australia's refocus away from Britain and Europe and towards engagement with Asia continued to be the government's primary economic focus. This was clearly reflected in the prioritisation of Asian languages but significantly, funding was directed only to the primary and secondary school sector not the tertiary sector.

A fourth theme is that of international influences. These can firstly be seen by the influence of British universities such as Oxford, Cambridge and Trinity College, Dublin as models for the colonial universities of Australia. Subsequent influences came from Europe and America as the post-Federation universities of Queensland and Western Australia widened the extent of their investigation of appropriate university models (Forsyth, 2014, p. 7). A further iteration of international influences has been the internationalising of the student body. Marginson quotes a rise of international student numbers from 24,998 in 1990 to 83,047 in 1998 following the deregulation of fee charging for international students in 1985. Australia became the third largest provider of international education in the world after the USA and the UK (Marginson, 2002, p. 424). The ABS data showed China, India, South Korea, Brazil and Malaysia as the top five countries from where international students came to study in Australia (ABS, 2011c, p. 4).

The international education sector had become very important to Australia's economy contributing $16.3 billion in export income in the financial year 2010/2011 (ABS, 2011c, p. 2). With Chinese language enrolments particularly, numbers rose significantly with an influx of Chinese-speaking international students. However, as McLaren commented, this could result in Chinese becoming a 'ghetto' language taken only by students of Chinese background (McLaren, 2011, pp. 4, 6). Coupled with significant international student enrolments, was the growing push for internationalisation of the curriculum within universities, which acknowledged the diversity of the student body, although, as I will show, languages have rarely been articulated as an essential part of that internationalisation process (Baik, 2013, p. 132; Li, 2012, p. 50; Rizvi & Walsh, 1998, p. 9)

Whilst this book is not one that is comparative in its investigation, it will show in Chap. 8, by its examination of language policy in Australian higher education, that the challenges for language learning in the twenty-first century parallel those in other countries. The issues relating to language teaching, which have been crucial in Australia, have been similar to the issues which concerned universities in other English-speaking countries such as the United Kingdom, the United States and New Zealand and several examples are cited. UK studies by the Higher Education Funding Council of England in 2009 (Worton, 2009), and the British Academy for the humanities and social sciences (Britac) in 2009 and 2013 (Britac, 2009, 2013) showed that the common issues were a decline in the numbers taking foreign languages, funding provisions and the crisis for university language departments. A report by the University Alliance in the UK traced the decline in secondary school language learning from 2004, the year when compulsory study of a foreign language for 14 to 16-year-olds was removed (Universities Alliance, n.d.). A 2013 international languages forum in the United States acknowledged the common issues faced by English-speaking countries: the vicious circle of monolingualism, the deficit of people with the language skills needed for global economies, and the range of languages taught not being sufficient for current or future demand (Brecht, 2013, pp. 3, 6, 37). Whilst issues in common were very apparent, this book will show how such concerns have been raised and tackled in the Australian context.

1.4 Discussion of Literature and Other Sources

A key framework for this discussion has been the successive government and institutional reports on both higher education reform and development, and on language teaching more specifically, that have been issues since the 1960s. These numerous reports produced from the mid to late twentieth century formed the bulk of literature on both higher education and language policy underpinning ongoing reforms. Much of the work undertaken in this extensive body of reports by academics, government policy-makers, and business people, has been in the form of surveys, gathering and interpreting data from Australian universities. These reports and surveys give an understanding of government and academic interest in higher education generally, and languages other than English specifically. The social, political and economic attitudes to languages are gleaned especially through foreign affairs and trade policies, as well as language policies. The 1966 Wykes Report (so called for its committee chair, Olive Wykes), the first to draw together data on language offerings in Australian universities, commented on apathy towards languages (Wykes, 1966). The 1975 AAH Report, which updated Wykes' data, expressed concern for the rapidly falling demand for languages (AAH, 1975, p. 41).

The 1975 Kramer Report (so called for its working party chair, Leonie Kramer) added to the data available on languages offered, although the Kramer Working

1.4 Discussion of Literature and Other Sources

Party had drawn on existing university submissions, whereas the AAH had drawn its data from a much wider variety of sources (AAH, 1975, p. 6; AUC, 1975a, p. 6). Daniel Hawley's 1982 report (Hawley, 1982, p. 1) detailed institutional language offerings and student numbers for individual languages. Hawley's report was significant and much more comprehensive, because he surveyed not only universities but also colleges of advanced education, teachers' colleges and institutes of technology. The earlier Kramer and AAH Reports had only included universities. The 1991 Leal Report (known for its chair, Barry Leal) contributed an enormous amount of data on language offerings in Australian higher education institutions (Leal, 1991a, 1991b). Academics such as Joseph Lo Bianco and Inna Gvozdenko considered the Report wide ranging in its analysis and important for its examination of modes of language delivery (Lo Bianco & Gvozdenko, 2006, p. 45).

Whilst there was no other government-commissioned report on languages after the Leal Report, it will be shown that academic researchers, such as Richard Baldauf Jr. and Peter White, kept the issues of language offerings well to the fore in the Australian tertiary sector in the late 1990s and into the 2000s. Their particular contributions were research on small and low candidature languages, alternative delivery modes and collaborative arrangements between various universities (Baldauf, 1995; Baldauf & Djité, 2000; Baldauf & White, 2010; White et al., 1997). They also collaborated in producing reports for the AAH and for the Deans of Arts, Social Sciences and Humanities, drawing attention to a serious situation for languages vis-à-vis under-resourcing and under-funding in the late 1990s (White et al., 1997; White & Baldauf, 2006). The 2000 AAH Report also highlighted the importance of maintaining languages with smaller enrolments 'in order to sustain a nationwide intellectual infrastructure' (AAH, 1998, 2000, p. 45). Together, these various reports constituted a solid history of data for language offerings, all of which demonstrated that tertiary languages were discussed increasingly from the 1960s into the 2000s when they were considered to be in a state of crisis going into the twenty-first century.

In the national context, the broader field of higher education and language policy has been explored through key sources such as the work of Simon Marginson (1997, 2002, 2013). Marginson has written extensively on the macro issues of the politics of education and the relationship between funding and the changing nature of the university in the global environment. In this context though, he does allude briefly to the monolingual environment of Australia and the need to develop its linguistic capability (Marginson, 2002, p. 426). Tony Coady's edited publication *Why universities matter* explores values, concerns and future directions of Australian universities and contains much about university policy making and tensions between academic and senior management in decision-making, although nothing at the micro level about languages in the curriculum (Coady, 2000).

To gain a broad perspective of the history of Australian higher education, the national context of its development and the language offerings of individual institutions, this book draws on the myriad of institutional histories which have been published. The early colonial universities reflected British traditions in their commitment to particular languages. The evolution of that colonial society into a distinctly Australian society was reflected in the changing attitudes to languages offerings in the universities founded in the latter half of the twentieth century. Discussion about languages curricula was included in the histories of the Universities of Sydney (Connell, Sherington, Fletcher, Turney, & Bygott, 1995; Turney, Bygott, & Chippendale, 1991) and Melbourne (Selleck, 2003), as was also true of the histories of the Universities of Queensland, Adelaide and Western Australia (Alexander, 1963; de Garis, 1988; Duncan & Leonard, 1973; Thomis, 1985). This showed the status which languages had as an essential part of those early university establishments.

It was Victor Edgeloe, a registrar emeritus[2] of the University of Adelaide, who documented the most extensive information on languages at that University (Edgeloe, 1990, 2003). As will be discussed, the ANU did not teach languages until, in 1960, the Canberra University College (CUC) with its established language offerings, was subsumed into the ANU (Foster & Varghese, 1996, pp. 144, 151, 303). In the first two of the three Monash University histories, there were references to languages being a part of the establishment of that University's offerings (Blackwood, 1968; Matheson, 1980) but, in the most recent history (Davison & Murphy, 2012) there were but two scant references to languages indicating that for those historians, the story of Monash's language offerings were not a priority.

Of the universities founded in the 1960s, the Flinders (Hilliard, 1991), Newcastle (Wright, 1992) and Macquarie (Mansfield & Hutchinson, 1992) histories made only brief mention of language offerings, whereas the La Trobe history discussed in detail the academic planning which took place regarding appropriate language offerings (Breen, 1989; Myers, 1989, p. 34). The histories of the universities founded in the 1970s are rather different stories. Both the James Cook and Murdoch University histories commented on Asian languages, reflecting the growing awareness for Australia of its relationship to Asia (Bell, 2010, p. 49; Bolton, 1985, p. 41). Deakin University (Hay, Lowe & Gibb, 2002) did not teach languages at all, because language laboratories were considered too expensive and funds were very tight when Deakin was founded (Hay, personal communication, 17 October, 2011). The Griffith University history clearly outlined the importance for that university of Asian languages and studies with its foundation School of Modern Asian Studies (Quirke, 1996, pp. 8, 11).

The 1980s and 1990s were the years of a period of reorganisation of the sector with either amalgamations of several institutions or the granting of university status to former institutes of technology. Much was written in the histories of these former institutes of their beginnings as providers of technological and industrial education when languages were simply not taught. Later histories have not necessarily updated changes in language curricula. The first Curtin University history (White, 1996), for instance, detailed that university's origins from the Western Australian Institute of Technology. The second Curtin history (Hart, 2014) however, made no reference to the current Asian language offerings. Languages have been considered marginal in some institutions and this was often reflected in histories containing no detail of

---

[2] Edgeloe was awarded this unique title when he retired in 1973.

1.4 Discussion of Literature and Other Sources

language teaching known to have existed. The Swinburne University of Technology (SUT) history (Love, 2007) had no detail of the several languages taught at SUT since 1969 (Swinburne College of Technology, 1970, p. 70). The 1987 RMIT history contained no details of languages offerings taught between 1975 and 1981 (Hawley, 1982, pp. 64, 66, 67; Murray-Smith & Dare, 1987).

Alongside the largely quantitative reports and surveys, key works in the field include the qualitative research on language teaching, including by Joseph Lo Bianco and Michael Clyne, both also prominent public commentators on languages. Clyne, who wrote extensively from the late 1960s, is well known for his work on the 'monolingual mindset' for English which he maintained was prevalent in Australia. He also described historical attitudes to languages in a series of differing phases: 'Accepting but laissez-faire, tolerant but restrictive, rejecting, and accepting' (Clyne, 2005, p. 143). Lo Bianco, whose research covers literacy education, language policy and language planning, also situated the history of languages in Australia in a series of phases though these related to policy direction and national identity: 'comfortably British, assertively Australian, ambitiously multicultural, energetically Asian, and fundamentally economic' (Lo Bianco, 2009, pp. 15, 16). Lo Bianco's fourth phase highlighted Australia's obsession with the Asian region and the much-repeated necessity of learning Asian languages as a matter of national interest, and continued to be a model for Australia's languages commitment although now intertwined with the economic imperative.

There are also specific studies of languages or languages groupings, such as Anne McLaren's 2011 work on Asian languages, David Hill's 2012 report on Indonesian, and Marko Pavlyshyn's historical work on the Ukrainian language in Australia (McLaren, 2011; Hill, 2012; Pavlyshyn, 1998). Both Margaret Travers (1971, 1977) and Harry Rigby (1992) documented Russian studies in Australian universities. A set of profiles about Australia's language potential, were published through the National Languages and Literacy Institute of Australia in 1993 and 1994. The original nine languages, Arabic, Modern Standard Chinese, French, German, Modern Greek, Indonesian/Malay, Italian, Japanese and Spanish, were the languages of wider teaching cited in the 1987 NPL (Lo Bianco, 1987, p. 124). To these were added a second series beginning in 1995: Hindi-Urdu, Korean, Thai, Vietnamese and Russian. These five languages although not widely taught at the time were considered 'an important investment … of cultural benefit and possible occupational advantage' (Lo Bianco quoted in Buzo, Dalton, Kimberley, & Wood, 1995, p. v). These profiles contain valuable historical information about the state of languages in Australia up to the early 1990s, demonstrating the language priorities of that time which, in the case of the languages of smaller enrolment, Thai, Vietnamese and Hindi-Urdu received no further attention.

University archives have been important for source material. In the case of the University of Melbourne which, because of its size and diversity of language teaching, is a central case study throughout this study, official records accessed have included registrar's correspondence holdings, council minutes and reports, faculty minutes and reports, calendars and faculty handbooks. The various official university reports and correspondence were particularly crucial for the case study in understanding the discussions and decision-making leading up to major structural changes for languages. The book has also drawn widely on other universities' archives. In addition to these sources, there are the rich archival sources of individuals giving contemporary views on languages such as the material contained in the personal papers of former University of Melbourne academics Nina Christesen (who established Russian) and Ian Maxwell (teacher of Old Norse). The Christesen papers were used to add depth to the official records on the establishment of Russian, whilst the Maxwell papers were used to cross-check other documentation on the teaching of Old Norse.

The archives of the Australian Federation of Modern Language Teachers Associations (AFMLTA) were a comprehensive source of academic writing about languages from the late 1940s up to the present although the main focus of AFMLTA has been the languages of the school sector. The proceedings of several colloquia of the Languages and Cultures Network for Australian Universities, and media releases from their website have provided significant and more recent information about the work of individual university language educators in effecting innovation in language teaching and lobbying for institutional and sector wide developments.

The oral history component was an essential part of the primary sources used in this book. Formal recorded interviews were conducted with 26 people with a further 38 people contacted by email for formal or informal information. The interviewees and others contacted ranged from vice-chancellors, deputy vice-chancellors, former professors and senior academics to current students, current staff and past graduates. These different interviewees were selected to include those involved in high-level decision-making about languages, those involved in curriculum development and those who had taught classical, Asian or modern European languages. Although some current and recent students were initially interviewed, it soon became apparent that to include the student perspective on language offerings and choice was outside the parameters of this book. Further research could fruitfully be conducted into student motivation and satisfaction with regard to language learning. The information gathered in this way, both formally and informally, was used to give individual perspectives to the historical reports and other sources about language offerings and teaching. There is a wealth of literature about issues to be considered when using interviews as sources of particular historical aspects which are being researched: issues of bias, forgetfulness, and mis-remembering (Jones, 2004, p. 23; Norrick, 2005, pp. 3, 11; Storey, 2004, p. 51). Understanding of such phenomena was important for this study in cross-checking official records with recollections of interviewees.

Whilst the research for this book has involved the collection and integration of archival, published and oral sources across a range of repositories and from a number of different contexts, there have been some limitations. Most of the university archives departments contacted were very forthcoming with data although in some cases, the historical data was not held electronically and could not be accessed. In the case of reports and surveys cited, these had been conducted over several decades and data had often been recorded in different ways, either by single years or ranges of years. Data had often been collected in different ways, sometimes by questionnaires, sometimes from websites, sometimes from existing reports. This resulted in piecemeal and fragmentary sources making it difficult to obtain consistent longitudinal data. The differences in data caused problems for the ease in which language statistics could be compared and conclusions drawn which are meaningful for this research (Baldauf & White, 2010, p. 42; Bettoni & Leal, 1994, p. 22).

The methodological approach used has been primarily an historical one which has aimed to add to the history of tertiary education and its language curricula. It has also aimed to provide an historical understanding as to whether languages have mattered to Australia in a national and international sense and how Australia's attention to languages has been reflected in its identity and its sense of place in the world. The use of case study material has also been part of the methodology examining the broader trends of the commitment to particular languages for the national interest through case studies of individual languages. An additional case study examines the particular language structure changes at the University of Melbourne firstly in 1992 and then in 1998. Including this case study has enabled analysis and evaluation of the consequences of differing perspectives articulated by influential individuals involved in high level decision-making at the University of Melbourne.

1.5 Overview of the Book

The book has been organised chronologically with an emphasis on educational policy and language teaching post-World War II. Chapter 2 explores tertiary education in colonial Australia specifically focussing on languages taught, why they were considered an essential part of university education and how language study related to the national interest of colonial times in educating future leaders. The classical languages, Latin and Ancient Greek, and the modern languages, French and German were taught at the University of Sydney founded 1851, the University of Melbourne (1853), the University of Adelaide (1874), University of Tasmania (1890), University of Queensland (1909), and the University of Western Australia, established in 1911. They were in line with developments in British universities and ideas of a liberal education. The funding of Japanese teaching by the Department of Defence from 1917 at the University of Sydney was, however, a significant change as its inclusion was justified for national security reasons.

Chapter 3 explores the post-World War II university context, a period marked by an expansion of foundations of universities and a proliferation of reports on higher education and language offerings. Universities founded reflected new priorities for the development of Australian industry and research and to accommodate expanding numbers of potential students. The ANU was founded in 1946, the New South Wales University of Technology (NSWUT) in 1949, Monash University in 1958, and Macquarie University and La Trobe Universities both in 1964. Another group of universities were created in the 1970s, when the increasing multicultural nature of Australia, as well as Australia's rising economic interest in the Asian region, influenced language offerings. The Dawkins reforms of the late 1980s ushered in the Unified National System, with a smaller number of large universities. Economic rationalism became the expected attitude for universities in their justification of courses and subjects.

Chapter 4 traces Australia's attitudes to migrants from the infamous White Australia Policy leading up to the large-scale migration post-World War II. Multiculturalism is discussed, as is the changing attitude to the rights of migrants to retain their language and culture. As I demonstrate, there was an upsurge in the teaching of the migrant or community languages in both schools and tertiary institutions, although this increase was not sustained over time. It is also shown that it was the teaching of English as a second language which became a key priority.

Chapter 5 concentrates on the growing prominence of three Asian languages, Japanese, Chinese and Indonesian, all of which have been important in Australia's growing involvement in the Asian region. Apart from Japanese teaching at the University of Sydney from 1917, it was not until the 1960s that there was a significant increase of Japanese language study in schools and universities. Although Chinese (Mandarin not Cantonese) had been introduced in the 1950s, it was not until the recognition of China in 1972, that more universities introduced Chinese along with other Asian languages. Indonesian teaching in universities began with Federal government funding in 1956. The numbers studying Indonesian increased in universities until 1975, and until 1983 in secondary schools (Worsley, 1994, p. x). Enthusiasm for Indonesian waned in the late 1990s in the face of terrorist attacks by fundamentalist Muslims in various parts of Indonesia and negative attitudes in the Australian community towards Indonesia (Hill, 2012, p. 25).

Chapter 6 considers three more languages which have been of national interest to Australia at different historical moments: Korean, Russian and Arabic. Korean teaching began in the university sector in 1982 and, although designated in 1994 as one of the trade languages with priority government funding for schools, it had never been as strong as the other three 'trade' languages, Chinese, Indonesian and Japanese. As will be shown, prioritisation of a language for economic reasons alone did not guarantee student demand. Russian was first taught in an award course in 1946 at the University of Melbourne and, as will be demonstrated, flourished through the Cold War period, although Russian was never a source of priority government funding. After the 1991 collapse of the Soviet Union, Australian students' interest in Russian declined. Arabic was first taught in Australian universities as a scholarly language but became an important community language in Australia with significant migration from the Middle East and from African and Asian Muslim countries. The Australian Government spent much effort on its Middle East trade, but has not extended this effort, or funding, to Arabic. As I will show, Arabic has been vulnerable to internal funding cuts even though designated by the Federal government as a nationally strategic language.

Chapter 7 reviews the 1990s with changes in language offerings and university language department structures. Federal government changes brought new policies and funding cuts for universities which, as will be shown, impacted on languages. A case study of languages at the University of Melbourne was undertaken to research how that university developed its language offerings and structures in 1992 in response to international, domestic and national influences (University of Melbourne (UniMelb), 1991a). However, as will be demonstrated, with later different internal priorities at the University of Melbourne, a separate academic structure for Asian languages was created from February 1998. To gain a wider perspective, the University of Melbourne's changes are contrasted with the attitudes to languages and the structures in other large universities to examine whether they followed the University of Melbourne's lead, specifically focussing on those known as the Group of 8 (Go8).[3] This Group had collectively signalled its commitment to languages in agreements listed on its website (Go8, n.d., Agreements). According to AAH reports, university languages were in a precarious state, by the end of the 1990s, with serious under-funding issues (AAH, 1998, p. 46; White et al., 1997, p. 25). Such a crisis, they said, required an urgent national renewed commitment to the languages capability of the universities as a matter of immense importance to Australia (AAH, 1998, p. 69).

Chapter 8 explores the contemporary situation for languages looking initially at the Labor Government's 2012 White Paper for the Asian Century, then the incoming Coalition Government's 2013 New Colombo Plan. In the midst of uncertainty about government interest in languages and national alarm about the state of languages, a new national organisation was created with federal funding, the Languages and Cultures Network for Australian Universities, bringing together Australian tertiary language educators. Universities' commitment to, and reasons for, language teaching are discussed, as are various innovations which have been important for the further promotion of language study. Comparisons with the fate of foreign languages in other English-speaking countries are briefly reviewed.

1.6 Conclusion

This book demonstrates that throughout the history of language teaching in Australian universities there have been waves of influences which have often been articulated in terms of the shifting priorities given to languages at many levels- federally, institutionally and by communities. Australia's changing demographics through extensive migration also influenced the linguistic diversity of the nation and hence the sense of national identity. Nevertheless, there has not been consistent support from governments or university decision-makers for languages in the university sector, although there have been some supportive policies implemented with necessary funding. As is shown, it is the changing context which is crucial for an understanding of the rise and decline of some languages, the shifting priorities of both Federal and State governments and those of the universities themselves. Through such an investigation of the social, cultural, political and economic situations which

---

[3] The Go8 was formally incorporated in 1999, comprising the Universities of Sydney, Melbourne, Adelaide, Queensland, New South Wales and Western Australia, Monash University and the Australian National University, some of the largest and oldest universities in Australia.

historically influenced language offerings, a clearer understanding can be gained of the factors impacting on the contemporary situation for languages in the Australian tertiary sector. Evidence suggests that social and economic environments and political agendas will continue to be powerful influences contributing to the shifting priorities.

Chapter 2
The Founding of Australian Universities

> The mission of the University is to form the character not of individuals but of the nation. (Selleck, 2003, p. 44). (Sir Redmond Barry, first Chancellor of the University of Melbourne, at the inauguration ceremony on 13 April, 1855)

Redmond Barry's view of the role of a university was typical of pre-Federation leaders in the individual colonies. They believed that the establishment of universities, based on the familiar traditions of Britain and Ireland, would develop the character of future leaders of colonial society and hence were essential for the national interest of the country as a whole. Nevertheless there were other different university systems overseas available as models and considered by different colonies. Each colony founded its university in the context of its own situation, albeit with knowledge of what other colonies were establishing. As Hannah Forsyth maintained, in relation to new ideas about universities, these were not incidental, but had power. 'Every new idea about tertiary education represents *someone's* interests' (H. Forsyth, 2014, p. 2). Thus, each new colonial university represented the ideas and interests of the founders in that particular colony. These beliefs continued to inform discussions of learning and teaching into the twentieth century.

For each of these colonial universities, languages other than English or foreign languages as they were known, were deemed to be an important part of the curriculum. They had before them the models of the British traditions of language learning, and the need to provide language training for the professions. This chapter will contextualise the beginnings of university education in Australia in the framework of the question of national interest, from the first university founded in the colony of New South Wales, followed by those in Victoria, South Australia, Tasmania, Queensland and Western Australia, each drawing on various models of British university education. For each of the universities founded, I will show which languages were introduced and why.

2.1 The Foundation of Universities in the Colonies

New South Wales was settled as a penal colony in 1788, the first European settlement in Australia. Although most of the population in the early years of the colony were men, the earliest schooling was mainly through working-class women caring for children and giving them basic instruction in reading and writing (Horne & Sherington, 2013b, p. 368). A simple system of government-assisted schools with education available to any children was gradually established, encouraged by Lachlan Macquarie, Governor of the colony from 1810 to 1821. Macquarie's efforts were hampered though by a lack of teachers (Barnard, 1962, pp. 129, 621, 622). The more prosperous families sent their children to private schools which also sprang up in the colony (Barnard, 1962, p. 623). It was in a despatch from Earl Bathurst, the Colonial Secretary in 1823 to Sir Thomas Brisbane, the Governor from late 1821 to 1825, that the hint of a future university is found. Bathurst instructed Brisbane about the setting up of schools, indicating that ultimately there should be 'an establishment of the nature of a University' (C of A, 1917, p. 140). This was, according to Frederick Watson, editor of the *Historical Records of Australia,* in 1917

> the first official reference by Earl Bathurst to a suggested university, but in private and unofficial correspondence the question had been mentioned several times. It is indicative of the advanced ideas which were under consideration for the future development of the colony. (C of A, 1917, p. 140)

Watson was referring to the origins of the colony as a penal settlement under the nearly autocratic rule of the governor and under the partial legal jurisdiction of the British Parliament. What the colony lacked were the institutions of a more independent society. And as more free settlers came for land, such structures needed to be established for the colony to move to a more democratic system of government. It was in the early 1820s that such structures were founded, with the Supreme Court of NSW, the NSW Legislative Council and a limited jury system (NSW Government Courts & Tribunals Service, n.d.). These social and structural changes provided a context for changing attitudes to education and what followed was the need for more formal educational structures. The National Schools Board was established in 1848 with a system of National Schools gradually established from then on, followed by the founding of the University two years later (Campbell & Proctor, 2014, p. 42). According to Clifford Turney and his fellow historians,[1] 'these developments were in many respects the expression of the interest and growing influence and power of the urban middle classes' (Turney, Bygott, & Chippendale, 1991, p. 4). Whilst the Colonial Secretary may have indicated in 1823 that eventually a university should be established in the colony, Turney and his colleagues maintained that the impetus had come from two quarters: the commercial leaders – the bankers, the manufacturers and the merchants on the one hand, and the professional leaders – the doctors, the lawyers, and the magistrates on the other hand. The commercial leaders

---

[1] Turney, Bygott, and Chippendale are the authors of *A History of the University of Sydney Volume 1.*

2.1 The Foundation of Universities in the Colonies

drove the financial development of the colony, and the professional leaders wanted educational reform which would enable colonists to qualify in Australia for entry into the legal and medical professions (Turney et al., 1991, pp. 4, 27).

The influence of these men points to how the social demographic of this colony had changed. Convict transportation had ceased in the eastern states in 1840 and Australian society was evolving into a diverse population comprising free settlers in both urban and rural areas, the ex-convicts, and of course rising numbers of those Australian-born. As the free enterprise economy grew, so did the middle classes of business people and people in the professions (Kingston, 2006, pp. 36, 37; Nadel, 1957, p. 15).

These commercial and professional men also formed the civic leadership of NSW, the colonial elite who believed a university would be 'fundamental to the development of a self-governing society and that it would raise the standard of education throughout the colony' (Turney et al., 1991, pp. 29, 31). It was William Wentworth who was credited, by Turney and his colleagues and the biographer Michael Persse, as leading the movement to found the University of Sydney. A landowner, barrister and member of the Legislative Council of NSW, Wentworth, who was educated at Cambridge University, believed passionately in the importance of advanced education for the enlightenment and understanding of men's minds and the training of men for high office. He also believed that university education would enable the colony's move towards responsible government (Persse, 1967, p. 8; Turney et al., 1991, p. 27). As an advocate for a university, Wentworth had stated in 1849 that it was 'the paramount duty of the Government to provide for the instruction of the people' (Wentworth, 1849, p. 2). These words, argued historians Horne and Sherington in their history of the University of Sydney, were carefully chosen (Horne & Sherington, 2012, p. 6). Wentworth's point was that the university was for the education of a governing elite; those who, being educated to such a standard to assume high office, would then lead the colony and thus all the population would benefit. This view of the purpose of a university would later underpin the concept of national interest which informed developments in the sector after Federation. As Horne and Sherington argued, this was a vision of a public university, not as an instrument of universal education, but one where, through a university education, those young men of merit would be groomed for future public office (Horne & Sherington, 2012, p. 6).

Horne and Sherington contended that, as an institution, 'established and maintained from public funds,' the University of Sydney was also to be secular and non-denominational (Horne & Sherington, 2012, pp. 6, 7). The universities of Oxford and Cambridge, and Trinity College Dublin were cited as models by the colonial universities of Sydney and Melbourne with their liberal arts education seen as the necessary education for those destined for careers in the church, the law, medicine or public office (Selleck, 2003, p. 26; Turney et al., 1991, p. 4). Indeed, it has been suggested by Horne and Sherington, that these universities were like 'the Church of England at study,' given the formal associations with the Established Church arising out of their foundations, and that around 1840 about half of the undergraduates were candidates for holy orders (Horne & Sherington, 2012, p. 8). So whilst the colonial universities had before them these examples of British university structures, the secular and non-denominational institutions founded in the colonies were in stark contrast.[2]

Whilst the founding fathers of the University of Sydney drew upon the models of British universities, those universities had hundreds of years of tradition and endowment behind them and long established academic schools. The colony had more pragmatic needs in the establishment of a university. Whilst there is no explanation of the 'peculiar circumstances of the colony' (University of Sydney (UniSyd), 1856, p. 13) mentioned in the 1856 University Calendar, this would seem to refer partly to the financial restrictions under which the Council of this new University had to proceed, and partly because there was no home grown educational tradition. Neither had there been any long standing push within the colony for higher education. This was rather a natural evolution from good secondary schooling towards higher education, as Bathurst had suggested would eventually happen, to advance the development of the colony (Turney et al., 1991, pp. 4, 27). Horne and Sherington, however, argued for the public purpose of the establishment of universities in stronger terms. It was, they said, 'part of the rising pride in colonial and national public enterprise, where support came not only from the state, but also from public-spirited citizens' (Horne & Sherington, 2013a, p. 285). Indeed, the greater push for such education was to show that colonial societies had the intellectual and cultural foundations of a maturing society. This was demonstrated by the establishment of public institutions for the people's learning, such as museums, libraries and art galleries (Fennessy, 2007, pp. 2–5; Horne & Sherington, 2013b, p. 376). The establishment of universities was therefore essential as a manifestation of that maturity.

2.2 Two British Colonies: Canada and New Zealand

By contrast two other countries, Canada and New Zealand, whose colonial foundation was also British, were settled for very different reasons from Australia. Whilst the French first settled Canada in the early seventeenth century, Canada was rapidly transformed from a French possession to a British colony after the Seven Years' War ended in 1763 (Nelles, p. 67). Explorers, traders, and missionaries, seeking to convert the indigenous people, were amongst the first European settlers, followed by those seeking gold. As cities developed so did the need for cultural and educational institutions. Just as in Australia, it was the general education of the future leaders of society which underlay the founding of universities (Harris, 1976, p. 27). By the early nineteenth century degree granting universities had been founded, with the University of New Brunswick, the oldest English speaking university in Canada gaining university status in 1828. As Glen Jones stated, higher education was part of 'the broad agenda' to strengthen British culture and values in this new British

---

[2] British universities had the denominational college structure and the Church of England, as the Established Church and training of its clergy, at their heart.

colony (Jones, 2014, p. 2). Not surprisingly, the University of New Brunswick taught the Classics including Latin and Greek from its foundation (University of New Brunswick, Classics and Ancient History).

The earliest European settlers in New Zealand were sealers, whalers, timber traders and missionaries, who sought to convert the indigenous Maori people. After the Treaty of Waitangi in 1840 between the British and many Maori chiefs, more British assisted settlers had arrived to work as farm labourers, builders and blacksmiths (Phillips, J., n.d., pp. 1–5). Sheep farming flourished in the South Island, where gold was also discovered in 1842. Large areas of land were opened up for development and the creation of infrastructure of roads, bridges, ports and public buildings (McLauchlan, 2004, pp. 97, 99). It was the Otago area of the South Island, with a history of Scottish settlement, where the city of Dunedin was founded in 1848, where gold mining boomed in the 1860s and the first university in New Zealand was founded in 1869. Not surprisingly one of the three founding professors taught classics (University of Otago – history and governance).

2.3 A Second University in Melbourne, Australia

Victoria, previously designated as the Port Phillip District and administered by NSW, had gained separation from New South Wales in 1851, and various sections of the community in Melbourne had begun to raise the issue of a university in Melbourne. Not only had Victoria gained control of its own affairs in 1851, but gold had been discovered in that same year. Richard Selleck described Melbourne as 'a raw, suddenly rich city… confronting political, social, demographic and economic pressures' (Selleck, 2003, p. 13). The population of Victoria increased dramatically, but thousands, including labourers, office workers, civil servants and seamen streamed up to the goldfields. As Michael Cannon observed of Melbourne, 'city and suburbs lost much of their adult male population' (Cannon, 1993, p. 18). In the midst of this social change, local newspapers continued to call for a public university which was open to all and reflected the university education of the mother country (Selleck, 2003, pp. 13, 14). The movement for a university in Melbourne needs to be seen in the context of the great civic impulse for the establishment of a range of publicly funded institutions which unfolded over the next 20 years.[3] It could also be argued that rivalry with New South Wales and Victoria's newly attained independence had prompted action in Victoria (Selleck, 2003, pp. 13, 14). In 1852, as the University of Sydney was enrolling its first students, a petition was presented to Governor La Trobe, the first Governor of Victoria, by a group of Melbourne citizens asking for the establishment of a university. He responded quickly, money was allocated, a committee formed, a bill drafted and presented and, by 22 January 1853, the bill had become the Act of Incorporation and received royal assent.

---

[3] State Library and National Museum of Victoria founded in 1854 and the National Gallery of Victoria founded in 1861.

Historians of the University of Melbourne such as Blainey, Scott and Selleck, have credited not just one but several prominent men with leading the movement to found the University of Melbourne (Scott, E. 1936, p. 4). One such was Hugh Childers, a member of the Legislative Council and Auditor General, who steered the legislation through the Council to its successful conclusion (Selleck, 2003, p. 14). He was also the first vice-chancellor of the University of Melbourne (Hall, 1969, p. 2). Blainey argued that Redmond Barry, who was the University's first chancellor, was the man who brought the university to life. By sustained effort, said Blainey, he steered it through its development and was its champion. Macintyre and Selleck alluded to Barry's 'thrusting leadership' and the demand of the city's professional men for a university (Macintyre & Selleck, 2003, p. 1). It could also be argued that Governor La Trobe should have some of the credit as it was he who, responding quickly, granted leave to Childers to bring the legislation before the Legislative Council. The more important point here is that as Scott put it 'there was no doubt about the capacity of the young colony to support a University, and public opinion on the subject was apparently unanimous' (Blainey, 1957, pp. 10, 209; Scott, E. 1936, pp. 1, 2, 3). The group of colonial gentry, clergy and public servants, who comprised the first University Council, wanted the new university to bring a sense of stability and social and moral improvement in the colony. Childers contended that the university would be conducive to the 'moral and social improvement of the colony.' This seemed particularly important at a time of huge social change in Victoria during the gold rushes when, according to Selleck, young men lured by the prospect of riches, left their educational pursuits all too readily. A university, Barry believed, would offer the discipline these young men urgently needed, as an alternative to seeking wealth on the goldfields (Selleck, 2003, pp. 14, 15).

Despite the unanimity of purpose to establish a university, there were diverse opinions as to the nature of this new university and what it should teach. The press, presumably claiming to represent the local population, made known their views of the proposed university. It should not be a 'caricature' of Oxford and Cambridge and should rather take heed of the experience of those universities rather than merely imitate them (Selleck, 2003, p. 19). The Council, however, aimed to establish a university which would bring the traditions of British education to the colony. The university was to be close to the city where middle-class businessmen and professionals and their sons worked. Whatever the popular press thought, the Council, in the Act it crafted, took elements from a number of British universities to form a distinct university (Selleck, 2003, pp. 22, 26). Initially the University of Melbourne was to be non- collegiate,[4] 'a state university, urban, secular, professorial, non-residential, centralised in government, controlled by a laity, and possessing power to teach and examine' (Selleck, 2003, p. 27). This was the University of Melbourne's distinct combination of attributes for a new mid-nineteenth century university, although the University of Sydney was also to be public, secular, and non-denominational. There were many similarities between these two early universities founded in such quick succession.

---

[4] The first residential college, Trinity College, was not established until 1872.

The areas of instruction set out by the Council to bring 'British civilisation' to the colony were: Greek and Latin with ancient history; mathematics, pure and mixed; natural science; and modern literature, modern history, political economy and logic. Barry did believe that academics coming from England would need to understand colonial society, but he also expected professors to be of such breeding as to 'stamp on their future pupils the character of the loyal, well-bred English gentleman' (Blainey, 1957, p. 10). Barry was very clear about the purpose of the university as an institution which had a national responsibility. He stressed in his inauguration ceremony speech at the University that, 'its mission was to form the character not of individuals but of the nation.' Just as with the founders of the University of Sydney, the building of the society of the colony was important to the founders of the University of Melbourne. The young men who would be educated at the University were to become the colony's leaders in the professions and government (Selleck, 2003, pp. 29, 30, 31, 44).

2.4 A Third Colonial University in Adelaide

The universities of Sydney and Melbourne had been founded within a few years of each other in the mid 1850s, however, there was a gap of some 20 years before the University of Adelaide was founded. Just as Sydney's schooling system and democratic infrastructure had evolved, so the same pattern could be seen in Adelaide. Through the 1860s and into the early 1870s the city of Adelaide grew in importance as the seat of government through which public works, manufacturing and agriculture were expanded. It became apparent, said J. J. Pascoe, an early historian, that the educational system established by the churches and private individuals, now needed to be advanced into higher education (Pascoe, 1901, pp. 173, 174). However, unlike Sydney and Melbourne, there had been no popular or business demand for a university. Adelaide was a much smaller city and it was Christian clergy who initiated the discussion for a university (Woodburn, 1983, p. 1). Union College was founded in February 1872 to train young men for the Christian ministry. This college was very successful and this type of education had such great appeal to those desirous of secular education that, within a few months, there was a further move to widen its base of instruction, and gather support to found a university (Duncan & Leonard, 1973, p. 2; Woodburn, 1983, p. 1). Subsequently, a group of 'gentlemen favourable to the establishment of a university', more than half of them clergy (Woodburn, 1983, p. 1), met in September 1872 and formed the University Association. Two key members of this group were the Vice-President, Augustus Short, Anglican Bishop of Adelaide (who subsequently became the first vice-chancellor) and Walter Hughes, a wealthy pastoralist, as President. Their vision of this university, just as with Sydney and Melbourne, was to provide a secular and non-denominational education to prepare the future leaders of that colony (Duncan & Leonard, 1973, p. 3; University of Adelaide, n.d.). Nevertheless, South Australia had a population of just under 200,000 in the early 1870s, compared with just over half a million in New South

Wales, and over 730,000 in Victoria. It is doubtful, argued the educational historian Alan Barcan, that such a small community could have established a university without the support of benefactors (Barcan, 1980, p. 126; Vamplew, 1987, p. 26).

The Association's effort was bolstered by Hughes' gift of £20,000 offered in January 1873, which was tied to the endowment of two professorships,[5] one in Classics and Comparative Philology and Literature, and the other in English Language and Literature and Mental and Moral Philosophy (Duncan & Leonard, 1973, p. 3). The University Association had to work hard to gain public and government support and, even when the bill for an Act of Incorporation was finally passed in October 1874, and the University formally established, it was reported that members of the legislature 'seemed to know little, and to care less, about universities, regarding them as little more than a colonial status symbol' (Duncan & Leonard, 1973, pp. 3, 4). The passing of the act to incorporate the university seemed to have prompted a second large gift of £20,000, this from Thomas Elder with no conditions stipulated (Duncan & Leonard, 1973, pp. 3, 4; Pascoe, 1901, pp. 229, 278; Woodburn, 1983, pp. 1, 2).

2.5 The Later Colonial Universities

To this group of three colonial universities already established came the University of Tasmania founded in 1890, just at the time of a national depression. Churchmen were also involved in the push for a university in Tasmania, as had happened in Adelaide, although local lawyers, doctors and graziers, all members of the state assembly, had their say about the need for a Tasmanian university. They all agreed about the necessity for a university but argued over the funding and governance for more than a decade, with the final compromise bill being passed in late 1889 (Davis, 1990, pp. 18, 19). James Backhouse Walker, a prominent solicitor and barrister in the colony, argued that a university is 'one of the necessities of a civilised and progressive people', not a luxury but an essential element of national progress. Having a university in Tasmania will keep young men here, 'a manifest advantage to our future progress.' This was to be a university for all the youth of the colony, which would enhance the colonial interests of Tasmania (Walker, 1896?, pp. 1, 2).

The last two of the six early universities were founded in the early years of Federation, the University of Queensland in 1909, and in 1911, the University of Western Australia. Although these two were not strictly colonial universities, they shared the same ideas as the earlier universities about the importance of a university for their previous colony (and now state of Australia), and are historically considered as part of the informal grouping known as the sandstone universities which

---

[5] According to the South Australian Register of Friday 1 August 1879, the Union College Council had been given the Hughes money and relinquished it to the University movement, believing that, through the University movement, the money would have greater benefit for the public than using the money for theological education.

represented the beginnings of the university sector in Australia. In both of these universities, there was a different founding outlook to the earlier four universities. Queensland saw itself as different – a pioneer society more concerned with the practical challenges of conquering the environment and developing industries, than with the pursuit of academic and intellectual needs. In a crucial ideological shift, those who advocated for the establishment of a university looked to the universities of the mid-west of the United States for their inspiration, believing them to be practical institutions for practical people (Thomis, 1985, pp. 4, 5, 6). In the Queensland parliamentary debate during the passage of the University bill, the proposed university was frequently referred to as 'a people's university' (Thomis, 1985, p. 23), apparently referring to the belief that the university should be open to all classes and free of fees, and that as the university developed, it would always 'be guided by the parliament who reflected the opinion of the people of the state' (Thomis, 1985, p. 22). Despite the supposed mid-west USA inspiration, when the University began teaching, its courses were modelled largely on those of existing Australian universities (University of Queensland Senate, 1935, p. 4) – the classics, mathematics and chemistry. In one respect though, Queensland was different, as unlike the earlier universities, Queensland's fourth foundation discipline was engineering.

Several men stood out in the development of this new university: Sir William MacGregor, a seasoned colonial administrator, chairman of the University Senate and first chancellor, Reginald Roe the first vice-chancellor, an experienced grammar school headmaster, and John Story, the permanent head of the Department of Public Instruction, and the link between the state government and the university (Thomis, 1985, pp. 32, 33). Here was the opportunity for a new outlook in university development – the first university to be created in Australia after Federation – although still with the common aims of being secular and non-denominational and important for the development of the economic and intellectual interests of that part of the nation.

The University of Western Australia (UWA) was founded in 1911. There was apparently a good spirit of bipartisanship between the state government initiating the act for the university and the new Federal government providing the funds. As had been the case in Queensland, there was also 'general agreement that the University should be practically oriented and that it should be open to all classes rather than a preserve of the elite' (de Garis, 1988, p. xx). The difference in Western Australia was that the Senate of the University, and particularly its chair and first chancellor, John Hackett, looked not only to the examples of the British and Irish university traditions, but also the models of universities such as Ontario in Canada, Cornell and Wisconsin in the United States and those in the eastern states of Australia (Alexander, 1963, pp. 16, 27, 28). He believed, too, that German universities with their utilitarian approach to research and teaching were more appropriate models than the 'elitist' British universities. He was particularly influenced by the 'Australian type' of university that had been established at the University of Queensland, based on the existing universities, but with 'some decided improvements' (Alexander, 1963, p. 28; Gregory, 2013, pp. 6, 7). Significantly, the foundation professorial chairs were in agriculture, mathematics and physics, mining and engineering, biology, history and economics, English, chemistry and geology, reflecting 'the belief that Western Australia needed university disciplines with relevance to its economy' (de Garis, 1988, p. xx). In fact, when the last chair was being decided between classics and geology, Hackett (a classics man who studied at Trinity College Dublin), used his casting vote in favour of geology, citing the importance of geology to the mining industry in Western Australia (de Garis, 1988, p. xx). The economy of the state and its consequent contribution to the national interest had the greater priority than a traditional curriculum. Across the 60 years of the early development of Australian university education it can be seen that the emphasis had changed from replicating British institutions to creating institutions that better suited Australian economic and social needs but always with a sense of what was in the national interest of the country.

2.6 The Language Offerings of the Universities

Just as British university traditions were the model for the early colonial universities, it will be shown that the languages initially taught in Australia followed the traditions of British language offerings, but only partially. The classical languages, the modern European languages and various Asian (or as they were known Oriental) languages were all offered at universities such as Oxford (Prest, 1993, p. 173), Cambridge (Brooke, 1993, p. 431), the University of London (Harte, 1986, p. 105) and Trinity College Dublin (McDowell & Webb, 1982, pp. 57, 270) in the middle to late nineteenth century. Just as the classical languages, Latin and Ancient Greek were an essential part of a liberal arts education at these British universities (Harte, 1986, p. 92; Turney et al., 1991, p. 5), so too was the primacy of the classical languages taken up wholeheartedly by the colonial universities. Whilst the modern European languages also had a place in the British university system, they were not as well established as the classical languages. So also in Australia, just two modern European languages, French and German were mostly taught from the beginning of those early universities, but did not have the status of the classical languages until the twentieth century. A significant point of divergence occurred with Oriental languages which were taught as scholarly languages in Britain. These languages did not gain any standing in Australia until the early twentieth century. As will be shown, scholarship in Oriental languages was not the initial focus, but rather language competency for an understanding of the contemporary affairs of certain Asian countries whose actions it was considered might impact on Australia's security.

2.7 The Importance of the Classical Languages

The first Vice-Provost of the University of Sydney, the Honourable Sir Charles Nicholson, made clear the fundamental importance of the study of the classics. 'No better discipline for the intellect of the young can be found than that which is afforded

2.7 The Importance of the Classical Languages

by a careful and thorough initiation into the structure and forms of the Greek and Latin languages.' He grounded the new University of Sydney in the traditions of the 'two most ancient and renowned seats of learning, Oxford and Cambridge' (UniSyd, 1853, pp. 32, 38, 39). The School of Classics at Oxford, was cited as the 'premier School in dignity and importance.' Nicholson's words were an echo of the attitude to the Classics held by Oxford (University of Oxford, 1903, p. 159; UniSyd, 1853, pp. 32, 67). The Principal of the University of Sydney, Dr. Woolley, the foundation Professor of Classics, followed Sir Charles' words by reflecting on the importance of the founding of the 'first colonial University of the British Empire'.[6] Woolley went on to say that the Faculty of Arts was in the tradition of the ancient universities, and the 'mother' of the other faculties. In the Bachelor of Arts, which was the first degree established at Sydney, all students had to pass Classics, Mathematics, Chemistry, Natural Philosophy, and Logic to obtain the degree. The classics required both the study of Ancient Greek and Latin language and history (UniSyd, 1853, pp. 50, 53, 77, 78). These curricular requirements clearly demonstrated the compulsory place which Latin and Ancient Greek had in the curriculum. Of the three foundation professors, the classics professor was designated as the senior professor and the Chairman of the Professorial Board, further cementing the premier importance of the classics (UniSyd, 1853, pp. 68, 69, 1856, pp. 13, 14, 69).

One of the motivating forces for the classical languages at the University of Sydney came from an emerging need for reform in the legal and medical professions. Latin and Greek were required by the legal profession. Medical students needed knowledge of Latin in the study of pharmacopoeia and some medical examinations were taken in Latin (UniSyd, 1856, p. 60). Degrees in Law and Medicine were listed alongside degrees in Arts in the act to incorporate the university (Turney et al., 1991, pp. 29, 30, 31, 33, 52), and all three faculties reinforced, by their curriculum requirements, the importance of these languages. Latin at this time had an economic and vocational function as a 'pathway to the professions' (Barcan, 1993, p. 45).

In Melbourne, the University began its teaching officially in 1855, also with compulsory classics included as in Sydney, but in Melbourne, unlike in Sydney, there was an outcry in the press. The Age newspaper spoke out against the money that had been spent on the University and again raised the issue of the questionable value of the classics. It was neither practical, nor suitable for the colony or its population at this time, and not the sort of education that colonists wanted. It may well be, as Scott suggested, that there was unanimity in the colony about the need for a university, but there was not unanimity about what this university should be teaching. Even two of the new professors, Hearn and Wilson, just days after the inauguration ceremony, had written to Chancellor Barry, insisting that compulsory classics would affect student enrolments, and that such was the state of secondary classics teaching that it could not be ensured that students would even be properly prepared for university study of the classics (Scott, E. 1936, p. 3; Selleck, 2003, pp. 32, 46).

---

[6] Turney et al. (1991. p. 4), disagreed with Woolley, saying universities had already been developed in British North America. However, the first universities in British North America were private universities. The University of Sydney was indeed the first colonial public university of the British Empire.

There was already disagreement about the value of classical languages, expressed not only in the press, but also within the University. However, the Council adhered to the traditional practice of compulsory classics with Latin and Ancient Greek. Regardless of the opposition to this practice, Barry, in what might be seen as educational arrogance, fought for his belief in what a university should teach: not only its educational instruction but also its role in the development of moral and social character. In the end Barry had his way and the Council in June 1855 agreed to compulsory classical languages in an Arts degree. Whilst this controversy raged, there was no actual classics professor in place. The professor appointed, Henry Rowe, who had died within weeks of his arrival in Melbourne in early 1855, was not replaced until Martin Irving arrived in mid-1856. Again in 1858, the other professors tried to have Greek made non-compulsory, but Barry used his casting vote and the proposal was lost (Selleck, 2003, pp. 32, 47, 48, 49, 50, 52). As Blainey put it, 'the classical languages retained their grip on the arts course for another half century' (Blainey, 1957, p. 21).

Classical languages at the new University of Adelaide had similar prominence as at both the Universities of Melbourne and Sydney. Latin and Ancient Greek were compulsory in the Bachelor of Arts up till 1886, whereas a Science student was required to choose two of Latin, Greek, French or German. Even at the University of Tasmania which had started in financially dire circumstances, the classical languages were among the first courses initiated and Latin or Greek were compulsory in a Bachelor of Arts (Davis, 1990, p. 29; University of Tasmania (UTas), 1891, p. 79).

Even though the University of Queensland was the first university founded after Federation and, had purportedly seen itself as more practical, and the 'people's university, the classical languages were taught from the beginning. There was also, just as had happened in Melbourne, a dispute within the University about classical languages. Chancellor MacGregor and the professors disagreed with Vice-Chancellor Roe over the place of classical languages for university matriculation requirements (Robertson, 2010, p. 9; Thomis, 1985, pp. 32, 33, 37). The resolution in November 1911 was that matriculation requirements would include 'Latin or Greek for Arts students and a modern language for the rest' (Thomis, 1985, p. 39). Chancellor MacGregor and the professors had prevailed. The issue was raised again in 1912 by Vice-Chancellor Roe and again the academics prevailed. Not even when the Senate of the University was approached by Queensland teachers in 1914 seeking the abolition of compulsory Latin, did the Senate resile from its position. Clearly there was a strong and resolute group of men who believed in the importance of the classical languages. They were determined not to dilute what they saw were proper standards of education, despite others seeking a people's university with a curriculum perceived to be more practical (Thomis, 1985, p. 60).

At the University of Western Australia, classical languages were also taught from the outset, but the Department of Classics and Ancient History had to be content with a lectureship. It was not until 1945 that Classics and Ancient History became a professorial chair and the foundation lecturer, George Wood, took up the chair (Alexander, 1963, pp. 55, 125, 231).

So as has been demonstrated, the classical languages were a part of the curriculum in all six of the early Australian universities, and in most had the greater priority over other languages. There had been dissention about their place in some universities, but the classics traditionalists prevailed at least into the twentieth century.

2.8 Modern European Languages

Whilst the classical languages held sway in those early Australian universities, French and German were the first of the modern or 'living' languages taught in the Australian university sector, and in most universities were taught from the beginning. As with the classical languages, the influence can be traced back to the British universities where several modern languages were taught including French and German although, as can be seen, they did not have the status of the classics. At Trinity College Dublin, professorships in French, German, Spanish and Italian had been established around 1770, although study in these languages was linked to other 'gentlemanly' accomplishments such as music and dancing. It was not until 1870 that there was a move to introduce these languages into formal academic courses rather than being seen as extra-curricular, 'fancy embellishments' (McDowell & Webb, 1982, pp. 57, 270).

At the University of Oxford, for instance, the Taylorian Institution had been established at Oxford in 1847 by dint of a benefaction of £65,900 from the estate of Sir Robert Taylor for the promotion of the study of modern European languages. French, German, Italian and Spanish instruction was available (Firth, 1929, pp. 24; University of Oxford, 1903, p. 93). French and German in particular were considered 'essential to diplomatic or commercial pursuits' (Brock & Curthoys, 1997, p. 633). However whilst the Taylorian Foundation had enabled modern languages to be developed, the University had not offered any inducement to undergraduates to learn these languages (Firth, 1929, p. 68). It was not until 1903 that modern languages were approved for examination at the University of Oxford (Firth, 1929, pp. 74, 75). The mixed fortunes of the modern languages at Trinity College Dublin and Oxford would have been known at the University of Sydney when French and German were introduced in 1853, as several of the foundation staff at Sydney were Oxford men (USyd, 1854, p. 36). There would have been academic networks across the British Empire between men who had studied and taught together (Horne & Sherington, 2013a, p. 285). Wykes and King, however, in their research on the history of languages, do assert that the introduction of French, for instance, in schools and the University of Sydney was an imitation of English practice. They also maintained that French grew in popularity in schools as it was considered a 'useful' subject, but they wondered at its usefulness, since it was taught as though it was a dead language with little emphasis on conversation (Wykes & King, 1968, pp. 3, 6).

The University of London (also stated as a model for the University of Sydney) (Turney et al., 1991, p. 27), required the classical languages and French or German. However there is no evidence that Sydney was influenced by the London language requirements (Harte, 1986, p. 105). Nevertheless, there is evidence that two of the original members of the University of Sydney Senate, Charles Wentworth (Persse, 1967, p. 1) and Edward Deas Thomson (Osborne, 1967, p. 1), were both fluent in French. It is suggested therefore that these two men may have influenced other members of the Senate about the usefulness of teaching the modern languages, both French and German. So for whatever reasons, a chair of French and German Languages and Literature had simply been established in 1853 (UniSyd, 1854, p. 125). However, it appears that the chair was not immediately filled as, in that same 1854 University Calendar noting the establishment of the chair, it was recorded that a Reader (not a Professor), Dr. Anselme Ricard, was in charge, and that classes in French and German language and literature were voluntary and not examinable for the Bachelor of Arts degree (Turney et al., 1991, p. 115; UniSyd, 1854, p. 36). Not surprisingly, student numbers for these voluntary classes were low. As Wykes and King argued, these languages remained second-class subjects without the prestige accorded to the classical languages (Wykes & King, 1968, p. 5). They did conclude, nevertheless, that in all Australian states, 'the link between the university department and the teaching in secondary schools was strong' (Wykes & King, 1968, p. 3). It was not until 1865 that changes were made to regulations at the University of Sydney allowing French or German language to be examined in the BA degree (Turney et al., 1991, p. 138).

Far from sharing their bumpy voluntary beginnings at the University of Sydney, the teaching of French and German at the University of Melbourne began in a formal and structured manner. Apart from the British universities' influence, it was clear that the particular impetus for these languages at Melbourne had arisen from experienced educators in the school system. Charles Pearson, former headmaster of Presbyterian Ladies' College, and member of the Victorian Legislative Council, gave a report on the state of public instruction in Victoria to the Legislative Assembly in March 1878. Amongst many educational matters, he indicated that, if the University of Melbourne was to offer a more practical education, it should teach modern languages with commercial value, such as French, German, Spanish[7] and Italian, in addition to the classics (Pearson, 1878, pp. 113, 114; Selleck, 2003, pp. 157, 159). Meanwhile, new faces and new voices came onto the University Council such that, on the Council in 1880, there were five men of a 'schoolmaster' background, including John Edward Bromby, an ex-headmaster of Melbourne Grammar. This group of men was powerful as they sought to make education more practical, and promoted training in the professions. Not only did their combined vote in March 1880 carry the motion to admit women to the University (Clark, 1969, p. 2), but Bromby's subsequent motion in May 1880, for the inclusion of French and German in an Arts degree, was carried. Here is the evidence of Wykes and King's assertion of the strong link between university and school modern language teaching and the evidence of voices other than university academics influencing language offerings.

---

[7] Pearson believed that Spanish and Italian were commercially important for the colony as trade was developing with new countries. However, Spanish and Italian were not taught until the 1920s and then only in the instructor mode.

2.8 Modern European Languages

Galbally contended that Barry had to 'swallow some very significant amendments pushed through his Council'. Galbally went on to say that 'Barry's notions of education were by now very outmoded and he could count on little support for them in the University and the wider community. His opponents were all educational specialists – Professor Pearson, Professor Hearn and Dr Bromby' (Galbally, 1995, p. 188). It is curious that the approval of a single chair of English, French, and German Language and Literature is not mentioned in either the Annual Report of Council for 1880/1881 or the Annual Report of 1881/1882. Probably this new chair was overshadowed by the death in November 1880 of Sir Redmond Barry, the 'first and during twenty-eight years the only, Chancellor of the University.' His remarkable career with its contributions to the cultural, educational and civic life of Victoria through his involvement in not only the University of Melbourne, but the National Gallery, the Public Library and numerous other institutions had come to an end (Blainey, 1957, p. 63; Galbally, 1995, p. 188; Scott, E. 1936, p. 106; Selleck, 2003, pp. 156, 163, 167; UniMelb, 1881, p. 246, 1883).

Modern European languages began at the University of Melbourne within a multi-language chair. Edward Morris, who had studied classics, law and modern history at Oxford, was appointed as Professor of English, French, German Languages and Literature, from January 1884. His name first appeared in the 1882/1883 University Calendar, and there was a brief reference about French and German being included in an Arts course for the first time in the 1883/1884 University Calendar, but no reference to his appointment was made in any University annual report over these years. It was as though he just slipped into the University and began teaching – an inauspicious beginning for the modern languages. The irony was that Morris had never studied these languages at Oxford because they were not offered as degree subjects when he was a student there. He had learnt French and German after spending some time in France and Germany. Morris had the task of teaching English, French and German language and literature by himself. Over several years he asked for assistance, but it was never granted. In the classics department, however, the professor, Thomas Tucker (who began in 1886) had, from the beginning of his tenure, a lecturer to assist him, illustrating the greater status of the classics and probably reflecting greater student numbers. The 1886 Annual Report recorded that the Council had considered classics teaching too onerous for a single teacher, hence their approval of this appointment (Scott, E. 1936, p. 127; Selleck, 2003, p. 200; UniMelb, 1883, p. 55, 1884, p. 259, 1887, p. 297). Just as in Sydney, the classical languages held sway in Melbourne, and the modern languages did not have the same priority regardless of the sentiments of the 1878 Pearson Report about the commercial value to the colony of other modern European languages (Pearson, 1878, pp. 113, 114).

Nevertheless, Morris struggled on by himself for the 18 years of his tenure. He died suddenly whilst on leave in England in January 1902. Unfortunately, at this time, the University's finances were in a bad state as fraud by the University accountant had been discovered the year before and expected state government grants were withdrawn or reduced. To save money, the University Council decided that French and German teaching was to be divided between two poorly paid lecturers, Fernand

Maurice-Carton for French and Walter von Dechend for German. The tide had turned away, it seems, from enthusiasm for modern languages and, when money was short, here was an area for saving a professorial salary. Only one of the five schoolmasters who had been instrumental in the Council vote to include modern languages still remained on Council – Alexander Morrison. There was a preponderance of lawyers and judges, with a couple of doctors, clerics and an engineer on Council that year who did not, it would seem, support modern languages to the same degree that the five school masters had. So much for the push for the modern languages as the necessary and more practical training; now they were dispensable when finances were tight. I argue that this was a short-sighted move, given the Matriculation student numbers in French and German. In the 1901 Matriculation examinations for the University of Melbourne, 135 candidates sat for Greek, 562 for Latin, 122 for German and 910 for French. There was clearly at this time a great interest from young people beginning university studies in those modern languages with the numbers of French and German candidates together surpassing the candidatures for Greek and Latin combined (Scott, E. 1936, pp. 175, 189; Selleck, 2003, p. 436; UniMelb, 1904, pp. 328, 344, 1902, p. lxxiii; UniMelb. Matriculation results (UMA), 1902).

It is difficult to determine the origins of French and German teaching at the University of Adelaide. There are no reasons suggested in any of the published sources as to why these languages were introduced six years after foundation (Duncan & Leonard, 1973; Edgeloe, 1990, 2003; Woodburn, 1983). Victor Edgeloe (Registrar Emeritus of the University of Adelaide) noted that it was only when a separate Science degree was established in 1882 that French and German were introduced. From then a Science student could take French and German in their 1st year program, whereas an Arts student at the same time had to take compulsory Latin and Greek, with no French and German available to them (Edgeloe, 2003, p. 324). There are no details in the University of Adelaide Calendars of the 1880s and up to 1898 of any French and German lecturers on staff. From 1886, French and German studies could count towards an Arts degree (Edgeloe, 1990, p. 1; University of Adelaide, 1882, 1889, 1898). However, as Edgeloe noted, 'no lectures were given in French and German' (Edgeloe, 2003, p. 325), and this accords with the absence of language staff in the listings of the University Calendars. There was, however, expertise in foreign languages amongst the staff who taught Mathematics, English Language and Literature and Mental and Moral Philosophy. These men served as examiners in French and German. Other assistance in examining foreign languages had come from staff at the Universities of Sydney and Melbourne. Informal classes were conducted in French and German from 1884 in the afternoon and evenings (Fornasiero & West-Sooby, 2012, pp. 138, 139, 143). Nevertheless, given the lack of formal teaching, it is not surprising to note that the number of students taking French and German between 1887 and 1900 was very small (Edgeloe, 1990, pp. 1, 2). These imprecise arrangements add weight to the argument that French and German had second-class status at that time.

An additional Elder bequest, given in 1897, enabled a part-time lectureship in German, although when the lecturer Ernst Eitel died in 1908 it was not until 1920

2.8 Modern European Languages

that another part-time German lecturer was appointed. It could be argued that the position was not filled because of negative feelings towards Australia's World War I enemy Germany, although no evidence could be found to explain the gap in teaching. There is also no information on what French classes were taught and by whom until 1918 when John Crampton was appointed to teach French in the Faculty of Arts and the Elder Conservatorium of Music. His daughter, Hope Crampton, joined him as assistant lecturer in French in 1930, and the two taught together until John retired at 75 years of age in 1937. At this stage, there was still no professorial chair of French or of German and there was no sign of interest in the teaching of Asian languages. James Cornell was immediately appointed to replace Crampton and subsequently made Chair of French in 1944. Just as at the University of Sydney and the University of Melbourne, modern languages at the University of Adelaide took a long time to be firmly established both in terms of student demand and commitment from the University (Edgeloe, 1990, pp. 9, 10, 11, 12, 2003, pp. 329, 335; Fornasiero & West-Sooby, 2012, pp. 156, 159; University of Adelaide staff records: Crampton, H & Crampton, J).

As with the Universities of Sydney and Adelaide, the modern languages, French and German at the University of Queensland did not have professorial status in the beginning. Moreover, even at the point of Queensland's foundation (1909), none of the older Australian universities had established individual professorial chairs in French or German let alone any other modern language. It might have been expected that German would have had a higher profile as engineering was one of the foundation faculties in Queensland (Thomis, 1985, p. 34). German was an important language for engineering and the sciences, thus it could be argued that there was a connection between German being taught from the beginning and the fledgling engineering faculty. Unfortunately, there is nothing in the recorded histories to support this conjecture. At Queensland, the same grouping of the modern languages, English, French and German occurred as had happened in Melbourne, Sydney and Adelaide. As Wykes and King commented, French and German were the 'handmaids of English' rather than initially standing on their own (Wykes & King, 1968, p. 6). An assistant lecturer of Modern Languages, Hermiene Ulrich first taught English, French and German, with Jeremiah Stable taking over at the beginning of 1912 when Miss Ulrich married Thomas Parnell, a Physics lecturer, and had to resign. Mr. A.K. Gray joined the department in 1913 (Thomis, 1985, pp. 35, 68, 69, 72; University of Queensland Senate, 1935, p. 26).

When both Stable and Gray were required for war service, Mrs. Parnell was conveniently recalled to manage the department until Stable returned in 1919. By 1919, a Department of Modern Languages was being officially referred to, although earlier groupings of subjects in the Faculty of Arts had been somewhat random. The Senate noted a decrease in student demand for German during the World War I, although they believed it was still an important subject. In 1922 when a Chair of English Language and Literature was created, Stable was appointed to the chair, with two lecturers of modern languages, French and German, also appointed. In the creation of modern language chairs, the pattern previously mentioned was repeated. Just as the University of Melbourne had created a chair of Modern Languages which grouped English, French and German together, so too did the University of Queensland, (University of Qld Senate, 1935, p. 30). However, even after the war when student enrolments rose, and staff numbers increased, the structure of the Department of Modern Languages, with its French and German teaching, remained the same for nearly another decade with still no professorial chairs in either modern language (Thomis, 1985, pp. 176, 192).

When the University of Western Australia was founded, the pattern of languages introduced was little different from that adopted by the other early universities, although at UWA, as previously mentioned, the classical languages and French and German all began with lectureships only (Alexander, 1963, p. 55). As with the other early universities, the published UWA histories did not record he reasons why French and German were introduced. This device, of introducing lectureships not professorial chairs, had been used in the early years of UWA to circumvent financial restrictions. Fred Alexander, the founding head of the Department of History at UWA, noted that this strategy persisted through the 1920s, 1930s, 1940s and even into the 1950s with modern languages being particularly affected. This tactic was not restricted to UWA and was, and sometimes still is, common at all universities. Whilst French and German eventually became independent departments they were headed by readers[8] not professors. It was not until the 1960s that professorial chairs in these two languages were established (Alexander, 1963, pp. 714, 715; de Garis, 1988, p. 232).

Whilst it can be seen that French and German had been established and continued to be taught in each of the colonial universities, what is also clear is that universities were slow to establish chairs in these languages either separately, or jointly. German, for instance, did not gain professorial status in Adelaide, Queensland, and Western Australia, until the 1960s. French did not have professorial chairs in Queensland and Western Australia until 1954 and 1963 respectively (Edgeloe, 2003, p. 341; Gregory, 2013, p. 270; Thomis, 1985, pp. 192, 282). Even at the University of Melbourne where a chair in Modern Languages had been established in 1854, then lapsed due to financial difficulties in 1902, that chair was not filled again until 1937 (Selleck, 2003, p. 642). I argue that the tardiness in establishing professorial chairs for these languages underlined the reluctance of universities to commit the funds required, and reinforced what can be seen as the lesser status of French and German at this stage.

Whilst classical languages and French and German were the languages first taught in universities, it was the modern European languages which further developed through the first half of the twentieth century, although, as will be shown, this was piecemeal development, and often subject to uncertain funding. French and German expanded in staff and student numbers in various universities, and other modern European languages were introduced with Italian being the first. By just one year, UWA led the way with its introduction of Italian. Italian had been accredited as a Leaving Certificate subject in Western Australia in 1920 due to the sus-

---

[8] The term 'reader' was generally used to denote a paid academic position ranked above senior lecturer but below professor.

2.8 Modern European Languages

tained effort of various academics at UWA supporting Italian as a language of Western culture (Klarberg, 1996, p. 155), and possibly because of the increasing Italian migration to Western Australia (Baldassar, 2004, pp. 270, 273). Italian was then taught at UWA from 1929 but, by 1931, was in danger of being eliminated as 'one of the necessary economies of the depression'. Its survival was assured by the gift of £120, specifically to help finance the retention of Italian, from Chancellor James to Pro-Chancellor Murdoch (Alexander, 1963, pp. 173, 174). According to Alexander, and the UWA 1929 Calendar, the part-time lecturer in Italian, Francis Vanzetti (who had begun teaching in 1929) was still teaching Italian part-time in 1963 (Alexander, 1963, p. 715; UWA, 1929, pp. 138, 155).

Generous philanthropy enabled the introduction of Italian language teaching at the University of Sydney in 1930. With a donation of £1000 from a Sydney medical graduate, Dr. Herbert Moran, and a further £1000 from the Countess Freehill,[9] a lectureship in Italian was established. No reason is stated in the Annual Report of the University Senate as to why these persons had an interest in the Italian language – their donations are simply acknowledged. A special grant was also given by the Italian government to enable an Italian academic to teach Italian at the University. However a professor in Italian was not appointed till 1963. It appears that apart from these benefactions in the 1930s, the University did not allocate much resourcing to this fledgling course. Neither had the University given much commitment to the modern languages in general (Turney et al., 1991, p. 510; UniSyd, 1931, pp. 788–9).

There were no new modern European languages introduced at the University of Adelaide before the middle of the twentieth century, and even at the University of Queensland, the extension of language offerings was not in award subjects for an Arts degree. The Institute of Modern Languages was created at the University in 1934, enabling the teaching of French and German and, 'any modern language for which there should be sufficient demand' presumably both from the general public and the university community (University of Qld Senate, 1935, p. 15). This teaching of modern languages was nevertheless outside of the Arts degree and thus was a non-credit bearing activity (Thomis, 1985, p. 132).

A national report from the Australian Council for Educational Research published in 1940 listed modern languages as one of the subject areas they were reviewing. French, German and Italian were the only languages mentioned, suggesting that these were the only modern languages taught in secondary schools in Australia at the time of their review which began in 1936 (Committee on the teaching of modern languages in the secondary school, 1940, p. 10). Whilst universities at the time controlled the secondary curriculum and examinations for the Leaving and Matriculation examinations, there is, unfortunately, no detail in this report about the state of secondary languages in the late 1930s and any connection there might have been to the development of other modern languages in the university sector.

---

[9] The first Australian woman to become a papal countess in her own right.

2.9 The Melbourne Solution for More Languages

The University of Melbourne had, quite early in the twentieth century, started to consider changes to the curriculum and the possibility of increasing the range of languages taught. But as will be shown, the University proceeded very cautiously, perhaps in the light of the financial difficulties at the beginning of the century. This discussion came in the midst of an investigation by a Joint Committee of Enquiry in early 1913, which included the general finances of the University, buildings, equipment, the library, and staffing (UMA-Registrar's Correspondence. 1913/190. 17 March, 1913. Masson). At their meeting in November 1913, the Committee recommended a systematic classification of teaching staff and, in stating that it was 'common knowledge' that the University was understaffed, they recommended that a new order of teachers, with the title of Reader,[10] should be established.

> It is believed that the creation of this office would do much to meet a recognized want. There are many subjects which ought to be taught in any great and progressive university, but which from lack of resources the University of Melbourne is at present unable to take in hand. Among such may be named as examples, Italian, Spanish, and other European languages, Chinese and Japanese, Semitic languages, Hellenistic Greek, Egyptology, Assyriology, etc. The Readers might also be able to give valuable assistance to the Professors and Lecturers by undertaking more specialized teaching within existing departments of study. It is proposed that they should receive no direct remuneration from the University...The amount of fees to be paid should be determined by the Council, who should also decide what proportion thereof should be paid into the University funds. (UniMelb. Joint Committee of Enquiry, 1913, p. 10)

Whilst the Committee had recognised the need for an expansion of the languages taught to include more European languages, Asian languages and ancient languages, they were not prepared to allocate resources to increased language teaching out of consideration for the financial priorities for the University. Whilst the Joint Committee's report, including the proposal for Readers,[11] was generally adopted by the Council, the Annual Report for 1913/1914, recorded that 'no general amendment of the University Acts has, however, been submitted to Parliament during the year (UniMelb, 1914, p. 631). So nothing had happened in the following 8 months to progress this new role of Readers.

Meanwhile by 5 August 1914, World War I had erupted, with Australia and other dominions joining Britain in the hostilities (Barnard, 1962, pp. 481, 482; Meaney, 1985, p. 217). The Annual Report of 1914/1915 detailed how the University of Melbourne had been affected by many staff and students going overseas on military service. It is not surprising that the 'comprehensive report' about the University submitted back in late 1913, was not acted upon and was overrun by those world

---

[10] Here the term 'Reader' is used in a different sense to that on page 44. AS indicated above, such Readers would not be paid by the University but directly by their students.

[11] Readers were to be paid directly by their students.

2.9 The Melbourne Solution for More Languages

events (UniMelb, 1915, p. 651). The University's cautious discussions about an expansion of languages came to naught. Once again the opportunity for the teaching of additional modern European languages and Asian languages was put aside, this time not by financial considerations but by the much greater issue of a world war in which Australia was involved. It can be argued that, had modern languages, specifically French, German and Russian been more widely taught, politicians, diplomats, public servants, and personnel of the Defence Forces who had knowledge of such languages might have found them particularly useful at this time, given the involvement of France, Germany and Russia in this world war.

However, the issue of teaching more languages had not been completely put aside. On 3 July 1916, Dr. Leeper raised the issue again in Council, for 'the appointment of Readers to provide teaching, particularly in languages such as Japanese and Russian, …as soon as possible' (UniMelb, 1916a, p. 391). His motion was carried and 'forwarded to the Professorial Board' (UniMelb, 1916a, p. 392). At a later meeting on 24 July 1916, letters from the Consul-General of the Netherlands, the Consul-General of Belgium and the Chamber of Commerce asked for Dutch and Japanese to be taught to further commercial relations with countries such as Japan and the Dutch colonies, such as the nearby Netherlands East Indies. These letters were referred by Council to the Professorial Board (UniMelb, 1916b, p. 400). There is no evidence that either Dr. Leeper's motion or the pleas of external organisations and other foreign governments' representatives were acted upon by the Professorial Board. Subsequently, in the Council meeting of 5 November 1917, the Arts Faculty submitted a proposal for Dutch to be introduced as a subject. But Council was not disposed to allow Dutch as an examinable subject 'until it had had further experience on the teaching of Dutch in the university through an instructor' (UniMelb, 1917a, pp. 84, 85). Dr. Augustin Lodewyckx's appointment as the instructor in Dutch was listed in the 1916/1917 Annual Report. As with the previously proposed role of reader, subjects studied through an instructor would not be part of a degree or diploma; students had to pay fees directly to the instructors who would receive no remuneration from the University. This, of course, was quite satisfactory for Dr. Lodewyckx as he was already a paid staff member of the Faculty of Arts (UniMelb, 1917b, pp. xxxvii, 20, 651). Again, the Council proceeded very cautiously as only one new language, Dutch, was introduced under these strict conditions. Even the obvious political and commercial advantages of teaching Dutch, given the proximity of the Dutch East Indies (later Indonesia), did not sway the Council to teach Dutch formally within a degree course. It is ironic that by the time Dutch was introduced as a degree subject in 1942, the Dutch had lost control of their colonial territory during World War II and never regained it.

Still the University prevaricated in the allocation of funds to modern languages other than the existing French and German teaching. The lists of Australian delegates to international conferences such as those of the Institute of Pacific Relations show that at this time various University of Melbourne academics were involved in these international forums (Walker, 2009, pp. 222, 225, 226). This suggests that there was academic and political interaction outside of the University of Melbourne as international affairs unfolded in the 1920s and 1930s and Australia expanded its national interests and diplomatic relationships. A commitment to the teaching of the languages of more European countries and their colonies in the Asia-Pacific region would have reinforced and strengthened Australia's position internationally. Nevertheless, instead, the system of fee-for-service instructorships which had begun with Dutch, had expanded by 1928 to include Japanese, Italian, Russian, Spanish, and Scandinavian languages (UWA, 1929, p. 79). In the University Calendar it looked as though the University of Melbourne had committed itself in the 1920s to a much wider range of languages but, as previously explained, this was an administrative commitment, not a financial one.

The picture for the modern European languages by the middle of the twentieth century was one where the teaching of French and German dominated in both secondary schools and in universities. Mario Daniel Martin has argued that the rise of the Direct Method of teaching, emphasising the spoken language, strengthened the teaching of two modern and 'living' languages, French and German. These languages had always been seen as commercially 'useful' by the businessmen of the colonies and in early Federation Australia (Martin, M, 2005, p. 56). The Wykes Report offered an explanation for the dominance of French and German: the numerical importance of subjects become self-perpetuating when there is steady flow of students to the university and a steady returning stream of teachers to schools (Wykes, 1966, p. 28). This self-perpetuating dominance was also demonstrated by the linguistic backgrounds of the delegates to the first Congress of University Modern Language Staffs held in Melbourne in August 1950: 83% of the delegates represented either French or German (Australasian Universities Modern Languages Association, 1950, pp. 37, 38). It was not until the second half of the twentieth century that the modern European languages expanded far more broadly and rapidly as Australia's population became more linguistically diverse through mass migration.

2.10 Asian Languages

The third group of languages considered for the early Australian universities are Asian languages. Again, as with the classical and modern European languages, Australian universities had before them the example of British universities. Oxford, for instance, had in the mid nineteenth century, when Melbourne and Sydney universities were founded, a long tradition of study in Oriental[12] languages with chairs in Hebrew, Arabic, Sanskrit and Chinese (Prest, 1993, p. 217). Cambridge University

---

[12] For British universities, languages of the Middle East and Asia were all included in the term Oriental Languages, reflecting British imperial interests of the time.

2.10 Asian Languages

also taught Indian, Oriental and Semitic languages (Brooke, 1993, p. 427). Notably, the University of Sydney established the first Department of Oriental Studies in an Australian university in 1866, appointing the Rev. Dr. Wazir Beg to a readership in Oriental Languages and Literature, with Arabic as the main teaching language.[13] However, there was no evidence to be found in the University Senate's annual reports as to why the Oriental Languages and Literature readership was introduced or whether languages other than Arabic were taught, although it could be argued that there was an attempt to follow the model of Oriental languages at Oxford. Student interest was apparently poor, the readership was short-lived and the subjects had disappeared from the University of Sydney Calendar subject listings by 1870 (MacLaurin, 1969, p. 1; UniSyd, 1867, pp. vi, 47, 1868, pp. vi, 83, 1870, p. 79).

Australia's trading interests with various Asian countries had already begun through the activities of the individual colonies in the nineteenth century (Walker, 2009, p. 72). As far as Asian languages were concerned, the University of Melbourne's Council had discussed additional languages, including Chinese and Japanese in 1913 and 1916, with no further action then. It was, nevertheless, at the University of Sydney where the short-lived Department of Oriental Studies had existed in the late nineteenth century, that an Asian language was first introduced as a subject for a degree. Whilst the call of tradition, commercial usefulness and the educational imperatives for the professions laid the foundations for the initial language offerings at the University of Sydney in classical and modern European languages, the first Asian language, Japanese, was introduced for very different reasons. Now the Federal government became involved, and for the national interest of Australia, both politically, and for matters of defence, the teaching of Japanese language was introduced near the end of World War I. Prime Minister Hughes distrusted the motives of the Japanese and was concerned about their influence in the Pacific (Meaney, 1985, p. 260). Consequently, knowledge of the Japanese language could have been very useful to Australia in understanding the intentions of the Japanese. The Department of Defence gave funds to the University of Sydney in 1916 to enable teaching to begin in 1917. The educational historian Ailsa Zainu'ddin quoted the brief from the Chief of General Staff to the Department of Defence about the appointment of James Murdoch, the first lecturer in Japanese.

> It is not considered desirable that it should be known that he was brought down from Japan expressly to teach Japanese in a Military College. We wish the public rather to take the view that we have taken advantage of his presence on the University teaching staff to add Japanese to the curriculum of the Royal Military College. (Zainu'ddin, 1988, p. 47)

It is apparent from this defence brief that the Australians whom the Federal government had in mind to learn Japanese were chiefly the army officer cadets of Duntroon Military College, which had been established just six years earlier (Moore,

---

[13] It was an Oriental Studies department in a very broad sense, encompassing mainly Semitic Studies.

2001, p. x). This brief further reinforced the strategic and defence reasons for the introduction of Japanese. Although Melbourne was the seat of the Federal government at this time, and the location of government ministers, including the Minister for Defence, Duntroon was located in Canberra in the newly established Australian Capital Territory, much closer to Sydney than Melbourne. The location of Duntroon underlined the real reason for the Department of Defence funding for Japanese at the University of Sydney rather than at the University of Melbourne: Sydney was the closest university to the College. Zainu'ddin further contended that as the Japanese had been allies of the British in World War I, the Government now needed to 'disguise the Australian suspicion that a present ally might be a future enemy, although this was clearly the motive behind the initial interest in promoting the study of Japanese in Australia' (Zainu'ddin, 1988, pp. 46, 47).

From 1917, James Murdoch formerly of Aberdeen University began teaching Japanese at the University of Sydney, travelling down to Canberra to teach Japanese at Duntroon. In October 1918, the University created a Chair of Oriental Studies, which Murdoch accepted in February 1919, an appointment which should have seen him through the next seven years. Further Commonwealth funds enabled him to visit Japan annually and report back to the Department of Defence on what he had noted of Japanese public opinion and foreign policy. Murdoch had, prior to coming to Sydney, lived in Japan for some 25 years, married a Japanese woman, written a history of Japan and was viewed as an international authority on Japanese matters. Unfortunately, Murdoch died in 1921 but his successor, Arthur Sadler, a Japanese language and culture specialist, further developed the Oriental Studies department over the next 25 years that he held the Chair. The military connections for Japanese language teaching still existed, and teaching was still presumably paid for by the Department of Defence, as Sadler also taught Japanese at the Royal Military College in Sydney for the six years that Duntroon was temporarily located there (Moore, 2001, p. 90; Selleck, 2003, pp. 642, 643; Turney et al., 1991, p. 524; UniSyd, 1919, p. 648; Zainu'ddin, 1988, pp. 47, 48).

Japanese language teaching began at the University of Melbourne in rather different circumstances. There were no government funds forthcoming but the University of Melbourne would have been aware of the Japanese teaching at the University of Sydney and Duntroon. It was via the fee-for-service instructor scheme, previously described, that the Rev. Thomas Jollie Smith, Presbyterian minister at East Malvern, was appointed as Japanese instructor with Mr. Mōshi Inagaki as assistant instructor (UniMelb, 1920, p. 772). Apparently, the Rev. Mr. Smith, who had a great interest in Japanese language,[14] had offered his services to the University of Melbourne to begin teaching Japanese in advance of a proper lecturer being appointed. This was a much poorer arrangement academically compared to the University of Sydney's Japanese lecturer and Japanese specialist, Murdoch. Zainu'ddin asserted in her review of the teaching of Japanese at Melbourne University that 'Melbourne University was less financial, less fortunate and less

---

[14] Thomas Jollie Smith had studied Japanese as he intended to undertake missionary work amongst the Japanese in Korea.

interested in Oriental Studies' (Zainu'ddin, 1988, p. 48). This opinion certainly accorded with the sentiments of the 1913 Joint Committee of Enquiry who were quite firm in their resolution that they could not afford to fund additional languages. The University of Melbourne's apparent lack of interest in, and unwillingness to commit funds to, Oriental Studies is particularly curious given that, as earlier mentioned, from the beginning of Federation in 1901 through to 1927, Federal Parliament was located in Melbourne. There would presumably have been opportunity for much formal and informal interaction between politicians, public servants and academics in what was not a very large city.

There was no impetus for any Asian languages at the University of Adelaide in the early twentieth century as there was at the University of Queensland. Queensland had been trading with various Asian countries since the late nineteenth century, and these commercial interests appear to have prompted interest in Asian languages from several quarters. Unfortunately, none of the proposals for Asian languages came to fruition (Tweedie, 1994, p. 224). One such a proposal in 1914 came from Edwin Fowles, a member of the University Senate, who had just returned from overseas with ideas for the expansion of the university's disciplines, including Eastern languages.[15] The University was approached in 1916 by the Ipswich Chamber of Commerce, who wished to support a chair in Eastern languages, long in advance of when the chair in Asian languages was actually created some 50 years later (Thomis, 1985, pp. 81, 82). The University was cautious about introducing new departments, believing that existing ones should be strengthened first. However, in 1936, the teaching of Japanese was again discussed after an approach to the Senate from the Japanese Consulate. Alexander Melbourne (a history lecturer with a keen interest in East Asia) who had reported on Chinese and Japanese universities after his second trip to the Far East, was influential in the appointment of a lecturer in Japanese history and culture who started in March 1938. Unfortunately, the events of World War II meant that the appointment, located within the Department of Social Studies, was short-lived. Seita Ryuunosuke, the highly-qualified lecturer, was investigated by Australian intelligence after the Pearl Harbour bombing. He was deemed to be a Japanese spy and repatriated to Japan in 1942 (Murray, J, 2004, pp. 184, 185; Thomis, 1985, pp. 132, 192, 1986, p. 3). Just as Australia's national and defence interests had prompted the introduction of Japanese at the University of Sydney, the same interests had done away with Japanese at the University of Queensland.

It was also commercial interests that prompted the introduction of an Asian language, again Japanese, at the University of Western Australia but this was not until the late 1960s. Significant trade in iron ore had developed between Australia and Japan, and funding for a Chair in Japanese Studies was given by a group of mining companies. This chair was located in the Faculty of Economics and Commerce at the insistence of the mining companies, not, as more traditionally happened with

---

[15] Eastern languages was the term Fowles used rather than Oriental or Asian languages.

languages, in the Faculty of Arts. The teaching of Japanese, which began in 1972, was to be slanted towards practical and commercial application and knowledge of Japanese society and culture, rather than towards literary knowledge. The first professor was to be 'fluent in Japanese, qualified in Economics and familiar at a scholarly level with Japanese society.' Such a multi-skilled person was found, Bernard Key, a young American (de Garis, 1988, pp. 249, 274; McLure, 2011, p. 72). This was an auspicious start for Japanese Studies.[16]

2.11 Conclusion

It has been demonstrated in this chapter that the earliest colonial universities had been greatly influenced by the traditions of British universities both in their foundations and languages taught, although the later post-Federation universities took more cognizance of what was pertinent to Australian conditions, both in university structures and subjects taught, including languages. The key motivation was the cultural and intellectual foundations being forged for colonial societies. Recognising that the British university model was the training of young men for political office and the professions, the colonial universities took on this model seeking to develop capable, educated leaders for the future. Training in classical languages was a part of this model which the colonial universities also adopted, as they did with the teaching of French and German which were deemed as modern, practical, and 'living' languages. Whilst the prime importance of the classics endured into the twentieth century, the modern languages, French and German began to take hold as more 'useful' and commercially valuable. These two languages dominated the school and university curriculum. Other modern European languages had been introduced in the early twentieth century, but there was no particular national imperative for other languages until after World War II.

As has been shown, the scholarly tradition of Oriental (or Asian languages) from the British university system was not emulated by Australia's early universities. An Asian language, specifically Japanese, was introduced at a point when it was deemed necessary for Australia better to understand its Asian neighbours. It was Australia's defence and strategic interests that prompted the funding of Japanese although, as has been demonstrated, there was not a wholesale embracing of Asian languages across the universities before World War II, apart from efforts to introduce Japanese for commercial reasons. It was in fact World War II and the events following when Australia was further precipitated into world affairs, that a commitment to providing a diversity of Asian languages, particularly Indonesian and Chinese, only became an imperative for a range of defence, strategic and economic reasons when Australia was further precipitated into world affairs following World

---

[16] According to McLure (2011, p. 4), J.B. Conyngham was the first candidate to be offered the chair, but it was Bernard Key who was subsequently offered the chair and took up the position. De Garis does not mention Conyngham at all.

2.11 Conclusion

War II. This chapter has demonstrated that the narrative of national interest, national progress, and national leadership punctuated the reasons for the development of university education in Australia. The next chapter extends the discussion about the expansion of the tertiary sector as the population increased rapidly. The consequent expansion of language offerings is also explored in the light of Australia's changing political, trade and defence considerations according to what was considered to be in the national interest.

Chapter 3
Post-War Expansion

> The Australian community needs 'those trained in the language, literature and culture of other nations. (Wykes, 1966, p. 3)

This challenge to Australia's language needs was voiced in the survey report of foreign language teaching in Australian universities prepared by Olive Wykes in 1966. Significantly, it was in this report that the national importance of languages other than English was stressed for the first time, although there was no immediate response by any government to give languages more prominence. Whilst six universities had been established by 1911, the events of World War I stalled further higher education development as staff and students of universities hastened to join up, and at home others threw themselves into various war service activities such as fundraising, drilling, voluntary teaching and caring for the sick and injured (Selleck, 2003, p. 529). It has been estimated that nearly 35% of Australian university students enlisted for service (Pietsch, 2013, pp. 127, 128). Some 60,000 Australians died in the war and more than 150,000 were wounded (Garton & Stanley, 2013, p. 47). It was a more sober and worldly-wise Australia which entered the 1920s and 1930s with a new and developing involvement in world affairs and the expansion of its higher university sector.

This chapter focusses on the development of universities from the 1940s to 1990s, in the context of the multiplicity of reports across this period, identifying trends in both general reports about higher education and those specifically relating to language offerings. The trend which was evident in language reports was the increasing concern about the decline of interest in languages from the 1960s right through into the 1990s. By contrast, the more general higher education reports showed an increasing trend towards economic rationalism as an imperative for the tertiary sector. This chapter also picks up the theme of national interest, a concept much used in Australia by politicians and media commentators. In the context of this book, it is taken to mean the justification of certain actions, decisions or policies which are upheld for the good of Australia. As will be shown, what is in Australia's 'national interest' has been applied in varying situations. It can relate not only to economic, cultural, defence, and strategic decision making, but also to decisions made for the social harmony or social cohesion of the nation. I argue that successive governments, politicians, influential speakers and writers have used 'national interest' to justify their decisions regarding university polices and funding. The establishment of more universities was a response to what was considered in the national interest at the time.

Firstly, this development was in response to the rapidly increasing population post World War II, the baby boomers[1] and the children of the post-World War II migrants (Mackinnon & Proctor, 2013, p. 440), and thus there were more people wanting to undertake tertiary study. So it was in Australia's interest to expand the sector to enable as many young people as possible to attend university to achieve that level of education and become productive members of Australian society. This development meant also relieving overcrowding in existing institutions, giving independence to regional university colleges, creating universities such as the NSW University of Technology, which addressed stated national priorities for training in science and technology. In the case of the Australian National University, a postgraduate university was created in 1946 with a focus on research rather than teaching and a priority for the development of Australia's research capability (H. Forsyth, 2014, pp. 26, 32, 33). The Federal government was involving itself more in the affairs of universities, and successive governments had different national priorities for tertiary education, each wanting to ensure that the sector was relevant in its courses and efficient in its structures. The sector was regularly reviewed and surveyed from the 1950s for the next 40 or so years. These reviews and reports, coupled with the recommendations of the Universities Commission (which later became the Tertiary Education Commission) also drove change in the sector.

The culmination of what were known as the Dawkins[2] reforms or Dawkins revolution of the late 1980s (Milne, 2001, p. 2), was massive change in the tertiary sector following the creation of the Unified National System. Through these reforms, 19 pre-1987 universities and more than 40 colleges of advanced education and institutes of technology amalgamated in various configurations to become 36 public universities (Moses, 2004, p. 2). This reduction in the number of institutions sought to bring about efficiencies and competitiveness in the sector, according to the higher education policy of the then Labor government. This was, according to Simon Marginson, a prominent educational researcher, a deliberate strategy to develop 'corporate-style institutions'. Whilst institutions had autonomy in educational matters, obligatory 'reporting and data collection were standardised and intensified' as the Federal government sought to make universities more accountable (Marginson, 1997, p. 232). This 'language of economic rationalism', as Marginson called it, typified the change of government thinking about the role of higher education (Marginson, 1997, p. 123). The focus in 1950 had been on the financial needs of those institutions, albeit noting the national importance of the development of

---

[1] Children born between 1946 and 1964 in the demographic spike of births post-World War II.

[2] These reforms were named after John Dawkins who was the Labor Government's Minister of the Department of Employment, Education and Training (DEET) from 1987 to 1991.

universities (Commonwealth Committee on Needs of Universities. (CCNU), 1950, p. 13). It then evolved by the late 1980s into a much stronger imperative about the national goals and priorities of those institutions and how they needed to be responsive to national needs and interests (CCNU, 1950, p. 1; DEET, 1988, p. 10).

It was through a relentless series of reports, policies and surveys, commissioned variously by the Federal government or academies, such as the Australian Academy of the Humanities (AAH), or undertaken by individual academics that the changing priorities of the sectors were revealed. In their totality, these reports were concerned with the development of Australia and its people across the second half of the twentieth century. Alongside these broad higher education reports were those which specifically focussed on foreign language teaching, one which related to the needs of migrants, and finally a report which dealt with language and literacy (DEET, 1991b).

Interwoven with this broader picture of higher education reform was the development of language offerings in the tertiary sector. It will be argued these offerings were shaped by successive changes in attitudes to languages and funding priorities. Evidence of these attitudes to languages is found in specifically language related reports and surveys, as well as in the submissions which tertiary institutions made to the Australian Universities Commission (AUC) and the subsequent Tertiary Education Commission (TEC), and the approval or non-approval of these submissions. It will be demonstrated that the rhetoric about the importance of languages also changed, from an emphasis on the educational and cultural aspects in the 1960s, to one of greater recognition of community or migrant languages in the 1970s. However, through the 1980s the emphasis changed again, until, by the 1990s, the government rhetoric was quite forceful: 'priority attention must be given to languages of broader national interest to Australia' (DEET, 1991a, p. 15). Those priorities were often couched in terms of Australia's economic interests.

As Lo Bianco and Aliani have commented, Australia has engaged 'robustly with language policy' whilst still being a 'steadfastly monolingual society'. Australia had certainly come to be seen as a multicultural nation but its concurrent monolingual attitude continued to pose a contradiction. The key is perhaps, as Lo Bianco and Aliani have also cautioned, 'how ambitious and often how unrealistic have been the aims of language policy' (Lo Bianco & Aliani, 2013, pp. xii, 6). This suggests that those passionately concerned with the needs of reform in language policy have been stymied by the indifference of those who have influence in decision making and who are still clinging to monolingualism whether they are in government or in the general population.

3.1 Post-World War II Australia

As Australia emerged from World War II, it had the opportunity to capitalise on the success of its wartime industries, converting them to the peacetime growth of the economy (Darian-Smith, 2013, p. 105). Australia was, said the historian Marjorie Barnard, because of its isolation from the troubled parts of the rest of the world, attractive to foreign capital (Barnard, 1962, p. 576). As service personnel returned home, there was a concentration of training under the Commonwealth Reconstruction Training Scheme (CRTS) which enabled them to undertake trade or technical qualifications or a university degree at public expense (Barnard, 1962, p. 575; Gallagher, 2003, p. 52). University enrolments surged in all six universities as almost a third of the student body in the immediate post-war years came from the armed services, taxing the meagre post-war staff. At the University of Melbourne in 1948, for instance, there were around 2700 fulltime CRTS students out of a total enrolment of 9500 (Mulvaney, 2003, p. iii). As John Mulvaney, ex-RAAF, and later an eminent archaeologist observed, 'the age and experience of these people enhanced and challenged the quality' of staff and students for teaching and learning (Mulvaney, 2003, p. iii, 2011, p. 41). The funds for CRTS students were a boost to universities' finances, although when CRTS students completed their courses, this specific funding declined (Ford, 1953, p. 57; Gallagher, 2003, p. 90; Poynter & Rasmussen, 1996, p. 105). However, apart from the importance of training ex-service personnel, Australia needed to develop economically, and for that a larger population was needed (Calwell, 1945, pp. 1, 2, 1948, p. 13). Coupled with these nation-building considerations, were issues of security. The Japanese attacks on Australia and in the Pacific during the War had heightened fears about Australia's ability to defend itself (Lack & Templeton, 1995, p. xiii; Ozolins, 1993, p. 5).

The idea of a national university was conceived quite specifically to meet the needs for research and the specialised knowledge to drive this revitalised development of Australia. Among those involved in the early planning for the Australian National University (ANU) in 1943 and 1944, was Herbert (Nugget) Coombs, Head of the Department of Post-War Reconstruction. Peter Baume, former Chancellor of the ANU, argued that Coombs was the driving force behind the creation of the ANU as part of the post-war reconstruction effort. It was Coombs' view that Australia ought to have a postgraduate and research university and, the success of the ANU in achieving that vision had much to do with Coombs' involvement in its academic and administrative life (Australian Electoral Commission, 2000). When the ANU was eventually established in 1946, it was the first university to be founded in Australia for 35 years. Its mandate was initially for postgraduate research in medicine, the physical sciences and the social sciences, with a fourth research school in Pacific Studies. As the ANU Act specified, its function was 'to encourage, and provide facilities for post-graduate research and study, both generally and in relation to national importance to Australia' (Australian National University Act, 1946, section 6a). With such a specific postgraduate research focus, there was no undergraduate teaching and languages were simply not taught (Australian Academy of Science, n.d.; Australian National University, n.d.; National Graduate, 2000, p. 1; Wigmore, 1963, p. 160).

In May 1927, Federal Parliament moved to the newly established capital, Canberra (Wigmore, 1963, pp. 29, 109), and a tertiary institution was required to enable public servants, all of whom were part-time, to continue or begin their studies. The Canberra University College (CUC), which was established in 1930, in association with the University of Melbourne, did teach languages. The CUC offered the same traditional education as did the existing Australian universities, including the languages French, German and Latin (Foster & Varghese, 1996, p. 144; Wigmore, 1963, p. 137), a selection which was almost identical to that offered at the University of Melbourne in 1930 (Burton, 1953, p. 4).

Just as the CUC served national needs by educating Federal public servants, so when the government sought training in Asian languages (or Oriental languages as they were then known) for diplomats and other public servants in Canberra (Foster & Varghese, 1996, p. 303), the CUC was the obvious place to establish such training. The historian, Marjorie Jacobs, disagreed at the time, seeing this as centralisation for the sake of economy. Whilst applauding the establishment of Oriental languages at CUC, she argued that the existing Oriental Studies department at the University of Sydney could be reopened to enable more students to study such languages. This, she said, would meet the national need by enabling the widest possible training for languages of such importance (Jacobs, 1953, pp. 82, 90). Nevertheless, the University of Sydney's Oriental Studies department was not revived at that stage and, in 1952, an additional Commonwealth government grant-in-aid[3] enabled the establishment of the School of Oriental Languages (later Oriental Studies) at CUC (Burton, 1953, p. 5; Ford, 1953, p. 56). This new School offered Modern and Classical Japanese, Modern and Classical Chinese, and subsequently Indonesian and Malay. Such studies were vital, according to Richard Casey, the Minister for External Affairs, and very important from both a cultural and practical point of view according to Ralph Farrell, Dean of Arts at the University of Sydney (A Staff Correspondent, 1953). By this specific Federal government funding, the language offerings of CUC were directed towards what was now deemed in the national interest, Asian languages and cultures.

The next phase of the post-war university development was also quite specific in its direction towards the needs of Australian industry. The New South Wales University of Technology (NSWUT) was founded in 1949, changing its name to the University of New South Wales (UNSW) in 1958 (O'Farrell, 1999, p. 31; Willis, 1983, p. 27). The impetus for the founding of this university was to supply the highly trained scientific and technical manpower that was needed 'to consolidate the rapid and extensive industrial expansion which has taken place in recent years in this State' (Willis, 1983, p. 13.) In the founding of the NSWUT, the NSW government saw itself as acting for the national interest by leading the way in technological education (O'Farrell, 1999, p. 22).

Not surprisingly, in line with the founding brief, the first departments of the NSWUT were branches of Science and Engineering (O'Farrell, 1999, p. 34; Willis, 1983, pp. 36, 37). There was also a small Humanities Department as it was deemed necessary graduates should not just be technical experts but have a broad understanding of the humanities (O'Farrell, 1999, p. 3). Languages, though, were not part of this humanities curriculum as they did not fit into the broad technological aims of this new university. Both ANU and the NSWUT were important new foundations:

---

[3] CUC's sole revenue (apart from students' fees) was an annual grant-in-aid from the Commonwealth Government.

the ANU in its research focus and NSWUT in its emphasis on leading technology for Australia's development (O'Farrell, 1999, p. 58). As its change of name suggested, the UNSW's emphasis gradually shifted to become more like the traditional universities, with a wider range of teaching areas, and the expectation that it would help relieve overcrowding at the University of Sydney (C of A, 1957, p. 88). To this end in 1960, the Faculty of Arts was created with a broad range of subjects which, from 1963, included French, then German and Spanish from 1966, with Russian following in 1969. In 1965, a Chair of Asian Studies was established but never filled, apparently because, according to Albert Willis, former Pro Vice-Chancellor of UNSW, a suitable candidate could not be found (O'Farrell, 1999, pp. 81, 82; Willis, 1983, pp. 102, 167, 185).

3.2 The Mills Report: The First Reckoning

With the creation of the NSWUT in 1949, there were now eight universities in Australia as well as the CUC. The universities were in financial difficulty due to rising costs, and the gradual loss of CRTS grants. There were very low levels of research in these universities because of inadequate funds. The vice-chancellors had collectively pressed the then Chifley Labor government for an enquiry into the needs of the universities and Chifley responded by setting up a committee (Ford, 1953, p. 57). Although the Labor government was defeated in December 1949, the vice-chancellors were relieved when the new Prime Minister Menzies confirmed the committee's appointment and reiterated the importance of a report on the needs of universities (Martin, A, 2007, pp. 181, 182; White, F, 1979, p. 5). The *Commonwealth Committee on Needs of Universities: Interim Report* (CCNU, 1950) was the first of the comprehensive reports into tertiary education since the Universities Commission had been formed in 1943 and the Commonwealth government began to have more substantial financial involvement with the universities (Groenewegen, 1986, p. 1). The chair of the CCNU committee, Richard Mills, was also the inaugural chairman of the Universities Commission, building good relationships with the universities, particularly through the administration of university places for the CRTS (Gallagher, 2003, pp. 68, 70, 74, 90).

The importance of the Mills Report for growth of the university sector was the States Grants (Universities) Act 1951 by which additional grants were made to state governments to assist universities. As Menzies said, 'encouragement of higher education in Australia was a matter of first-rate national importance' (Govt. Will Grant Extra Money for Universities, 1951). This report did not contain details of courses and curricula and certainly not languages; it was concerned with broad issues about the involvement of the Commonwealth with the universities, the financial difficulties of the universities, their immediate needs, and the basis on which Commonwealth grants would be made (CCNU, 1950,

3.2 The Mills Report: The First Reckoning

p. 1). The only reference to languages in the Interim Report, under special needs, was that 'the Committee has given some consideration to the need to promote Oriental Studies and in particular the immediate need to promote studies in Oriental Languages' (CCNU, 1950, p. 13). The Committee's recommendation was 'that action should not be taken by the Commonwealth government towards establishing a School of Oriental Studies in any University until the Committee has had a further opportunity of considering the various possibilities' (CCNU, 1950, pp. 13, 22). Those further enquiries by the Committee resulted, as has been previously mentioned, in an additional grant being made to CUC through the Commonwealth Office of Education to establish the School of Oriental Languages (Auchmuty, 1959, p. 25; Burton, 1953, p. 5; CCNU, 1950, p. 13).

There were good economic and geo-political reasons for Australian diplomats and public servants to have better knowledge of Asian cultures and languages, such as was now offered through courses at CUC. The end of World War II had seen the emergence of China as a Communist country, the Korean War of 1950–1953 and progressive decolonisation in a number of South-East Asian countries: Indonesia, Burma, the Philippines, Vietnam and Malaya. Australia's international arena and interests were changing considerably and, although it may still have seen itself as a Western nation in an Asian region, it could not ignore the fact that, rather than the 'Far East', Asia was for Australia the 'near north'. These sentiments had been expressed by Governor-General McKell at a meeting of the United Nations Economic Commission for Asia and Far East held in Australia in November 1948 (Far East is near north to Australia, 1948). In the Asian region, Australia had been involved in the British Commonwealth Occupation Force in Japan from the late 1940s to the early 1950s (Gerster, 2008, pp. 4, 5), and had also taken a first-hand interest in the Indonesian push for independence which it gained in 1949. Australia was growing its trade with China in spite of Australia's non-recognition of the communist regime and seeking to re-establish its wool trade with Japan in spite of post-war community hostility (Tweedie, 1994, pp. 119, 154).

As staff numbers in the Department of External Affairs substantially grew, the Department had, in 1944, introduced and funded a course in diplomatic studies to recruit and train its own cadets (Foster & Varghese, 1996, pp. 146, 149). This course only lasted till 1953 when the Federal government decided it was no longer necessary (Foster & Varghese, 1996, p. 151; Gyngell & Wesley, 2007, pp. 59, 60; McDougall, 1998, pp. 6, 7). This was quite contradictory behaviour on the part of the government when clearly, with the rapidly changing situations in the Asian region, Australian diplomats needed more comprehensive training than ever. It is fortuitous, however, that the CUC had established a School of Oriental Languages in 1952, adding to the already established Far Eastern History course. Such Asian language training was therefore available at the university level to those who might wish to undertake it, whether they were public servants, diplomats, those pursuing trade and business opportunities, or those with simply an interest in the languages, culture and history of the Asian region.

3.3 Murray Report and More Commonwealth Control

Although the Government had acted on the recommendations of the Mills Report to make grants to the states for the funding of universities, it became increasingly apparent that the states still did not have sufficient finance to meet the growing demands for tertiary and technical education. There was still reluctance on the part of some vice-chancellors to accept the idea of a Commonwealth committee supervising their development, and apprehension at an intrusion into their autonomy (White, F, 1979, p. 6). The funds granted through that 1950 Mills Report were simply not enough and 'by the beginning of 1952 were in any case seriously eroded by inflation' (Martin, A, 2007, p. 186). The vice-chancellors again pressed their case about the financial crisis for universities, citing 'the importance of the universities to national development and defence' (Australian Vice-Chancellors' Committee. (AVCC), 1952, pp. i, 7, 8).

Eventually, in 1956, Menzies responded by commissioning another report on higher education. Keith Murray, who chaired the committee of enquiry, was considered eminently suitable as he was chairman of the British University Grants Committee and very skilled in assessing the financial needs of universities. The other committee members were Charles Morris of Leeds University; Alex Reid, Chancellor of the University of Western Australia; Ian Clunies Ross, Chairman of CSIRO; and J.C. Richards, a senior manager at BHP (C of A, 1957, p. 4; Martin, A, 2007, pp. 197, 198). Their brief was to investigate the financial needs of universities, additional facilities needed, university technological education and the role of the university in the Australian community (C of A, 1957, pp. 5, 86; Martin, A, 2007, p. 197). In their report, known as the Murray Report, the Committee expressed alarm: the situation they said was 'critical'; 'we had hoped to find that they [the universities] were at present adequately staffed and equipped to discharge their heavy responsibilities to the students and to the nation. This is, unfortunately, far from the case.' They recommended an immediate injection of funds into the universities for both capital and recurrent expenditure for the next 3 years. It was critically important, they said, for universities to be able to cope with the increased enrolments expected and to avoid the situation becoming catastrophic. The Committee could not have expressed with more urgency the pressing financial needs of the nation's universities (C of A, 1957, pp. 4, 125).

The Murray Report cited the need for more graduates of science and technology to ensure for Australia's industrial and technological development, and also a need for more tertiary institutions to relieve the overcrowding in existing institutions (C of A, 1957, pp. 49, 68). With Australia's expanding external responsibilities, additional diplomatic and consular graduate-trained staff were required overseas although there was no detail as to the academic disciplines required in these graduates (C of A, 1957, p. 15). It could be argued that such expanding external responsibilities would require greater language capacity, but no such conclusion was drawn by the Committee. A permanent University Grants Committee was recommended to formulate acceptable policies and programs to serve the national

3.3 Murray Report and More Commonwealth Control

interest, for both the government and the people. This was the first time that the term national interest applied to the university sector appeared in a government document. Here its use was economic: the Government had to be confident that the programs which universities submitted for financial consideration had been comprehensively discussed, and represented a concerted policy before universities received grants (C of A, 1957, p. 93).

The Vice-Chancellors' Committee, said the Murray committee, would need to take even more responsibility and initiative in speaking collectively for the universities (C of A, 1957, p. 92). The Government accepted the recommendations of the Murray Report, increasing the Commonwealth grant to the states for universities and setting up, in 1959, the AUC to recommend university grants and ensure the balanced development of Australian universities (C of A, 1964, p. 13: White, F, 1979, p. 8). Menzies did indeed carry through the recommendations of the Murray Report as he had done with those of the Mills Report, and it could be argued that he, in these actions, had single-handedly revolutionised the universities in the 1950s. However, as Allan Martin reminds us, the Mills committee was first approved by the Chifley Labor government, and confirmed by the incoming Menzies Liberal government. And, as has been previously described, it took Menzies several years to agree to the need for another committee of enquiry on the universities (Martin, A, 2007, pp. 177, 197). Now the development of the university sector was orchestrated through the AUC, since universities made their funding submissions for buildings, equipment, and new courses. These measures of checks and balances presumably satisfied the national interest as articulated by the Murray Report recommendations.

That the Commonwealth now had greater control of universities can be seen in Menzies' decision, in 1959, that Canberra could not financially sustain two tertiary institutions. After the non-negotiable amalgamation of the CUC and the original ANU in 1960, the ANU now consisted of its original four research schools, and the School of General Studies comprising the Faculties of Arts, Economics, Law and Science (Foster & Varghese, 1996, pp. 155, 161). Then in 1961, there was a significant first in the university sector as the School of Oriental Studies from CUC became the fifth faculty of ANU, the Faculty of Asian Studies. No other university had yet supported Asian Studies in this way by giving it faculty status (Foster & Varghese, 1996, p. 303). The original national purpose for ANU, as a postgraduate research university only, had changed. The pessimists saw the amalgamation as a shotgun marriage, whilst the optimists saw potential for academic benefits for both students and researchers (Foster & Varghese, 1996, pp. 155, 159).

The newly amalgamated ANU built on the language foundations of the CUC, adding Classics, German, and Indonesian languages and literature, although Asian Studies was a particular flagship. Through the 1950s and 1960s, the Oriental Studies department (later renamed Asian Studies) was fostered by two Swedish professors, Hans Bielenstein and Nils Malmqvist (Foster & Varghese, 1996, pp. 173, 185). The historians of the ANU, Foster and Varghese, whilst noting the strong foundations built by these two academics, commented that 'they also tended the make the faculty perceive Asia through European rather than Australian eyes' (Foster & Varghese,

1996, pp. 241, 303). Rafe de Crespigny, who studied under both Bielenstein and Malmqvist, disagreed about this supposed teaching bias: 'Sweden has a long and very strong tradition of contact with China – so it was not really a matter of Eurocentricity' (De Crespigny, personal communication, 28 September, 2012).

Further university expansion in Australia was needed, given a growing demand for higher education that was forecast to escalate over the following years (C of A, 1957, p. 81). After the low birth rate in the early 1930s (C of A, 1957, p. 81), and with the growing prosperity of the early 1950s (Fadden, 1950, p. 229), the birth rate had returned to a more normal rate, resulting in increasing numbers of young people to be educated. It was the Murray Committee which strongly recommended a second university in Victoria specifically for more scientific and engineering training (C of A, 1957, pp. 86, 87). According to Robert Blackwood, chairman of the Interim Council and first Chancellor of Monash University, the brief was 'the urgent need for the establishment of courses in applied science and technology and for the training of more engineers and scientists for industry and agriculture' as well as 'the relief of those faculties at the University of Melbourne which have reached' or were nearly reaching their limits (Blackwood, 1968, p. 12; Davison & Murphy, 2012, pp. 10, 15). Whilst Engineering, Science and Medicine were the first faculties established, the Interim Council saw a more urgent demand for arts and economics places, so the Arts and Commerce faculties soon followed, with Monash commencing teaching in 1961 (Blackwood, 1968, p. 14).

The first professorial chairs in Arts were in English, history and mathematics, with senior lectureships in philosophy, economics, and modern languages – French with a second language, preferably German (Blackwood, 1968, p. 61; Davison & Murphy, 2012, p. 41). Apparently, the Interim Council was trying to constrain the initial number of professorial chairs and it was thought that modern languages could quite adequately be looked after by senior lecturers. Here was that same cost-saving measure seen in the establishment of languages at UWA. Nevertheless, as funds became available through State government grants and the AUC (1963, pp. 75, 76), other language professorial chairs soon followed: French in 1962, German and classical studies in 1964, although the language taught in classical studies was Latin, not a modern language (Blackwood, 1968, pp. 125, 132; C of A, 1957, p. 86; Matheson, 1980, p. 6).

Significantly, the Interim Council decided that there would be no matriculation subjects required as prerequisites for entry to any Monash courses. Despite this decision, it was made clear to commencing students that 1st year instruction in certain subjects would assume matriculation-level knowledge of that subject (Blackwood, 1968, p. 61). The publication, *Monash University General Information for Students for 1964,* stated that there was also a requirement that 'one of the first year courses must be either a branch of Mathematics or a language other than English' (Monash University, 1963, pp. 4, 8. This was not a new trend. Wykes and King, and Lo Bianco, had noted that over several years in the 1960s leading up to 1968, a number of Australian universities dropped the entry requirement of a foreign language, and new universities as they were founded simply did not have such a requirement. This had the effect of making universities more accessible but also immediately resulted in a drop in Year 12 language candidatures (Lo Bianco, 2009, p. 20; Wykes & King, 1968, p. 54). However, the stated Monash requirements of the period 1964–1970 suggest that there was not a wholesale abandonment of foreign language prerequisites. They were still there in some form, as can be seen in subsequent editions of the Guide for Prospective Students (the official joint publication of the universities listing courses and prerequisites), even as late as 1985 (Blackwood, 1968, p. 117; Victorian Universities Admissions Committee (VUAC), 1970, p. 58, 1975, p. 19, 1979, p. 55, 1984, p. 45).

Menzies continued to be very committed to a balanced expansion of higher education in the best interests of Australia. In his address to the Australian College of Education in 1961, he had referred to the great challenges to the university system, acknowledging that

> without growing numbers of trained and dedicated teachers we cannot meet the demand in Australia and elsewhere for the scientific, technological and managerial and administrative skills demanded by the task and the time…. However, a specialist without some reasonable degree of basic education of a humane kind can do more harm than good. (Menzies, 1961, pp. 2, 3)

He went on to say,

> We must not achieve a lop-sidedness in our education. A scientist who was unaware of literature and history or of the principles of social responsibility would be dangerous. A humanist who turned his back upon the discoveries in natural science, who did not know something of their impact upon life and living would be condemning himself to a socially fruitless life in a non-radio-active ivory tower. (Menzies, 1961, pp. 7, 8)

However what is significant in Menzies' rhetoric is what he omits to say: there is no reference at all to the importance of modern languages in the 'balanced' Australian university education which was Menzies' vision. His personal vision for Australia's education was one where people should be imbued with a sense of history, ethics and philosophy, and an appreciation of the richness of the English language (Menzies, 1961, pp. 8, 9). Percy Joske in his biography of Menzies reiterated Menzies' interest in history, literature and languages and 'studies of the mind and spirit of men' (Joske, 1978, p. 235). John Bunting in his biography of Menzies commented that Menzies had a 'passionate belief in pure learning which he took universities to embody' (Bunting, 1988, pp. 187–8). His 'national interest' expressed in this way harked back to the British manifestation of a liberal university education in the nineteenth century, rather than a uniquely Australian vision for universities of the mid-twentieth century.

3.4 Martin Report: A New Framework for Higher Education

Regardless of the reports already undertaken and recommendations implemented, the need to evaluate the higher education system continued to be felt. Another review had been called for by Menzies in 1961 'to consider the future development of tertiary education in relation to the needs and resources of Australia' (C of A, 1964, p. 13). This review committee which presented its report in 1964 was chaired by Leslie Martin, the chair of the AUC (Caro, Martin & Oliphant, 1987, p. 403). Whilst further expansion of higher education was supported by the Committee on both social and economic grounds, they also emphasised a need for a model of higher education, comprising the universities, institutes and teachers' colleges, so that higher education was not simply considered by the community to be university education (C of A, 1964, p. 175). This expanded pattern of education, the Committee believed, would 'meet the demands of the nation over the next decade and would also provide a satisfactory basis for future developments' (C of A, 1964, p. ii). What was important, they said, was that it was 'in the best interests of Australia if facilities for tertiary education are provided' so that those young men and women of adequate ability will profit from higher education' (C of A, 1964, p. 36).

Consequent to this way of framing all higher education, the Committee recommended that an Australian Tertiary Education Commission (TEC) should be created through which Commonwealth grants would be made to universities, teachers' colleges and institutes, thus always working to ensure 'a balanced development of all forms of tertiary education' (C of A, 1964, pp. 195, 196). However this recommendation for a Tertiary Education Commission was not taken up immediately, as the TEC was not established until June 1977 (TEC, 1977, p. 1). Most importantly, the Martin Report commented on the need for a rationalisation of the courses offered, and for reciprocal cooperation to occur. Languages, as time would show, were particularly vulnerable to the sort of rationalisation and suggested reciprocal cooperation which was referred to.

Now the economic demands for education to further Australia's interests can be seen emerging as the Martin committee argued that 'education was a form of national investment in human capital', and that 'a dynamic economy must be prepared to devote a relatively high proportion of its resources to tertiary education.' Investment of the national resources in tertiary education was justified because there would be 'a return in terms of increased efficiency and economic growth' (C of A, 1964, pp. 4, 10, 11). Marginson contended that Murray and Martin were 'the two major reports of the system-building period', with 'the university seen as a principal tool of modern nation-building' (Marginson, 2002, p. 411). Whatever the importance of universities as investment in human capital producing educated professionals, there was nothing in the Martin Report about the importance of language skills as a national resource. The scant references to languages related to the difficulty for graduates without a language wishing to do further study where a foreign language was required.

The Martin committee endorsed the action of the newly-established University of Essex where the study of Greek, Latin, French and German was excluded in favour of the study of Russian, and the languages and cultures of North America, Latin America and the Far East. However the Committee made no further mention of the immediate need for such prioritisation of languages in their recommendations. They did note the importance of each of these geographical areas as Australia's international interests broadened, but counselled a strategic approach, considering what reciprocal arrangements might be set up between tertiary institutions (C of A, 1964, p. 54, 1965, pp. 9, 14). The warning against duplication of language offerings and the suggestion to set up cooperative language arrangements between universities is a recurrent theme in the reports of the 1950s and 1960s. It should be said, though, that the warning against duplication of courses was not, at least in this Report, only levelled against languages offerings but rather was a warning to all universities not to try to teach a complete whole range of courses (C of A, 1964, p. 54). This was a cautionary approach in university development that expenditure had to be justified.

So, as the Martin Report was received and considered, Monash University continued to expand its languages, beginning Russian in 1964, Indonesian and Malay in 1965, Spanish and Greek in 1966. Wanting to fill gaps in language offerings in Victoria, and noting that the University of Melbourne had a chair in Chinese, Monash created a chair in Japanese, with Jiří Neustupný appointed in May 1966. It could be argued that Monash at least was heeding the duplication warnings of Murray and Martin. However Louis Matheson, the first vice-chancellor, contended that Monash was deliberately developing courses, not just to fill gaps, but to provide distinctly different offerings from those offered by the University of Melbourne, and to build Monash's identity (Blackwood, 1968, pp. 142, 156, 157; Matheson, 1980, pp. 5, 13).

The same justification used to establish Monash was now put forward for a third university in both Melbourne and Sydney. More universities were necessary, said the AUC and the Martin Report, to accommodate the numbers of qualified young people wishing to attend university. The Martin Report also commented on these increasing numbers resulting from the rapid increase in the birth-rate during the period 1944–1948 (AUC, 1963, pp. 3, 13). According to Borrie and Rodgers' demographic research of 1961, this birth rate had remained consistently high through the 1950s (Borrie & Rodgers, 1961, pp. 6, 7). Macquarie University, the third metropolitan university in New South Wales established in June 1964, began teaching in 1967 (C of A, 1964, pp. 178, 179). Macquarie University opted for chairs in both French and German, the justification being their importance as major secondary school languages, even though both Sydney and UNSW already taught French and German. Subsequently, in 1968, Chinese was introduced at Macquarie, and Japanese commenced at UNSW, even though the University of Sydney had developed both Chinese and Japanese. These arrangements suggest that the broad principles of the Murray and Martin Reports about avoiding duplication of courses in the same city were not being adhered to in the metropolitan universities of Sydney as far as languages were concerned (Mansfield & Hutchinson, 1992, pp. 48, 49, 57).

La Trobe University, Melbourne's third university, was established in December 1964, with teaching beginning in March 1967. Whilst La Trobe did address the areas of special student demand stated in the Martin Report, namely, arts, social sciences and physical and biological sciences (C of A, 1964, pp. 178, 180), it was in language planning that La Trobe identified the importance of Australia's developing global role. Asian languages were considered, but not introduced at this stage, as other universities had already established such courses. La Trobe thus decided to concentrate on French and Spanish (Glenn, 1989, p. 27; Myers, 1989, p. 34). This was another example of the rationalisation of languages recommended by the Murray and Martin Reports; the acceptance that all universities cannot teach everything. What this implied though, was that universities would need to cooperate with each other in allowing their students complementary credit studies so that a full range of languages might be open to them.

Notably, La Trobe had no pre-requisite requirements for any courses other than passing the Matriculation examination. The one exception was French where in order to study first year French, a student had to have passed Matriculation French (Jenkins & Richards, 1989, p. 77). This requirement was insisted upon by the foundation professor of French, Elliott Forsyth (E. Forsyth, personal communication, 9 February, 2012). For some years, only French and Spanish were taught. By 1977, Italian was being offered (through the French department) but apparently in only a small way and with 'considerable help from the University of Melbourne' (E. Forsyth, personal communication, 9 February, 2012; Scott, J, 1989, p. 178). La Trobe now wished to establish its own Italian program as there was a great demand for it, not only from those of an Italian background but also from other interested students. Despite this demand, the Federal government through the TEC, did not wish another Italian studies department to be established, and would not fund it. As John Scott, a former vice-chancellor recollected in 1989, 'the authorities in Canberra were none too keen to see another department of Italian in the Melbourne metropolitan area'. Nevertheless, in spite of Government wishes, it was through the enormous generosity of the Vaccari Foundation that a Chair of Italian Studies was endowed for eight years, a professor being appointed in 1982 (Scott, J, 1989, p. 178). Such philanthropic endowments enabled universities to establish, for their further development, what they believed were important areas of teaching, rather than being tied solely to the government for funding. This was important for La Trobe as a university located in the northern suburbs of Melbourne, in areas of substantial post-war migration settlement.

The establishment of the University of Newcastle was another product of the recommendations of the AUC and the support of the Martin committee, and an example of the importance of the expansion of regional university facilities. Newcastle University College was granted independence from UNSW in 1965, an event which the Newcastle community and the head of arts and social sciences, James Auchmuty, had long argued for as important for that region. Initially the university was heavily weighted towards the sciences and engineering, given the concentration of industry in the area, although a general range of university courses, including languages, was offered by the University to fulfil its regional role. French and German as the most important secondary school languages, were the first languages offered, with Japanese following in 1975. Whilst Japanese flourished, French and German numbers slumped due to a move to optional language study (Croft & Macpherson, 1991, p. 44; NSW Committee appointed to survey secondary education, 1957, p. 86) in schools under the Wyndham Scheme,[4] and it was only through

---

[4] The Wyndham Scheme was a major reform of the secondary school curriculum in New South Wales implemented in 1962.

the introduction of beginners' courses that these languages survived at the University of Newcastle. Latin and Greek were also taught, but by the mid-1970s, numbers dropped in these languages also (Wright, 1992, pp. 40, 48, 78, 88, 132, 160).

Now it was in South Australia that a second university, named The Flinders University of South Australia, located in Bedford Park, was formally opened in March 1966. Whilst a second university for Adelaide was noted in the Martin Report, Flinders University owed less to Federal government moves and more to the push from the South Australian government for a second university when they first set aside the necessary land in 1960 (Flinders University, n.d.-b, Flinders University established). The AUC had, in its 1963 Report, certainly recommended an additional grant to assist the University of Adelaide to develop the Bedford Park campus (AUC, 1963, p. 74). Nevertheless, from the beginning there was a movement for the Bedford Park campus to become independent of the University of Adelaide and this was executed by the State government by the time the first students arrived in 1966 (Flinders University, n.d.-b, First staff and students).

The Schools structure, characteristic of Macquarie and La Trobe Universities, was also adopted by Flinders University. Just as Macquarie had begun with modern languages as one of its ten Schools, Flinders also gave some prominence to languages, as one of the four foundation Schools was Languages and Literature, comprising English and Romance languages. Spanish was taught in 1966, the first undergraduate Spanish course anywhere in Australia. It was significant also that, just as philanthropic funds enabled Italian to begin at the University of Sydney and at La Trobe University, so too did the Flinders University in Italian, first taught in 1971, benefit from the financial support of the Italian community. The financial support of the Greek community was subsequently very important when the languages program was extended to include Modern Greek in 1988 (Hilliard, 1991, pp. 12, 13, 26, 27, 31, 99). The establishment of such programs corresponded to a growing trend within the university sector: where funds were not approved by the Federal government and where there was sufficient community support and benefaction, universities could, and did, initiate additional language programs.

3.5 The First Survey of Language Teaching

Whilst the Federal government had initiated the three major educational reports of the 1950s and 1960s, the first major enquiry into foreign language teaching was commissioned by the Australian Humanities Research Council (AHRC) in 1963. The AHRC were concerned that honours and postgraduate students were not linguistically equipped for their research, but data were needed to make a case for more attention to languages. Data were gathered about the 'extent, aims and efficacy of the teaching of foreign languages in Australia' through a questionnaire sent to all the heads of foreign language departments in Australian universities (Wykes, 1966, p. ix). In 1966, the survey, known as the Wykes Report, was presented to the AHRC which adopted its recommendations and endorsed the importance of the teaching of foreign languages. The Report specifically suggested support for those European languages currently given insufficient attention, and stressed the importance of Asian languages both culturally and for international relations. The Report signalled serious concerns for languages in Australia, citing the apathy in the Australian community towards languages and the low numbers of students taking languages in schools and universities. Further investigation was needed, they said, into 'the Australian community's need for those trained in the language, literature and culture of other nations' (Wykes, 1966, pp. iii, 2, 3).

This Report was crucial, being the first major survey of foreign language teaching in which the national need for languages was raised, and the concern first expressed about declining interest in languages. Nevertheless, the AHRC did not have the power itself to make the changes they believed necessary. They suggested that the Report be distributed widely to all educational authorities in universities and colleges, relevant state and federal educational bodies and ministers and directors of education, presumably to galvanise government into mounting the further enquiry which the Wykes Report recommended (Wykes, 1966, pp. iii, v). Wykes had argued that a wide-ranging enquiry was necessary to understand Australia's requirements for foreign languages – an enquiry which would survey not just schools and universities but also 'the needs of business houses and government departments' (Wykes, 1966, p. 1). By now however, Menzies, who had been instrumental in three previous major higher education reports, had retired. Regardless of yet another plea by Wykes and King in 1968, for research into 'our national need for linguists in the fields of commerce, industry, government and international affairs', no such general enquiry into languages was commissioned by the Federal government (Wykes & King, 1968, p. xii). Although Wykes and her colleagues saw language capability as in the national interest, the government at this stage did not see it as a priority.

3.6 Auchmuty Report: The First Asian Languages Report

It was a different matter in 1969, when the government did focus on languages, but specifically on Asian languages, as the then Minister for Education and Science, Malcolm Fraser, explained: we have a need for 'greater emphasis on Asian affairs in our education systems' (C of A, 1970, p. 7). Whilst there had been a 'steady growth in the economic, cultural, political and military links between Australia and Asia during the last two decades', he said, the number of Australian students studying an Asian language was small (C of A, 1970, p. 7). The Committee, chaired by James Auchmuty, the Vice-Chancellor of the University of Newcastle, was to conduct a comprehensive survey of 'Asian languages in Australian schools and other educational institutions' (C of A, 1970, pp. 7, 8). This was ironically at a time when Australia still did not officially recognise Communist China despite continuing to forge trade links with that country.

This Report, presented in August 1970 was, according to Lo Bianco and Gvozdenko, 'the earliest wide-ranging investigation of the position of Asian languages and cultures in Australian education' (Lo Bianco & Gvozdenko, 2006, p. 29). The Committee noted Australia's reorientation towards relations with Asia and the 'new and expanding opportunities for trade development'. They also noted that an increasing number of Asian students were now living in Australia undertaking secondary and tertiary education (DFAT, 2005) following Australia's engagement in a number of Asian countries through the Colombo Plan.[5] An increase in the teaching of Asian languages was recommended, as well as an increase in teacher numbers. By its recommendations the Committee had reinforced all of the political, economic, and trade issues mentioned by Minister Fraser (C of A, 1970, pp. 11, 12, 13). Nevertheless, the Committee contended that universities should 'co-ordinate with State education authorities on the question of deciding which Asian language to introduce' in each state as a first step (C of A, 1970, p. 99, 100). Asian languages were being prioritised and tied to Australia's economic, political and cultural interests with Asia, but still, as has been seen earlier, rationalisation of languages and cooperation between institutions was expected rather than each institution being able to decide on its own language offerings.

Here was a very clear change of direction when it came to determining the importance of certain languages in the political and economic national interest of Australia. As Deborah Henderson, a Queensland University of Technology academic, observed in 2011, 'the report harnessed the argument that it was in Australia's national interest to challenge the prevailing Eurocentric traditions which dominated Australian intellectual and cultural life' (Henderson, 2011, p. 5). Jim Quinn, a researcher in languages, argued that Auchmuty's holistic approach, addressing all sectors of the education system, presented a better approach to understanding how the study of Asia ought to be represented in the curriculum of Australia education (Quinn, 2005, p. 106). The Auchmuty Report was important, Quinn went on to say, in providing, some years later, much of the impetus for the Whitlam Labor government's funding of significant Asian studies, and the establishing of the Asian Studies Coordinating Committee (Quinn, 2005, p. 94).

3.7 Concurrent Language Surveys: Kramer and the Academy of the Humanities

At the same time as Australia was focussing more on how its national interest could be served by its links with Asia, there was in Australia a growing awareness of the multicultural nature of society. The next chapter will deal in detail with the rise of multiculturalism, its causes and effects on society and on attitudes to languages. It was under the new Labor government and from the backdrop of that multicultural

---

[5] The Colombo Plan was an initiative of Commonwealth countries launched in 1951 to assist the economic and social advancement of the peoples of South and South-East Asia.

movement, that yet another language report (known as the Kramer Report after its chair, Leonie Kramer) was commissioned in June 1973.

The impetus for this Report had come from several quarters, with a number of factors combining to influence the Federal government to initiate this enquiry. Universities had regularly been proposing to the Government, through their AUC submissions, the need for expansion or establishment of more language courses, and there was growing interest amongst ethnic groups for their languages to be taught (AUC, 1975b, pp. 1, 2). The original request for such information had come to the AUC from the then Minister for Education, Kim Beazley. As it was the AUC which had advised the Government that a general enquiry into the provision of languages in universities, particularly migrant languages, would be advantageous to the Government, it can be argued that the Government was not simply motivated by altruism in mounting this enquiry (AUC, 1975b, p. 2).

What the Kramer Report captured in its survey was the pattern of language teaching which had emerged by 1974, where the languages important for the early colonial universities – Latin, Ancient Greek, French and German – still dominated. Of the 15 universities in existence in 1974, all taught French, 12 taught German, and 10 Latin and Ancient Greek. Asian languages were still not widely taught despite the encouragement of the 1970 Auchmuty Report for an expansion of Asian languages. Japanese was offered at seven universities; Chinese was offered by six, and Indonesian/Malay by five of the 15 universities. Clearly, as French and German still dominated in the university and the school sector, other modern European languages were in less demand and sparsely taught. Seven universities taught Italian, five taught Russian, and Spanish was taught in just four universities, of which two were in Melbourne. Dutch, Modern Greek and Swedish were offered in only two, three and two universities respectively (AUC, 1975a, pp. 11, 12). Hebrew, taught in only two universities, had very small student numbers. When the language cohorts were investigated, the pattern was more revealing. The most popular languages by student load in 1973 as reported by Kramer were: French 952, German 746, Indonesian/Malay 241, Japanese 221,[6] Italian 219, Latin 149, and Spanish 135. Clearly the modern European languages together commanded much greater student numbers and had overtaken the classical languages. Asian languages, whilst not widely taught, were quietly increasing their numbers (AUC, 1975a, p. 15).

The Working Party concluded that there was 'no evidence of any significant unsatisfied demand for enrolment in language courses offered by Australian universities…given the current level of student demand.' They therefore did 'not believe that a major expansion of existing languages offerings' or greater financial commitment to university language teaching was justified (AUC, 1975a, p. 7). This was contrary to the expansion for which universities had been arguing, and which had been acknowledged in the terms of reference for this enquiry (AUC, 1975a, p. 1). Whilst the Working Party had noted that there was a relationship between school and subsequent university language enrolments, they did not investigate this rela-

---

[6] This figure is a conservative approximate as the University of Sydney could not give separate figures for Chinese and Japanese enrolments.

tionship further, or comment on why student demand was declining and what factors might have contributed to this (AUC, 1975a, p. 17). They did not explore the effect that dropping compulsory language prerequisites for university entry, leading up to 1968, might have had (AUC, 1975a, p. 29). They warned institutions against the duplication of courses and the creation of too many small language departments, and they endorsed cooperation between institutions in language offerings as the key to improving language offerings. This was not a new mantra and was a further indication of the trend towards rationalising language offerings. The need for such inter-institutional negotiation on courses had been stated in both the Murray and Martin Reports as a general principle (C of A, 1957, p. 86, 1964, p. 45).

The Working Party did acknowledge the lack of teaching of the languages and cultures of significant migrant groups at tertiary level, recommending funding to remedy such a language deficiency. They believed that some languages, such as classical languages, which had intrinsic academic benefits, should still be offered, even if student demand declined and such teaching were to be considered uneconomic (AUC, 1975a, pp. 7, 8). Whilst much could have been achieved for languages from these recommendations, there was a change of government and changes in overall university funding, and the Kramer Report was not considered (AUC, 1975a, p. 47).

In the same year as the Kramer Report, the Australian Academy of the Humanities (AAH) had also received a report which they had commissioned, the *Survey of Foreign Language Teaching in the Australian Universities (1965–1973)* (AAH, 1975). Whilst there were apparently some discussions between the Kramer Working Party and the AAH committee, these were quite separate reports. The AAH committee's brief was to update the material of the 1966 Wykes Report. Unlike the Kramer Report, the AAH survey obtained its information from 'a great variety of sources including state education departments, public examination boards and various published and unpublished reports and studies' (AAH, 1975, p. 6). Although endorsing the need for the teaching of migrant languages, the Kramer Working Party was concerned about the financial implications of course duplication and small uneconomic departments.

By contrast, the AAH Report stressed other issues: societal concerns, a crisis in the demand for languages, and monolingualism as an insular Australian attitude. What was required, they said, was a balanced range of languages, the major European and Asian languages as well as migrant languages. However, they could but *ask* that universities 'recognise the special budgetary and staffing needs of language departments', and recommend that the Academy *suggest* to the Universities Commission that they encourage universities to extend their language offerings to 'include additional Asian and migrant languages' (AAH, 1975, pp. 1, 41, 42). Nevertheless, what is not discussed in either the Kramer or AAH Reports is that, in order to support the teaching of a better balance of languages in universities and schools, the supply of trained teachers and lecturers was crucial.

Whilst the 1970s represented not only a time of rising interest in multiculturalism and a grappling with Asian languages and cultures, tertiary expansion continued with the establishment of five more universities. James Cook University in

North Queensland had become independent of the University of Queensland in 1970 (Bell, 2010, p. 35), the University of Wollongong had become independent of UNSW in 1975 (Castle, 1991, p. 25), and three new universities had been founded: Griffith in Queensland in 1971, Murdoch in Western Australia in 1973 and Deakin, Victoria's fourth university, in 1974. Griffith's structure was particularly significant, as it reflected the imperatives of Auchmuty for the study of Asian languages and cultures. One of the four foundation Schools, the School of Modern Asian Studies (a first in Australia), was to be concerned with 'the development of commercial, industrial and cultural contact with Asian Societies' (Quirke, 1996, p. 8). This university had clearly emphasised its commitment to Australia's engagement with Asia. Murdoch University also reflected the Auchmuty Report's recommendations since its foundation languages were Chinese and Malay (Bolton, 1985, p. 41; Hawley, 1982, p. 56).

It was Deakin, however, that was caught by the change of government in late 1975. The incoming Fraser government cut higher education funding for 1976 just as the foundation Vice-Chancellor, Fred Jevons, took up his position at Deakin. According to the historian Roy Hay, a foundation Deakin academic, Jevons said 'the University had to make hard choices about what they would do'. Deakin consequently taught no languages when teaching began in 1977. Hay noted that one likely factor prohibiting the teaching of languages was the expense of setting up language laboratories. The cuts, expected in the Australian Federal budget for August 1977, were reported in UK Times Education Supplement perhaps because the new Deakin vice-chancellor was a prominent UK academic (Hay, Lowe, & Gibb, 2002, p. 14; Hay, personal communication, 17 October, 2011; Purvis, 1977).

The consequence of this political and financial turmoil was that the Kramer funding proposals for migrant languages in universities were delayed for two years because of unavoidable cost increases impacting on university funding, and other priorities such as supporting the teaching of the newly established universities. This meant that, even given the differences between the two reports in their interpretation of the data and in the concerns they expressed about languages, neither the findings of the Kramer Working Party nor those of the AAH committee bore fruit for some years. However, whilst it could be argued that again languages expansion was not being addressed, the AUC stated, in its 1976 Report for the 1977–1979 triennium, that numbers of priority items, apart from languages funding, could not be accommodated till later. The greater priorities were funding three new universities, veterinary studies at Murdoch University and two new medical schools (AUC, 1976, pp. 4, 40, 72).

Compounding the difficulties in obtaining funding for the development of languages was, as has been previously mentioned, the abandonment of the foreign language entry requirement, and the dropping of internal requirements to complete a language in degree studies around the late 1960s. As new universities began without these requirements, said Mario Martin, an ANU language academic, the older universities also waived these requirements. This resulted in a downturn in secondary school language enrolments as students no longer needed to take a compulsory language. There was now a growing need for universities to teach elementary or *ab initio* languages courses. In addition, the situation for language enrolments became more complex once more universities introduced a wider variety of languages which were not taught in the schools (Martin, M, 2005, pp. 58, 59, 62). Added to this complexity was a significant change in the control of upper secondary school curricula, as universities relinquished this control and this function was assumed by state curriculum authorities. In all, a whole series of countervailing pressures were adversely affecting the health of university language enrolments.

3.8 The Galbally Report: Migrant Services and Programs

The boost to university languages, specifically migrant languages, came out of the recommendations of quite a different report, the 1978 Galbally Report. It was neither an educational report nor a report into the teaching of languages, although both general and specific educational issues and issues about language teaching were raised in its recommendations. The Fraser government had commissioned the Report to 'examine and report on the effectiveness of the Commonwealth's programs and services for those who have migrated to Australia, including programs and services provided by non-government organisations which received Commonwealth assistance, and shall identify any areas of need or duplication of programs or services' (C of A, 1978, p. 1). This Report was very much concerned with Australia's national interest, given growing concerns about migrants and the need for adequate programs and services to enable them to settle successfully in Australia. The lead up to, and ramifications of, this Report will be examined in detail in Chap. 4.

Significantly, for the promulgation of this Report, it was published in English and nine community languages: German, Greek, Turkish, Italian, Spanish, Serbo-Croatian, Vietnamese, Dutch and Arabic. In the proposed major initiatives, Galbally noted a significant need for migrants to be fluent in English, a need that was relevant in 'virtually all areas of program and service delivery, such as health, welfare, education, employment and law.' Here was a change in emphasis about language needs: the first time that the need for English literacy was mentioned as crucial although migrant language initiatives were also proposed. The Committee recommended a package of measures with suggested financial allocations to be introduced over three years. These included English language teaching, support for ethnic groups, measures for communication such as ethnic media, interpreting services and the teaching of migrant or community languages and cultures (C of A, 1978, pp. 6, 14).

Education for a multicultural society was a particular theme, with the proposed setting up of an Institute of Multicultural Affairs whose functions were to include the commissioning of research into multiculturalism, and the preparation of materials on cultural and ethnic backgrounds for use in schools and universities (C of A, 1978, pp. 106, 109, 110). Nevertheless, whilst an increase in the profile and teaching of community or migrant languages in Australian universities did eventually occur, it was not until the 1980s. What was significant about the Galbally Report, commented Lo Bianco and Gvozdenko, was that 'both conservative and labour parties now endorsed multicultural principles' (Lo Bianco & Gvozdenko, 2006, p. 34). Fortuitously, given all the happenings of the 1970s, an updated survey of tertiary language offerings (Hawley, 1982, pp. xx) was completed in 1982 by Daniel Hawley, a specialist in French language and literature from the University of Wollongong (University of Wollongong (UoW), 1980, p. 8, 1982, p. 1). His survey, funded by a two year grant from the Commonwealth Education Research and Development Committee, covered foreign language study in Australian tertiary institutions from 1974 to 1981. Hawley's survey was of particular interest to the Commonwealth Department of Education which was working at the time on a paper about the lack of coordinated language policy (UoW, 1982, p. 1).

The value of Hawley's Report was not only the data it listed covering such a wide period and showing the diverse range of languages taught, but the comprehensiveness of that data and the indication of new language programs and changes to existing programs. These new and changed programs were made possible by TEC funding granted to tertiary institutions following recommendations made in 1980 by the Australian Institute of Multicultural Affairs (Hawley, 1982, p. 14). At last it could be seen that the funding for migrant languages in universities recommended back in 1975 in both the Kramer and AAH Reports, was coming to fruition not only in the universities, but also in the colleges and institutes.

Taking the nine languages of the Galbally Report as the government's understanding of which were the community or migrant languages, it should be noted from Hawley's data that seven of those nine languages (German, Italian, Modern Greek, Dutch, Serbo-Croatian, Spanish and Arabic) were already being taught in the tertiary sector, whilst Turkish and Vietnamese were not. Significant funding from the TEC enabled Macquarie University to introduce Slavonic Studies, initially teaching the languages Serbian, Croatian, Macedonian and Polish. Italian had been introduced at seven more institutions[7] between 1974 and 1981, in addition to the four where it was already taught, and Modern Greek had been introduced at three institutions.[8] New departments of Asian languages were founded and enrolments in Japanese, Chinese and Indonesian also grew. TEC funding also enabled the introduction of new languages at colleges of advanced education in all states: specifically Arabic, Turkish, Vietnamese, Maltese, Portuguese, as well as Croatian and Serbian. The one Aboriginal language funded was Pitjantjatjara at the South Australian CAE (Hawley, 1982, pp. 7, 9, 14, 15). (As previously mentioned Aboriginal languages have not been researched as part of this book.)

Whilst the Galbally Report was ostensibly designed to survey migrant services, the funding which flowed to tertiary languages from initiatives recommended in that Report, covered not only migrant languages but also Asian languages. This was in line with the sentiments of the 1982 Commonwealth Department of Education (ComDepEd) discussion paper, *Towards a national language policy*, which noted the recommendations for expanded English teaching and migrant languages teach-

---

[7] ANU, Griffith, James Cook, La Trobe, New England, Tasmania and Wollongong Universities.

[8] Universities of Melbourne, New England and Western Australia.

ing (ComDepEd, 1982, p. 2). Significantly, as they worked towards the formulation of a national policy on languages, they stressed that 'language skills are rapidly becoming important national resources for Australia.' They further commented that it was no longer in Australia's best interests to rely on English alone for global communications in trade and defence. Australia's international relations required a greater proficiency in other languages, particularly Asian languages (ComDepEd, 1982, pp. 2, 3). Twelve years after the Auchmuty Report had stressed the national importance of knowledge of Asian languages (C of A, 1970, p. 11), the same comments were being made again.

Since the publication in the 1970s of various government reports on education and languages, the springing up of new universities and the push for community languages and Asian languages, it is instructive to see how the older universities had responded to these imperatives. By the mid-1980s, the University of Sydney, for instance, offered Ancient and Modern Greek, Latin, French, German, Italian, Chinese, Japanese, Arabic, Hebrew, Bengali, Hindi, Urdu, and seven different Indonesian/Malayan languages (Connell, Sherington, Fletcher, Turney, & Bygott, 1995, p. 100). There was just one *new* language which could be deemed a community language – Modern Greek, which added to the existing community languages taught, German, Italian and Arabic. At about the same time, the University of Melbourne taught Arabic, Chinese, Dutch, French, German, Ancient and Modern Greek, Ancient and Modern Hebrew, Hindi, Old Norse, Indonesian, Italian, Japanese, Latin, Russian, and Swedish, as well as a range of ancient languages such as Syriac, Akkadian and Ugaritic (UniMelb, 1985, pp. 35, 36, 37, 38, 39, 40). Just as with the University of Sydney, Modern Greek was the only relatively new language which could be deemed a community language, and similarly, community languages already being taught were Italian, German, and Arabic.

The University of Adelaide taught French, German, Chinese, and Japanese, but Russian, Italian and Spanish were only offered as complementary studies from Flinders University. They also offered Ukrainian externally through Macquarie University. Languages offered at the University of Queensland were even fewer in number: French, German, Russian, Japanese, and Chinese. A significant range of community languages was offered through their Institute of Modern Languages but these were all non-award programs. The University of Western Australia offered only French, German, Italian and Japanese, although Modern Greek was introduced in 1980. Essentially it seemed the older established Australian universities had not embraced the community languages, but rather had continued with their traditional European language offerings and their Ancient Near Eastern language offerings, and had ventured into the teaching of the larger Asian languages. This may well have been a deliberate policy whereby the older universities were quite happy for the more recently established universities and the colleges and institutes to introduce the newer community languages, rather than venture into this uncertain area themselves (Connell et al., 1995, p. 100; Leal, 1991a, p. 57, 1991b, pp. 10, 97, 139; Hawley, 1982, p. 7).

3.9 National Policy on Languages

Whilst tertiary institutions were responding to government funding initiatives regarding community languages, a Senate Standing Committee Enquiry Report had been produced in 1984.[9] Many of the submissions to this enquiry commented on the problem of a lack of coordination of language policies across the various levels of governments, suggesting the need for national coordination (Senate Standing Committee on Education and the Arts, 1984, pp. x, 3). There was a level of optimism and goodwill for this proposed national policy but, as Lo Bianco and Gvozdenko commented, 'despite having a level of bipartisanship, the Senate's Report languished, with no response to its many recommendations ever being issued by either side of politics.' This was, they maintained, because the recommendations did not link up with essential government priorities (Lo Bianco & Gvozdenko, 2006, pp. 35, 36). As Lo Bianco later recollected: the relatively new Hawke government was not persuaded by the Senate Report, the recommendations seemed too unwieldy and they delayed doing anything more about a language policy. However the impetus was not lost, public comment had been aroused and did not abate. By 1986, the Government needed to take some action towards a national language policy, and Lo Bianco, who had been very involved in submissions and lobbying for action, was commissioned by the then Minister for Education, Susan Ryan, to research and prepare a formal language policy (Lo Bianco & Gvozdenko, 2006, p. 37; Lo Bianco, personal communication, 12 September, 2014).

The *National Policy on Languages* issued in 1987, was significant as the first language policy for Australia. The policy aimed to take a 'coordinated approach' on issues of language, be a 'framework of nationally shared and valued goals', and recognised that various bodies, would be 'responsible for the implementation of aspects of the policy'. 'Competence in English, maintenance and development of languages other than English, provision of services in languages other than English, and opportunities for learning second languages' were four guiding principles of the policy (Lo Bianco, 1987, pp. 4, 5).

The significance of this policy was in its prioritisation. Lo Bianco specified a group of languages of wider teaching, important for 'Australia's economic, national and external policy goals': Mandarin Chinese, Indonesian/Malay, Japanese, French, German, Italian, Modern Greek, Arabic and Spanish (Lo Bianco, 1987, pp. 124, 125). It is important to note that in arriving at the substance of this policy, Lo Bianco had consulted widely with academics, professional organisations, ethnic communities, relevant government departments and State and Territory ministers (Lo Bianco, 1987, p. vi). The languages in which the Galbally Report was published reflected the needs of migrants and how the languages of migrants were important for the social cohesion of Australia, but now the NPL was looking globally at which languages were in the economic and political national

---

[9] The Fraser government lasted from 1975 to 1983 with the Hawke Labor government taking power in March 1983.

interest. Lo Bianco, when commenting later on the NPL, explained that the languages of wider learning category was the group of languages that were, or could readily become, languages of widespread teaching and learning, and were not a category of greater or lesser importance. He reiterated that it was important to recognise that there were two categories of action in the NPL: firstly the mother tongue maintenance and secondly the languages of wider learning, which in some cases fell into the mother tongue maintenance group (Lo Bianco, personal communication, 21 January, 2014). The NPL, commissioned and accepted by the Federal government, was a nationally endorsed document of languages considered to represent Australia's national interest.

Clyne commented in 1997 that the NPL had certainly been worth waiting for, as it provided a rationale for multilingualism with a balance of social equity, cultural enrichment and economic strategies. It suggested key strategies for implementation, and was informed by Australian and overseas research. Moreover, most of its budgetary allocations were accepted by the Federal government. Nevertheless, as Clyne further commented, 'when the portfolios of Education and Employment and Training were merged, the balanced approach of the Lo Bianco Report gave way to an emphasis on short-term economic goals, such as the fulfilment of labour market needs, as with other aspects of the education system' (Clyne, 1997, p. 67). What was in Australia's national interest as defined by the NPL, and accepted by the Federal government now changed, as that government's educational and economic priorities shifted.

3.10 The Dawkins Era: Reforms and More Reports

There was now huge change coming for the tertiary sector as a whole. In mid-1987, a 'super' Federal department of Employment, Education and Training, was created, bringing together employment, training, education and research 'on the basis of national economic goals', with Dawkins, the minister of this department (Williams, 2013, p. 93). The reforms, known as the Dawkins reforms, have been described as 'dramatic and extensive' and 'far more ambitious than any other single set of reforms initiated previously or since then in the Australian higher education system' (Harman, 2005, p. 169). This far-reaching policy of the Labor Federal government published as a White Paper in July 1988, set the scene for the future development of the higher education system with what was known as the Unified National System. In this new system there were to be 'fewer and larger institutions' and 'more effective co-ordination between them on such issues as course provision, disciplinary specialisation and credit transfer' (DEET, 1988, p. 27).

In setting the context for such a policy Dawkins reiterated the importance of 'familiarity with the languages of our region'… and 'knowledge of the history and culture of the countries involved and their ways of doing business.' He also affirmed, on behalf of the Government, 'its intention that an increasing share of total higher education resources should be directed to those fields of study of greatest relevance to the national goals of industrial development and economic restructuring' (DEET, 1988, p. 8). In speaking of business, national goals of development and languages with the same degree of importance, this suggested that languages would receive priority attention. What was clear was that the tertiary sector was to be aligned with the Government's national economic goals.

When Dawkins' policy was published some mergers were already being negotiated and others were being considered with the expectation that all proposals for consolidation of institutions would be put forward by the end of 1988. Marginson called this a national market of competing institutions (Marginson, 1997, p. 166). To be successful, institutions would have to be entrepreneurial as they presented the distinct profile of their activities to secure additional sources of funding to expand their activities. Dawkins expected institutions to become more responsive to 'market pressures and interests' (Marginson, 1997, pp. 161,162). However it was with the abolition of the TEC that, according to Marginson, the Government was then freed 'to reset the policy agenda, and weaken 'the capacity of education institutions and interest groups to retard government initiatives' (Marginson, 1997, p. 163). By 1994, following these reforms, a new group of 36 universities had emerged, replacing the 70 tertiary institutions of 1987, as former institutes of technology and colleges of advanced education became universities that were expected not just to teach, but do research and offer doctoral study (Marginson, 1997, p. 233). The shakeup of the tertiary sector was immense, couched in terms of efficiencies, market forces and national development, with an expectation that tertiary institutions would act accordingly. It was a clear indication of the economic rationalist trend apparent in government education policy.

Whilst Dawkins argued for the importance of 'the languages of our region' (DEET, 1988, p. 8) and affirmed that, in larger institutions, students will 'have the potential for access to a more comprehensive range of course and program options' (DEET, 1988, p. 42), according to Mario Martin, the Dawkins reforms were detrimental to languages, and had

> an immediate impact on the overall language provision in higher education as the merger of universities and colleges reduced the overall percentage of students studying a language. Because the CAEs had a significantly lower proportion of students studying languages compared to universities, the merger of the two systems not only reduced the overall percentage of students studying a language – which had modestly increased during the multicultural years – but also created universities in which languages were not taught at all. (M. Martin, 2005, p. 66)

There was one notable exception. Deakin University which, from its establishment in 1974, had not taught languages, amalgamated with the Victoria College in 1990. The now enlarged Deakin University had picked up the total language capacity of Victoria College which, in 1990, was Hebrew, Chinese, Indonesian, Modern Greek, and Arabic (VTAC, 1990, pp. 119, 120). Jim Quinn, in his doctoral research, also agreed that the Dawkins reforms did not assist the development of

3.10 The Dawkins Era: Reforms and More Reports

languages. New aspects of resource allocations, he argued, negatively affected the time academic programs could devote to languages and the courses which could be offered to students (Quinn, 2005, pp. 123, 124).

Dawkins had commissioned, late in 1989, a review of the teaching of modern languages in higher education, under the auspices of the Australian Advisory Council on Languages and Multicultural Education (AACLAME) (Leal, 1991a, p. xxi), chaired by Barry Leal, Deputy Vice-Chancellor (Academic) of Macquarie University. The review brief, which seemed to augur well for languages, required 'a co-ordinated plan for efficient, effective and high quality teaching in the higher education sector... identification of the balance and range of language programs required to achieve four social goals of cultural and intellectual enrichment, economics: vocations and foreign trade, equality: social justice, and external: Australia's regional and global role' (Leal, 1991a, pp. vii, xxiv). Whilst acknowledging the cultural and intellectual, the sentiments of this brief were very evidently slanted towards Australia's national and international interests. Such a review was long overdue. There had not been a comprehensive review of languages in higher education since the Kramer and AAH Reports of 1975 although Hawley had produced quite a sizeable report in 1982.[10]

The review which 'was to proceed in the context of the National Policy on Languages' was presented to Minister Dawkins in 1991.

In their Report, the Leal Review Panel expressed concern for the declining numbers in some languages and the problems this posed for universities, in another manifestation of that trend which had been first expressed in the 1960s. It reinforced the opinions of individual academics by stating that the 'establishment of the Unified National System appears to have accelerated the process' of the disappearance of some languages from the curriculum (Leal, 1991a, p. 170). They stressed the cultural, trade, tourism, equity, and access reasons for ensuring that interested Australians were able to study a wide range of languages (Leal, 1991a, pp. 9, 19). Three languages, Arabic, Spanish and Russian, which represented areas of cultural, strategic and trade importance for Australia, needed better support (Leal, 1991a, p. xxxii). Also mentioned was the need for adequate teacher training to meet present and future language delivery needs (Leal, 1991a, p. 48). Strategies were proposed to enable languages of lesser demand to be offered on a continuing basis. Unfortunately, as Lo Bianco and Gvozdenko noted, the Report 'failed to attract government support'. None of the recommendations were adopted. Lo Bianco and Gvozdenko argued that this reflected 'policy priorities ... which had moved away from a comprehensive and multilingually oriented policy towards a more targeted [one] specifying a narrow range of languages of priority' (Lo Bianco & Gvozdenko, 2006, p. 45). By this they meant the next policy which Dawkins released in August 1991, the Australian Language and Literacy Policy (ALLP), which had a much narrower focus.

---

[10] However, the 1991 Leal Report covered only modern languages so corresponding data for the classical and ancient languages are not available for all universities.

Even whilst the Leal review panel was completing its work, another report was submitted to the Federal government in May 1990 in which AACLAME had reviewed the implementation of the NPL. AACLAME endorsed the effectiveness of the NPL and recommended its extension for a second term but this recommendation was not approved (AACLAME, 1990, p. iv; DEET, 1991b, pp. vii). Meanwhile a Green Paper, *The Language of Australia: Discussion Paper on an Australian Literacy and Language Policy for the 1990s,* issued in December 1990, appeared to have taken no notice of the AACLAME Report, just as the later Leal Report had been disregarded. The title of the Green Paper signalled to the critics that already a major shift in policy was being contemplated by Dawkins before discussion had even happened (Herriman, 1996, pp. 51, 52). He had already moved on to different national priorities.

Although Dawkins had indicated that the ALLP was building on the NPL, it was in fact significantly changed just as had been foretold by the critics of the Green Paper (AACLAME, 1990, p. iv). The ALLP stressed the need for 'proficiency in English for all Australians', an expansion of the learning of languages other than English, and attention to the 'special needs of Aboriginal and Torres Strait Islander languages' (DEET, 1991a, p. 4, 1991b, p. 1). Dawkins took a different line to the NPL's languages of wider learning. He specified a group of 14 priority languages: Aboriginal languages, Arabic, Chinese, French, German, Indonesian, Italian, Japanese, Korean, Modern Greek, Russian, Spanish, Thai and Vietnamese. He indicated that the States and Territories should choose eight languages from the 14 on which to concentrate. Funding was tied to enrolment targets in these specified languages (DEET, 1991a, pp. 16, 17). The landscape had changed: more languages had been specified as being of importance, but now a choice had to be made, and targets met to secure funding. This group of 14 included four key Asian languages, several long established European languages and a mix of older and more recent migrant languages.

On the face of it, it could be argued that this was quite an equitable solution. The authors of the ALLP certainly thought so, stating that the ALLP sought to 'strike a balance between the diversity of languages which could be taught and the limits of resources that are available' (DEET, 1991a, p. 15). They further asserted, in relation to the prioritised languages, that 'this selection of priorities accords well with our broader national interests' (DEET, 1991a, p. 16.) Again, as has been demonstrated earlier, the national interest was cited to justify changed priorities in the matter of languages. However, commented Lo Bianco and Gvozdenko, many language professionals and the wider community did not agree, and saw the ALLP as 'weakening the multicultural and multilingual character of existing policy [the NPL]' (Lo Bianco & Gvozdenko, 2006, p. 46). Michael Herriman, a researcher in language policy, branded the ALLP as a policy with a 'general utilitarian and economic rationalist spirit', far removed from the academic, social justice and multicultural concerns that drove the NPL' (Herriman, 1996, p. 54). The ALLP demonstrated the cumulative impact of the reports over the Dawkins era: as the period during which the imperative for prioritisation of languages had been established and the emphasis on the national economic interest as the justification for language teaching grew stronger.

David Penington, the then Vice-Chancellor of the University of Melbourne, criticised in 1993 the language used to justify the 1988 Dawkins reforms: 'The Green Paper stressed the importance of national priorities and national planning. National priorities were in reality the priorities of Dawkins and the Department of Employment, Education and Training (DEET)' (Penington, 1993, pp. 27, 30). The Labor government's priorities for the national interest were very evident when they were re-elected in March 1993. One particular priority was trade in the Asia-Pacific region and the role of the Asia-Pacific Economic Cooperation forum (APEC).

In 1992, the Council of Australian Governments (COAG), which brought together Federal and State governments, had already 'discussed the importance of proficiency in Asian languages and an understanding of Asian societies to the enhancement of Australia's economic interests in the Asia-Pacific region.' This COAG meeting agreed on the necessity for a report on the current situation for Asian languages and cultures programs in schools, and a 'strategic framework for a new comprehensive Asian languages and cultures program' (National Asian Languages & Cultures Working Group (NALCWG), 1994, p. i). The report, presented to the Federal government in February 1994 by the Chairperson, Kevin Rudd, reiterated the national importance of Asian language development and emphasised the relationships between 'national linguistic skills and improved economic performance' (NALCWG, 1994, pp. vi, 1). Henderson argued that the report was a 'political, and eventually, a practical solution to the inertia' developing over a national strategy for Asian literacy. It was significant, she said, because it linked both domestic and external economic policies for second language provision to Australia's geopolitical future in the Asian region (Henderson, 2008, pp. 171, 172). Although the Rudd Report mentioned the need for increased second language capability for Australia in general, the key recommendation was the prioritisation of four Asian languages. The national interest in languages, as expressed by the Government, was to focus solely on East Asian languages as being 'of greatest significance to Australia's economic future' (NALCWG, 1994, pp. iii, 43).

3.11 Conclusion

As this chapter has shown, the development of tertiary education shifted from universities as autonomous institutions with little government intervention to a situation where universities became nationally accountable. It was in the context of Australia's national interest that the Federal government exercised much more rigorous control over funding not just for the actual buildings and infrastructure but also over decisions on what courses would be funded. More universities were developed to enable the growing population of young people to gain a tertiary education – an important priority for the prosperity of the nation. The needs of research, of science and technology, and of regional areas were all taken into account in the expansion of the tertiary system – each contributing to the national interest of Australia.

Whilst acknowledging that the study of languages other than English had always been part of university curricula, this chapter has also shown how the focus shifted in language offerings through the second half of the twentieth century. The earliest language surveys showed the importance of languages in a cultural and educational sense. Successive reports emphasised the growing sense of Australia as a multicultural nation, and the Federal government responded strategically. It now became expedient to give recognition and funding to migrant or community languages. However, as has been demonstrated, Federal government priorities changed with Australia's national interest now turned towards Asia and emerging world markets to be captured in that region. Australia's sense of which languages were important for its national interest also changed. The rhetoric justifying Government policy and funding shifted firstly to languages of broader national interest and then to languages of economic national interest.

Chapter 4
Australia: Both Multicultural and Multilingual

> We are clearly a multicultural community… the study of migrant languages and cultures is essential in a multicultural society. (Brennan, 1974, p. 41)

In October 1973, the Migrant Workers' Conference issued this impassioned statement attesting to Australia's multicultural identity that had been forming since the huge post-World War II migration program and was continuing to shape Australian society. The demographic shifts shown by official censuses illustrate the changed identity. The population had diversified from one where in 1947, 66.7% were born in the United Kingdom, to one where by 1971, 40.6% of the population were born in the United Kingdom (Department of Immigration and Multicultural Affairs (DIMA), 2001, pp. 18, 19) with many thousands of people migrating to Australia from non-English speaking countries. As a result of that growing cultural and linguistic diversity, attitudes and policies towards those settlers of different ethnic origins had to change as this chapter will show. It was from the early 1960s that the Federal government began to review its existing migrant policies. Concurrently, issues such as the inappropriateness of the White Australia Policy, the ineffectiveness of the assimilation policy, migrant welfare, the education of migrant children and employment prospects for migrants, all began to be part of academic discourse and serious research in universities as well as government departments (Jupp, 1966; Zubrzycki, 1968). In the early 1970s, migrant groups began to lobby both the Federal and State governments to achieve their demands, including the recognition of migrant languages. Such languages started to assume an importance for Australia's national interest.

According to Clyne, a variety of terms were used to describe ethnic languages as State and Federal governments sought to formulate policies that accurately represented multilingual Australia (Clyne, 1991, p. 231). The term which came to have precedence in the 1970s, 'community languages' was the term Clyne strongly preferred. He went further, suggesting that all languages used in Australia – aboriginal languages, migrant languages or the *lingua franca* English – should be considered community languages, and thus given their rightful place (Clyne, 1982, p. 134).

The huge post-war migration program that was to boost the population, and enable the further development of industries, was clearly a program serving Australia's national interest. Between 1949 and 1954, 650,999 people (DIMA, 2001, p. 26) settled in Australia of whom large numbers were of non-English speaking background. Successive governments assumed that all would assimilate into the Australian way of life with English as their sole language. Subsequently the Federal government was forced to review its attitudes and policies as evidence showed that migrant settlement programs were failing and many migrants were returning home. Given the resources which the Federal government had put into migration programs, it was in the best interests of the nation that such programs were revised so that the rate of returning migrants did not escalate. While Australia grappled with the diverse ethnic origins and languages of migrants, governments turned their attention to policies formulated about languages other than English in Australia. For some time community languages flourished with government funding and the benefaction of ethnic communities, but such languages were vulnerable to student demand and inconsistency of funding. Philanthropy was very significant for some community languages. Ukrainian and Yiddish will be discussed in detail to illustrate the powerfulness of philanthropy.

This chapter also demonstrates that community attitudes and government policies coincided in the advent of multiculturalism as an official stance of government. This stance had consequences for both the languages of the communities of migration and English as a second language. The evidence shows that, rather than governments granting significant ongoing funding to underpin the teaching of other languages, it was literacy in English which came to have primary importance in government language policy. Literacy in English for all had greater priority in the national interest than the linguistic diversity of Australia.

4.1 Migration to Australia

From the initial European settlement of Australia as a series of British colonies, English was the dominant language transplanted into Australia (Ozolins, 1993, p. 3; Romaine, 1991, p. 2) Nevertheless, by the second half of the nineteenth century, there were already significant migrant communities whose first language was not English. Through various waves of immigration to cities, country settlements and the goldfields, diverse language communities had developed by the 1860s: Irish and Scots Gaelic, Chinese, German, Welsh, French, Italian and speakers of Scandinavian languages. The strength of that multilingualism was seen in the ethnic language press, the ethnic clubs, churches, and a number of mostly private bilingual schools. There were, for instance, many German Lutheran schools in communities such as Hahndorf in South Australia, the Riverina district of New South Wales and Sydney, as well as in Toowoomba in Queensland. There were French-English schools in Melbourne, Gaelic-English schools in Geelong and Ballarat, and Welsh chapels in the Ballarat-Sebastopol area (Clyne, 1988, pp. 96, 97, 99,101, 1991, pp. 7, 8; Kipp,

2008, p. 70). A 'multicultural and multilingual nation' was already starting to develop, although it was 'not always viewed, acknowledged or promoted' as such, as the primacy of the English language and British heritage was (Clyne, 1991, p. 12; Kipp, 2008, p. 69). Australia was created as part of the British Empire, and governed on British principles (Hirst, 2010, pp. 230, 231). That loyalty to Britain was a strong foundation and as Clyne argued, 'English monolingualism was a symbol of the British tradition' (Clyne, 1991, p. 2).

In the 40 years to 1900, almost 95% of migrants were of English, Scots or Irish origin (DIMA, 2001, p. 33). After Federation, this largely monocultural population was further reinforced by the Immigration Restriction Act of 1901, the so-called White Australia Policy. Through this Act, an immigrant arriving in Australia had to pass a dictation test in any European language directed by an officer appointed under the Act, or any Officer of Customs (C of A, 1901, pp. 1, 2). In 1905, the wording was changed to 'any prescribed language' in order to minimise offence to the Japanese with whom Australia was developing promising trade (Walker, 2009, p.77).

Similar sentiments had been expressed in New Zealand with an amendment act in 1920 that was effectively an undeclared white New Zealand policy seeking to target anyone not of British or Irish stock (Mein Smith, 2005, p. 141).

The underlying assumption of Australia's Immigration Restriction Act was that all migrants 'would assimilate, non-Europeans were undesirable because they looked different and therefore could not assimilate' (Romaine, 1991, p. 3). As this restrictive policy was applied through the 1920s and 1930s, both the numbers and sources of migrants were affected (Clyne, 1991, p. 14). As Clyne indicated, 'xenophobic and monolingual attitudes between the wars and during World War Two' had a negative effect on the languages of the migrant communities. Instead of being a source of pride in cultural identity, those languages became private, particularly when speakers were abused for using foreign languages in public (Clyne, 1991, p. 15). At the outbreak of World War II, Federal government attitudes hardened towards those migrants deemed to be enemy aliens and a security risk. These people, often German and Italian males, were interned in camps across the country (Lowe, 2013, p. 503). Prejudice towards German-born Australians, and internment of German subjects had also happened during World War I (Garton & Stanley, 2013, p. 49).

The Australian population grew steadily from 3.7 million at the beginning of the twentieth century to 7.6 million in 1947 as a result of the natural birth rate and small scale migration (DIMA, 2001, p. 18). It was the large scale migration after World War II which had such a dramatic effect on the size, the ethnic and linguistic composition of the population, and on subsequent attitudes to those immigrants who were non-English speaking and not of an Anglo-Celtic ethnic background. Romaine put it succinctly: 'In 1947, Australians were 99% white and 90% of British origin, and virtually all spoke English' (Romaine, 1991, p. 3). These percentages did not, of course, include Aboriginal or Torres Strait Island people[1] who were not counted in censuses until after 1967 (Haebich & Kinnane, 2013, pp. 347, 349). However, after that war, Australia needed to increase its population, requiring a larger workforce to

---

[1] Economically, socially and politically, indigenous people had extremely limited rights.

develop industries and resources. British migration, which had been a steady source of new arrivals, had decreased dramatically during the years of the Depression and was not large in the pre-war years but post-war, was to be the largest group. Significantly too, the Federal government was worried about national security and Australia's ability to defend itself, given the attacks on Australia and in the Pacific during the war and changes in regional security (Ozolins, 1993, p. 5). The issues of a declining birthrate, a need for skilled workers and concern for the national defence prompted New Zealand also to look to ways of increasing its population (Phillips, n.d., p. 23).

The aim of the Australian government's immigration policy, to maintain the relative ethnic and cultural homogeneity both pre-war and post-war, was that immigrants would be largely British (Lack & Templeton, 1995, p. 9; Lopez, 2000, p. 43; Ozolins, 1993, p. 5). As there was insufficient British migration to supply the necessary population increase, Australia responded to the growing European refugee problem and processed some 170,000 displaced persons for settlement in Australia between 1947 and 1954 (Lack & Templeton, 1995, p. 11; Ozolins, 1993, p. 6).

New Zealand also had accepted many displaced persons from Europe but also sought those of British stock and Western Europeans by preference, seeking those who might easily be assimilated (Mein Smith, 2005, p. 172; Phillips, n.d., pp. 22, 24). Likewise, Canada had opened its doors to thousands of displaced persons from war-torn Europe, in what was not only a humanitarian gesture, but also the means of expanding the Canadian economy through the influx of skilled workers (Nelles, 2004, p. 203).

From the 1950s onwards, refugees from other European countries arrived in Australia, together with Italian, German, Dutch, Greek and Yugoslav economic migrants (Kipp, Clyne, & Pauwels, 1995, pp. 21, 22). Appendix 1 illustrates the variety of settler backgrounds in the years 1949–1954, with a large proportion (37%), from the United Kingdom, Ireland and New Zealand (241,130). A larger proportion of people (48.3%) migrated from Western European countries where English was not the first language (314,389): Germany (122,890), Italy (96,563), the Netherlands (51,355), Malta (17,553), Austria (13,603), and Greece (12,445).

By the end of 1954, the total population was nearly 9 million as shown in Appendix 2 with 86% of that population Australian-born, swelled by the post-war baby boom and the children of the waves of different migrant groups. For those who were overseas born, the largest single group were UK-born (626,035 or 48.7%). The next in size were Italian-born (119,897 or 9.3%), German (65,422 or 5.1%), Polish (56,594 or 4.4%), and Dutch (52,035 or 4.0%). The 1970–1975 settler arrival statistics, however, showed changes in percentages from non-English speaking countries. Now Yugoslav-born were more numerous (8.7%), followed by Greek (4.1%), Italian (3.6%), Lebanese (2.3%), Turkish (2.2%) and Indian (2.2%) (DIMA, 2001, p. 26).

The post-World War II program was, according to the first Labor immigration minister, Arthur Calwell, writing in 1948, scientifically planned over three years. It was designed to gain the extra population needed to benefit the country economi-

4.1 Migration to Australia

cally and defensively, given the fear of invasion which was now a constant preoccupation of government (Calwell, 1948, pp. 14, 15, 17). Rather than cautioning Calwell's notion of careful planning, John Lack and Jacqueline Templeton, writing 50 years later, couched their analysis of the migration program in starker terms. It was not, they said, simply a humane response to the tragedy of displaced persons and refugees. It was all about Australia's calculating self-interest, a response to opportunities to increase the population of Australia as they presented themselves (Lack & Templeton, 1995, p. 11). Nevertheless, Calwell had presented the immigration plan quite candidly as the solution to Australia's population deficit, a plan which enabled Australia to take in war refugees and displaced persons. What it was all about, argued Lack and Templeton, was what 'the new immigration would do *for* Australia, rather than what it would do *to* Australia (Lack & Templeton, 1995, p. xiii). What that Labor government and successive Federal governments did not envisage were the social consequences of mass European migration (Lack & Templeton, 1995, pp. xiii, 2).

It was the process of assimilation that initially directed the government's settlement policy for migrants. Assimilation, meaning absorption into the Australian 'way of life', was used both officially and unofficially to indicate the government's policy direction (Lopez, 2000, pp. 46, 49). The Australian Council on Population and Ethnic Affairs (ACPEA) stressed that assimilation was not an actual policy written into law, but more 'the expression of a point of view' used officially (ACPEA, 1982, p. 9). Assimilation meant that migrants were discouraged from using their own language in public, and parents were encouraged to speak only English to their children at home (Clyne, 2005, p. 144; Ozolins, 1993, p. 57). The over-riding concern was to build a socially cohesive Australia where minorities would adopt the 'language, lifestyle and culture of the majority', and thereby fully participate in Australian life (ACPEA, 1982, p. 9; Lopez, 2000, p. 47). The Federal government pressed on with assimilation as the key to successful settlement (Ozolins 1993, p. 4), a policy seen as very much in the national interest. Nevertheless as Jean Martin[2] argued in 1978 from her research, it was becoming clear that not all migrants readily assimilated into Australian society (Martin, J.I., 1978, p. 30). The substantial departure rate of migrants was an inescapable fact. Various calculations of settler losses between 1966 and 1971 were reported in a 1973 Federal parliamentary inquiry as between 22% and 24% (Parliament of Australia, 1973, p. 4; Jupp, 1966, pp. 159, 180).

It was clear though that Australia's security concerns were influencing the assimilation strategy. The Government was keen to encourage migrants to become naturalised, fearing that non-naturalised and therefore unassimilated migrants might form ethnic enclaves with un-Australian tendencies (Foster & Stockley, 1984, p. 47). Monolingualism was one of the keys to the social cohesion of Australia, and assimilation was deemed successful where there was a decline in the use of foreign languages (Lopez, 2000, p. 49). As Jean Martin contended, whilst many migrants

---

[2] Jean Martin was a prominent sociological researcher.

had language skills in interpreting and translating, no one had any official use for the knowledge and competence these skills represented (Martin, J.I., 1978, p. 211).

4.2 Academic Interest in Migrant Languages

Given the developing new migrant communities of Australia, some official government or university interest in the languages of these communities might have been expected. Nevertheless, there is no reference to languages in the 1950 Mills Report, nor in the Australian Vice-Chancellors' Committee Report of 1952. Both these reports were concerned with the financial difficulties of universities and their future needs, not with specific disciplines. There was no pedagogical or academic impetus for the teaching of the languages of the migrant communities who were changing the nature of Australian society as the 1950s proceeded. The 1957 Murray Report said much about the need for more science and technology courses, and the shortage of teaching graduates, but nothing about languages (AVCC, 1952; CCNU, 1950; C of A, 1957).

University interest in languages was still very much a traditional one of academic scholarship and research. In a 1959 survey of *The Humanities in Australia,* Richard Samuel, Head of Germanic Languages at the University of Melbourne, wrote of the importance of teaching modern languages other than French and German. Whilst Russian, Italian and Dutch were already being taught in some universities, he argued these languages should be expanded and Spanish introduced (Samuel, 1959, pp. 140, 142). Even though these languages were those of the new migrant communities, the emphasis in university language teaching was oriented towards the study of the literature of foreign languages (Barko, 1996, p. 7). The only mention of any migrant languages in this survey was the reference to students from the German communities in the Barossa Valley studying German at the University of Adelaide (Mitchell, 1959, pp. 57, 59; Samuel, 1959, pp. 139–143). The irony, of course, is that numbers of university language academics of the 1950s and 1960s were themselves of a non-English speaking background, but it was their academic scholarship in the literature of foreign languages which was important, not their language fluency. Even the Martin Report of 1964 brought no new insights into the university study of foreign languages and certainly nothing that hinted at the importance of migrant languages at university level. Languages were mentioned only in the context of postgraduate students learning languages to aid their research by being able to read the literature in the original language (C of A, 1964, Vol. I. p. 171, 1965, Vol. III. p. 9).

As mentioned in Chap. 3, the 1966 Wykes Report into foreign languages in Australian universities was commissioned by the Australian Humanities Research Council, not by the Federal government. It was significantly different to previous reports which had investigated higher education generally. The AHRC brief was very specific: gather data about the 'extent, aims and efficacy of the teaching of foreign languages in Australia'. Data was gathered through a questionnaire sent to all heads of foreign language departments in Australian universities (Wykes, 1966, p. ix).

4.2 Academic Interest in Migrant Languages

Their findings showed no significant differences from the 1959 survey. Apart from the classical languages, French and German dominated, followed by Italian, Indonesian, Russian, Chinese, Japanese and Dutch. Spanish was apparently on the horizon for several universities (Wykes, 1966, pp. 2, 28, 29, 30, 31, 32). Survey participants gave rather disparate reasons for the possible introduction of new languages, but together they demonstrated a need for wider uses of languages than just studying the literature. Reasons cited were 'practical' ones such as 'the numbers of Italian migrants in Australia, our trade ties with Japan, the rise and importance of the new China, the importance of Arabic as a key to how the Moslem world thinks, our proximity to Indonesia, and the political importance of Russia in the contemporary world.' Even though it was slipped in amongst those other languages, the mention of Italian was critical because it was the first time it was acknowledged in a report as a migrant language of significance (Wykes, 1966, p. 41).

There were ten resolutions put forward, covering issues such as languages for postgraduate study, *ab initio* courses, the teaching of migrant languages, the avoidance of duplication of languages, and the need for an increase in language teachers. Although not explaining which languages they were referring to, they clearly identified growing language diversity (Wykes, 1966, pp. iii–v).

> A special demand which it would be desirable to encourage is that, in the diversity of national origins created in our community by immigration, opportunities should be given to migrants and their children to maintain the study of their original tongue. (Wykes, 1966, p. iii)

The Wykes committee widely commended its findings to both relevant government authorities and educational institutions, stating a necessity 'for Australians in a changing society and a changing world situation to become acquainted with foreign languages and civilisations' (Wykes, 1966, p. v). They did not elaborate on the 'changing world situation' to which they referred; whether, for instance, it was the Vietnam War, the decolonisation of Africa, the Cultural Revolution in China, the Cuban Missile Crisis, leadership changes in the Soviet Union, or the aftermath of the construction of the Berlin Wall. All these events were part of a changing world in the early 1960s, but not necessarily events which so impinged on Australia as to prompt action towards the teaching of new languages. There was encouragement for *ab initio* or beginners' language courses in universities (specifically in Italian, Modern Greek and Russian). However, these languages were treated as foreign academic languages and not acknowledged as migrant languages, and there was no consequent recommendation that specifically stated that migrant languages should be taught.[3] There was a lack of connection between the academic study of languages and awareness that numbers of languages already being taught were languages of migrant communities. The university sector just did not speak in terms of 'migrant languages' at that stage, still using the term 'foreign languages' for any languages other than English (Wykes, 1966, p. 48).

One academic voicing concerns was Ronald Jackson, Head of the French department at the University of Melbourne. He emphasised the need for the learning of

---

[3] Russian was not only a migrant language but a scientific one and the language of a Cold War country of which more will be discussed in Chap. 6.

foreign languages, including those of migrant communities (Jackson, 1968, p. 3). He advocated a range of developments, including modern teaching materials, 'recruitment of sufficient native speaker assistants', and exchange arrangements in the secondary school system to encourage students to study languages because, he believed

> these developments would help make the foreign language something real and living for Australian schoolchildren. So would extension of the teaching of European languages actually spoken by migrant children in the schools and the replacement of the present short-sighted emphasis on unilateral assimilation by an official policy of educated bi-lingualism. More generally, further diversification of foreign language studies would help to undermine the false linguistic absolutes of our still largely monolingual community. (Jackson, 1968, p. 4)

Jackson was farsighted in advocating the teaching of migrant languages in schools. Italian was the only migrant language taught in any significant numbers in Australian schools in 1964 although not specifically positioned as a migrant language (Wykes & King, 1968, pp. 75, 76). He went on to say that universities were already diversifying their language offerings, but only to a small extent. Spanish, both a migrant language[4] and a language spoken widely internationally, had been introduced at four universities by 1967 (AAH, 1975, pp. 12, 13, 32). Swedish had been introduced at the University of Melbourne in 1962 and Italian introduced at several more universities. There was some diversification, as Jackson suggested, but these were not major changes in language offerings in the nearly 10 years since the 1959 survey (Hunt, 1959, pp. 166, 167; Jackson, 1968, pp. 3, 4; Samuel, 1959, p. 140). Many university language departments, according to Jackson, were still traditional in their commitment to the language-literature-civilisation mode rather than practical language proficiency (Jackson, 1968, p. 4).

4.3 Assimilation to Integration

Whilst the universities had been slow to embrace migrant languages in the late 1960s and the Holt Coalition government of 1966–1967 had apparently not responded to the Wykes' recommendations, the population of Australia continued to expand with more diverse groups of non-English speaking people arriving as migrants. In 1958, as part of a revision to the Immigration Restriction Act, the controversial dictation test had been abolished (Australian Citizenship Convention, 1958, p. 12; Parliament of Australia, 2009, p. 7; Tavan, 2005, p. 105). What was also apparent was that the settlement policy of assimilation was not working for all migrants (Tavan, 2005, p. 89), as many were experiencing problems which existing social welfare, health, and legal institutions were not managing effectively (Lopez, 2000, p. 46). The Federal government was forced to recognise these issues and, by the end of the 1960s, there was a shift in the terminology used in the Department of Immigration and in Parliament. Integration was the new strategy for dealing with

---

[4] Migration from Spanish-speaking South American countries was increasing.

4.3 Assimilation to Integration

migrant issues (Jordens, 1997, p. 112). The renaming in 1964 of the Assimilation Unit of the Department of Immigration to the Integration Section had underlined the beginning of this change of attitude within the Commonwealth bureaucracy. James Jupp, a key researcher into immigration issues and also a British migrant, argued that the name change was 'more than symbolic and created an obligation to redefine social and political objectives' (Jupp, 2011, p. 46).

As a later report by the Australian Council on Population and Ethnic Affairs noted, it became increasingly obvious that mature adults could not be expected to entirely 'discard their language, culture and ethnic identity' (ACPEA, 1982, pp. 9, 10). Yet, all the time that the government was working on issues of migrant settlement and welfare, they were still actively seeking migrants. More migrants could have been encouraged from Asian countries but there were still restrictions on Asian migration. As Tavan pointed out the legacy of the White Australia Policy still held sway (Tavan, 2005, p. 95).

Billy Snedden, Minister for Immigration in the Gorton Coalition government, explained at a meeting in July 1969 that the government's understanding of integration was 'a willingness on the part of the community to move toward the migrant, just as it requires the migrant to move towards the community' (Committee for Economic Development of Australia (CEDA), 1969, p. 8; Ozolins, 1993, p. 105). But later in that same meeting he said, 'we must have a single culture, those of different ethnic origin must integrate and unite into our community' (Snedden, 1969a, Mixed race society, p. 2). A couple of months later, Snedden said, 'I am quite determined we should have a monoculture, with everyone living the same way, understanding each other, and sharing the same aspirations. We don't want social pluralism' (Snedden, 1969b, We are not in Asia, p. 10). Even two years later Phillip Lynch, the next Coalition Minister for Immigration, advocated an 'essentially cohesive society without self-perpetuating enclaves and undigested minorities' (Lewins, 2001, p. 754). These statements do not demonstrate a change in those politicians' thinking. As Lewins has argued, they 'gave mixed messages from old and new thinking' (Lewins, 2001, p. 754). Jupp summed up: 'integration was never effectively defined in public policy; … it was a transition phase in which the continued reality of organised diversity was accepted by policy makers' (Jupp, 2011, p. 47).

Adding to the growing knowledge of migrants' difficulties were the results of the 1966 inquiry into poverty in the City of Melbourne. Subsequently a Commission of Inquiry into Poverty in Australia was set up in August 1972 by the Liberal Prime Minister McMahon and extended by the Whitlam Labor government elected in December that year. This inquiry, under the direction of Ronald Henderson, subsequently showed high levels of poverty in migrant communities (Department of Immigration and Multicultural and Indigenous Affairs (DIMIA), 2003, p. 27). Coupled with these findings, was the growing awareness of the difficulties migrant children experienced learning English that came from various quarters: State government education departments, unions, parents' groups and churches (Ozolins, 1993, p. 82). A counter view had been put back in 1960, in the report of a committee chaired by Mr. Justice Wilfred Dovey, *The Progress and Assimilation of Migrant Children in Australia* Report (Commonwealth Immigration Advisory

Council (CIAC), 1960). According to Jean Martin, that committee had 'screened out information that ran counter to prevailing views', implying that there were no problems and there were adequate resources for the teaching of English to migrant children (CIAC, 1960, pp. 7, 8), and this, said Martin, was simply not true (Martin, J.I., 1978, pp. 97, 98).

Whilst the Coalition governments of the late 1960s and early 1970s struggled to give adequate attention to migrant concerns, and give credence to its changed policy emphasis from assimilation to integration, issues about the effects of assimilationist policies on the languages of the migrant communities began to be raised in two quarters: those concerned with language maintenance such as language teachers and linguists, and academics involved in sociological research. Clyne was foremost in advocating the study of migrant languages and cultures and promoting bilingualism and had argued this as early as 1964 when he taught German at Monash University (Clyne, 1964, p. 13). He led the debate about the coining of an appropriate term whilst arguing against the use of the term, 'foreign languages' as unsuitable for languages 'that are very much part of Australian life'. He also argued that the term 'ethnic languages', did not account for the use of particular languages by other ethnic groups. Languages other than English (LOTE) he said, was a term usually confined to the policies of the educational sector (Clyne, 1991, p. 3).

The other strand of research and debate that fed into public policy came from social scientists. Jerzy Zubrzycki, the Polish-born foundation Professor of Sociology at the Australian National University, referred to these stirrings of the 1960s in a speech he gave in Sydney in 1995 (Zubrzycki, 1995, p. 1). Zubrzycki paid tribute to Jean Martin and her research work on the 'disadvantages experienced by migrants during and often well past the initial settlement period', and also to Sir Peter Heydon, former secretary of the Department of Immigration. Heydon had, in 1964, drawn up proposals for the modification of immigration selection and settlement policies, modifications which were seen as the dismantling of the White Australia Policy. Martin and Heydon, said Zubrzycki, were important 'in establishing a conceptual link between equity and cultural pluralism' (Zubrzycki, 1995, p. 1).

Foreign language preservation, said Zubrzycki, was important in making use of the diversity of culture which migrants brought to Australia, but there were difficulties in the introduction of migrant languages in schools. New Matriculation subjects for secondary schools generally depended on the existence of corresponding university departments to set the examination (Zubrzycki, 1968, p. 27), and, as has been previously noted, such migrant language departments (as Zubrzycki called them) in universities did not exist. There was also a dearth of opportunities to train teachers of migrant languages. Zubrzycki presented his ideas of the importance of the retention of ethnic identity and ethnic community groups to the 1968 Citizenship Convention attended by public servants, a few politicians and community group members. However, these sentiments said Zubrzycki, 'fell like a lead balloon'. Nevertheless, said Zubrzycki, a beginning had been made in putting publicly an alternative view to the current migrant settlement policies (Zubrzycki, 1995, p. 3, 1968, p. 25).

Jupp produced a comprehensive report in 1966 on migrant life and attitudes, including why some were returning home. He saw their return as an 'enormous waste of human resources, public money and years of life' and proposed reform in the Immigration Department (Jupp, 1966, pp. 160, 163). It was not just a matter of trying to stem the rate of loss of discontented migrants, but to improve opportunities for all migrants. The government had invested such resources into the immigration program that they needed migrants to settle in and become economically productive for the good of Australia (Jupp, 1966, p. 167). These many strands of responses to migrant settlement issues, commentary on government policies of assimilation and integration, and on the importance of migrant languages on new concepts of Australian identity such as Zubrzycki's cultural pluralism, continued throughout the 1960s and into the early 1970s. However, there was not, at this time, an official policy that addressed issues of languages other than English nationally. Policies about language meant opportunities for migrant children and adults to learn English.

4.4 The End of the White Australia Policy and the White Zealand Policy

By the beginning of the 1970s, the Coalition government, despite the economic prosperity of Australia, was losing popularity and credibility, particularly as support for the Vietnam War was declining (Jordens, 1997, p. 18). Labor in Opposition was framing its social welfare and justice policies in a way which accorded with Zubrzycki's cultural pluralism (Castles, Cope, Kalantzis & Morrissey, 1992, p. 70), which now gained traction politically as multiculturalism. Multiculturalism was a term borrowed from Canada, first used there in 1971 to publicly recognise the equality of all Canadian citizens (Canadian Museum of Immigration at Pier 2, n.d.). This policy of multiculturalism appealed to the Australian electorate and aided Labor's election in 1972 (Lopez, 2000, p. 85). Commentators such as Romaine, have called the 1970s the decade of multiculturalism (Romaine, 1991, p. 5), citing a number of events as evidence: The Labor Party, with its policies of social justice and welfare, gained government in 1972; the White Australia policy officially ended in 1975 with the immigration policy no longer based on racial classification. The Minister for Immigration Al Grassby spelled out in 1973 the official government policy in an address entitled, *A Multi-cultural Society for the Future* (Grassby, 1973, p. 1).

According to Herriman, this reformist and socially conscious Labor government fostered 'a sense of equality of opportunity that had been missing' (Herriman, 1996, p. 41). Additionally, Herriman suggested, a gradual move towards change was building, brought about by the sheer weight of numbers of migrants, their hard-won access to positions of some authority in the community, and their growing political awareness, as many quickly sought Australian citizenship and the opportunity to exercise their compulsory vote (Herriman, 1996, p. 41). Christine Inglis agreed that there was a political and economic expediency to the Whitlam government policies, when she said:

> Underlying the changes was a redefinition of the national interest. The United Kingdom ... had signalled its own redirection by joining the European Economic Community.[5] Also ... potential economic partners and diplomatic allies, such as the newly independent nations in Asia, resented discriminatory policies based on ethnicity. (Inglis, 2004, pp. 188, 189)

Grassby, himself trilingual (Clyne, 1982, p. 121), enthusiastically celebrated the ethnic diversity and multilingual nature of Australian society, suggesting that it was time that all Australians were encouraged to develop a better understanding of what that implied (Grassby, 1973, p. 3). Tavan contended that this 'shift to multiculturalism was further evidence that the abolition of White Australia was now almost complete' (Tavan, 2005, p. 201). Along with it had gone the doctrine of assimilation which was transitional, Tavan argued, facilitating the shift from a monocultural definition of Australia to one conceptualised in pluralistic and multicultural terms (Tavan, 1997, p. 89). Significantly though, she pointed out, the abolition of the White Australia Policy was not just the legislative efforts of the Whitlam Labor government, the Policy had been gradually dismantled by various administrative changes in the 1950s and policy reforms of the period from 1966 to 1975 (Tavan, 2005, p. 235).

The demise of the White New Zealand Policy had also occurred over a number of years beginning with the Immigration Amendment Act 1961 and the Immigration policy review of 1974, although as the historian Ann Beaglehole indicated, it was not until the Immigration Policy Review of 1986 when there was 'a real break with the earlier emphasis on nationality and ethnic origin as the basis for admitting immigrants (Beaglehole, n.d., pp. 4, 5). In Canada, although there had never been a policy quite as blatant as the Australian and New Zealand policies on 'White' migration, previous discriminatory immigration policies against non-Europeans were gradually being dismantled through the 1960s and 1970s, culminating in the Immigration Act of 1976 (Foot, 2017, p. 4; Nelles, 2004, p. 203, 229).

It was clear that in Australia there were many strands of influence, ethnic, academic, and political, already coming together in the early 1970s, underpinned the fact that Australia simply was a multicultural nation. This was decisively stated early in 1973 in a significant document: *Statement on Immigrant Education, Cultures and Languages* (Brennan, 1974, pp. 40–43). It had originated from Greek community organisations, and had been signed by 40 individuals and organisations from four states – members of ethnic communities, teachers, academics, teacher organisations, and trade unionists. In essence, it appealed to the education system to reflect the needs of a culturally diverse society and demanded the study of migrant languages and cultures in schools and universities to give migrant languages the status they believed was deserved (Clyne, 1997, p. 63, 2005, p. 146; Brennan, 1974, p. 41). It can clearly be observed that the discourse concerning migrant/ethnic groups had changed over time. Whilst in the 1960s, academics were writing

---

[5] The United Kingdom eventually joined the European Economic Community in 1973.

particularly about migrant issues, Grassby, in 1973, emphasised how multicultural Australia had become, turning from a narrow focus on migrants to a broader one encompassing the whole population.

But it was not just about embracing multiculturalism, there was still concern for migrant settlement issues. The Labor government had already received in July 1973, a report (requested by the previous Government) from the Immigration Advisory Council inquiring into settler departures from Australia. This report followed on from a previous one in 1966–1967 (Parliament of Australia, 1973). Whilst noting that there were a myriad of reasons for migrants to leave Australia, they concluded that the rate of departure was not excessive given the size of the immigration program, but did suggest that regular enquiries of departure movement should take place. There were recommendations in the 1973 Report for improvement to various services for migrants but no recommendations for government funding (Parliament of Australia, 1973, pp. iv, 13–15). Significantly, it was the descendants of the post-war migrants who, as they began to take up positions of influence, took up these issues and channelled the agitation of the grassroots concerns. This, according to Lo Bianco, was a shift from dealing with the eradication of problems to an assertion of rights. It was also the time, in Ozolins' view, of the development of representative community structures for ethnic groups, such as the Ethnic Communities Councils in the middle 1970s, 'who from this time maintained a conspicuous presence in policy discourse on ethnic affairs' (Lo Bianco, 2009, p. 19; Ozolins, 1991, pp. 333, 334). This was the building of momentum to which Herriman had referred.

It was during the 1970s that a national infrastructure of services was introduced, responding to the increasing linguistic pluralism of Australia. The Telephone Interpreter Service was established in February 1973. Up until then, interpreting services had been scattered, largely private, with little quality control and targeting of needs (Martin, J.I., 1978, pp. 59, 60; Ozolins, 1993, p. 147). Experimental ethnic radio stations 2EA in Sydney and 3EA in Melbourne went to air in June 1975 (Ang, Hawkins & Dabboussy, 2008, p. 276). The National Accreditation Authority for Translators and Interpreters was set up in 1977 with a brief for testing in various languages, accrediting courses and establishing a professional body (Ozolins, 1993, p. 148). SBS, the Special Broadcasting Service was established in January 1978 to provide multilingual radio services, with a permanent ethnic television service established in September 1978. SBS Radio picked up the operation of the existing Sydney and Melbourne ethnic radio stations that were already broadcasting for over 100 h a week in more than 30 languages (Ang et al. 2008, p. 278). All these services allowed an expanded voice for the ethnic communities. It gave their languages and culture much more visibility within the wider Australian community through the media there were opportunities for employment and the ability to obtain accurate information about welfare services in the case of the interpreting and translating services (Clyne, 2005, pp. 148, 149; Djité, 2011, p. 56; Ozolins, 1991, p. 336). The national interest was well served by these expanded measures of communication and the media. As Kalantzis and Cope have argued, it was not a matter of introducing multiculturalism, Australia already was multicultural (Kalantzis & Cope, 1983, p. 20).

4.5 Kramer Report: A Timely Report into Languages

Whilst multiculturalists such as Zubrzycki and Martin had argued for more attention to migrant languages it was the urgent demands from ethnic community leaders, which propelled the Minister for Education, Kim Beazley in April 1973, to initiate a report into the study of languages (particularly Modern Greek), cultures, and linguistics in Australian universities.[6] Nevertheless, Zubrzycki and Martin were also doing their lobbying through their connections with the Department of Immigration. The Working Party appointed to undertake this enquiry into languages, cultures and linguistics in Australian universities did not include any multiculturalist members, and Leonie Kramer, who replaced Peter Karmel as the Chairman of the Working Party in May 1974, was not known to hold multiculturalist views (Lopez, 2000, p. 271).

The Working Party relied only on submissions from universities, the justification being that they did not want to raise the expectations of ethnic communities to 'unrealistic levels' – a rather dampening attitude with which to begin the enquiry. They did not seek views from members of the public or organisations as they 'had not been asked to conduct a formal public enquiry'. Regardless, they did receive a large number of informed comments and several detailed statements as there had been wide publicity for their work. Nevertheless, the lack of formally solicited comments did not bode well for a report to contain any innovative recommendations for migrant languages funding which was presumably what the ethnic communities were hoping for (AUC, 1975a, pp. 6, 7; Lopez, 2000, p. 272). However, in making statements about 'no significant unsatisfied demand' for languages, and the paucity of migrant language study available in the universities, it was as though the Working Party was treating migrant languages as something quite apart from the *normal* student demand for foreign languages.

The Working Party went on to recommend that in the 1976–1978 triennium, funding be made available of 'four establishment grants of $75,000 each to those universities wishing to introduce studies in the migrant languages and cultures' in specified countries 'or major cultural groups represented in the Australian community': Czechoslovakia, Hungary, Latvia, Lithuania, Lebanon, Malta, Poland, Turkey, Yugoslavia (AUC, 1975a, p. 47). These seeding grants were to enable universities to set up such language programs until course enrolments 'attracted recurrent grants in the normal manner' (AUC, 1975a, pp. 47, 48). The 1971 Census statistics indicate that people from these nine specified countries were indeed amongst the major non-English speaking cultural groups in Australia, but were often newer arrivals (DIMA, 2001, p. 19).

The Working Party acknowledged that for other large cultural communities, key languages such as German, Greek, Italian, Dutch, Russian, Arabic, Malay and Hindi

---

[6] Modern Greek classes already planned for since the late 1960s, began at the Universities of Sydney and Melbourne in 1974, encouraged by the universities and Federal government as the language of one of the largest migrant communities and supported by funds from the Greek community.

4.5 Kramer Report: A Timely Report into Languages

were already being taught in universities. This was a sweeping statement as Dutch, Modern Greek, Arabic, and Hindi each had very small tertiary cohorts: less than 20 students nationally in 1973 (AUC, 1975a, p. 13). Curiously, Chinese was not mentioned at all as its inclusion might have been expected as representative of a larger cultural community. The Working Party's own figures indicated more than 100 equivalent fulltime student load (EFTSL) for Chinese language study in 1973. In addition, Chinese-born Australians were at least as numerous as Czech-born Australians in the 1971 Census (AUC, 1975a, p. 15; DIMA, 2001, p. 19).

The oversight in this whole investigation was not to survey languages offered in colleges of advanced education (CAEs) that offered tertiary education alongside the universities. The Working Party acknowledged this by saying it was not part of their brief but that 'both types of institutions [universities and CAEs] should have regard for each other in their plans and aspirations' (AUC, 1975a, p. 36). It is unfortunate that the Working Party did not seek to have the brief widened so that a joint report of the Universities Commission and the Commission on Advanced Education could have been presented. Such a report would have given much more comprehensive data on the state of languages teaching in all Australian tertiary institutions, both universities, CAEs, institutes of technology and the training of language teachers in teachers' colleges. The Working Party Report was presented on 19 May 1975, and then, on 30 May 1975, Prime Minister Whitlam announced the amalgamation of the Universities Commission and the Commission on Advanced Education into a Tertiary Education Commission (Poynter & Rasmussen, 1996, p. 440).

There is little data on migrant languages available at CAEs and other institutions in 1974 to compare with the Kramer Report data on university languages in 1974. Despite this, some relevant data can be extracted from Hawley's Report on foreign language study for the years 1974–1981. Modern Greek was taught at the Adelaide College of the Arts, and Modern Greek, Modern Hebrew, and Yiddish at the Prahran CAE. The expansion of migrant languages in the CAEs was yet to come (Hawley, 1982, pp. 62, 65, 66, 69). However Lopez's conclusion rang true: although recommending the provision of migrant languages at the tertiary level, the Working Party 'treated these changes as incremental adjustments to the existing system rather than intrinsic to the development of a multicultural society' (Lopez, 2000, p. 398).

As mentioned in Chap. 3, there was another report on foreign languages presented in 1975, this one by the Australian Academy of Humanities (AAH, 1975, p. 31, 41). That report referred to the problem of monolingualism and the keenness of migrant groups for their languages and cultural heritage, but there was little detail. By this time, 1975, according to Clyne, the terminology to describe migrant languages had changed. There had been considerable debate about an appropriate term from both ethnic community groups and academics working in the field of languages but there was no consensus (Clyne, 1982, p. 133). Even the 1973 statement about migrant languages mentioned previously had, whilst using the term, 'migrant languages', also referred to Italian, Greek, Serbo-Croatian and German as 'Australian languages' (Brennan, 1974, p. 41). Later, said Clyne, this 'kind of rhetorical justification of ethnic languages' was expressed by 'community languages'. The first Migrant Education Action (MEA) Conference held in Melbourne in 1974 used 'community languages' interchangeably with 'migrant languages' in its discussions, with the MEA organisation gradually shifting to the exclusive use of 'community languages' later in the decade.

Clyne also pointed out that the term 'community languages' started to appear in both Victorian and NSW Education Departments' documents as state governments responded at the pre-tertiary level to the rhetoric of the migrant communities (Clyne, 1982, p. 133). Clyne himself strongly approved of the term 'community languages' as referring to 'languages spoken in the Australian community' and again, in another context, community languages are those 'resulting from immigration from an increasing diversity of source countries' to Australia. He had misgivings, though, about how the term might be politically manipulated to promote some languages and disenfranchise others, rather than 'justify the place of all languages' (Clyne, 1982, p. 134, 1991, p. 231; Clyne & Kipp, 2006, p. 7). Nevertheless, there was a change in thinking, however slowly it was happening. It might have been supposed that an impetus now existed for the promotion of community, migrant or ethnic languages, whichever term the Federal and State governments might be using, but this was not to be. Larger issues of university funding overtook whatever national profile had been temporarily gained for migrant languages.

4.6 A New Government in a New Era

After the dismissal of the Whitlam Labor government in November (Fricke, 1990, p. 220), Malcolm Fraser formed a Coalition (Liberal/Country Party) government in December 1975. Unfortunately for the growth of community/migrant languages in universities, the Sixth Report of the Universities Commission (with its recommendations for establishment grants for migrant languages in universities) was not adopted for legislative action (AUC, 1975b, pp. 101,102). Emergency funding arrangements for 1976 had been announced in October 1975. 'The triennial planning pattern on which all universities had learned to rely was broken' (UniMelb, 1976, p. 2). Nevertheless, contended Ozolins, there was some bipartisan continuity of purpose with the Fraser government signalling its interest in ethnic affairs by reconstituting the old Department of Immigration as the Department of Immigration and Ethnic Affairs (Ozolins, 1991, p. 334.) The next opportunity for the Fraser government to demonstrate its commitment to ethnic affairs came with the reception of a report, *The Teaching of Migrant Languages in Schools* (Department of Education (Dept of Ed), 1976). This Report had been commissioned in November 1974 by the then Labor government but was not presented to the new Fraser government by the chair, John Mather, until March 1976 (Ozolins, 1993, p. 135). The Report recommended language learning from the primary years including intercultural studies and improvements in teacher training. The committee noted the difficulties of increasing language studies in an already crowded curriculum, but pointed out that there was significant interest in the study of migrant languages from non-migrant students, particularly in Italian and Modern Greek in secondary schools (Dept of Ed, 1976, pp. 25, 55, 100).

Despite these positive signs for action, the Report was not tabled in Parliament until December 1976 and its findings were buried in the rush of business before the end of 1976. Ethnic groups were concerned that such an important report had not been acted on by the Government let alone even properly announced. Despite promises made for a further study, nothing by way of an action-oriented report from the Federal government on migrant languages, was forthcoming (Ozolins, 1993, pp. 139, 140). This was a lost opportunity for the Government to show its commitment to migrant languages. For those lobbying for an increase in the teaching of migrant languages, this was very frustrating. Not only were the Kramer Report recommendations for migrant languages in universities put on hold, but the Mather Report on migrant languages in schools was not acted on either. All this lack of action suggested that migrant languages were not a priority for the Fraser government in spite of its rhetoric.

Clyne reported that whilst there was some progress in the teaching of migrant languages in primary and secondary schools at the state level, it was fairly slow (Clyne, 2005, p. 147). Zubrzycki had pointed out in 1968, that there generally needed to be a university migrant language department to examine a secondary school language subject (Zubrzycki, 1968, p. 27). As mentioned in Chap. 3, that barrier was no longer there in the late 1970s (Clarke, 1987, pp. 17, 19, 2005, p. 111; Research Data Australia, n.d., Victorian Institute of Secondary Education). With the increasing responsibilities of state institutes of secondary education, universities no longer controlled the Year 12 curriculum. Development of any new Year 12 subject was the province of state education authorities. As Clyne insisted, university language courses in migrant languages were important 'to provide a two-way link with schools, to develop language skills from where students left off in Year 12 and for the training of teachers, as well as preparing them linguistically for their careers' (Clyne, 2005, pp. 111, 117, 147). Consequently, as Ozolins noted, Federal government initiatives in this area did not come until the Galbally Report of 1978 (Ozolins, 1993, p. 140).

4.7 Galbally Report: A Report for Migrant Services

Apart from the debate about the teaching of migrant languages, migrant settlement and welfare problems persisted regardless of the policies set in place by government across the 1970s. The next opportunity for government action came with the announcement in 1977 of an enquiry into the wide range of post-arrival services for migrants, to be chaired by Frank Galbally, a prominent criminal defence lawyer. Economically there was a cost to the Government for those migrants returning home, increased pressure on welfare services for those migrants not coping with life in Australia, and a 'need to retain the migrants that the social purse had supported' (Kalantzis & Cope, 1983, p. 16). In the face of all the criticism, the Government needed to do something. Contemporaneously in 1978, a discussion paper on multiculturalism was prepared by a group of representatives from a range of bodies, including the Tertiary Education Commission and the Schools Commission under the aegis of the Commonwealth Department of Education. This discussion paper was much more blunt about the electoral need for action, attributing changes in government attitudes to growing awareness of the needs of migrant communities and of the importance of the migrant vote, particularly in marginal electorates (Department of Education, 1979, p. 10; Jupp, 1966, p. 160; Ozolins, 1993, p. 150).

Clyne commended 'the commitment of the Fraser government to continue the agenda of a multicultural Australia initiated by Whitlam' (Clyne, 2005, p. 150). According to Jupp and Clyne, the Galbally Report contained the classic definition of multiculturalism in its imperative of services to non-English speaking migrants: migrants have the right to maintain their culture and racial identity, a multicultural society would benefit all Australians, and ethnic organisations would be the most significant bodies to preserve and foster migrant cultures (Jupp & Clyne, 2011, pp. xvii, xviii).

Importantly, for a publication of the Commonwealth government, the terminology for languages other than English in the Galbally Report was almost exclusively 'community languages'. It was the first multilingual bill to pass through parliament and was published in ten major community languages including English' (Bradshaw, Deumart, & Burridge, 2008, p. 19; Ozolins, 1991, p. 334). The sociologist, Robert Birrell, was cynical about this exercise, suggesting that the recommendations had been shaped towards gaining the ethnic vote (Birrell, 1978, p. 28). And, as Foster and Stockley pointed out, whilst the main Report was multilingual, the appendices, 'extensive and central to the Report, were published only in English' (Foster & Stockley, 1984, p. 79). For Zubrzycki, the Galbally Report was a 'major landmark in multicultural practice… in its application of the philosophy of multiculturalism in the formation of government policies', and in addressing the twin issues of equity and cultural maintenance in settlement services, English language teaching to adults and children, translation services, migrant resource centres, and grant-in-aid programs to community groups (Zubrzycki, 1991, p. 131). However, summing up the effects of the Galbally Report, he said that not all the issues for migrants had been adequately tackled and they surfaced again in subsequent years (Zubrzycki, 1991, p. 135).

The Report was well received by the various ethnic groups and had bipartisan support from the Opposition and in the Government (Herriman, 1996, p. 43; Ozolins, 1993, p. 150). Funds for multicultural education in schools were recommended to include pilot projects for the teaching of community languages and cultures (C of A, 1978, p. 108). Funds were also allocated for interpreting and translating services so that migrants could better access information about services available (C of A, 1978, p. 19). More interpreting and translating accreditation courses were introduced in colleges of advanced education although some of these courses were quite short-lived (Hawley, 1982, pp. 64–67). The maintenance of ethnic identity was to be encouraged, but not at the expense of the broader society. Thus the benefits of multiculturalism would be available to all Australians, including opportunities to learn languages other than English (Herriman, 1996, p. 43; Ozolins, 1993, p. 150, 151, 152).

4.7 Galbally Report: A Report for Migrant Services

Ozolins, an Australian academic, and a refugee from Latvia, contended that 'ethnic activism was now publicly asserted so strongly as to motivate considerable response on the part of governments' and thus influence language policy. He described the Galbally Report as the summing up of the growing 'conspicuousness of significant language interests' as they began 'to affect major Australian institutions.' However he felt that even though ethnic activism had brought migrants rights to more prominence, 'there was often little incentive for Australian institutions to turn their endorsement of language rights (now broadly conceded) into practical programs, whether in education or elsewhere' (Ozolins, 1993, p. 155). Ultimately he said, the Report 'sees the most important instance of migrant needs as that of language, or rather lack of language', and that 'the implications of inability to reach a satisfactory level of English are repeatedly referred to.' This was a major emphasis - the learning of English, not the maintenance of migrant languages, nor the teaching of migrant languages to the wider Australian community (Ozolins, 1993, pp. 152, 153). Others such as Jean Martin criticised the paucity of funding for particular areas of need and particular groups such as young children, women, the handicapped, and the aged. She felt that the Commonwealth was moving away from 'direct welfare services towards a largely consultative and information giving role' (Martin, J.I., 1978, p. 83).

Arthur Faulkner, a researcher with the Centre for Urban Research and Action (CURA), maintained that, whilst the Report properly acknowledged the economic and political role of migrants, it seemed to have something of a 'free enterprise attitude to welfare' and offered only 'piecemeal solutions to problems'. The Ethnic Communities Council (ECC) contended that the Report did not fully understand the underlying structural basis of migrant disadvantage. The strategies proposed to redress the issue of inadequate migrant English skills were deemed inadequate. The establishment of the Institute of Multicultural Affairs was seen by the ECC as unnecessary since, they believed, there were already organisations which engaged in such research (Ethnic Communities Council, 1978, p. 19; Faulkner, 1978, pp. 16, 17, 18). The general thrust of the critical comments was that the compilers of the Galbally Report understood the issues to be addressed for migrants, but that their recommendations did not always adequately cover the issues.

It could be argued that the Galbally Report was the turning point for Australia to acknowledge the importance of its multicultural population. Multiculturalism, as far as the national interest was concerned turned on two aspects: working towards the social cohesion of a multicultural and multilingual population and ensuring that this population could fully benefit economically as Australians. It is important to judge the Galbally Report according to its primary purpose: to assess and recommend changes to programs and services for migrants and how migrants might best access those programs and services through the dual aims of better opportunities for learning English, and better facilities for interpreting and translating. Any recommendations about the importance of and funding for community language teaching were, however, secondary to the main purpose.

As the 1970s came to a close, there had still been no implementation of the funding recommendations for the teaching of migrant languages from either the 1975

Kramer Report or the 1976 Mather Report. The Galbally Report had recommended $5 million for multicultural education over 3 years, for initiatives such as special projects for curriculum, training and seminars for teachers, pilot projects for the teaching of community languages and bilingual programs in schools (C of A, 1978, p. 107). There was nothing, though, that linked the importance of the teaching of community languages in schools to such teaching in universities. Tertiary institutions were mentioned only in very specific contexts: ethnic cultural curriculum components to be included in appropriate professional courses such as medicine, education and social work; bridging courses for the upgrading of overseas qualifications; and advice to tertiary institutions about the need for, and content of, interpreting and translating courses. There was nothing specific about the teaching of community languages in tertiary institutions in general (C of A, 1978, pp. 26, 51, 52, 110).

One Galbally Report recommendation which did ultimately work positively for community languages was $1.8 million over 3 years for the establishment of an institute for research into multiculturalism and related issues. Whilst the government accepted this recommendation, this was not a lot of money to make a significant difference to multiculturalism policies. But then, of course, the Galbally Report was essentially an enquiry into programs and services for migrants covering a wide range of areas of which education was just one. Despite this, the Australian Institute of Multicultural Affairs (AIMA) when it began its research in 1980, did make some inroads into the promotion of community languages. In the AIMA *Review of Multicultural and Migrant Education,* eight recurrent grants of $50,000 each either for the teaching of community languages not already taught in any university or to increase the teaching of community languages already being taught but under-represented, were recommended. The Review did not specifically define what a community language was, it simply referred to the 'languages used in the Australian community' and named six community languages not taught anywhere in the tertiary sector: Czech, Slovenian, Ukrainian, Lithuanian, Hungarian and Turkish (AIMA, 1980, pp. vi, 63). In their next report for the 1982–1984 triennium, the TEC took up this recommendation, endorsing the allocation of 'up to $1 million' over the next 3 years for new community languages to be introduced in universities and CAEs. Hawley listed the actual TEC funding allocated and languages to be supported. However, of the six community languages identified in the AIMA review as not taught anywhere in the tertiary sector, the only one for which funding was sought and granted was Turkish, in two colleges of advanced education (TEC, 1981, Vol. 1, Part 1, p. 186; Hawley, 1982, p. 15). There seemed to be no synergy about appropriate languages between the AIMA research findings, tertiary institutions' funding submissions and TEC allocations.

4.8 The Consequences for Community Languages

Over the period of nearly 40 years from 1974 to 2013, several community languages flourished in the tertiary curriculum. Others were discontinued for lack of student demand. Student demand itself can be affected positively or negatively by the relative value in which the language is held by its own ethnic community and by the myriad of other reasons that may prompt language study. As Clyne has pointed out not all community languages have equal status. He cited variables such as the numerical strength of a community, and whether a community believes its language is a core value to be passed on to successive generations. To these Clyne added the recency of migrant arrival, changing migration patterns, and the political and economic importance of a particular language (Clyne, 1982, pp. 31, 32, 40, 142, 145, 1991, pp. 230–231). There are also community languages of Australia which are significant global languages given how many people speak that language internationally, and whether the language is one of the official languages of the United Nations, other than English: namely, Arabic, Chinese, French, Russian and Spanish. The complexity of categorising languages is exacerbated by the overlap in terminology where a language is for some a community language, for others a cultural language, and yet again, by dint of the number of global speakers, an international language.

Data are certainly available for this period from the Hawley, Kramer, Leal, White and Baldauf, and Dunne and Pavlyshyn surveys and these are listed in Appendix 3. The first column lists the 1975 Kramer Report language recommendations. The second column lists languages taught across the period 1974–1981 according to the Hawley survey. The third column lists White and Baldauf data for 1981. The fourth column lists languages for which institutions gained TEC grants for the 1982–1984 triennium. In columns 5–7, further White and Baldauf's data is shown in three discrete years, 1988, 1990, and 1994. In the final two columns the Dunne and Pavlyshyn data of 2011 and then 2013 is shown (Dunne & Pavlyshyn, 2011, 2014). It was difficult to draw conclusions about the health of community languages study as the data were not contiguous: some surveys listed student enrolment figures and the equivalent fulltime student load (EFTSL), others listed the number of institutions teaching a language, some data were listed in blocks of years, others by single years. White and Baldauf pointed out, in relation to their own data, that figures from 1981, 1988 and 1990 could not easily be compared. The number of higher education institutions in Australia had reduced significantly between 1988 and 1990 due to the many institutional amalgamations prior to the Unified National System. Statistically there was a decrease in the number of institutions offering a given language between 1981 and 1990. This may have been due to decreasing student demand or to an institution's strategic decision not to continue a particular language (White & Baldauf, 2006, pp. 7, 8).

The data in Appendix 3 does not attempt to show which institutions offered these languages nor whether the languages were offered as majors, minors or one year subjects. What it shows is the incidence of offering various languages across the 39 year span. Some community languages were steadily offered in the tertiary sector in this period of time – those of the larger or more well-established community groups such as Italian, Russian and Spanish. In addition, these three languages all had cachet as cultural/international languages. These were not languages that had been singled out for special funding needs in either the Kramer Report recommendations or the later TEC grants of the 1982–1984 triennium. Greek and Modern Arabic had been cited as under-represented languages and therefore gained new TEC grant funding in some institutions for the 1982–1984 triennium, but were still quite well established in this period. Yet another group of these community languages – Polish, Portuguese, Turkish, Vietnamese, and the languages of the former Yugoslav Republic, Serbian and Croatian (sometimes taught as Serbo-Croatian) – had been offered, but not consistently, across this period and according to White and Baldauf were 'lesser taught' languages (White & Baldauf, 2006, p. 8) and according to Dunne and Pavlyshyn, 'less commonly taught' but still available.

An inspection of the immigration figures from these countries for this period 1974–2013 did not offer an explanation for these languages to be 'lesser taught' or 'less commonly taught' and thus presumably less in demand. In each case, for those whose birthplace is another country, the percentage of the Australian population which they represented was calculated. The data of the 1971, 1981, and 1991 censuses showed increases in the proportion of the Australian population born in Yugoslavia, Poland, Turkey, and Vietnam. There was no separate data available for immigration from Portugal or Brazil (DIMA, 2001, p. 19). The 1991 Leal Report signalled Portuguese as important for tourism and a recent Department of Foreign Affairs and Trade (DFAT) brief indicated that Australian trade with Brazil had grown steadily since the mid-1990s, but these imperatives have not translated at any point into a demand for, or prioritisation of, Portuguese (DFAT, 2013a).

Yet another inspection of migration data for 1996–2013 came from the Australian Government Department of Home Affairs website into which the previous Immigration Department had been subsumed (Department of Home Affairs, n.d.). This data showed an increase in the Australian population for people from Vietnam, a decrease in those who were Turkish-born, and steady migration figures for people from Poland. Conclusions could not be drawn on migration from the countries of the former Yugoslavia as the breakup of that country happened over a long period of time and clear data was not available.[7]

However an explanation for decisions about which languages should be taught may be found back in the National Policy on Languages of 1987. In this policy, Lo Bianco advocated a group of nine languages of wider learning: Mandarin Chinese, Indonesian/Malay, Japanese, French, German, Italian, Modern Greek, Vietnamese, Arabic and Spanish. None of the 'lesser taught' languages, Serbian, Croatian, Polish, Turkish were mentioned in the context of this prioritisation. Lo Bianco stressed, however, that not to prioritise a language in the NPL did not imply devaluation of that language (Lo Bianco, 1987, p. 125).

---

[7] Explanatory notes from the migration data suggest that figures on the former Yugoslavian countries are significantly understated.

4.8 The Consequences for Community Languages

Ozolins argued nevertheless, that the result of this prioritisation meant that the languages of wider learning were 'targeted for system-wide initiatives' in curriculum and teacher training, and 'gave a lead to schools in choosing languages that had major systemic support.' Consequently it followed that, without that systematic support, non-prioritised languages would struggle to gain and maintain a foothold in the education system (Ozolins, 1993, p. 245). Even the next prioritisation of languages set out in the 1991 ALLP, complete with tagged funding, did not aid the community languages of smaller ethnic groups. According to that policy, nine of the 14 prioritised languages had importance for Australia's trade: Chinese, Japanese, Arabic, Indonesian, Korean, Thai, Spanish, German and French. Of the remaining five, Italian and Modern Greek had special recognition, presumably as languages of large community groups. The Report made no particular comment on the remaining three languages – Russian, Vietnamese and Aboriginal languages, although clearly Aboriginal languages were languages of the Australian community, and Vietnamese and Russian were languages of significant migrant community groups (DEET, 1991a, p. 16).

The final group of community languages that require comment are those which have, according to White and Baldauf, never been taught in the tertiary sector or are those of much lesser demand, or those which were no longer taught by the middle of the 1990s (White & Baldauf, 2006, pp. 8, 9). Latvian, Lithuanian, Maltese and Czech struggled with lessening demand and have now all been discontinued in tertiary programs. Similarly, the data of Dunne and Pavlyshyn showed no revival of these community languages of lessening demand (Dunne & Pavlyshyn, 2011, pp. 18, 19, 2014, pp. 16, 17). Clyne quoted from the 2001 census the first generation language shift which has occurred in speakers of Latvian, Lithuanian, Maltese and Hungarian. These four languages feature amongst the higher percentages of those using only English at home, rather than their community language (Clyne, 2005, pp. 13, 68).

The vulnerability of these languages to declining student demand, followed by funding cuts and inevitable discontinuation, was linked to the relatively high rates of language shift in the first generation with presumably less interest in that generation for pursuing their community language in formal education. Whilst Czech did not appear in the data which Clyne has quoted, a comparison of the Victorian Certificate of Education (VCE) candidature for 1990 showed Czech with a similarly very small candidature as the other languages: Czech 3, Hungarian 15, Latvian 6, and Lithuanian 5. I argue that, at least in the state of Victoria, this VCE data showed Czech in a similarly vulnerable position to the other languages when considering the language interests of the first generation (Victorian Curriculum and Assessment Board (VCAB), 1990, table 2.2).

Not only were some of these smaller community languages not surviving in the tertiary sector as undergraduate subjects, they were not being offered as language method subjects in postgraduate teaching qualifications. The 1991 Leal Report showed that in 1990 in teacher training programs, French, German, Japanese, Chinese and Indonesian were widely taught as language method subjects; so too were the major community languages, Italian and Modern Greek. Less common in available teaching methods were Vietnamese, Arabic, Spanish and Turkish. Russian, Croatian, Polish, and Serbian were available only in two institutions in Melbourne (Leal, 1991a, pp. xxx). By 1995, only the University of Melbourne offered Arabic, Turkish, Russian and Vietnamese as language methods in its postgraduate Bachelor of Teaching program (Victorian Tertiary Admissions Centre (VTAC), 1995, p. 13). If there were few opportunities for the training of language teachers of smaller community languages, then obviously there was less chance of these languages being taught in secondary schools to then feed students into university language programs. What was growing, by contrast, was the teaching of English as a second language. Whilst data were not available for the whole of the Australian tertiary sector, the data on the Victorian postgraduate admissions for teacher training showed a growing prevalence of Teaching English as a Second Language as a teaching method through the 1980s and 1990s (VTAC, 1986, 1987, 1988, 1989, 1994, 1995; VUAC, 1985). This was in line with the Federal government's priority in its language and literacy policy for literacy in English.

4.9 The Fortunes of Ukrainian and Yiddish: Case Studies

The languages Ukrainian and Yiddish have been chosen as two examples of community languages which do not have large numbers of speakers, and are quite unambiguously minority languages which have not figured in any government language priority reports. According to the population statistics of the Australian 1976 census, there were 11,434 people who were born in Ukraine, and by the 1981 census, this figure had dropped to 10,942, probably due to deaths, emigration and no new immigration. This census listed 17,584 people claiming to speak Ukrainian regularly (Seneta, 1986, pp. 17, 18, 21). There was no census evidence for the number of people regularly speaking Yiddish, a language of Eastern and Central European Jews, for the census years 1976, 1986, 1991, and 1996 as Yiddish was not listed as an individual language but simply in 'Other'. The 2001 census listed 2666 people speaking Yiddish at home but it could be expected, as suggested by the Yiddish Studies department at Monash University, that this figure was a lot lower than those who spoke Yiddish at home 25 years earlier (Department of Immigration and Citizenship, 2008, p. 30; Monash University, n.d., Yiddish Melbourne, p. 2). Whatever the case for Yiddish, the communities where both Yiddish and Ukrainian might be spoken were not large. They had not attracted government funding and had no clout as languages of economic importance for Australia. Both these languages illustrated the wider context of philanthropy and the effect of that philanthropy on community language teaching. They were both significant because, at different times, the financial support of their communities was crucial for teaching of these languages to continue. However, as it will be shown, the situations of Yiddish and Ukrainian have been rather different in the institutions where they were, and are now, offered. In the case of Yiddish, teaching began in 1974 at what was then the Prahran College of Advanced Education and ceased in 1981. It was revived at

4.9 The Fortunes of Ukrainian and Yiddish: Case Studies

Monash University in 2003, and was still being taught there in 2018. Ukrainian was first taught at Monash University in 1983 and, at the time of writing had been offered continuously for 35 years. However, at Macquarie University where Ukrainian teaching began in 1984 (Pavlyshyn, 1998, p. 7), the language gradually became unsustainable and was last taught in 2008.This was due partly to declining student demand and institutional support, as well as insufficient community support to cover rising costs.

For Macquarie University, 'Ukrainian was a special case: the community funded a full academic development entirely out of its own resources' (Mansfield & Hutchison, 1992, p. 179). A Ukrainian Studies Foundation had been set up in 1974 aiming to raise funds from the Ukrainian community to establish a teaching program. Macquarie University was the university where the Foundation wanted this to happen (Mansfield & Hutchison, 1992, pp. 179, 180). Macquarie had the facilities for distance education and the 'Commonwealth government insisted that this program be accessible throughout Australia… and be offered in distance teaching mode' (Koscharsky & Pavković, 2005, pp. 149, 150). No reason was given as to why the Commonwealth government's wishes were taken into account as, has been previously mentioned, they gave no funding for Ukrainian. The likely explanation is that the Commonwealth government was funding other Slavonic languages at Macquarie University in external mode and wished all these languages to be offered in the same way. Fortuitously, Ukrainian already had a champion there in Ihor Gordijew, a senior Economics lecturer, who became the chairman of the Ukrainian Studies Foundation. By 1983, a formal agreement between Macquarie University and the Foundation enabled the establishment of both a teaching program and a Centre for Ukrainian Studies and teaching began in 1984.

The program attracted not only undergraduate students but also large numbers of non-degree students reaching a total enrolment of 60 in 1985 (Gordijew, 1986, p. 146), although it was not a large program in terms of students enrolled in award programs. The 1991 Leal Report showed an EFTSU[8] enrolment in 1990 of just 10.70. By the late 1990s, said a former senior lecturer in Ukrainian, Halyna Koscharsky, the University picked up 50% of the costs of offering the language (Koscharsky, personal communication, 17 July, 2013). Unfortunately, student numbers had dropped in the early 1990s when, with the collapse of communist regimes in Eastern Europe, potential students could now travel more freely in countries such as Ukraine. Koscharsky and Pavković maintained that such travel was a more exciting alternative than distance education study at Macquarie (Koscharsky & Pavković, 2005, p. 160). By 1994, the EFTSU had dropped drastically to 2.70 (Baldauf, 1995, p. 34; Leal, 1991a, p. 66). Whilst in many institutions such a low EFTSU would have meant the immediate phasing out of the teaching of such an uneconomic language, White and Baldauf confirmed that Ukrainian continued to be taught at Macquarie right through to 2005 which was as far as their survey extended (White & Baldauf, 2006, p. 56.) In fact, it continued for three more years. Koscharsky explained the last few years of teaching. Student numbers continued to decline,

---

[8] Equivalent Full Time Student Unit (Australia).

reaching a point where there had been an enrolment of less than 20 for three consecutive years (a measure set by the University) and the teaching of Ukrainian ceased at the end of 2008 (Koscharsky, personal communication, 17 July 2013).

Ukrainian at Monash University, which began in 1983, has been a more successful story. Like Macquarie, the Monash program was made possible through the Ukrainian Studies Support Fund by which, according to Baldauf, 'practically the full cost of the program [was] borne by the Ukrainian community' (Baldauf, 1995, p. 13). According to Marko Pavlyshyn (who was the first lecturer in Ukrainian at Monash and was, at the time of writing, the convenor of Ukrainian Studies at Monash University and Director of the Centre for European Studies), the Ukrainian 'community paid 100% of the costs' in the early years and 'continued to bear the full costs until the late 1990s (Pavlyshyn, 1986, p. 136). By then, the contribution of the community, whilst growing in dollar terms, became only a proportion of the running costs' (Pavlyshyn, personal communication, 19 July, 2013). Baldauf's survey also revealed that 'while research support [to the program] has been available from government and non-government granting bodies, there has been no support of the core language teaching program' (Baldauf, 1995, p. 13). The Ukrainian program at Monash, as at Macquarie, had small numbers – an EFTSU of 1.76 in 1990, and 2.21 in 1994 (Baldauf, 1995, p. 34). Nevertheless, Ukrainian survived at Monash University (White & Baldauf, 2006, p. 56). As Pavlyshyn went on to say: 'most of the funding for Ukrainian nowadays does come from the university in the same way that funding for say, French or Chinese does.' It was also important to note, he said,

> that there is an acceptance at various levels of the University that Ukrainian Studies is one of the distinctive areas of its activity, and that having this discipline is of value. But it is hard to see that this situation would have been reached without a long lead-time during which the community bore the full costs. (Pavlyshyn, personal communication, 19 July, 2013)

Thus, for Ukrainian, it can be argued that it was the acknowledgement of its importance by Monash University that enabled it to continue, notwithstanding the importance of community funding to found it and sustain it until it became a continuing language. However, it is also true to say that philanthropy has played an enormous part. In June 2014, Ukrainian Studies at Monash were the beneficiaries of $1.52 million for either PhD scholarships or inter-disciplinary areas involving Ukrainian studies. This was 'the largest single philanthropic donation that Australia's Ukrainian community has seen to date' (Monash University, 2014). By contrast, Ukrainian studies at Macquarie University did not have that same level of philanthropy, nor the same commitment from the University for the ongoing teaching of the language, and to sustain it through difficult periods so, when student numbers dropped, it was allowed to die.

Yiddish has been another example of a community language for which community funds were important although not in the first iteration of its tertiary teaching. The teaching of Yiddish language, as previously mentioned, began in 1974 at what was then the Prahran CAE. The Director of the College, David Armstrong, had a particular interest in community education, and envisaged Prahran CAE as a community college which would take its shape and form and learning needs from the

4.9 The Fortunes of Ukrainian and Yiddish: Case Studies

community in which it was located (Armstrong, 1979, p. 39). According to Louis Waller, formerly of the Monash Law School, who was, at that time, on the Prahran CAE Council (Waller, personal communication, 25 July, 2013), David Armstrong was especially concerned where a particular community's culture was not represented in tertiary education. In the newly established Liberal Arts department, Jewish Studies, including Yiddish and Modern Hebrew, was taught under the leadership of Henry Shaw.

The impetus for this teaching and the means to fund it had not come from the Jewish community (save for a very insignificant amount), but was an initiative from the College itself (Waller, personal communication, 25 July, 2013). Danielle Charak, the first and only teacher of Yiddish at Prahran CAE recalled that there were about 10–12 students from a variety of backgrounds: Jews who had a nostalgia for Yiddish because their parents and grandparents spoke it, and various non-Jews who just wished to learn the language, in some cases, to aid their academic research. However by 1980, Henry Shaw had retired, David Armstrong was no longer the director, and Prahran CAE was in negotiations to become part of the new multi-campus Victoria College. Yiddish was moved to the Toorak Campus, and student numbers were declining. When Danielle Charak resigned, Yiddish was discontinued at the end of 1981 (Charak, personal communication, 17 July, 2013). The original champions of Yiddish, Shaw and Armstrong had gone, and there was no community financial support or institutional support to keep it going.

It was a different story in 2003 when Yiddish was revived, this time at Monash University within its Centre for Jewish Civilisation. The Centre was encouraged to raise funds through its connections with the Jewish community. A small committee from the Jewish community organised a large fundraising event in 2004 and raised $¼ million,[9] all of which went to the funding of Yiddish teaching (Charak, personal communication, 19 July, 2013). Since then funding has continued in the form of several endowments from the Jewish community. As Mark Baker, Director of the Australian Centre for Jewish Civilisation remarked, 'Yiddish language study is therefore secured on a sessional basis' (Baker, personal communication, 21 July, 2013). This example of Yiddish teaching at Monash demonstrates that what was required for its continuation was not only the commitment of Monash University to teach it, but equally the commitment of the community to provide adequate funding.

These languages, Yiddish and Ukrainian, are but two examples of how small community languages have fared. Whilst there may have been great hopes for the flourishing of the teaching of community languages through the greater awareness of the multicultural and multilingual nature of Australia in general in the 1970s and 1980s, this trend did not continue. The 1991 Australian Literacy and Language Policy showed that by then there was a greater emphasis on the teaching of English as a second language than on languages other than English.[10] Whilst the ALLP

---

[9] Here is the philanthropy of the Jewish community supporting Yiddish just as the Ukrainian community supported Ukrainian.

[10] This emphasis on English was not new. The 1978 Galbally Report had said the teaching of English was the highest priority.

spoke of 'the right of all Australians to express... their individual cultural heritage, including their language,' and the importance for all Australians of the development of skills in languages other than English (DEET, 1991b, p. 13), it was also stated that 'it is not feasible to expect that all languages can be taught on an Australia-wide basis' (DEET, 1991a, p. 16). In fact, the principal focus of the ALLP was on literacy, and that meant literacy in English (Herriman, 1996, pp. 54, 55). The breakdown of the total funding package for the ALLP showed clearly that priority. In the first of four years of funding, programs for the teaching of English as a Second Language (ESL) represented 80% of the total budget; funding for literacy programs was 8.8% of the budget; and funding for the teaching of Languages Other than English (LOTE) represented just 9.5% of the total funding. By the 4th year of the funding package, ESL programs commanded 71.4%, literacy programs 17.3% and LOTE programs just 6.8% of the budget (DEET, 1991a, p. 25).

Not only were literacy and the teaching of English as a second language now the primary issues but, argued Baldauf and Djité, the ALLP was a retuning of the National Policy on Languages because there had been a downturn in the Australian economy, and there was a need to 'provide an appropriate response to the rise to economic power of a number of countries in the Asian region' (Baldauf & Djité, 2000, p. 233). The attention that had been focussed by the Federal government on issues of multiculturalism and migrant languages as an expression of the social cohesion and changing identity of Australia, was moving in another direction. Now it was turning towards the economy and the languages of Australia's major trading partners, as it was determined that Australia's ability to interact with the key Asian economies would be enhanced by greater knowledge of Asian languages and cultures (Baldauf & Djité, 2000, p. 234). The national interest was restated for what was now the priority, the economic interests of the nation.

4.10 Conclusion

This chapter has shown that with the influence of the many different nationalities that had come to Australia in the post-war period, there was a gradual change of attitudes towards migrants and their languages and cultures. There was indeed a period from about 1974 to 1988 when many migrant or community languages did flourish in the university sector. However whilst there seemed to be an opportunity for such languages to become embedded in the educational system, the reality was quite different. There were certainly some languages such as Italian, Modern Greek and Spanish (representing larger community groups) which had become firmly established but smaller languages were quite vulnerable. Other languages were vulnerable because of first generation language shift of migrants to speaking English by preference at home. Often when student numbers declined, or community funding could not always be sustained, it was usually the case that the teaching institution did not pick up the funding and the language did not survive in that institution, although examples have been shown against that trend. It had certainly

4.10 Conclusion

been in Australia's national interest across this period to pay attention to issues of migrant welfare, community languages and cultures and to encourage a sense of social cohesion in the multicultural nation which Australia surely was.

Through several changes of Federal government, priorities had changed such that by the middle 1990s there was a stated national interest in Asian trade. Targeted funding was put forward for key Asian languages important for Australia's trade and this was a fillip for the increased teaching of those languages. The reality of that huge migration starting in 1947 was a realisation that, by the early 1970s, Australia was a multicultural country. There was a short-lived boost in the teaching of community languages, an increase in the number of translating and interpreting courses and the establishment of a permanent ethnic languages media. In the long run though, there was a much stronger stated national interest for language proficiency in English and thus the teaching of English as a second language. The emphasis on the benefits of trade with Asian countries and the Federal government funding given for the study of Asian languages and cultures, as well as English literacy showed clearly the national language priorities that now took precedence.

Chapter 5
Three Trade Languages: Japanese, Chinese and Indonesian

> Asian languages are a priority for expansion as 'a matter of national importance' for Australia. (National Asian Languages & Cultures Working Group (NALCWG), 1994)

In 1994, the NALCWG Report, *Asian languages and Australia's economic future* gave the strongest possible imprimatur for Asian languages in the late twentieth century and encapsulated government and academic opinions of that time. The Report was popularly known as the Rudd Report after its chair, Kevin Rudd, a Mandarin-speaking former diplomat, who became Prime Minister in December 2007. The Report's sentiments were a far cry from the earliest years of the twentieth century, when the Immigration Restriction Act (known as the White Australia Policy), aimed at limiting Asian migration was in force, a policy which did not finally end until the 1970s.

From the latter half of the twentieth century, Australia's trade with Japan was increasing with Japan becoming Australia's major trading partner in the early 1960s. Trade with China in wool and wheat was also increasing despite the Federal government's non-recognition of China's communist regime. Indonesia was important to Australia as its nearest Asian neighbour and as a newly independent country developing as a democracy. Australia needed to diversify its trade from the United Kingdom to include other markets as the UK looked to the European Economic Community for its trade development.

In this chapter I show how Australia's Asian trade interests and defence and security concerns influenced tertiary language offerings. Aspects of this discussion will be achieved through the analysis of the role of a range of individuals who were the key players both in government and academic circles. In exploring Australia's broad relationship with three Asian countries, Japan, China and Indonesia, this chapter investigates how the languages of these countries, which developed differently in the Australian tertiary sector, came to be considered important in Australia's national interest. Each was enhanced by government imperatives for Australians to hone linguistic competence in such 'trade 'languages.

It was for political and security reasons, rather than educational or pedagogical reasons, that each of these Asian languages, Japanese, Chinese and Indonesian was first introduced into the university sector. It was after World War II that the Asian region and Asian languages came to have more strategic importance for Australia, with diplomatic and security issues, in the ensuing years. The attitudes held both by governments and the general population towards Asian countries had an impact on the popularity of these languages, and it was only later that trade interests became important motivators for such languages. As a series of language reports demonstrate, it was in the context of Australia's economic future that these three languages became priority languages for successive governments. Nevertheless, later in the twentieth century and into the twenty first century, geopolitical and security issues in the Asia-Pacific region again had a bearing on the popularity of Indonesian.

However, by 2014 government priorities for relationships with China, Japan and Indonesia had swung firmly towards the economic benefits of engaging with the region. The New Colombo Plan (of which more will be discussed in Chap. 8) emphasised the economic benefits of young Australian studying and working in Asia. The importance of proficiency in the relevant languages was not emphasised in this Plan.

5.1 Australia/Japan Contact Begins with Trade

In 1917, Japanese was the first Asian language introduced into the Australian university sector. However, contact between the two countries had begun in the 1870s as Japan sought Australia's wool (Tweedie, 1994, p. 19). Small numbers of Japanese immigrants began to settle in Queensland as pearl fishermen and indentured labourers in the sugar cane fields (Millar, 1991, p. 47). By the 1890s, trade in wool and coal was flourishing, there were regular shipping services between the two countries, and regular or honorary consulates operating in most Australian colonies. Small import and export businesses had grown up, principally in Sydney but also in Melbourne, with larger Japanese companies establishing themselves, again chiefly in Sydney (Frei, 1984, p. 79; Oliver, 2001a, p. 1). The late nineteenth century was also a time in Australia of enthusiasm for things Japanese, especially the decorative arts, although there was not enthusiasm for learning the language (Broinowski, 1996, p. 27). Walker contended that 'there is no question that, in the 1890s, Japan had become the object of considerable sympathetic interest in Australia' (Walker, 2009, p. 66).

But these sympathetic attitudes were not to last. Frei suggested two issues which made Australia uneasy about Japanese intentions. The Japanese success in the 1894–1985 Sino-Japanese War was seen by Australia as aggressive foreign policy, whilst the fear of the increasing numbers of Asian immigrants (including Japanese) fed anti-Asian racism. The numbers of Japanese immigrants however, were very small. Even by the 1911 census, only 3474 people were listed as Japanese-born (C of A, 1911, p. 116). The colonies, whilst enthusiastically trading with Japan, were concerned not only about security issues but that improved trade might bring unfettered Japanese immigration. Consequently, there were moves to restrict all Asian immigration (Frei, 1984, p. 80; Millar, 1991, p. 47; Tweedie, 1994, pp. 23, 28). In 1926 Edmund Piesse, a former Head of the Pacific Branch of the Prime Minister's department, wrote of that change in attitude of the colonies towards Asia that had come at the very end of the nineteenth century. The colonies feared Japan and the immigration to Australia of 'coloured peoples' (Frei, 1984, p. 80; Millar, 1991, p. 47; Piesse, 1926, p. 476; Tweedie, 1994, pp. 23, 28). That fear was illustrated by Australia's negative attitude towards Japan at the Versailles Peace Conference in 1919.

This unease resulted in the passing of the Immigration Restriction Act of 1901 by the end of the first year of the existence of the Commonwealth of Australia. This Act, according to its authors, was aimed most immediately at Japan (Meaney, Matthews, & Encel, 1988, p. 18). From then on, commented Frei, relations between Australia and Japan were carried out in a much more subdued climate. It became a general assumption that the Japanese were spying in Australia (Frei, 1984, p. 80; Piesse, 1926, p. 479; Walker, 2009, p. 173). Still Australia pushed on developing trade in Asia, with Japanese trade in the ascendant as Japanese companies in Sydney expanded rapidly through the first two decades of the century (Oliver, 2001a, pp. 2, 5). Numbers of businessmen, the then NSW Governor, Lord Chelmsford, and John Suttor, the trade commissioner, promoted the value of Australians learning Asian languages and culture in both the school and university sectors. These suggestions gained some publicity through reports in the press in 1905 and again in 1910. However, such suggestions were not acted upon until just before the end of World War I, a war in which the Japanese were allies of Britain and Australia (Walker, 2009, pp. 82, 83).

5.2 Japanese Language

Although Australia and Japan may have been allies, there was still suspicion within the Australian government about Japanese intentions. That Government took steps to support the teaching of Japanese in Australia which Zainu'ddin contended in her history of Japanese teaching was clearly motivated by concerns about Japanese imperialism in the Pacific (Zainu'ddin, 1988, p. 47). James Murdoch was engaged as a lecturer in Japanese at the University of Sydney in 1917, with the Defence Department bearing the greater share of his salary costs. The public reason given for Murdoch's appointment was teaching at the University but, in reality, the major reason was for him to teach Japanese at the Royal Military College, Duntroon near Canberra. Murdoch was closely associated with Piesse, the then Director of Military Intelligence. The historian Neville Meaney suggested it was Murdoch who had assisted Piesse to learn Japanese to enable Piesse to read Japanese documents (Meaney, 1988, p. 1). It is more credible though, according to Zainu'ddin, that Mōshi Inagaki taught Japanese to the Melbourne-based Piesse (Zainu'ddin, 1988, pp. 47, 49). It is highly likely, given their documented correspondence, that it was to

Piesse that Murdoch, after his annual visits to Japan, reported back about trends in Japanese public opinion and foreign policy (Meaney, 1988, p. 1). Those annual visits to Japan had been required by the Department of Defence as part of his employment conditions.

Murdoch was made a Professor of Oriental Studies in 1918 but there was no hint of including Chinese language, the government funding was for Japanese.

Murdoch's influence went further than the teaching of Japanese. When writing to Piesse in 1919, he pointed out 'the need for a clear policy towards Japan as a necessary basis for an independent Australian foreign policy attuned to the role that Pacific trade would come to play in Australian affairs' (Walker, 2009, p. 212). His opinion was sought by Prime Minister Hughes about the renewal of the Anglo-Japanese alliance which was due to expire in July 1921 (Vinson, 1962, p. 264). Hughes had already revealed his views about the Japanese when he vigorously opposed a Japanese amendment about equality of nations and equal treatment of their nationals at the Versailles Peace Conference in early 1919. Hughes saw this amendment as a threat to Australia's White Australia Policy (Fitzhardinge, 1983, p. 7). Each of these three men were influential in their own field but had diverse views: Hughes, the Prime Minister, suspicious of Japanese foreign policy and committed to the White Australia Policy (Akami & Milner, 2013, p. 541); Piesse, Head of the Pacific Branch in the PM's Department most critical of Hughes' anti-Japanese posture, and Murdoch, the Professor of Oriental Languages, a Japanese specialist with a keen interest in Australian foreign affairs. However, this relationship was not to continue as Murdoch died in late 1921, Hughes was deposed as Leader of the Government in early 1923 and Piesse resigned from the Public Service in frustration, joining a Melbourne law firm in 1923 (Ball, 1969, p. 26; Meaney, 1988, p. 2; Sissons, 1986, p. 2).

Whatever had been the true motivation of the Government in funding such studies, Japanese language was now established in the university sector. According to the historians Tokomo Akami and Anthony Milner, 'the wider Australian public still had little knowledge or interest in Asia and the Pacific' (Akami & Milner, 2013, p. 544). Nevertheless, groups of influential academics, public servants and businessmen were writing articles and meeting with each other to discuss trade, Australian defence and foreign policy and Asia-Pacific cultural affairs, both Japanese and Chinese. Walker continued: this 'well-travelled, well-informed group of internationalists saw the Asia-Pacific as a region of vital importance to Australians and the world at large' (Ackroyd, 1988, p. 1; Walker, 2009, pp. 204, 222, 226). These people, although a minority, kept alive the debate about the value of knowledge of Asia throughout the late 1920s and 1930s, in a spirit of reciprocal cultural and intellectual exchange, hoping to better inform the Australian public (Akami & Milner, 2013, p. 543).

The reciprocal goodwill visits between Japan and Australia of External Affairs Minister Latham and Japanese diplomat Katsuji Debuchi in 1934 and 1935 demonstrated that the Federal government did seek a strengthening of the relationship with Japan and peace and stability in the Asia-Pacific region, although still fearful of Japanese intentions. Peter Russo, a Melbourne University graduate and linguist, who was travelling as Debuchi's adviser and speech writer, told the press on a visit

5.2 Japanese Language

back to Australia, how important the visits had been for cultural understanding and closer ties between Australia and Japan. More visits between Australia and Japan were planned for the future when it was hoped that international tensions might have lessened (Andrews, 1988, p. 68; Torney-Parlicki, 2001, p. 353; Walker, 2009, pp. 209, 221).

Whilst Japanese had first been introduced at the University of Sydney, it would have made good sense for Japanese to have begun at the University of Melbourne, especially as the Federal government was based in Melbourne from 1901 to 1927. Japanese language expertise would then have been readily available to the Federal government. However, there is no evidence that the Government had any influence or interest in assisting that University to introduce such studies. The University of Melbourne had neither the resources nor an official interest in Japanese whereas the University of Sydney had been granted Commonwealth government funds. The University of Melbourne had instead, in 1919, enabled the teaching of Japanese by an instructor (who was not a University staff member) to whom students paid fees directly. This instructor, Mōshi Inagaki, who had Japanese tertiary qualifications, had been endorsed for the position by Russo and by Eric Longfield Lloyd, who was the Australian Trade Commissioner in Japan from 1935 (Murray, J. 2004, p. 176; Oliver, 2001b, p. 123; Zainu'ddin, 1988, pp. 49, 50).

Despite the lack of formal support for Japanese language at the University of Melbourne, Japanese classes began at the Macrobertson Girls' High School (MGHS) in 1935 on Saturday mornings and also through the Correspondence School (Zainu'ddin, 1988, p. 51). Public Examination records show that those classes were at the Intermediate and Leaving Certificate levels (The University of Melbourne Matriculation Rolls and Handbooks of Public Examinations). In addition, the Australian Broadcasting Commission (ABC) had begun broadcasting a Japanese language and history course in late 1935 which was immensely popular up until December 1941 when Inagaki, who was involved in these broadcasts, was interned (Murray, 2004, p. 177). Russo, who had maintained professional connections with the University whilst he was teaching in Japan, had argued for Japanese as an examinable subject in his discussions with University of Melbourne academics which, at that time, controlled these examinations (Torney-Parlicki, 2001, p. 355). The Japanese teaching at MGHS can be attributed to the influence of Russo. Bruno Mascitelli and Frank Merlino, in their discussion of the origins of Saturday morning language classes, disagree. They suggested that the Saturday classes were simply a 'special experiment', not a particular plan of the government, but more an initiative of visionary individuals (Mascitelli & Merlino, 2012, pp. 41, 42).

Whilst World War II had begun in September 1939 and Japan had signed a pact with Germany and Italy by September 1940, Australia, anxious about Japanese intentions, appointed Sir John Latham, in December 1940 as Australia's first Minister to Japan. Latham reported on firm and frank discussions with Japanese foreign ministers hoping to curb Japanese aggression. Nevertheless, Australia's fear of Japan pushing south was confirmed by Japan's entry into the war in late 1941 (Akami & Milner, 2013, p. 546; Andrews, 1988, p. 75; McDougall, 1998, p. 6; Macintyre, 1986, pp. 5, 6). Australia acted swiftly against Japanese living in

Australia and interned them in camps, such as Tatura in Victoria, Loveday in South Australia and Cowra and Hay in NSW. In all, 4301 Japanese from Australia and from overseas were interned, including the University of Melbourne Japanese instructor, Inagaki (Nagata, 1996, pp. 77, 91).

Inagaki's appeal against internment was not supported, despite his connections with influential men whom he had taught or knew professionally: Piesse, the former Director of Intelligence, Alexander Melbourne, an academic, at the University of Queensland, Longfield Lloyd, trade commissioner to Japan, and Russo, an Australian teaching with Tokyo but with connections to the University of Melbourne. In addition, the then Chancellor of the University of Melbourne, Sir John Latham, had approved Inagaki's initial teaching appointment (Murray, 2004, p. 176). However, Inagaki was probably of little consequence to Latham given the palpable national fear of Japanese invasion. Selleck, in his history of the University of Melbourne, reported that Latham had made some 'mild' efforts on Inagaki's behalf and that the Registrar was sympathetic, but not willing to do anything further because Inagaki was not a regular member of staff, but merely an instructor. Inagaki certainly had no support from other language academics. He had in fact been criticised about the suitability of his teaching materials by the Professor of French, Alan Chisholm, and Harold Hunt, from the Classics department, himself a former student of Inagaki's (Chisholm & Hunt, 1940, pp. 74, 75; Selleck, 2003, p. 644). The instruction in Japanese limped along for another few years, with various part-time instructors, but disappeared from the University of Melbourne calendar listings by 1946 (UniMelb, 1946).

5.3 Defence Needs Japanese Skills

After the Japanese had entered the Pacific War, knowledge of the Japanese language was of crucial importance for Australia's national defence and security interests. Duntroon had discontinued its Japanese language training in 1937. However, Army command in Melbourne, anticipating the entry of Japan into the war, set up a Japanese language school in Melbourne in August 1940 to train the urgently needed Japanese linguists. Several linguists employed had studied Japanese with the ill-fated Inagaki. That Army language school lasted for five years and had been 'Australia's first attempt to produce armed services linguists in any numbers' (Funch, 2003, pp. 38, 39, 43, 50). Navy and Army Intelligence in a joint operation also sought Japanese linguists to decode Japanese messages (Pfennigwerth, 2006, p. 163).

Still more Japanese linguists were needed. Max Wiadrowski, an RAAF Intelligence officer with Japanese language ability, argued persuasively for a Japanese language training facility which was established in March 1944 in Sydney (Turner, 1983, p. 21). Classes were conducted at the University of Sydney, reinforced by further evening instruction by military linguists. The first class was composed entirely of RAAF personnel, but subsequent courses included army and navy personnel. The University of Sydney taught Japanese for the RAAF School of Languages from July 1944 to July 1945. When the training premises in Sydney were closed at the end of the war, the School transferred to new accommodation available in Melbourne. Japanese language trained military personnel were still needed after the war, principally in the governorship of Japan and in war crimes trials of which some 300 were conducted. The School continued till 1948 when it was closed, but not for long. It was reopened in 1950 under the leadership of Flight Lieutenant Garrick, who had skills in both Russian and Japanese (Darian-Smith, 2013, p. 104; Funch, 2003, pp. 69, 239; Turner, 1983, pp. 21, 22, 23).

The Occupation of Japan lasted from 1945 to 1952 with Australians involved in both military and civilian roles for almost the whole time as part of the British Commonwealth Occupation Force. Gerster suggested that many of those personnel came to have an understanding of the Japanese people in a way that was entirely unexpected. Some made an effort to learn the language, and meet Japanese people in a spirit of goodwill, with numbers of men marrying Japanese women. These experiences were difficult for those back home in Australia to understand. Many Australians were vehemently anti-Japanese because of Japanese war atrocities and brutality towards POWs (Gerster, 2008, pp. 2, 16, 18, 231, 263).

So, whilst the evidence showed that it was the Defence Forces whose need for Japanese linguists facilitated the training in the latter war years and into the 1950s, Japanese was dropped from the RAAF School's curriculum in 1948 when it was no longer deemed a defence imperative, not resuming till 1969. The Japanese department at the University of Sydney, which had flourished through the first half of the twentieth century, and whose staff had assisted with military Japanese language instruction in 1944/1945 had, by 1952, just one part-time staff member and only five students, suggesting a lack of student demand. The University said it had been unable to find anyone with the necessary qualifications to replace the Japanese language professor who resigned in 1949. Thus, the remaining staff taught the last of the students who finished at the end of 1952 and 'the department ceased to function' (A Staff Correspondent, 1953, p. 2).

Whilst Japanese was languishing at the University of Sydney, the Canberra University College had established its School of Oriental Studies in 1952 introducing Chinese in 1953. Now Chinese had become a priority language for Australia given the government's suspicion of Communist China. Japanese was taught at CUC from 1955 (Bielenstein, 1962, pp. 257, 259), although it was less of a national priority given the defeat of the Japanese. CUC had maintained the link with the wartime Japanese language training as their Japanese lecturer was Joyce Ackroyd who had taught Japanese at the University of Sydney in the 1940s, and in the RAAF School of Languages from 1944 to 1945 (Funch, 2003, p. 55).

5.4 From Defence Needs to Trade Needs

Whilst there was understandably some post-war hostility towards Japan in the general community, there was enthusiasm from the Australian government to resume trading with Japan (Tweedie, 1994, pp. 150, 154). Through the late 1940s and the

1950s Japan again became one of Australia's more important trading partners. As the economic historian Boris Schedvin noted, by the mid-1960s 'Japan had displaced the United Kingdom as Australia's most important trading partner' (Schedvin, 2008, p. 209). Schedvin noted the difficulties with both Japanese language and business etiquette that trade commissioners encountered, implying that enthusiasm for trade alone was not enough without cultural understanding (Schedvin, 2008, pp. 208, 210, 211). Sandra Tweedie highlighted the complexities of the relationship with Japan: 'Sharing none of the political and cultural links that marked the UK-Australia trading partnership of the past, the relationship between Australia and Japan is now entirely economically based, relying as it does on the strong complementarity between the different resource endowments of the trading partners' (Tweedie, 1994, p. 170).

Given the economic importance of Japan to Australia, it could be argued that more interest might have been be shown by widespread government funding for Asian languages as well as cultural and contemporary affairs in universities, other than the University of Sydney and subsequently the Australian National University which took over the CUC in 1960. Even the 1964 Martin Report on tertiary education, an obvious vehicle for raising priorities for particular subjects, was silent about Asian languages. It was therefore up to the universities themselves to use their triennial funding to introduce languages they felt were important. In the case of Japanese, it was introduced both at the University of Queensland and the University of Melbourne in 1965, and Monash University in 1966. The historian Malcolm Thomis indicated that the University of Queensland had been considering Asian studies since 1959, seeing such studies as important to further Australia's 'national interests within her sphere of influence' (Thomis, 1985, p. 284). Subsequently, a University Senate committee on university expansion, guided by the wishes of the vice-chancellor, 'recommended a department of Japanese Language and Literature' in August 1964. In 1965, Joyce Ackroyd formerly of CUC and the University of Sydney, was appointed as founding Professor of Japanese (Thomis, 1985, p. 284). The University of Melbourne, it will be remembered, had taught not-for-degree Japanese from 1919 until approximately 1945. The reintroduction of Japanese in 1965, enabled degree studies to be taken in that language for the first time although this was not through University triennial funding, but rather by the endowment of funds from the Myer Foundation. As Monash University expanded academically in the mid 1960s, Jiří Neustupný was appointed to the Chair in Japanese in May 1966. According to Blackwood, the first chancellor of Monash, it was important for Monash to develop quickly into a full university with the normal range of courses. The choice of Japanese was, according to Matheson, then first vice-chancellor of Monash, to differentiate Monash from Melbourne which specialised in Chinese (Blackwood, 1968, pp. 99, 142; Matheson, 1980, p. 13).

5.5 The Influence of Universities on Japanese in Schools

In New South Wales, secondary and tertiary Japanese began almost simultaneously with the first Japanese language classes in Australian schools starting at the Fort Street Boys' High School in Sydney in 1918. The clear connection between secondary and tertiary Japanese here is demonstrated by the report, in the *Fortian*, of Professor Murdoch's weekly school visits. By 1927 it was discontinued due to lack of student interest, but subsequently reintroduced in 1947 (Fort Street Boys' High School, 1918). Olive Wykes' national language statistics (covering government and non-government schools) show that in NSW by 1961 a small number of Form One pupils studied Japanese, but none at Form Five, the last year of secondary school (Wykes & King, 1968, p. 40). Japanese teaching had started in 1935 at MGHS in Melbourne. According to both Les Oates who studied Japanese at MGHS in 1941, and the historian Zainu'ddin, the teachers were all ex-pupils of Inagaki from the University of Melbourne. Oates remembered Inagaki attending those classes to monitor the students' progress and assist in the teaching. Oates sat the Leaving Japanese Examination late in 1941, but, as Inagaki was interned straight after the Pearl Harbour attack, Oates recollected that it was Inagaki's wife, Rose, who marked his examination paper (Jones & Oliver, 2001, p. viii; Oates, personal communication, 2 July, 2012; Zainu'ddin, 1988, p. 52).

Wykes' Victorian statistics (covering only formal weekday language classes) indicate that, in 1961, no students were studying Japanese although it is possible that the Saturday morning classes still continued. Wykes and King's 1961 figures also show there was no Japanese taught in Queensland, South Australia, Western Australia and Tasmania (Wykes & King, 1968, pp. xi, xii, 50, 58, 62, 65, 69). They did acknowledge however, the difficulties in comparing data because of differing school systems and variations in the data obtained (Wykes & King, 1968, pp. 32, 34, 76). G. A. Browne, of the Teachers' Training College Brisbane, reported the first teaching of Japanese in Queensland at Year 10 Level in 1939 (Browne, 1967, p. 16). Other data on Japanese language teaching in schools was reported by Anne Bonyhady in *Babel,* the journal of the Australian Federation of Modern Languages Teachers Associations, in 1965. This data showed that only five students sat for Matriculation Japanese in 1964, and these were all in New South Wales (Bonyhady, 1965, p. 32). This rather disparate group of data illustrate the paucity of Japanese language teaching in Australian schools up to 1964.

It was only in NSW where Japanese language teaching in schools gained any foothold. Although in Victoria the Saturday morning Japanese language classes had been supported by the University of Melbourne Japanese instructor, he was not a salaried academic. Combined with the fact that Saturday classes were not considered mainstream formal teaching, this may account for why Japanese language teaching was not more established in Victoria. One final group of data complete this picture of Japanese language teaching in Australian schools. From the 1975 Kramer

114   5   Three Trade Languages: Japanese, Chinese and Indonesian

Table 5.1 Matriculation Japanese candidates 1967–1974

Year	Student numbers
1967	5
1968	43
1969	33
1970	56
1971	134
1972	183
1973	214
1974	250

Report on university languages (AUC, 1975a, p. 18), a table of the number of students sitting Matriculation Japanese nationally showed a rapid increase (Table 5.1).

The evidence of this table underlines the point, made by the writers of the Japanese profile of *Unlocking Australia's Language Potential*, that there were two major factors contributing to the radical change in Japanese teaching in the mid-1960s. Firstly, Japanese had now been introduced at a number of universities, and secondly there was a growth in secondary Japanese language teaching and 'systematic introduction of Japanese as a subject for school examinations, including Year 12 examinations' (Marriott, Neustupný, & Spence-Brown, 1993, p. 1). This also suggests that there was an increase in the number of teachers trained and registered to teach secondary level Japanese. Most certainly there was a growth in the number of universities offering Japanese. Wykes reported just two universities offering Japanese in 1964 (Wykes, 1966, p. 27), whilst the 1975 Kramer Report indicated for the year 1973, that six universities taught Japanese (AUC, 1975a, p. 15). Hawley's 1974 tertiary languages survey showed (Hawley, 1982, pp. 10, 62, 68) major studies in Japanese being offered at now 11 universities, and four tertiary institutes/colleges of advanced education, with some other tertiary institutions offering just a terminal one year course.[1]

However, as far as the impetus for increased Japanese language learning is concerned, it was not the mid-1960s, when Japanese was systematically introduced for school examination, as Marriott and her colleagues contend, but several years later (Marriott et al., 1993, p. 1). It has already been shown that sub-matriculation Japanese examinations were already held in Victoria and New South Wales by 1961. Matriculation Japanese is illustrated by R. F. Holt's first candidature statistics for 1967–1974: NSW already offered by 1964, South Australia (1968), Queensland (1969), Victoria (1970), Western Australia and Tasmania in 1971. Thus, it was the late 1960s and early 1970s, not the mid-1960s, when most Matriculation Japanese candidates started to come through the school system and be eligible for university-

---

[1] There are discrepancies in some reports about the date a language began. Some use the date of the decision to introduce the language, others the date when the first teaching staff were appointed and others still the date of first classes. Often the terminology is loose, and it is not possible to determine which date is being reported.

level Japanese. Of course, in several of these universities there may already have been elementary or beginners' courses, entry for which did not require any previous knowledge of Japanese (Holt, 1976, p. 31). From this data it appears that the contiguity of the development of Japanese in both university and school sectors can be noted, but available information does not allow a causal connection to be clearly demonstrated.

Nevertheless, as can be seen from the 1991 Leal Report statistics, Japanese flourished during the general expansion of Asian languages throughout the 1980s and by 1990 was offered at 28 tertiary institutions. Such was its popularity that the number of institutions offering Japanese, and the number of students enrolled in Japanese, exceeded all other individual languages offered in 1990 (Leal, 1991a, pp. 64, 66). The profile of Japanese was considerably strengthened by its designation as one of the key languages in the 1987 National Policy on Languages, its prioritisation by both DFAT and Austrade, as well as its designation as a key language for inbound tourism (Leal, 1991a, pp. 20, 54). The later 1980s was also a period of considerable growth in services exports to Japan, particularly in tourism (Tweedie, 1994, pp. 174, 175). The sociolinguist, Florian Coulmas, agreed with Neustupný that what marked Japanese teaching in Australia was the quality of Japanese curricula in secondary schools and teaching of Japanese as an 'instrument of communication' (Coulmas, 1989, p. 128). Coulmas further contended that the popularity of Japanese language was due to Australian awareness of the weight of the Japanese economy and an awareness of Japanese culture, and the Department of Foreign Affairs and Trade and Austrade priorities support this argument of national interest (Coulmas, 1989, p. 128).

5.6 Chinese Migration to Australia

Whilst Chinese migration for the 1850s gold rushes marked the largest influx of Chinese, small numbers of Chinese had migrated to Australia in the 1840s. Some came as indentured labourers (Tweedie, 1994, p. 24), but others came as free settlers, setting up businesses such as cabinet making, or working for families of white colonists (Fitzgerald. S. [Shirley], 1997, p. 17; Rolls, 1992, pp. 32, 33). Various schemes for settling Chinese in Australia to increase the population had been mooted in the early 1800s but came to nothing (Levi, 1958, p. 10; Rolls, 1992, pp. 18, 19). In addition, more well-to-do Australians picked up the trend from Europe acquiring Chinese porcelains, lacquerware, and silks (Broinowski, 1996, pp. 26, 27). All these strands of Chinese society – labourers, craftsmen and the goods of Chinese high culture – permeated colonial Australia. These were vastly different images of Chinese people and Chinese civilisation portrayed to Australians in the nineteenth century – a far more complex picture than just the diggers who came to seek gold.

By 1859 there were estimated to be around 50,000 Chinese in Australia (Walker, 2009, p. 36), and that Chinese population was 'overwhelmingly' male (Andrews,

1985, p. 21). As their numbers increased, the Chinese became the largest foreign group on the goldfields. Racial intolerance and violence grew, and colonial governments instituted a poll tax on Chinese arrivals. As the gold petered out, and many Chinese returned home, their numbers in Australia declined (Andrews, 1985, pp. 8, 9; Walker, 2009, p. 36). Those who remained were employed in market gardening, hotels, restaurants, the furniture trade, and laundries. Many of the population were threatened by the Chinese work ethic and business acumen and there was increasing intolerance towards Chinese immigration (Andrews, 1985, pp. 12, 13, 17).

It is not surprising then, that upon Federation the first substantive Act passed was the *Immigration Restriction Act* 1901, (the White Australia Policy). This policy was, as Andrews argued, 'the natural outcome of nineteenth-century Australian-Chinese relations' (Andrews, 1985, p. 34). The aim of this Act seems to have been twofold: a fear of Japanese imperial aggression but also, a fear of the sheer numbers of Chinese settlers who might come to Australia, notwithstanding that by 1901, there were some 30,000 Chinese already in Australia. Given these numbers already settled, it was simply not possible to completely exclude the Chinese, even if this was desired by members of Federal Parliament (Andrews, 1985, pp. 33, 36; Walker, 2009, p. 38). Whilst Andrews saw the White Australia Policy as emanating from the growing racialism of nineteenth-century Australia, Dutton suggested that the 'policy was less a continuation of the colonial system of immigration restriction than the outcome of a new nation-building population regime.' The point of the White Australia policy was to ensure a 'white' population was developing which would be more socially harmonious and have similar values. Australia, contended Dutton, sought to be a 'racially harmonious' nation and racial exclusion was thought to be necessary to prevent non-European enclaves (Dutton, 2001, pp. 30, 33).

In the early twentieth century, trade with China was quite small, and for many Australians this was the only interest in China. Others, such as the 'internationalists' (Broinowski, 1996, p. 47) mentioned earlier, were keenly interest in Asian cultures and societies for their own sake (Dutton, 2001, p. 50). Dutton further argued though that 'the efforts of such individuals to transmit their Asian enthusiasms to the public, made only a limited impact.' Australians in general had a parochial outlook and a lack of interest in Asia. The country's political leaders broadly shared this cultural insularity, which perhaps explains why they made no serious attempts to expand education about Asia (Dutton, 2001, p. 51).

Herbert Gepp, industrialist and public servant, and Alexander Melbourne, a history lecturer at the University of Queensland, who both visited Asia in 1932, stressed to the Government the importance of understanding Asian societies, languages and cultures in order to further develop trade, and to make diplomatic and commercial appointments accordingly (Andrews, 1985, pp. 71, 72; Smith, 2001, pp. 70, 71, 78; Tweedie, 1994, p. 87; Walker, 2009, pp. 204, 205). However, whilst large exports of wheat to China were important to Australian primary producers and new markets were desperately needed, the suggestions of Gepp and Melbourne went unheeded, and there was no move by either governments or universities in the early twentieth century to promote Chinese language teaching. There was just one introductory course in Eastern history, covering Chinese, Indian and Japanese culture taught by

Arthur Sadler, Head of Oriental Studies at the University of Sydney from 1923 until 1947 (Turney, Bygott, & Chippendale, 1991, p. 524; UniSyd, 1925, p. 217). Sir John Latham's previously mentioned visit to several Asian countries including China and Japan in 1934 also emphasised trade. Latham believed that trade commissioners could bridge the gap between Australian and its northern neighbours, combining a trade development role with that of a diplomat (Schedvin, 2008, p. 51; Walker, 2009, p. 205).

5.7 Trade and Diplomacy with China

Australia continued to pursue its trade and diplomatic relations into the 1940s. Unfortunately, the very experienced trade commissioner, Gordon Bowden, was killed after he had fled to Singapore from the advance of the Japanese in September 1941. Bowden had been a great asset to Australian trade with his Chinese language skills, his knowledge of Asian markets, and his family business experiences particularly in Shanghai (Schedvin, 2008, p. 54). Meanwhile Australia continued to be represented by Sir Frederic Eggleston appointed as Minister to China from November 1941. This appointment, along with that of Sir John Latham to Japan, was seen as very important given the seniority and distinction of both men in the Australian community. Although not a linguist, Eggleston developed valuable relationships with Chinese intellectuals, educationists and politicians. Effective as he was, his was a small legation of three of whom only one spoke Chinese: Charles Lee, a young Australian-born Queensland University graduate of Chinese descent. Andrews summed up the interest in China shown by Australia's leaders in the early 1940s even though Australia and China were allies in World War II: 'None showed deep sympathy for the Chinese or real effort to help them. Their appointment of Eggleston was a pragmatic move at a crucial time for Australia, not part of a commitment to China.' Eggleston's poor health eventually forced him back to Australia in 1944 (Andrews, 1985, pp. 98, 100; Osmond, 1981, pp. 2–4; Schedvin, 2008, pp. 68, 69; Smith, 2001, p. 95; Tweedie, 1994, p. 89, 111; Watt, 1967, p. 239). Australia continued to demonstrate that its only interest in China was to maximise trade possibilities, without developing any further knowledge of Chinese culture or language, ignoring the advice of those with a deeper understanding of China.

Post World War II, diplomatic and trade relations continued with Douglas Copland, an economics professor from the University of Melbourne, as the next Minister to China from 1946 until late 1948 when he was appointed the founding vice-chancellor of the Australian National University (Andrews, 1985, p. 120; Harper, 1993, pp. 3, 4). Copland was certainly an influential person both in the university world and in Australian politics. Despite Australia's trade post re-opening in Shanghai in 1946, it closed again in December 1948, when civil war broke out and the Chinese economy was collapsing. Australia's diplomatic mission was withdrawn by the Labor government in October 1949, and Menzies, as incoming Prime Minister of the Liberal government in December 1949, chose not to recognise the

People's Republic of China. Copland chided the Government over its short-sightedness, declaring that this non-recognition of China was due to an upcoming federal election. Percy Spender, the External Affairs Minister, in an angry press release, took exception to Copland's remarks (Spender critical of Professor's China speech, p. 7). He declared that Copland was 'over-simplifying the problem', insinuating that, as External Affairs Minister, he understood the situation better. Copland retorted by reminding Spender that he, Copland, 'had far more expert knowledge of China than' Spender 'would probably ever have' (Andrews, 1985, pp. 152, 157; Schedvin, 2008, pp. 106, 107; Watt, 1967, p. 240).

5.8 The Imperative for Chinese Language Teaching

The first teaching of Chinese language studies in an Australian university commenced in 1953, at the School of Oriental Languages established in 1952 at the Canberra University College. It had taken over a century of contact between the Chinese people and Australia before such language study had been introduced. Whilst there is no evidence of direct Federal government funding of Chinese language teaching for political reasons, there are certainly factors which suggest this link. Australia had been involved in the Korean War against North Korean and communist Chinese forces. China's stance fed Australian fears that communism could spread throughout the rest of South-East Asia. It is my view that it was this fear that finally impelled the establishment of the School of Oriental Languages, as at last the Federal government saw the need for Australia to become more China-literate (Andrews, 1988, p. 127; Bielenstein, 1962, p. 257; Foster & Varghese, 1996, p. 151). That China-literacy imperative had not been prompted by trade interests, but by Australia's strategic national interest with the Asian region. Subsequently the Menzies' government instituted Asian studies scholarships for the study of Chinese and Japanese. As Rafe De Crespigny, (a retired Adjunct Professor with the College of Asian and the Pacific at ANU) who studied Chinese at CUC through this scholarship commented, 'this was the beginning of serious academic interest in Asia, and the very existence of the scholarships was a mark of the Menzies' government's concern that there should be a body of home-grown knowledge of the countries in our region' (De Crespigny, personal communication, 28 September, 2012).' Whilst it could be argued that academic interest in Asia had begun much earlier with the introduction of Japanese at the University of Sydney in 1917, this had been primarily for defence reasons.

I argue therefore, that the Menzies Asian studies scholarships were the real catalyst for Australia to seriously engage with Asia academically. The remarks of Colin Mackerras, an eminent Asian Studies scholar, who also studied Asian languages through the CUC Menzies' government scholarship, support this view. Mackerras said: 'There had long been a feeling we in Australia should take more notice of Asia. …In my own case, I had the opportunity to study both Chinese and Japanese, … and quickly came to think Chinese more important, and China more interesting'

(Mackerras, personal communication, 14 July, 2012). Mackerras, later Deputy Head of the School of Modern Asian Studies at Griffith University, spoke of the scholarship he gained in the 1950s that had no conditions attached. Although he recalled that in his small class his colleagues had not taken up the scholarship for employment reasons, nevertheless, his career developed from that early love of Chinese (Mackerras, personal communication, 14 July, 2012).

Hans Bielenstein, a Swedish academic, was the first Head of the School of Oriental Studies teaching modern and classical Chinese. He had been recommended by Charles Fitzgerald, who at that time held the Chair of Far Eastern History at the Australian National University. Fitzgerald himself had lived and worked in China for over 20 years before coming to Australia. Michael Lindsay was another academic at ANU in the Research School of Pacific Studies. He had also lived in China, knew the communist leadership personally, and had good connections with Australian parliamentarians (Cotton, 2010, pp. 4, 7). So, there were in Canberra around 1952 and 1953, four China specialists: Fitzgerald, Bielenstein, Lindsay, and Copland. Fitzgerald, Lindsay and Copland particularly, had the ear of government and made their views about the non-recognition of China known. The influence of all four men should have augured well for the Federal government to become better informed about China. This situation was reminiscent of the 1930s when men like Gepp, Melbourne and Latham had lobbied the Government in vain for the further development of diplomatic and trade relations with, and cultural knowledge of, Asia (Andrews, 1985, p. 69, 73; Walker, 2009, p. 204). Now in the early 1950s, the voices of the China specialists were again being ignored and, according to Wang Gungwu, an eminent Chinese scholar who had taught at the ANU, speaking particularly of Fitzgerald and his influence, this was unfortunate:

> his [Fitzgerald's] was the fresh voice that the country vitally needed to hear if it was to lose its deep-rooted fears of the Chinese that had contributed to the tragic White Australia Policy. What he had to say about the Chinese revolution was not always what most Australians wanted to hear. Only his colleagues, some journalists and a few diplomats appreciated that he possessed that rare commodity, an authentic and authoritative view. (Gungwu, 1993, p. 162)

I argue that the Government's concern for the teaching of Chinese for political and security reasons is underlined by two factors: firstly, the comments of Richard Casey, the Minister for External Affairs who was quoted in the Sunday Herald in 1953, as saying that Oriental Studies had now become much more vital. Casey was known to personally believe that Asia was important for Australia's future and encouraged younger diplomats to take a particular interest in Asia rather than Europe – an attitude rather different to that of Prime Minister Menzies who held strong anti-communist views. Secondly, I argue that there was a connection with the timing of the revival of language teaching in the RAAF School of Languages. This School, which had closed in 1948, reopened in 1950 just as the Korean War was breaking out, with Chinese language classes beginning in 1951 (A Staff Correspondent, 1953, p. 2; Hudson, 1993, p. 3; Turner, 1983, p. 22).

Just two years later in 1953, the Department of External Affairs – which had requested and funded the Diplomatic Studies course which included language training, taught mainly at the CUC from 1944- dropped the funding. The Department had decided it was more cost effective to train cadet diplomats in-house (Beaumont, 2003, pp. 28, 29, 31; Foster & Varghese, 1996, pp. 146, 151). This was an unfortunate waste of an opportunity for solid language training, particularly when, in the years to come, there was a chronic problem with a lack of language competence in diplomats (Beaumont, 2003, p. 33). It was fortunate, nevertheless, that the Menzies government had initiated Asian language scholarships, and that Asian languages were still being taught at CUC even though External Affairs had dropped its connection with CUC.

Yet Asian relations, particularly Chinese communism, were very much on the mind of the government. Gifford described the period, from 1950 up as far as 1963, as 'one of extremely active diplomacy by Australia and its major allies', as they sought to construct 'security arrangements that would contain China and provide the means to combat communism throughout the region' (Gifford, 2001, p. 218). Casey, who had become Minister for External Affairs in 1950, argued in Cabinet for a re-evaluation of Australia's position on China but again and again his view was defeated. Nevertheless, as Andrews recorded, 'Australia continued trading with China' (Andrews, 1988, p. 178; Gifford, 2001, p. 192). Australia was ever pragmatic in the issue of trade. Some in government and in the community, felt that trade with China amounted to de facto recognition of the communist government. However, as Schedvin put it: 'the government was intent on picking its way through the minefield by taking advantage of the trade opportunity and at the same time maintaining reasonable ideological purity' (Andrews, 1988, p. 179; Schedvin, 2008, p. 212; Tweedie, 1994, pp. 122, 123).

5.9 Oriental and Asian Studies Expand

Apart from the CUC, other universities were slow to commit themselves to the teaching of Chinese. It was not until the end of 1953, that the University of Sydney Senate decided to advertise the Oriental Studies Chair[2] which had been vacant since 1949. Albert Davis, a Chinese and Japanese scholar, was appointed to the Chair in 1955, with a temporary lecturer, W. P. Liu. Liu was presumably the 'native' speaker required by the University Senate in its approval of staffing. There is no reference in the University Senate reports as to why it took six years to fill the Chair of Oriental Studies, with now both Chinese and Japanese taught in equal standing, or whether there had been any pressure from the Federal government on the University to begin Chinese language studies (Stefanowska, 1984, p. 18; UniSyd, 1955, p. 1058, 1956, p. 43, 1957, p. 41).

The University of Melbourne now entered the fray, announcing in its 1960 Annual Report, that, until 1959, 'the wider field of the languages and civilizations of Australia's neighbours had not been touched' other than 'a small department in Indonesian and Malayan Studies'. However, 'fortunate circumstances' now allowed

---

[2] Only Japanese had been taught in Oriental Studies since the creation of the Chair in 1918.

5.9 Oriental and Asian Studies Expand

them to expand their offerings (UniMelb, 1961, p. 600). This was a reference to the generous offer of Kenneth Myer through the Myer Foundation which gave substantial funds for a Chair of Oriental Studies. It had been nearly 20 years since such a Chair had first been discussed. In April 1941, the Dean of Arts, Boyce Gibson wrote to Vice-Chancellor Medley stating that the Faculty of Arts felt that 'the kind of understanding of other civilizations which is likely to be useful to the nation can be acquired only through permanent and advanced courses of University standard' (UMA- Registrar's Correspondence. 1961/1987-28 April 1941. Gibson). The Faculty further argued that the teaching of Japanese and Chinese was of national importance, both languages 'vital for a nation fronting the Pacific'. It is not too much to claim, they said, that in the long run it would greatly strengthen Australia in her cultural, commercial and diplomatic relations with the "Near North" (UMA-Registrar's Correspondence 1961/1987-28 April 1941. Gibson). Percy Spender, the Minister for the Army replied to Medley in June 1941 indicating his personal interest in such language studies, and the need for Commonwealth funding. He promised to put the matter before Prime Minister Menzies as soon as possible, agreeing with Medley, that under efficient control it (a School of Oriental Studies) could no doubt give the Army and the other services extremely valuable help (UMA-Registrar's Correspondence 1961/1987- 5 June 1941. Spender).

No further correspondence on this matter is to be found in the Archives for nearly two years. This lack of correspondence supports my interpretation that, although Spender had been positive about the proposal for Oriental Studies at the University of Melbourne, the Federal government had not deemed the matter urgent in 1941 when the war in Europe was still of uppermost concern, and the war in the Pacific had not yet started. In 1943, Chisholm, Dean of Arts, put the same political and strategic arguments, that External Affairs would need 'competent linguists for the development of Australian relations with the Far East after the war' and that 'Australia's geographical situation is the more eloquent argument in favour of such a scheme'. Chisholm pressed on: 'The proximity of Army Headquarters would enable the University to co-operate usefully with the Army in the training of potential linguists' (UMA – Registrar's Correspondence 1961/1986 -18 February 1943. Chisholm).

All this argument was to no avail. In his reply to Medley in July 1943, Lieutenant Colonel Hodgson, Secretary of the Department of External Affairs, indicated it was not an opportune time to put up the scheme. As Hodgson said, the University of Sydney already had a School of Oriental Studies and 'I should hardly think that there would be room in Australia for two Schools'. Hodgson agreed to put the proposal to his Minister, Herbert Evatt, in the Curtin Labor government, and inform Medley of his response: 'Though you appreciate that even then, pending the outcome of the Federal Elections, they cannot be definitive.' It cannot be known if Hodgson ever did put the proposal to Evatt, although subsequently, Melbourne did not receive Government funding. The proximity of Army headquarters in Melbourne made no difference. Politically, Sydney already had the running for Government funds and the established department (UMA – Registrar's Correspondence 1961/1986 -14 July 1943. Hodgson).

The Federal government did not bestow any grant on the University of Melbourne to establish a School of Oriental Studies, nor did the University find the funds internally, but significantly the funds came from a large external endowment of eight annual donations of £8000 each. Harry Simon, a specialist in Chinese, from the University of London accepted the Chair. This endowment demonstrated a crucial change in funding from government imperatives to individual philanthropy. In the announcement of his gift, Kenneth Myer said:

> I have been deeply impressed on visits overseas by the increasing influence of the peoples of Asia in world affairs. I feel that we should be better informed on the great historical cultures of China and Japan, their languages and their current aims and aspirations. The importance of such understanding to Australia scarcely needs stressing. Although the main and early emphasis will be on China and Japan I envisage that the Department will ultimately cover the broader field of Asian studies in general. (Edwards, 1983, pp. 106; UMA-Registrar's Correspondence 14 July 1943. Hodgson; 149; UMA – Registrar's correspondence 1961/1986 – 12 October 1960. Myer; 1961/1987 – 5 September 1961. Simon)

There was a little dig at the Federal government when Vice-Chancellor Paton announced this philanthropic gesture: 'That we can now take these steps despite the financial difficulties of the University is very largely due to the generosity of private citizens and of foreign governments.' (By foreign governments he was referring to monies given by the Government of Pakistan for the creation of the Department of Indian Studies) (UMA-Registrar's Correspondence 1961/1986 -12 October 1960. Paton). Chinese language teaching staff were appointed in 1962, with appointments for Japanese teaching from 1963 (UMA-Registrar's Correspondence 1961/1987-Department of Oriental Studies Report – February 1962). Thus, by the early 1960s, the University of Sydney had revitalised its School of Oriental Studies with Chinese and Japanese, and the University of Melbourne had finally established its School of Oriental Studies. The Canberra University College with its School of Oriental Studies had been subsumed into the ANU in 1960 where that School became, in 1970, the Faculty of Asian Studies, the first in Australia (Foster & Varghese, 1996, pp. 185, 303; UMA-Registrar's Correspondence 1961/1986, Fac/Arts 18/7/61 Item no. 3 (a) in Appendix A). This was a solid beginning for Asian languages with, according to the Wykes Report, 123 undergraduate students taking Chinese in 1964, although this number was much smaller than the European and classical language cohorts (Wykes, 1966, p. 26).

Monash University, as a new university attracting additional funds, was able to establish a Centre for Southeast Asian Studies in 1964 with John Legge, a specialist on modern Indonesian history, as the foundation director. The Centre offered interdisciplinary studies in history, politics, economics, anthropology, sociology, with Indonesian and Malay as the only Asian languages taught until a Professor of Japanese was appointed in 1966 (Blackwood, 1968, pp. 142, 156). Chinese was not introduced until 1974. Monash University historians, Davison and Murphy, quoted Legge, as saying that 'since Melbourne and ANU had together annexed the major fields of China, India and Japan, Monash was left with "little room to manoeuvre"' (Davison & Murphy, 2012, p. 159). However, Centres, said Davison and Murphy, 'were more nimble, more capable of improvisation' (Davison & Murphy, 2012,

p. 159) – a quite different model to the traditional, although very well resourced, Department of Oriental Studies at Melbourne. There is a hint here of the developing competition between Melbourne and Monash which contrasted with the cooperation which the 1964 Martin Report suggested should be the hallmark of the introduction of languages.

The University of Western Australia established a Centre for Asian Studies in 1966, although at that time they could not teach Asian languages as this speciality had been appropriated by the soon to be created Murdoch University. According to the Kramer Report there was an agreement in Western Australia that tertiary institutions would not duplicate existing languages. This was, in hindsight, a retrograde step because although discussions for Murdoch had begun in 1966, it was not until 1975 that Chinese Studies and Southeast Asian Studies were offered. Ironically, 1975 statistics for UWA and Murdoch University show Chinese and Malay language enrolments at both universities. The previously mentioned agreement was clearly not working. The impetus for the teaching of Asian languages in Western Australia could have been harnessed nearly ten years earlier (AUC, 1975a, p. 58; Bolton, 1985, p. 41; de Garis, 1988, p. 232).

5.10 Official Recognition of China

Whilst universities were embracing Asian studies, including Chinese language offerings, the McMahon Coalition government still stood firmly against recognition of China. In July 1971 the Opposition Leader, Whitlam, boldly led an Australian Labor Party delegation to China in to meet with Premier Chou En-lai, with Stephen Fitzgerald as adviser and interpreter. Henry Kissinger, on behalf of President Nixon, was in China at the same time as Whitlam. By October 1971, China was recognised by the United Nations and given a seat in the Assembly and on the Security Council. Australia had voted against this resolution. Still the Coalition government stuck to its position of separation between trade, politics and diplomacy, keeping the Country Party on side, and sales of wheat to China continuing (Andrews, 1988, p. 180; Goldsworthy, Dutton, Gifford, & Pitty, 2001, p. 334; Tweedie, 1994, pp. 128, 129).

Despite the Government's intransigence, public and academic opinion was slowly changing. A group of academics organised a conference in Melbourne in June 1972, of Australian and overseas China specialists with a theme of China and the world community. Stephen Fitzgerald, a Fellow in the Department of Far Eastern History at ANU, and adviser to Whitlam, said it was in Australia's interest to adopt a flexible and 'agile' policy towards China (Legge, 1999, p. 174). This advice, to be more flexible, was coming from China specialists, not from Government departments such as Defence or External Affairs. The Government had lost the impetus for greater knowledge and understanding of China created by the establishment and revitalisation of Oriental Studies Departments at the Australian National University and the Universities of Sydney and Melbourne some ten years earlier. As Andrews commented, 'External Affairs had its own weaknesses, including a lack of personnel with training in Asian languages, frequent changing of posts and no central organisation. Its permanent heads were increasingly amenable to the government and its hard line on China' (Andrews, 1985, p. 207). The Government needed to move with the rest of the international community in relation to China. It was not listening to the Australian China specialists, and its own department heads were apparently not able to provide the international expertise necessary. As Andrews put it so succinctly, Australia's 'stand was beginning to look both lonely and illogical' (Andrews, 1985, p. 203).

The radical change to Australia's China policy came with the Labor victory in December 1972. Within days, the Whitlam Labor government had recognised the People's Republic of China, establishing diplomatic and trade relations. Whitlam set a new tone in foreign policy, to be 'more flexible and constructive, and less militarily oriented', maintaining relations with both Western and Asian countries (Andrews, 1985, p. 210, 1988, pp. 180, 190). Not surprisingly, Fitzgerald, a China specialist fluent in Mandarin, was appointed as the first ambassador to Beijing. Speaking at a gathering in 2002 to mark the 30th anniversary of diplomatic relations, Fitzgerald said that he considered himself lucky to have learnt Chinese as he had been told to learn it when he first arrived in Canberra to enter the foreign service in 1961. Having had many years' experience in China he pointed out, in those early months of this new relationship, that for China trade and politics were interrelated with each serving the other. His knowledge and experience served the Whitlam government well. Not only was the new ambassador a skilled linguist but also the first trade commissioner, John Clark, who was fluent not only 'in Chinese but had a working knowledge of several other Asian and European languages' (Fitzgerald, S. [Stephen], 2002; Schedvin, 2008, p. 277). These events set a new and informed environment for Federal government policies and understanding of China, aided by experienced specialists with language skills.

Following the diplomatic recognition of China, one university after another introduced Asian studies, many creating centres of Asian studies rather than separate language departments for Chinese and Japanese as happened with European languages. The University of Adelaide created a Centre for Asian Studies in 1974 teaching Chinese and Japanese, whilst Murdoch University taught Chinese through its School of Human Communication from 1975. However, at the University of Western Australia, Japanese, which was taught from 1975, was located within Economics rather than Arts (Bolton, 1985, p. 28; de Garis, 1988, p. 249; Edgeloe, 2003, p. 348; Hawley, 1982, p. 56). It was the newly-established Griffith University where teaching began in 1975 which was the most significant in its recognition of Asian languages. Of the four foundation Schools, one was the School of Modern Asian Studies with a brief to concern itself with 'the development of commercial, industrial and cultural contact with Asian Societies' (Quirke, 1996, p. 8). The foundation Chair was Ho Peng Yoke, an established Asian scholar, fluent in Mandarin, Cantonese, Japanese and basic Malay. The Deputy Chair was Colin Mackerras (Quirke, 1996, p. 9). This was the first School of Modern Asian Studies in Australia for undergraduate students.[3] Here was a university boldly shaping its courses towards Asia. Theodor Bray, Chairman of the Interim Council, had said: 'If we do nothing else in this university we will teach Asian studies and we will cultivate good relations between Asia and its neighbours around the Pacific Rim' (Quirke, 1996, p. 11).

In this flurry of enthusiasm for Asian languages and cultures, so it went on: Macquarie University introduced Chinese in 1978, the University of Tasmania taught Japanese from 1975, Newcastle (having received special AUC funding) and James Cook University introduced Japanese in 1976. But there was not wholesale approval for funding for Asian language courses. The Universities Commission made it clear in 1972 that it was against the proliferation of small and necessarily weak Asian language departments in all universities and strongly suggested inter-university collaboration for Asian language offerings (AUC, 1972, p. 98). The Commission's Working Party on Languages and Linguistics (the Kramer Report) was also cautious in its reaction to funding submissions for new Asian languages and studies programs. They rejected some submissions, suggested delayed starts for others, or that cooperative arrangements with other universities should be entered into. This was to avoid duplication and wastage of resources that could result, they said, if universities expanded their language programs 'in an uncoordinated fashion' (AUC, 1975a, pp. 1, 52–58; Hawley, 1982, pp. 5, 10). Despite the caution of funding authorities, the 1991 Leal Report noted that Chinese was now being offered at 19 tertiary institutions, as well as having key language designation in the NPL, prioritisation by DFAT and Austrade, and key language status for inbound tourism. However, despite the expansion of Chinese teaching, Japanese student enrolments exceeded Chinese enrolments significantly by 1990 (Leal, 1991a, pp. 20, 54, 62, 64, 66).

5.11 Indonesia: Trade First Then Security and Defence

Whilst Australia was concentrating on its trade interests with Netherlands East Indies in the early twentieth century, a nationalist movement in that country for a united state called Indonesia was emerging. The young intellectuals of that movement adopted Malay as the language of unity, renaming it Indonesian. The Dutch, alarmed by the rising nationalism, moved quickly against the independence movement, shutting down the party and imprisoning its leaders (Grant, 1964, p. 2; Sneddon, 2003, p. 5; Zainu'ddin, 1968, pp. 171, 172). Australia continued to cement its trade with the Netherlands East Indies, appointing a trade commissioner, Charles Critchley, in 1935. Critchley's successor, Herbert Peterson, an experienced Foreign Affairs officer, fluent in Dutch, developed new markets for Australia, but had to flee, escaping just before the Dutch surrendered to the Japanese in March 1942 (Schedvin, 2008, pp. 50, 62, 70).

---

[3] ANU had only postgraduate Asian Studies at the time.

Subsequently, in 1945, the Japanese were defeated, and the new Republic of Indonesia was declared. Now Australian interest in Indonesia had security and defence overtones. William Macmahon Ball, political scientist and diplomat, was sent to Indonesia in November 1945 by the Chifley Labor government which had come to power in July 1945. Evatt, the new Minister for External Affairs particularly wanted Macmahon Ball to report first hand on what was turning out to be a very complex situation in Indonesia as the Dutch tried to resume their colonial administration over the newly proclaimed Republic (Lee, 2001, pp. 140, 142; Ryan, 1990, p. 10). It was clearly in Australia's national and security interests to have an influence on the resolution of Indonesia's declaration of independence. From Indonesia Macmahon Ball wrote: 'Australia's interests are comparatively simple. We cannot afford to have South-East Asia neatly divided into simple sections in each of which some European power enjoys complete sovereignty. There is ill will between the Dutch and the Indonesians and this ill will could spread to other South East-Asian countries.' Macmahon Ball counselled Australia in whatever involvement it might have in the conflict between the Dutch and the Indonesians, to do it through the auspices of the United Nations, noting the strategic and political importance of Indonesia in Australia's own future (Rix, 1988, pp. 6, 265).

Australia, said Forsyth of the Department of External Affairs, has a special position in the area and long term interests in the 'cultivation of political, economic, and social strength and maturity among the' Indonesian native community (Lee, 2001, p. 140). Australia was looking towards its own role in South-West and South-East Asia as new countries emerged from colonialism to independence. The support which Australia gave to Indonesia's independence, asserted Rawdon Dalrymple, a former Australian ambassador to Indonesia, 'constituted a capital store of good will towards Australia in Indonesia which was very helpful in the years ahead and through some difficult times' (Dalrymple, 2003, pp. 163, 165; Lee, 2001, p. 147). It was not until late 1949 that the Dutch finally gave up their claims to Indonesia. In December 1949, the former Dutch colony became the sovereign Federal Republic of Indonesia, although West Papua remained under Dutch administration until 1962 (Grant, 1964, pp. 29, 33; Joint Standing Committee on Foreign Affairs, Defence & Trade (JSCFADT), 1993, p. 2).

Now Australia sought to revive its trade with Indonesia, re-opening its trade post in 1950 and beginning formal diplomatic relations with the new Republic (Schedvin, 2008, pp. 76, 116). Whilst the Indonesian economy needed revitalisation also (Grant, 1964, p. 29; Tweedie, 1994, p. 180), Schedvin maintained that, by the mid-1950s, conditions were more settled and the number of Australian visitors to Indonesia increasing. Indonesia was emerging as one of Australia's more important trading partners in the region (Schedvin, 2008, p. 118). Australia's other strategic relationship with Indonesia was through the Colombo Plan, a program of economic and technical assistance to improve the economies of under-developed countries in South and South-East Asia, conceived at a meeting of Commonwealth foreign ministers in Colombo in January 1950. Spender, the External Affairs Minister in the Menzies government, was a key advocate of this Plan. Central to Australia's involvement was the sponsoring of students to study or train in Australia, although there were many other aspects to this venture such as strategic planning, economic and cultural engagement. Indonesia was one of the many recipients of the aid which flowed from this Plan (Gifford, 2001, pp. 175, 176; Watt, 1967, pp. 197, 198). Casey, the next Minister for External Affairs, welcomed Indonesia's decision to join the Colombo Plan in January 1953, stressing, in a newspaper interview, the importance of discussions with Indonesia as to how Australia might assist Indonesia's economic and technical development (A Staff Correspondent, 1953 p. 2).

5.12 Government Commitment to Indonesian Language Teaching

It is surprising that – with the trade relationships which had existed between Australia and Indonesia for some 50 years, the Colombo Plan which helped to engender positive contacts, and the diplomatic support which Australia had given to Indonesia in its quest for independence – there was still no formal study of Indonesian language in Australian schools and universities. It also appears that amongst Australian trade and diplomatic representatives dealing with Indonesia, none were fluent in Indonesian. Since the early twentieth century, Australia had been dealing with the Netherlands as a colonial power, and probably saw no need either for trade or security reasons to have Australians trained in the Indonesian language. The initiative for the establishment of such language studies, said Worsley, a noted Indonesianist, came not from the Indonesian community,

> not from the scholarly community nor even from public demand. The impulse came from the Commonwealth government, which announced its interest in the teaching of Indonesian and Malayan Studies in a letter from William Weeden, Director of the Commonwealth Office of Education, to the Vice-Chancellor [of the University of Sydney] in June 1955. (Worsley, 1994, p. 54)

Charles Coppel, Indonesianist and political scientist, writing recently about the introduction of Indonesian in universities, reported that the same communication took place in June 1955 between Weeden and George Paton, the Vice-Chancellor of the University of Melbourne, and with the Canberra University College, presumably with Bertram Dickson, the Director of the CUC (Coppel, forthcoming, p. 3). The Government wanted these tertiary institutions to establish Indonesian and Malayan Studies and offered funding for this teaching to begin in 1956, if possible. According to Worsley, the letter did not state that the request had in fact originated in the Departments of External Affairs, Defence and the Office of the Prime Minister, not in the Department of Education (Worsley, 1994, p. 54).

I argue therefore, that it was the political climate, not an educational priority, which prompted Government interest in the teaching of Indonesian. For security reasons it behoved Australia to know more about Indonesia, and the key to understanding its culture and people was its language. This funding eventually stopped, late in 1965 in the case of the University of Sydney. As Worsley reported, the Commonwealth government had decided that the 'particular and clearly defined Commonwealth needs' that had prompted the original funding had ended. The Government had not spelled out these needs but, said Worsley, these needs were considered "Commonwealth" and not "scholarly". Worsley ended rather cynically that one could well understand 'the diplomatic and strategic imperatives attached to Australia's relationship with a newly independent Indonesia, but no doubt the same enlightened self-interest which informed the government's support of the Colombo Plan and Australian Volunteers Abroad also encouraged it in its desire to establish the study of Indonesian in Australian universities' (Worsley, 1994, pp. 54, 55).

So Indonesian and Malayan Studies teaching began at the University of Melbourne and the CUC in 1956, and at the University of Sydney in 1958. Apparently, in order to comply with the urgency of the Commonwealth government's request, the University of Melbourne offered not-for-degree studies in Indonesian for the first couple of years taught by a native Indonesian speaker, Zainu'ddin, who was himself undertaking undergraduate degree studies. According to Coppel, that first class included several public servants (Coppel, forthcoming, p. 3). It was not till 1958 that Indonesian was first taught as a degree subject when James Mackie, who had been working in Jakarta as a Colombo Plan expert, was appointed as senior lecturer. CUC had also hastened to comply to receive the funding as lectures were given by a visiting Indonesian academic for the first two years until an Indonesian and Malayan Studies curriculum was developed in 1958 (Bielenstein, 1962, p. 258). Monash University began teaching Indonesian/Malay in 1962 although this was not through the Defence Department funding but was enabled by the establishment funds of this relatively new university (Blackwood, 1968, pp. 62, 122).

The 1966 Wykes Report, including 1964 enrolment statistics, stated that Indonesian 'is the most important of Asian languages taught here' as the language of our nearest neighbour. The Report continued:

> since Indonesian is scarcely taught in the schools the elementary courses are essential and are counted as full first-year subjects. There is a big drop-out after the first year, and this is an interesting phenomenon. It might be thought that those who tackled a new Asian language at the university would be eager to continue, but the drop-out is as great as in any other language. (Wykes, 1966, pp. 30–31)

The Report concluded that 'the number of students taking the language of our nearest neighbour is insignificant and it would be desirable to increase it. It is abundantly clear that it should be taught outside the three cities', namely, Sydney, Melbourne, and Canberra (Wykes, 1966, p. 31). It is ironic that in the year this Report was published, Commonwealth government funding for Indonesian had already ceased the year before. Presumably the government now intended that the universities concerned would find the funding to maintain Indonesian teaching.

Meanwhile, Australia became involved in an Indonesian/Malaysian conflict over territory when the Federation of Malaysia came into being in September 1963 (Australian War Memorial, n.d., Indonesian confrontation). Australia was reluctant at first, not wishing to fracture its relations with Indonesia, but eventually Australian troops were sent in January 1965 to help defend Sarawak against

Indonesian incursions, with the Royal Australian Navy and Air Force also involved (Australian War Memorial, n.d.; JSCFADT, 1993, p. 3). In 1956, the RAAF School of Languages, according to Mark Doran, a military reporter, had already introduced Indonesian language training. This, said Doran, in a 2012 article in the Australian Army newspaper, *Army,* was indicative of the fact that languages taught at the School reflected the current requirements of Australia's defence operations (Doran, 2012, p. 194). Barry Turner, an Indonesian linguist and Director of the RAAF School of Languages when writing in 1983, had pre-empted Doran's comments about the timely introduction of Indonesian, although Turner states it was 1963 not 1956 (Turner, 1983, p. 23). Both years are relevant, as the mid-1950s were a time of instability in Indonesia and 1963 marked the beginning of *Konfrontasi* (the conflict between Indonesia and Malaysia) in which Australia was involved. Subsequently, as a later Australian Parliamentary report reviewing relations with Indonesia noted, President Sukarno was overthrown, and by 1967 General Suharto had become the new President. Diplomatic relations between Australia and Indonesia greatly improved over the next eight or so years (JSCFADT, 1993, p. 4; Zainu'ddin, 1968, p. 273).

In trying to gauge the strength of Indonesian language teaching in schools, it is difficult to find statistics for the 1960s, although such teaching had begun in some states. In Bonyhady's 1964 statistics no Indonesian teaching is listed at matriculation level (Bonyhady, 1965, p. 32). Holt's matriculation language statistics showed that in 1967 and 1968 only NSW students sat for Indonesian. For the next three years 1969–1971, Victorian, NSW and Tasmanian students sat for Indonesian, and from 1972 to 1974, South Australian students also sat for Indonesian. The matriculation numbers were always larger in NSW, e.g. 979 candidates in 1972, compared to Victoria's 93 candidates. Holt made no comment about particular languages, but the total figures he listed showed Indonesian with greater numbers than each of Italian, Japanese and Chinese in these eight years from 1967 to 1974. Indonesian had eclipsed Latin candidature by 1972 although it had nowhere near the numbers which French and German commanded (Holt, 1976, pp. 31, 32). Clearly Indonesian language was making serious inroads in schools as the most popular Asian language in the 1970s.

5.13 Auchmuty and Kramer Reports: Stocktakes for All Languages

The major evidence for the health of Indonesian language teaching on both schools and tertiary institutions is found in two comprehensive language reports. The 1970 Auchmuty Report indicated Indonesian was the dominant Asian language in secondary schools in NSW and Victoria. Indonesian and/or Malay was taught at only four universities, ANU, Monash, and the Universities of Melbourne and Sydney. These universities' Indonesian language enrolments in 1969 were larger than those for either Japanese or Chinese. It should be noted that whilst universities list the subject as Indonesian/Malay or Indonesian and Malay, the nomenclature used in the Auchmuty Report was largely just Indonesian.

Whilst no more universities had begun to teach Indonesian and/or Malay by 1969, other tertiary institutions, mainly teachers' colleges in Adelaide, Sydney, and Perth, were teaching either one or two year courses. This was clearly necessary to support the growing need for teachers of Indonesian in schools. The Western Australian Institute of Technology and the Sydney Technical College both taught a three year sequence of Indonesian. In addition, South Australian teachers' colleges had offered an Indonesian/Malay teaching methodology course since 1964. The Auchmuty Report emphasised the need for Asian languages to have the same level of importance as European languages particularly in the secondary school system. Whilst not mentioned in this Report, this comment suggests that there may have been adverse reactions from European language academics towards the increasing interest in Asian languages being taught, and perhaps the fear of competition. Certainly Wykes in her 1966 survey encountered academics disdainful of the merit of Asian languages, giving reasons such as the paucity of literature behind Asian languages, and the imprudence of introducing them for 'so-called practical reasons' (C of A, 1970, pp. 40, 56, 64, 65, 99; Wykes, 1966, p. 41).

Worsley commented on the substantial student numbers of the first 15 years of tertiary Indonesian/Malay teaching from 1955 to 1970 (Worsley, 1994, p. 40). With James Cook University in North Queensland teaching Indonesian from 1974, now all states taught Indonesian at the tertiary level. Not all university funding submissions for Indonesian for the 1976–1978 triennium were approved. The University of New England submission was not endorsed as Sydney and ANU were already teaching Indonesian. Griffith University's submission for Indonesian language teaching was endorsed as a more important priority than Japanese language teaching, but the University of Queensland's submission was not endorsed as that would have been a duplication of Griffith's teaching. Flinders University's submission was endorsed with the expectation that cooperative teaching arrangements would be made with the University of Adelaide. Murdoch University's submission was turned down as the Western Australian Institute of Technology already offered Indonesia. Clearly the Working Party of the Universities Commission had taken very seriously the economic concerns of duplication and wastage in their recommendations for or against the funding of new Indonesian language programs (AUC, 1975a, pp. 12, 52, 53, 56, 59).

5.14 The Testing of Diplomatic Relations and Language Popularity

Australia's seesaw relationship with Indonesia was seriously affected in 1975 when Indonesia invaded East Timor and incorporated this country into Indonesia. Dalrymple, a former Ambassador to Indonesia, said that the Fraser government,

5.14 The Testing of Diplomatic Relations and Language Popularity

which took office in late 1975, 'sought to keep things going despite anger on the Indonesian side and discomfort on the Australian side.' Dalrymple continued, 'the technocrats maintained other programs and business, or at any rate frequent contact, between the respective foreign ministries continued' (Dalrymple, 2003, pp. 175, 185; JSCFADT, 1993, p. 4). The Ambassador to Indonesia in 1975, Richard Woolcott, reflected on the challenges for the embassy in keeping the normal activities going:

> I regarded the embassy's role as critical to the better understanding in Indonesia of Australia and in Canberra of Indonesia. The embassy needed to continue to identify trade and investment opportunities as well as to ensure that our technical assistance and defence cooperation programs were well targeted and effective. I also encouraged officers to build up as wide a network of contacts as possible in order to sharpen their insights into Indonesian thinking. (Woolcott, 2003, pp. 127, 130)

Given these events in Indonesia it could be argued that the popularity of Indonesian with Australian students was negatively affected. However, this appears not to be the case, as tertiary student numbers, according to Worsley, increased up until 1975 and only then started to decline, whereas secondary student numbers increased up until 1983. Dalrymple[4] himself had said that, by the early 1980s, the relationship between Australia and Indonesia was becoming more cordial, to the extent that when the Hawke Government took office in 1983, it was possible for Prime Minister Hawke 'to make a well-publicised and generally positive visit to Indonesia' (Dalrymple, 2003, p. 175). Worsley contended that the rise of multiculturalism in Australia had a negative effect on Indonesian. He argued that the push for an increase in the teaching and learning of migrant languages, meant that 'a vastly greater number of languages' were now 'available for studying in Australian education'. There was now competition for Indonesian as well as other Asian languages and 'multiculturalism contributed little directly to the wider teaching of Indonesian/Malay. The Indonesian community in the period was small and had no profile in the national debate about, or large share in, the benefits of multiculturalism' (Worsley, 1994, pp. ix, x). There was another boom period for Indonesian in both schools and the tertiary sector, reported Worsley, from the middle 1980s up to the early 1990s.

Firdaus, an Indonesian lecturer at Flinders University, maintained that Indonesian was the most popular Asian language in the 1980s, aided by the fact that Indonesian used the Roman alphabet. She suggested also that there was an economic imperative for the language because the Indonesian economy was booming, Australian tourists were flocking to places like Bali, and Indonesian ability was seen as advantageous by students for jobs in Australia and Asia (Firdaus, 2013, p. 31). This claim is refuted by the 1988 Asian Studies Council statistics which show that, whilst Indonesian was certainly popular in secondary schools, Japanese still commanded slightly higher numbers. At the tertiary level, Japanese and Chinese also commanded larger numbers than Indonesian (Asian Studies Council, 1988, p. 15).

---

[4] Dalrymple was minister in the Australian embassy in Jakarta from 1969 to 1972 and Australian ambassador to Indonesia from 1981 to 1984.

However, a factor which is not discussed in these various commentaries is whether secondary school students had a wide choice of languages or whether Indonesian was sometimes chosen because it was one of a narrow range of languages available at a particular school. Nevertheless, according to the 1991 Leal Report there were now 21 Australian tertiary institutions teaching Indonesian with student enrolments of 408 EFTSU (Leal, 1991a, pp. 64, 66).

It was the recommendations of the 1994 Rudd Report which next boosted Indonesian language enrolments. This Report designated Mandarin Chinese, Japanese, Indonesian and Korean as priority languages as a matter of economic national importance for Australia with funding recommended to meet increased school enrolment targets (National Asian Languages & Cultures Working Group, 1994, pp. v, xviii, 1). As Henderson commented, this funding did boost school enrolments in all these Asian languages with Indonesian enrolments doubling by the year 2000 (Henderson, 2003, p. 25). Now the national interest for Indonesian had a different complexion, this was for trade reasons not for defence and security as the previous university funding of 1955 had been.

But, said Firdaus, Indonesian language school enrolments slumped again. In May 2002 it was announced that Government funding for the National Asian Languages and Studies in Australian Schools program (NALSAS) (Department of Education, Science & Training. (DEST), 1994, About NALSAS) would cease at the end of 2002, earlier than previously intended. This was unfortunate timing as, in October 2002, the Bali bombings created significant fear in Australia about terrorism and negative attitudes towards the Indonesian language (Firdaus, 2013, p. 31). Given the important role of school language enrolments feeding into the tertiary sector, an examination of data for that period is important. Whilst Chinese language tertiary enrolments continued to grow from 2001 to 2005 and Japanese enrolments had plateaued, Indonesian enrolments had dramatically dropped across the same five years (White & Baldauf, 2006, p. 14). This situation was exacerbated by a further spate of bombings in Bali in 2005. I argue therefore, that the economic factors which had previously promoted Indonesian as a language worth learning, had been severely cut across by the fear of terrorism in, and from, an Asian country so near to Australia.

Further reports, commissioned in 2011 and 2012, showed that the situation for Indonesian had not improved. Anne McLaren, Asian language academic of the University of Melbourne wrote in her report of February 2011, *Asian Languages Enrolments in Australian Higher Education 2008–2009*, 'Indonesian is a language of crucial national significance for Australia. However, one can only describe the picture for Indonesian as dire. Indonesian enrolments in Australia's largest programs have declined year by year from the mid-2000s' (McLaren, 2011, p. 7). A comprehensive report, *Indonesian Language in Australian Universities,* was completed in February 2012 by David Hill, a South-East Asian studies academic of Murdoch University. He emphasised the crisis for Indonesian language with declining student numbers in both schools and universities, making the crucial point that 'Australians' preparedness to learn the Indonesian language is a key indicator of the perceptions of Indonesia that exist within the Australian community'. It is a quantifiable measure of Australians' interest in, knowledge of, and engagement with Indonesia' (Hill, 2012, p. 1). This point, I argue, is borne out by the rise and fall of Indonesian language enrolments. He also contended that 'a healthy working relationship with our northern neighbour is vital to both our present and future national interest' (Hill, 2012, p. 1).

Henderson had written, a little earlier in 2008 about Australia's national interest in relation to Asian languages. She contended that the Rudd Report,[5] in developing a 'national strategy for Asian literacy…demonstrated the use of political power in determining the kind of knowledge deemed most useful to the national interest' (Henderson, 2008, p. 190). She further contended that the Howard government's 'decision to terminate the funding agreement before the scheduled time, was short-sighted and undermined Australia's future capacity for regional engagement' (Henderson, 2007, p. 17). Strategically however, the new Labor government did provide more funding for four years for 2008–2009, and 2011–2012 in the form of the National Asian Languages and Studies in Schools Program (NALSSP). This funding was engineered by Kevin Rudd, when he became Prime Minister in 2007 (Slaughter, 2011, p. 169).

Hill also argued in his 2012 Report for more NALSSP funding. One of the 20 recommendations of that Report was that 'the Program (at least for Indonesian) be maintained and extended, with a government commitment until at least 2020', with significant funding to support it (Hill, 2012, p. 4). For Hill, significant government funding was clearly the key to revitalising the study of Indonesian. As he pointed out, Indonesian had been designated as a "Nationally Strategic Language" in 2006 in the DEEWR funding agreements with universities. 'Yet, he said, no accompanying funding has been provided to support this "Nationally Strategic Language"' (Hill, 2012, pp. 2–3).

Thus, the issue for Indonesian language is twofold. On the one hand commentators have argued that Australia needs to reinvent itself in Indonesian studies. Community support needs to be engaged so as not to lose the comparative advantage provided by linguistic expertise and the consequent political, economic and strategic benefits for our relationship with Indonesia. According to Kate McGregor, an Indonesianist at the University of Melbourne, there is a more pragmatic dimension to student decision making about languages than in years past, but the economic significance of Indonesia for the future, has not reached student awareness yet (McGregor, personal communication, 27 September, 2012). On the other hand, to encourage and support this awareness, there must be, Hill argued, from both Government and Opposition, 'an explicit public commitment to supporting Indonesian language in Australian universities' (Hill, 2012, p. 4). This funding should include not only the extended NALSSP program, but also student scholarships, development of contemporary teaching materials, and in-country study programs. This range of strategies, said Hill, is designed to increase Australian interest in and knowledge of Indonesia (Hill, 2012, pp. 4, 5, 6). As Henderson maintained,

---

[5] The NALSAS program of funding for Asian languages in schools had been particularly important to Kevin Rudd following his 1994 Report on Asian Languages.

governments have used their political power for programs in the national interest before, and it should be done again now.

5.15 Conclusion

This chapter has shown the rising importance of three key Asian languages for Australia's national interest across the second half of the twentieth century and into the twenty-first century. The initial reasons for encouraging such language study had been diplomatic and security based, but these, as has been shown became compelling economic reasons. What marked the rise of these languages was the Federal government's funding initiatives to boost the numbers of school students studying an Asian language. These initiatives aimed to increase Australia's linguistic competence in key Asian languages as Australians interacted economically with these key countries (DEST, 1994, NALSAS). The 2010 Asia Education Foundation Report funded by DEEWR showed a decline in the proportion of school students studying the four NALSSP languages in 2008 with the most significant decline in Japanese and Indonesian (C of A, 2010, p. 4). As the Report suggests, aspirational targets for Asian language fluency sufficient to engage in trade and commerce in Asia and/or tertiary study, require new and sustained efforts and a persuasive vision, tailored for each language (C of A, 2010, p. 9).

As far as the health of Asian languages in the university sector is concerned, whilst all three languages were classified as widely-taught in a study, *Swings and roundabouts: Changes in language offerings at Australian universities 2005–2011* (Dunne & Pavlyshyn, 2014, p. 18, 19), this study did not deal with actual student numbers. Nevertheless, a picture can be obtained from the summary comments about Asian languages in the 2013 LCNAU (Languages and Cultures Network for Australian Universities) submission to the Asian Century country strategies. 'Indonesian is in serious crisis throughout the school and university sectors', whereas Japanese 'has relatively stable enrolments nationwide'. Chinese on the other hand has expanding school and university enrolments. However, this 'involves a large percentage of Chinese background speakers, matched by a worrying decline in non-native demand' (LCNAU, 2013, pp. 3–5). These comments all suggest that whilst Asian languages may continue to be important for Australia's economic future, their continued development in both the secondary and tertiary sectors cannot be taken for granted. The new vision for schools suggested by the Asia Link Foundation, with sustained effort, customised to each language with its particular issues, would also be required for the university sector.

LCNAU has been a key organisation in highlighting the reality of Asian language teaching, however there is no evidence that governments are convinced that Asian language proficiency should go hand in hand with economic and business knowledge about Asia. Indeed, the lack of mention of Asian language capability in the

5.15 Conclusion

Federal Government is quite stark in its 2017 Foreign Policy White paper (Australian Government, 2017). That White paper underlined just where the government believes its priorities should lie: in economic growth, opportunity, prosperity, and security. As far as young Australians were concerned the emphasis has been to increase the opportunities to expose them to the challenges of working and living in Asia, rather than encouraging Asian language proficiency. The New Colombo Plan outlining opportunities for young Australians in Asia (previously mentioned) will be discussed in more detail in Chap. 8.

Chapter 6
Three Strategic Languages: Russian, Korean and Arabic

> The language pluralism of Australia is a valuable national resource enhancing and enriching cultural and intellectual life and a valuable economic resource in its potential for use in international trade. (Lo Bianco, 1987, p. 6). [National Policy on Languages]

Australia's language pluralism was celebrated in the 1987 National Policy on Languages (NPL) authored by Lo Bianco. This policy had sought to place the languages of Australia in a context of both 'the external, economic and political needs of the nation, and the wishes and needs of Australia's citizens' (Lo Bianco, 1987, p. 4). In this chapter a detailed case study of three languages, Russian, Korean and Arabic is undertaken. These three have been chosen as examples of languages which have had significance as a language of national interest depending on relationships Australia has had with the countries represented by these languages at various times in the twentieth and into the twenty-first century. Each of these languages is examined for evidence of government support and student demand.

Unlike the case studies of the three Asian trade languages discussed in Chap. 5, this chapter demonstrates that it has been Australian government policies both in geopolitical and security issues which have at times prompted interest in these languages. The military connections for each language are illustrated by the events of various wars and conflicts. Australia and Russia were initially allies in World War I, until the Russian Revolution when individual Australians fought briefly in Russia against the Bolsheviks as part of the British Army's North Russian Expeditionary Force. Australia and Russia were again allies in World War II although they became opponents with the beginning of the Cold War. Australian defence forces served in the Korean War in the early 1950s when communism was considered a threat to be countered in Asia. Australian defence forces have served in the Middle East region where Arabic is often the official language, not only in the two World Wars, but also as combat troops and peace-keeping forces in the 1990s and into the twenty-first century. It was not only for military reasons but also for trade opportunities that successive Federal governments focussed on the areas represented by these languages. That national interest has been played out in Australia's trade and diplomatic relations.

Australian defence and geopolitical interests since the Cold War have been important in all three regions represented by these languages, and indeed Russian and Arabic are two of the six working languages of the United Nations (UN at Glance, n.d., p. 1). Nevertheless, successive Australian governments have never given Russian and Arabic the same funding priority as they have given to the major Asian languages, although Korean was given Federal government funding in 1994 along with the other trade languages, Chinese, Japanese and Indonesian. Regardless of being a prioritised language, Korean has never commanded the volume of tertiary student numbers as have the other Asian trade languages. It appears that trade related to the countries of these three languages, Korean, Russian and Arabic, has not been significant enough for Federal governments to prioritise these languages. I also argue that defence and geopolitical issues relating to contemporary events in the countries of these three languages should warrant greater attention to build increased cultural and linguistic understanding.

After World War II, Australia's relationship with the Soviet Union entered a new phase of security and defence concerns through the heightened tension of the Cold War period.[1] Many Russian-speaking migrants came to Australia after World War II and throughout the next three decades in various waves. By 1954 there were over 13,000 Russian-born immigrants in Australia, with another 7000 arriving by 1961 (Christa, 2001, p. 640). Whilst it was not one of the migrant languages in which the 1978 Galbally Report was published, neither was Russian one of the languages of wider learning prioritised in the 1987 National Policy on Languages. Nevertheless, it was a language which commanded consistent student numbers in the tertiary sector, from its beginnings in 1946 as a language of scientific research, culture and literature, for about 50 years.

The importance of the Arabic language to Australia is significantly different to that of Korean and Russian. Arabic has a global geographic significance, not only as the official language of some 22 countries, but also as a language of religious importance for Muslims including those whose national language is not Arabic. Arabic was first taught in Australian universities after World War II as a scholarly language along with other Semitic languages. By the time of the 1978 Galbally Report, Arabic was being acknowledged as a migrant language, and featured in the 1987 National Policy on Languages, and the Australian Language and Literacy Policy of 1991. It is difficult to isolate figures for Arabic-speaking migrants to Australia. However, Ibtisam Abu-duhou, a tertiary lecturer, quoted 119,187 persons over five with Arabic as their home spoken language according to the 1986 census, and Arabic as the fifth most spoken language in Australia (Ab-duhou, 1989, p. 33). Into the next century, the Arabic language became associated with Australia's concern about global terrorism, particularly that emanating from Islamic extremism. Whilst Australia reiterated its national defence and strategic interests against such threats, Arabic became an important language for security reasons, apart from being the language of many migrants from the Middle East. This chapter shows that whilst all three languages

---

[1] The Cold War between the Eastern and Western Bloc superpowers, chiefly between the USSR and USA, lasted from the late 1940s to about the early 1990s.

have had periods of demand by university students, ultimately each has, in the late twentieth and early twenty-first century, struggled to maintain a secure place in tertiary languages curricula. Apart from Korean's promotion as a trade language in the 1990s, these three languages have not galvanised the attention of successive Federal governments as being languages worthy of funding for the economic, defence and geo-political aspects of Australia's national interest.

6.1 Early Australian Relationships with Russia

Australia's relationship with Russia began early in the nineteenth century, documented as starting around 1807 with the regular visits of Russian ships to Sydney. The place where they docked became known as Russian Point, but is now known as Kirribilli Point, the site of the Sydney residence of the Australian Prime Minister (Barratt, 1988, pp. 56; Christa, 2001, p. 636; Protopopov, 2006, p. 1). Those early cordial relations did not last. By the Crimean War of 1853–1856, the Australian colonies became obsessed by the possibility of a Russian invasion as the Russian Imperial fleet cruised in the Pacific region. Several fortifications were built around the eastern coast of Australia in Port Jackson, Queenscliff, Portsea, Launceston and Hobart (Barratt, 1988, pp. 196; Govor, 2001, p. 572–7; Protopopov, 2006, pp. 1, 6). This anxiety gradually subsided presumably because Russia did not invade Australia.

By 1891 Russia sought to formalise its diplomatic relations with the Australian colonies and appointed a permanent consul who took up his post in Melbourne in 1893. Both trade and diplomatic relations flourished, with the Russian-Australian Bureau of Commerce and Information being formed in January 1917 and Russians continuing to migrate to Australia. This was in the midst of World War I when Australia and Russia were allies, although when the Russian Revolution broke out, all diplomatic connections ceased (Govor, 2001, p. 572; Protopopov, 2006, pp. 10, 184). In fact, in July 1918, a small contingent of Australian soldiers fought with a British-led force in Northern Russia against the Bolshevik revolutionaries in a futile attempt to overthrow the Bolshevik government (Challinger, 2010, pp. ix, 192). Back in Australia, the Communist Party of Australia was formed in 1920 taking its political philosophy from Russia. It was never a large party but did gain influence during the Depression years (Bongiorno, 2013, p. 77; Brett, 2013, p. 116). There was a further wave of Russian migration to Australia in the early 1920s as the 'White' Russians (defeated by the communist 'Reds') fled to various countries. Most gravitated to Queensland where labouring work was readily available in cane fields and on farms (Christa, 2001, pp. 636, 638; Protopopov, 2006, p. 32).

These late nineteenth and early twentieth century relationships with Russia were partly trade-related, but also governed by Australia's involvement in World War I as a dominion of Britain, responding to British foreign policy strategies. Whilst in the 1920s and 1930s there were no diplomatic relations between the Soviet Union and Australia, there were cultural and literary links, and visits from celebrated opera singers and ballet companies. This was a time, said Bernard Smith, the Australian art historian, when everyone talked of Russian culture (Petrikovskaya, 2007, pp. 294, 296, 297). Whatever trade there was continued on into the 1940s, but it was highly variable trade (Schedvin, 2008, p. 206). Three universities, Sydney, Melbourne and Queensland were already teaching Russian but only as a not-for-degree subject.

When Germany invaded Russia in June 1941, Australia, along with other British dominions and the USA, was allied with Russia. Australia was seeking to expand its trade and re-open diplomatic relations with Soviet Russia (Poole, 2007, p. 211). In December 1941, the Japanese entered the Pacific War. The new Prime Minister Curtin,[2] who was very concerned for Australia's national security, sought strategic assurance from other countries. As he said: 'Australian external policy will be shaped towards obtaining Russian aid, and working out, with the United States … a plan of Pacific strategy, along with British, Chinese and Dutch forces… We should be able to look forward with reason to aid from Russia against Japan' (Curtin, 1941, p. 10). Such aid for the Pacific allies was not forthcoming; Stalin had apparently made this quite clear two weeks earlier (Barclay, 1977, p. 6).

Meanwhile by July 1942, Stalingrad was under siege and needing aid itself. Australia, as part of the Commonwealth initiative, sent aid to the Soviet Union. Prime Minister Curtin, and Evatt, the Minister for External Affairs, were still keen to have positive diplomatic relationships with the Soviet Union. In October 1942, William Slater, of the firm Slater and Gordon, and Speaker in the Victorian Legislative Assembly, was appointed as the first Australian Ambassador to the Soviet Union (Poole, 2007, p. 213). Slater spent only a few short months in Russia finding it difficult to establish working relationships with the Soviet government. He became seriously ill and had to return to Australia in June 1943. The posting was considered unfortunate, and Slater's appointment not well thought out as he had no foreign policy experience, scant knowledge of Russia, no Russian language skills and was located nearly 540 miles from Moscow with little opportunity to discuss trade issues or undertake diplomatic discussions (Cannon, 2002, p. 2; Poole, 1992, pp. 191, 193, 197, 2007, pp. 211, 213, 215). Later appointments were more successful. Keith Officer became the next chargé d'affaires until March 1944. Two other staff with him, Max Crawford, the First Secretary, (on leave from the history department of the University of Melbourne), and Peter Heydon, as Second Secretary, had pursued Russian language studies and made such good progress that they were able to make some use of their language ability in official business (Fewster, 2009, pp. 234, 256).

Meanwhile Minister Evatt had instituted a diplomatic cadet scheme to train recruits for a more professional foreign service. Recruits undertook the two year University of Sydney course (later moved to the Canberra University College) which included public administration, political theory, diplomatic practice, international law and a language nominated by the cadet. There is no evidence of the range of languages which a cadet could choose (Beaumont, Waters, & Lowe, with

---

[2] John Curtin became Prime Minister on 7 October, 1941 after the Australian Labor Party had won the election.

Woodard, 2003, pp. 25, 28, 29), although it was recognised that language skills were important for successful foreign diplomacy. John Rowland, newly graduated from the University of Sydney, completed the diplomatic cadet course in 1944 and 1945, and was then posted to Moscow as Third Secretary from 1946 to 1948. Rowland quickly began to learn Russian (which he had not studied in the diplomatic cadet course), becoming quite fluent – a useful skill in the extensive contacts he made both in political, literary and artistic circles (Historical Documents Branch, DFAT, 1996, pp. 1, 2, 5, 9).

In Australia, interest in Russia and the Russian language was growing in the years immediately after World War II. Margaret Travers, who taught Russian at the University of Melbourne from 1963, saw this as a time of 'realisation of Russia's growing scientific, economic and political importance.' This, she said, contributed to a greater interest in the study of Russian, with 'many of the early students being returned servicemen' (Travers, 1971, p. 223). It was a time of significant advances in space technology and the 'space race' between the USSR and the USA. Regardless, the fortunes of Russian language fluctuated, depending not only on the Australian government's involvement with Russia, but also on the fluctuating student interest in Russia politically, scientifically and culturally.

6.2 Russian Language Begins at University of Melbourne

The University of Melbourne, in an Arts Faculty report of November 1943, had already noted that Russian was a language 'likely to be of world importance', and a language which should be taught if the means for teaching were provided (UniMelb. Faculty of Arts Minutes, Book 5, 16 November 1943, p. 291). The matter was not discussed again until April 1945 when the Science Faculty raised the question of a reading course in Russian within a Science course. The Professorial Board thought it impracticable to establish only a Science Reading Russian course, suggesting that elementary Russian should be made available to students in all courses. The Arts Faculty subsequently resolved at its meeting of 17 April 1945 that, given the importance of Russian literature and Russian scientific publications, Russian should be established as a course in the Bachelor of Arts degree. The Arts Faculty also recommended that Matriculation Russian should be established concurrently. It was not, however, until 1951 that the first candidates had sat for Matriculation Russian (the University of Melbourne Handbooks of Public and Matriculation Examinations, 1951, p. 49). Subsequently the Council of the University resolved 'to establish a Lectureship in Russian to enable Russian to be introduced' as a subject for an Arts degree and as an 'optional reading course for Science students' (UniMelb. Faculty of Arts Minutes, Book 5, 17 April 1945, p. 423; 10 July 1945, p. 445).

In 1946, the University of Melbourne was the first Australian university to begin teaching Russian as a subject credited towards a degree. Nina Christesen, the lecturer appointed to set up the Russian program, was a Russian émigré, who had been a secondary school teacher in Queensland. She had also taught Russian both privately and as a not-for-degree subject at the Institute of Modern Languages at the University of Queensland from 1936 before coming to Melbourne in late January 1945. Many of Christesen's students in the early 1940s were servicemen and Christesen was an examiner for Russian for the Australian Army. Travers reported that it was Christesen herself who argued for the introduction of Russian at the University of Melbourne with the support of senior Arts Faculty staff. Christesen was not appointed as a member of the Arts Faculty until May 1946, but it can be seen from the Faculty minutes that the introduction of Russian had been discussed and endorsed by April 1945. It is unlikely therefore that she had the access to senior Faculty staff to influence the introduction of Russian as strongly as has been suggested (Armstrong, 1996, p. 64; Christesen, 1982, pp. 72, 73, 74; UniMelb. Faculty of Arts Minutes, Book 5, 21 May 1946, p. 491). What is not clear from the archival documentation about the introduction of Russian is whether funds had been found to support such teaching, or whether the arrival in Melbourne of Christesen was 'the means for teaching' which the Arts Faculty back in 1943 had said was required.

Michael Protopopov, a Russian Orthodox priest and historian, contended that Australia and Russia's joint involvement in the Allied war effort contributed to much warmer diplomatic relations between the two countries. By 1948, the Australian Government had invited the Soviet Union to establish an embassy in Canberra. This was also the time of a yet another large wave of migration to Australia of many thousands of displaced persons from Europe, including people from the Soviet Union. Protopopov was himself, as a child, part of this migration wave (Protopopov, 2006, pp. 55, 184).

Russian language grew slowly at the University of Melbourne. Richard Woolcott, later a senior Australian diplomat, learned his Russian under Christesen from 1946. He said that 'for people of my generation in Australia, Russia had an aura, a certain romantic mystique…it was a massive, suffering land of harsh winters, huge social upheavals and great talent.' Woolcott was posted as Third Secretary to the embassy in Moscow in 1952 (Woolcott, 2003, pp. 5, 7). However, as the Cold War atmosphere of suspicion and mistrust between the USSR and the US and its allies intensified, this, argued Travers, had an effect on the rather slow growth of the numbers of students choosing to take Russian (Travers, 1971, p. 223). Nevertheless, numbers of students did take up Russian. Travers, who excelled in languages at school, decided to take up Russian at university after reading the Tolstoy novel *Anna Karenina* in translation; it 'made me want to learn Russian'. Her mother was very concerned at her learning Russian and her mother's friends aghast, presumably as Russia was a Cold War enemy. Travers remarked that Australian passports at that time, before Stalin died in 1953, were marked "not valid for the Soviet Union" (Travers, personal communication, 27 February, 2013). Travers subsequently went on to teach Russian at the university level for many years. Robert Dessaix was another academic and writer who began learning Russian in the Cold War era of the 1950s. Meanwhile the RAAF School of Languages added Russian to the cohort of languages they taught in 1951 when Toby Garrick was the commanding officer of the School. Although Garrick was of Russian parentage, there is no evidence that this directly influenced the introduction of Russian. Inexplicably, given the political and defence implications of the Cold War, Russian did not survive very long in the language offerings of the School, and was dropped in 1954.

How useful it would have been for diplomats in Australia to have had that expertise in the events shortly to unfold that year (Turner, 1983, pp. 22, 23). As Russian was also being established at the Canberra University College with the first permanent teaching staff appointed in 1954, what became known as the Petrov affair, erupted. Petrov, an intelligence agent at the Soviet embassy in Canberra, defected in April 1954 and was granted political asylum by Australia. Soviet diplomats were immediately withdrawn from Canberra and, in Moscow, the Australian embassy staff were expelled and told to leave within 48 h. Woolcott's first posting ended very abruptly. It had not been an easy couple of years, he wrote. 'The Soviet government was deeply suspicious of foreigners especially Russian-speaking Western diplomats.' In such a closed and suspicious country, 'it was very difficult to establish genuine friendships' (Protopopov, 2006, p. 187; Travers, 1977, p. 3; Woolcott, 2003, pp. 5, 8, 16, 17).

Such was the political fallout from this incident with the communist Soviet Union, contended Woolcott, that the re-election of the Menzies government in May 1954 was ensured. Menzies was an avowed anti-Communist, and a Royal Commission into suspected Soviet espionage, began in the same month of his re-election. The political ructions extended to the Australian Labor Party (ALP), with the infamous split in the ALP resulting in the formation of the strongly anti-communist Democratic Labor Party (DLP). Those who became the DLP were fearful of the influence of the Communist Party in the ALP-affiliated unions (Protopopov, 2006, pp. 189, 191; Woolcott, 2003, p. 18). When diplomatic relations were restored in 1959, it was Woolcott who was sent to re-open the embassy because he spoke Russian and knew the Soviet Union from his earlier posting. Woolcott's appointment was fortuitous as the senior chargé d'affaires appointed, Bill Cutts, did not speak any Russian (Woolcott 2003, pp. 38, 40).

Concurrent with the restoration of diplomatic relations, interest in Russian language had increased from its slow growth in the early 1950s. Dessaix who taught Russian at ANU spoke of the motivations of his former students for learning Russian:

> they thought it would open doors to a diplomatic career… business was hardly a drawcard during the communist era… but there were also many students who were of Russian or Slavic background who thought it would be an easy option. They were rarely amongst our best students. Sometimes, but very rarely, students with a Jewish background were an exception – they were usually more culturally motivated. (Dessaix, personal communication, 1 March, 2013)

Former students of Nina Christesen quoted her remark that 'enrolments in Russian shot up along with the first sputnik in 1957' (Travers, 1971, p. 224), indicating the great interest in Russian scientific and technological achievements. Russian was now being taught in Victorian secondary schools with the first candidates having sat Matriculation Russian in 1951. Student interest in Russian language was surging ahead with 44 Russian Victorian Matriculation candidates in 1963. Bonhady's survey of 1964 matriculation languages in Australia recorded Russian language candidates in New South Wales, Victoria, Queensland and Tasmania as the language became firmly established in secondary schools (Bonyhady, 1965, p. 32; Rigby, 1992, p. 268; Travers, 1977, p. 3; The University of Melbourne Handbooks of Public and Matriculation Examinations, 1963, p. 39).

Chairs in Russian language were founded at both Monash University and the University of Queensland in 1966, and at UNSW in 1967. The ANU established a Chair in Russian in 1962 although they did not find a suitable candidate until Reginald de Bray, from the University of London, accepted and took up the Chair at the end of 1971. Only the University of Melbourne lacked a Chair in Russian and this eventually came to pass in 1977 when Roland Sussex was appointed. Travers maintained that a number of factors had caused student numbers for Russian language in universities to level out by the end of the 1960s: the dropping of a compulsory language unit in arts courses, the competition from a wider choice of languages available to students, and possibly the negative influence of changes in the political climate (Travers, 1971, pp. 224, 225). Joseph Zajda who taught Russian at Monash University expressed the same reasons as Travers, adding that the ethnic obscurity of Russian and its perceived difficulty (presumably its Cyrillic script) were also factors (Zajda, 1976, p. 30).

One aspect of the Cold War between East and West was the even greater need to keep up to date with Russian scientific research, particularly its space programs and for this an ability to read Russian was essential (Sussex, 1980, p. 4). At the University of Melbourne, for instance, a Science Russian Reading course was offered between 1954 and 1988, corresponding roughly to the length of the Cold War. Science Russian was also taught at Monash University, the University of Queensland and the ANU (Travers, 1971, p. 231).

During the 1960s, as numbers of Russian language students grew in universities, the Australian government, through the Department of Trade, was investigating new trade opportunities in the Soviet Union. The Vienna trade post opened in 1964 with the brief to cover Vienna, Belgrade and Moscow. The experienced trade commissioner appointed, Dutch-born Rudi Schneemann, was fluent in Dutch, German and English, and competent in Russian, other Slavonic languages and Javanese. His language ability was important in the slow and often difficult trade negotiations he undertook. As Schedvin explained in his history of Australia's trade commissioner service, this expansion of 'trade with the Soviet Bloc went some way to replace the loss of markets in the UK and the European Economic Community' (Schedvin, 2008, pp. 204, 205, 207).

The year after Schneemann began, the new ambassador appointed to the Soviet Union was the Russian-speaking Rowland who had been Third Secretary back in 1946 during which time he had travelled widely in the Soviet Union (Historical Documents Branch, DFAT, 1996, pp. 2, 9). In both diplomatic and trade positions with Russia, Australia was recognising, for its own strategic and economic interests, the importance of appointing experienced professionals with the appropriate language skills. This was a very positive precedent for this new chapter in Australia's exploration of its national interest in relation to Russia. It was not however, until 1972, that an Australian trade post was opened in Moscow itself with the appointment of Laurie Matheson, a fluent Russian speaker. Said Schedvin, 'language proficiency was not always given priority in trade commissioner positions but in this case, [the opening of the Moscow post] it was the overriding consideration' (Schedvin, 2008, p. 249). According to Gill, there was a reorientation of Australian foreign policy with the incoming Whitlam Labor government: new cultural, scientific and technological agreements signed and provision for more exchange visits by parliamentarians. Significantly, Gough Whitlam himself visited the Soviet Union in 1975, becoming the first Australian Prime Minister to do so (Gill, 2007, p. 241).

Whilst Australia was consolidating diplomatic and trade relations with the Soviet Union, no new Russian courses had begun in Australian universities. The impetus which these new relations had gained for Australia could have been further reinforced by government initiatives for more Russian language teaching, but this did not happen. The five universities who offered Russian in the 1960s, were the same five offering Russian in the 1970s: the Universities of Melbourne, New South Wales and Queensland, Monash University, and the ANU. The Kramer Report detailed Australian university student numbers in Russian as 149 in 1970, dropping to 126 in 1973. Hawley's (1982) statistics for the years 1974–1981 showed university and college student numbers ranging between 145 and 179 (AAH, 1975, p. 20; AUC, 1975a, pp. 13, 18; Hawley, 1982, pp. 60, 80). These were not large numbers but had shown no appreciable decline even when the Soviet Union invaded Afghanistan in December 1979. Although Australia was highly critical of the Soviet invasion, diplomatic representation was not withdrawn, although relations were strained. Australia put its trade with the Soviet Union 'on hold' just when the Soviet Union had become Australia's third largest export market. Existing trade continued but no new trade initiatives were allowed. This meant a loss of opportunities over the next four years until trade connections were gradually restored by the Hawke government after May 1983 (Gill, 2007, p. 244; Schedvin, 2008, pp. 307, 308).

The 1987 National Policy on Languages had initiated a time of reckoning for languages in Australia, as this policy included a prioritisation of languages of wider teaching. Whilst Russian was seen as an important language for Australia's trade and diplomatic relationships, it was not included as one of the nine languages of wider teaching. Those nine languages were 'languages of importance to Australia for external and national reasons. Although some of these languages overlapped with languages widely spoken in Australia' they were to have 'the addition of a specific focus' (Lo Bianco, 1987, pp. 124, 125). As Lo Bianco reiterated, the NPL was not just about the languages of wider learning but also about the importance of mother tongue maintenance and community languages as second languages (Lo Bianco, personal communication, 21 January, 2014). Lo Bianco further explained: 'the nine languages of wider learning were "in addition" to their presence as mother tongue maintenance languages in some cases and would also be in demand as languages of wider teaching i.e. as second languages not mother tongues' (Lo Bianco, personal communication, 21 January, 2014). Russian would be supported through mother tongue maintenance. Nevertheless, Russian was not emphasised in the NPL as having national importance for Australia despite the government's trade and diplomatic activities at the time.

The 1991 Australian Literacy and Language Policy did include Russian in its specified 14 priority languages from which individual states could choose eight to gain priority funding. This policy emphasised Australia's location in the Asia-Pacific region, trade patterns for that region and the broader national interest, as factors in prioritising languages. The far eastern parts of Russia were clearly in that Asia-Pacific region with the strategically important commercial city of Vladivostok and its marine base for the Soviet fleet. Another survey, commissioned by DEET, submitted to the Australian Advisory Council on Languages and Multicultural Education, and published in 1990, explored the relationship between international trade and linguistic competence. The researchers, in examining the use of languages by Australian companies, surveyed employers' stated language needs for international trade, indicating nine languages most in demand: Mandarin, Japanese, Arabic, Indonesian, Korean, Thai, Spanish, German, and French in roughly that order. There was no mention of Russian (DEET, 1991a, pp. 15, 16; Stanley, Ingram, & Chittick, 1990, pp. iii, 53, 98). So, whilst the Federal government had ongoing diplomatic and trade relationships with Russia, its policies did not exhibit a consistent interest in promoting Russian as an important language for Australia's national interest.

6.3 Collapse of Soviet Union

By 1991 the world was adjusting to the collapse of the Soviet Union and forming new relationships with the constituent republics which were being established, principally with Russia. The 1991 Leal Report predicted that 'Russian would obviously become of increasing importance to Australia and the Western world,' and that 'the potential of the USSR to develop stronger cultural, political and economic links with Australia has changed in a very short time.' Nevertheless, the Leal Report noted that whilst eight institutions were now teaching Russian, there was only 'limited growth in real terms', given the actual student numbers (Leal, 1991a, pp. 61, 168). Yet the authors of the 1995 Russian volume in the series *Unlocking Australia's Language Potential*, emphasised Russia as having increasing economic importance for Australia, being a country which uniquely straddled Europe and Asia. It was the north east of Russia, Pacific Russia, which had a particular focus for Australia. They also pointed out that Russian was 'the *lingua* franca for official and trade relations' between all the newly emerging states of the former Soviet Union (FSU). There was also a significant Russian speaking community in Australia strengthened by yet another wave of migration to Australia since the breakup of the Soviet Union (Phillips, Akbarzadeh, & Mathew, 1995, pp. 68, 69). Such a wave of Russian migration added weight to Lo Bianco's mother tongue maintenance imperative. Australia had certainly recognised Russia in December 1991 (Rich, 1993, p. 46), and indeed opened a combined consulate and Austrade office in Vladivostok in December 1992 (Phillips et al., 1995, p. 66). Regardless, the government did not seem to hasten to capitalise on the economic opportunities predicted by Russian language specialists in Australia.

6.3 Collapse of Soviet Union

It could be argued that it was the breakup of the Soviet Union that caused a downturn in the numbers of students studying Russian in Australia. However, according to Dessaix, whilst it was not the breakup of the Soviet Union which first affected Russian language numbers, this was the final blow to its popularity. He maintained that, although there had been a surge in enrolments during Gorbachev's perestroika years from 1986 to 1989, by 1991 enrolments were declining. He quoted, for instance, a 30% fall in enrolments at UNSW in 1990 from the previous year (Dessaix, 1997, p. 2). Phillips and his colleagues noted in 1995 that 'no state or territory has selected Russian as one of its eight national priority languages' at the secondary school level to receive priority ALLP funding. They also quoted the view of languages academics at the University of Melbourne that suggested the breakup 'of the Soviet Union and the economic crisis currently being experienced in the countries of the FSU may have contributed to a diminishing of the status of Russian in the eyes of students' (Phillips et al., 1995, pp. 56, 71).

Whatever the truth of the matter is for the decline in the number of students studying Russian, Phillips and his colleagues maintained that Russian came out a poor second in competing for resources when pitted against a national push for the learning of Asian languages for Australia's economic future, and a national emphasis on learning the major European languages (Phillips et al., 1995, p. xvi). As ABS statistics show this was a time when Asian immigration was increasing (DIMA, 2001, p. 21). The committee commissioned by the Council of Australian Governments (COAG) to produce a report into Asian languages met for the first time in December 1992 (COAG, 1992, para. 8). I agree with the argument of Phillips and his colleagues that resources for, and interest in, Russian suffered not only because of political changes in that country, but also because the Australian government's priority for languages had now turned clearly towards Asian languages (Phillips et al., 1995, p. xvi).

Dessaix in his article entitled 'Russia: the End of an Affair' wrote lyrically of Russian language and its great literature: 'Russian as the language of a great and growing empire – ethnically diverse, geographically vast, utterly and confrontingly different… mysterious.' Dessaix had studied Russian at secondary school and then at the ANU in the early 1960s (Dessaix, personal communication, 1 March, 2013). He explained further how Russia was viewed when he was a student: 'Moscow was the epicentre of a brutal totalitarian empire. A sympathetic interest in things Russian was idiosyncratic, if not downright politically suspicious…. Yet, at Melbourne University, at precisely that time, Russian studies were in their heyday.' For him the decline in interest in Russian was because Russia was no longer mysterious and fascinating, but a country finding a new post-USSR identity. It was not just disillusionment with what Russia has become that has dulled our interest, he argued, but also that students nowadays no longer seek to understand this strange other world through its language and literature. Quite bluntly he said, 'The eroticism of Russia partly vanished, I think, when she was revealed to be little more than a vulgar, backward version of America' (Dessaix, 1997, pp. 1, 2, 3).

Even the 1997 White Paper on foreign and trade policy did not accord Russia much of a role in the Asia Pacific in the short term. It was acknowledged that there was potential advantage for Australia's trade and investment interests 'as Russia puts its economic house in order' (C of A, 1997, p. 31). Macquarie University had recently promoted Russian language as 'one of the most important languages of broader national interest to Australia', one of the official languages of the United Nations, a language giving access to the great Russian literary masterpieces. Russia is one of the world's boom economies; more than a quarter of the world's scientific literature is published in Russian (Macquarie University, n.d., Russian studies). Nevertheless, it appeared that those reasons were no longer compelling to students as they had been in a bygone era. I also argue that what university academics, such as those at Macquarie University, have thought, and currently think, of the importance of Russian language to Australia, is at odds with what successive Australian governments have thought about the importance of Russian as demonstrated by official statements on foreign and trade policy.

6.4 Australia's Relationship with Korea

It might be assumed that Australia's relationship with Korea began with the Korean War which started in June 1950, in which the Australian defence forces were involved. It was, however, Australian Presbyterian missionaries who had Australia's first documented contact with Korea in the late 1880s (Kerr & Anderson, 1970, p. 7; Lee, 2009, pp. 29, 61; Shapley, 2008, p. 1). Nevertheless, it was for trade possibilities with Korea that two Australian state governments appointed trade commissioners: John Suttor, appointed NSW trade commissioner to Japan in 1903, included Korea in his territory. James Sinclair, appointed as a Victorian trade commissioner in 1906, also included Seoul in his visits. Other Australians such as Alexander Melbourne of the University of Queensland and Ian Clunies Ross, a veterinary scientist, both of whom had an interest in Asia, particularly China and Japan, included Korea in their professional visits to Asia in the 1930s (Schedvin, 2008, p. 4; Walker, 2009, pp. 76, 205, 207). In spite of this collective interest, it appears that there was little trade with Korea in the first half of the twentieth century. Japan, after years of intervening in Korea's affairs, took advantage of the Korean government's instability and annexed Korea which, from 1910, became a colony of Japan. Korea completely lost its independence which it did not regain until Japan's defeat in 1945 (Dutton, 2001, pp. 42, 43; Lone & McCormack, 1993, p. 50).

It was at this point that Korea became important for Australia's national interest as Australia was pulled into a new relationship with Korea, shaped by security and defence concerns after World War II. What had followed World War II was a 'troubled and divided' independence (Waters, 2001, p. 122), with Soviet and American troops converging around Korea, with what has been described as 'nascent Cold War rivalries' (Lone & McCormack, 1993, p. 94). The antagonism between the communist North and the anti-communist South Korea descended into war in June 1950 when North Korea invaded the South. Australia joined a multi-nation United Nations force to defend South Korea from what was viewed as an 'unprovoked,

6.4 Australia's Relationship with Korea

deliberate and planned' invasion (Goldsworthy, 2001, p. 394; Lone & McCormack, 1993, p. 106), a war halted by the armistice signed in July 1953. Ben Evans, a military historian, maintained that Australia's involvement was a 'major factor in defining Australia's place in the post-World War Two world' (Evans, 2001, p. 2). Whilst it was a small nation, Australia had shown itself to be a good global citizen by contributing to collective regional security. The closer alliance which Australia forged with the US through Australia's Korean War involvement assisted Australia's own regional security which of course was in Australia's national interest (Evans, 2001, pp. 2, 3).

Through the later 1950s and into the 1960s, the Korean economy grew rapidly, albeit assisted by enormous amounts of US aid. It was not until 1972 that a full trade post was opened in Seoul by Australia to facilitate interest in exports such as beef and live cattle, barley and wheat, and consultancy services. In the private sector, the Australia-Korea and Korea-Australia Business Councils were formed in 1978 (Evans, 2001, p. 85; Schedvin, 2008, pp. 113, 237). Around the early 1980s, suggested Goldsworthy, there seemed to be much that Australia and Korea had in common: 'economic complementarity, shared strategic world views, and close security and economic relations with the United States' (Goldsworthy, 2003, p. 150). But, given the lack of Korean language studies in Australia at that time, all this 'political and economic courting' was not underpinned by any substantial knowledge of South Korean language and culture. Whilst Korean trade was important for Australia, Korean language was not. As Cotton maintained as late as 1997, the burgeoning relationship was still hampered by the 'lack of a cultural dimension' (Cotton, 1997, p. 193).

An investigation of the various language reports of the relevant decades demonstrated that knowledge gap through the paucity of teaching of Korean language and culture. In the 1966 Wykes Report, the 1970 Auchmuty Report and the 1975 Kramer Report, there is no reference to Korean being taught anywhere in the Australian tertiary sector. The 1975 Australian Academy of the Humanities Report recorded that Korean was available as a non-credit bearing subject at the University of Queensland's Institute of Modern Languages in 1973, but there was no evidence for the longevity of this teaching. It was not until 1982 that Korean was introduced at the Australian National University. The instigator of this program was the Head of the Department of Far East History at ANU, Professor Wang Gungwu. He recollected that he had been visiting Korea since 1967 and had discussed his desire to start Korean at ANU with a Korean colleague, Professor Kim Jun-yop of Korea University. Kim was able to secure funds from a Korean business federation. Wang put this proposal to the ANU Faculty of Asian Studies, which proposal was gratefully received. A young academic was sent from Korea and classes began (Wang, personal communication, 31 May, 2013).

It was not, however, until the late 1980s that interest in the Korean language appears to have increased with growing trade interdependency as a key factor. Whilst Korean was not one of the priority languages for Australia specified in the 1987 NPL, it was noted in the 1991 Leal Report, that DFAT was placing 'increased emphasis' (Leal, 1991a, p. 27) on Korean and Russian particularly for the foreign language competency of their consular staff. That increased emphasis on Korea can be seen firstly in the 1988/1989 exchange of visits between Prime Minister Hawke and President Roh Tae-Woo of South Korea. These visits aimed to strengthen cooperation between the two countries and identify new directions for the ongoing relationship.

South Korea was also one of the 12 founding member economies which attended the inaugural meeting of Asia-Pacific Economic Cooperation (APEC) held in Canberra in November 1989. Subsequently, the Australian government established the Australia-Korea Foundation, allocating funds in the 1991 Budget, with Korea establishing the Korea-Australia Foundation. Whilst the objectives of the Australia-Korea Foundation included the promotion of Korean language studies, there were no substantial resources allocated by the Australian government to meet such an objective according to Foundation's annual report of 1992–1993, and no direct evidence of DFAT resourcing Korean language teaching for its staff (Australia Korea Foundation, 1993, pp. 1, 6). Despite this, at least by 1990, eight institutions taught Korean: ANU, Griffith University, Monash University, University of Queensland, Swinburne Institute of Technology (soon to become the Swinburne University of Technology), University of Sydney, Victoria College (a college of advanced education), and the Victoria University of Technology (Leal, 1991a, pp. 13, 37, 64, 98, 116, 118, 130, 134).

As previously mentioned, the Federal government issued its language and literacy policy (ALLP) in August 1991. One of the goals of this policy was the expansion of the learning of languages other than English. Fourteen priority languages were listed: Aboriginal languages, Arabic, Chinese, French, German, Indonesian, Italian, Japanese, Korean, Modern Greek, Russian, Spanish, Thai, and Vietnamese. Each state or territory was required to prioritise eight languages from this list to receive specified grants for year 12 students completing a priority language (DEET, 1991a, pp. 4, 16, 17). Not one state or territory prioritised Korean (NALCWG, 1994, Attachment E).

In 1994, the NALCWG Working Group with Kevin Rudd as Chair, had recommended four Asian languages for priority expansion, Japanese, Mandarin Chinese, Indonesian and Korean based on a 20 year range of economic forecasts made by DFAT. As the title of this 1994 Report suggested (*Asian languages and Australia's economic future*), the recommendations were set firmly in an economic framework. Asian languages and cultures education was required as 'a means of enhancing Australian economic interests in East Asia,' a clear indication of language promotion for Australia's national interest, but couched in economic terms. What was urgently needed, said the Working Group, was Asia-literate Australians possessing 'the range of linguistic and cultural competencies...to operate effectively at different levels in their various dealings with the region – as individuals, organisations and as a nation' (NALCWG, 1994, pp. v, 2). This was a long term strategy encouraging the study of second language learning, to begin in primary schools from Year three. A follow-up report was suggested to assess the impact that the schools' language strategy had on university and TAFE Asian languages/cultures courses (NALCWG, 1994, pp. v, xiii). The subsequent strategy was The National Asian Languages and

6.4 Australia's Relationship with Korea

Studies in Australian Schools (NALSAS) with substantial funding (over $208 million) provided from 1994 to 1995 to the end of 2002 (DEST, 1994, p. 1).

Despite the ALLP prioritisation of Korean with funding attached to targets, and the promotion of Korean as one of the priority trade languages in the Rudd Report, such prioritisation was simply not enough to galvanise more schools into offering Korean or tertiary students into taking Korean. Yvette Slaughter, a language education specialist, contended that whilst Chinese, Japanese, and Indonesian flourished under the NALSAS funding, 'Korean never gained a strong foothold in Australian schools...The impact of socio-political events was seen as a significant factor in the decline of Korean' (Slaughter, 2007, p. 104, 2011, pp. 163, 165). As Slaughter maintained: Together, the continued division of the country, the disruptive political situation with the North Korean nuclear program, the ongoing US military presence, and militant unionism in South Korea, have worked against the image of South Korea and Korean language programs (Slaughter, 2007, p. 104). Slaughter argued that promoting Korean on the basis of its economic importance does not [and has not] guaranteed success (Slaughter, 2011, p. 166).

The tertiary sector did receive a boost in the promotion of Korean language and studies when the National Korean Studies Centre (NKSC) was established in 1990 with Commonwealth government funding of approximately $900,000 over four years. The establishment of this Centre was the result of a specific recommendation in the Garnaut Report which had analysed the implications for Australia of economic growth and change in North East Asia (Buzo, personal communication, 23 April, 2014; Garnaut, 1989, pp. 34, 304, 305; Swinburne Institute of Technology, 1992, p. 38). After a nation-wide tendering process, the NKSC was awarded to a consortium of four Melbourne tertiary institutions: Swinburne Institute of Technology (SIT), La Trobe, Melbourne and Monash universities, operating out of Swinburne from 1990. The University of Melbourne offered Korean from 1994 as a complementary subject from SIT, coincidentally the same year as the first Victorian Year 12 candidature sitting for Korean language. Each university undertook to provide $25,000 p.a. over this period making a total of $400,000. From various sources, the NKSC raised about $2 million during its lifetime, but, indicated Adrian Buzo, a former director of NKSC, when Federal government funding ceased, in the general climate of reduced Federal government interest in funding Asian Studies, the Centre was unable to become self-supporting and closed after five years of operation (Buzo, personal communication, 23 April, 2014).

Swinburne continued to offer a double degree in Business/Arts (Korean) only until 1997 (Swinburne University of Technology, 1997, p. 141). So, just as the secondary sector could not sustain solid numbers for Korean, neither could the tertiary sector. As Baldauf and White noted, from 1990 to 2005, Korean continued to be taught in only eight or nine institutions across Australia (Baldauf & White, 2010, p. 44). By 2011, only seven institutions offered Korean, classified then as a moderately taught language, compared to Chinese, Japanese and Indonesian all classified as widely taught (Dunne & Pavlyshyn, 2011, pp. 18, 19). By 2013, only one additional university offered Korean (Dunne & Pavlyshyn, 2014, p. 19). Whilst various Australian government strategies had sought intermittently to bolster Asian languages in schools and universities, such strategies did not have the same significant effect on the growth of Korean, as they did for the numbers of students taking Chinese, Japanese and Indonesian (Baldauf & White, 2010, pp. 50, 51). Korea is a country which has figured importantly in Australia's economic interests, however, as Slaughter had said, economic importance alone was not enough to stimulate greater interest in the Korean language.

6.5 Arabic: A Pluricentric and Religious Language

Whilst through the defence forces, there had been a century of Australian involvement with many of the Middle Eastern countries where Arabic is spoken, the nature of that relationship was quite different to Australia's relationship with Korea and Russia. As previously indicated, the importance of Arabic to Australia relates to the unique position of that language both internationally and from a religious point of view. Any discussion of the Arabic language must acknowledge also that, from the latter half of the twentieth century, Arabic was, in Australia, an excellent example of a pluricentric language. Such a language, according to Clyne, is one that has 'been brought to Australia by people from different countries with separate national varieties and with different sets of linguistic norms' (Clyne & Kipp, 1999, p. 2). Currently, Arabic is one of the six official languages of the United Nations, and is the official language in some 22 countries. Arabic is also important as a religious language for the Qur'an, the sacred text of Islam. Thus, it also has deep religious resonance in countries where the national language is not Arabic but where the population is overwhelmingly Muslim (UN at Glance, n.d.; Victorian Arabic Social Services: Mission, n.d.). In Australia, the largest Muslim communities have their origins in Lebanon, Turkey, Afghanistan, Pakistan, Bangladesh, Iran, Iraq, Indonesia, and Bosnia and Herzegovina, with just over a third of these people speaking Arabic. The 2006 census showed that the majority of Muslims lived in NSW (49.6%) or Victoria (32.1%) (Department of Immigration and Citizenship, n.d., Muslims in Australia).

6.6 Arabic as a Scholarly Language

It was, nonetheless, as a scholarly language that Arabic was first taught in 1946 in an Australian university, the University of Melbourne, in the Department of Semitic Studies. In 1944, Chisholm, as Dean of Arts, was approached by Abraham and Lazarus Sicree, two Jewish businessmen strongly committed to Jewish philanthropic values, who wished to endow a Chair for five years with the broad purview of Semitic Studies (Waller, 1995, p. 72). This generous offer was accepted and, in 1945, Maurice Goldman, a gifted linguist, was appointed to the Chair. Goldman, who had fled from Nazi Germany in 1938, arrived in Australia in 1939. He had

6.6 Arabic as a Scholarly Language

already been giving guest courses in Hebrew and Arabic since 1942, there being no funds at that stage to establish a department of Semitic Studies (Chisholm, 1958, p. 127). According to Chisholm, Goldman 'knew some forty languages and spoke at least fifteen of them fluently' (Chisholm, 1958, p. 128). Apart from Hebrew, Yiddish, Ethiopic, Syriac, Aramaic, Polish, Russian and German, he had an excellent knowledge of both classical and vernacular Arabic, as well as Islamic thought and modern Arabic literature. To those at the University, wrote Chisholm, 'Goldman was a gift from heaven' (Chisholm, 1958. pp. 128, 129, 131, 132). Under Goldman for just 11 years, the Department of Semitic Studies flourished till his untimely death in 1957.

Goldman was followed in 1959 by the Rev. Dr. John Bowman, also a notable Semitic Studies scholar, but with a wider perspective on the importance of Arabic language. He had introduced Arabic at Leeds University in the 1950s 'because he recognised the growing importance of Middle East oil and the risk of further regional conflict, due to ignorance' (Bowman & Bowman, 2006, p. 1). With great enthusiasm and 'missionary zeal' he set about to 'develop his department as a centre to advance the understanding of Middle Eastern culture and civilisation, ancient and modern' (Sagona, 2006, p. 5). The department, which taught both modern and classical Arabic, with some tuition in colloquial Egyptian Arabic, was renamed the Department of Middle Eastern Studies from 1968 (UniMelb, 1967, p. 73). A significant microfilm collection of unpublished manuscripts of Hebrew, Arabic and Syriac works was built up and, although Semitic Studies and then Middle Eastern Studies flourished, Arabic language did not (Bowman, 1976, pp. 3, 5). Wykes' 1966 survey reported very few students taking Arabic at the University of Melbourne, and showed that Arabic was not taught in any Australian secondary schools in 1964 (Wykes, 1966, p. 77).

Curiously, the 1970 Auchmuty Report listed Arabic as an Asian language and referred to the West Asian[3] studies of the Department of Semitic Studies at the University of Melbourne. Bowman also used the term West Asian to refer to Middle Eastern studies (Bowman, 1976, p. 7). Arabic was available at three institutions only, the University of Melbourne with eight students in 1969, the ANU with nine students and the University of Sydney with none. Teaching in Arabic at Sydney did not actually begin until 1970 when classical Arabic was to be offered as a support to Aramaic, Syriac and Hebrew; whereas at the University of Melbourne, Arabic was a four year sequence offered in its own right (C of A, 1970, pp. 42, 53, 56, 57, 72, 141). Bowman, writing in 1976, noted that the particular bias at ANU was literary Arabic, with Arabic being located in the Department of Indonesian Languages (Bowman, 1976, p. 8). Up to this point Arabic remained a scholarly language and had not yet been picked up by any tertiary institution as a language of migrant groups in Australia.

---

[3] This academic linguistic designation is perhaps because Arabic is a Semitic language in the Afro-Asiatic group.

6.7 Arabic as a Migrant Language

Some five years later, the Kramer Report showed still very small numbers of students of Arabic across the three universities, Melbourne, Sydney and ANU. Nationally between 1970 and 1973, the enrolment figures were 10, 12, 8, and 13 (AUC, 1975a, p. 13). Additionally, Kramer reported that Arabic was not a matriculation subject in any state, commenting how secondary enrolments can affect tertiary enrolments (AUC, 1975a, pp. 18, 29). Kramer did, however, refer to Arabic as the language of both Lebanon and the United Arab Republic, countries representing a significant proportion of Australia's migrant intake. Arabic was mentioned, not only as one of the migrant languages neglected at the tertiary level, but also a language for which interpreting and translating courses were needed (AUC, 1975a, pp. 42, 45, 47). That same Kramer Report recommended that funds be allocated in the 1976–1978 triennium to redress the neglect of the teaching of Arabic and other migrant languages (AUC, 1975a, pp. 12, 13, 18, 44). This was the first time that the Arabic language had been mentioned in an official report as requiring funds to promote its teaching and acknowledging Arabic as a migrant language. These grants, according to the AUC, would be determined on the basis of submissions made by interested universities (AUC, 1975a, p. 47, 1975b, pp. 101, 102). Unfortunately, as has been previously mentioned, such funding was not forthcoming. The AUC Report for the 1977–1979 triennium stated that 'no provision was made in the Commission's recommendations for 1976 for the new initiatives proposed in the Sixth Report.' The new Coalition government had suspended the triennial system of funding and proposed new arrangements from May 1976 (AUC, 1976, pp. 1, 72). An opportunity for the promotion of Arabic as a significant migrant language of Australia was missed.

When the Galbally Report into migrant services and programs was presented in May 1978, it boded well that Arabic was one of the ten community languages in which the Report was published and thus recognised officially as a language of migrant groups. 'Significantly increased migration from the Middle East' was one of the Report's themes (C of A, 1978, p. 3). The extension to all states of the ethnic media was one of the costed recommendations of the Galbally Report (C of A, 1978, pp. 12, 14). In January 1978, SBS Radio had already commenced operation taking responsibility for 2EA in Sydney and 3EA in Melbourne. Each of these ethnic radio stations had been broadcasting in several migrant languages for three years, including Arabic (Ang, Hawkins, & Dabboussy, 2008, pp. 58, 278).

Nevertheless, as the 1982 Hawley Report recorded, only one more university now taught Arabic, and that was Classical Arabic at the University of New England. Nationally, tertiary enrolments for Arabic averaged only 29 across the eight years of Hawley's survey (Hawley, 1982, pp. 5, 60). What Hawley did contribute by way of data were the college Arabic offerings: an intensive three month course at the Canberra CAE and an external course in Arabic at the Goulburn CAE. The Milperra CAE had Tertiary Education Commission funding to begin 'an award course in community languages including Arabic, Turkish and Vietnamese' in the 1982–1984 triennium. Goulburn CAE was already teaching Contemporary Middle East Cultures to promote better understanding of such cultures (Bowman, 1976, p. 9; Hawley, 1982, pp. 15, 70). Thus, from about the middle of the 1970s, the national interest in Arabic had begun to change. It was now listed as a migrant language which warranted a contemporary focus, rather than being a language embedded in a Semitic or Middle Eastern Studies department along with other studies of ancient cultures, religions and languages.

Arabic gained further recognition being listed as one of the nine languages of wider learning in the NPL of 1987. This policy recognised the language pluralism of Australia of which Arabic was a part, valuable both economically and culturally, both domestically and internationally (Lo Bianco, 1987, p. 6). This momentum was subsequently lost, because, although in the 1991 ALLP, Arabic was one of the 14 priority languages, not one State government prioritised Arabic (Clyne, 2005, p. 157; DEET, 1991a, p. 16). Such non-prioritisation at the school level was quite counter-productive for raising the profile of Arabic within schools which could have helped to increase enrolments for Arabic at the tertiary level. Even the writers of the 1991 Leal Report, who represented government, school and tertiary sectors, commended Arabic as a language of international significance with strategic, trade and cultural importance to Australia. They believed though that Arabic was seen as just a community language for those of Arabic background, noting that student demand nationally was still weak. They recommended that an advisory council be established to make specific proposals designed to make Arabic attractive to students of non-Arabic speaking backgrounds (Leal, 1991a, pp. 61, 169).

Nevertheless, there were a variety of Arabic programs offered in 1990: teacher training courses with very small numbers of students; a Diploma in Education with an Arabic Method Unit at the University of Melbourne, La Trobe University and the University of Sydney; and a Bachelor of Education (Primary/LOTE- Arabic) at Victoria College (Leal, 1991b, pp. 45, 56, 58, 118, 130). Both the University of Melbourne and the University of Sydney offered an Arabic major. At these two universities, a total of 66 students were enrolled across all year levels in Arabic language subjects (Leal, 1991b, pp. 59, 120). Other tertiary institutions around 1990, offered Arabic in more vocationally-oriented courses, such as the major in Arabic at Phillip Institute of Technology in the School of Community and Policy Studies, an Arabic major in a Bachelor of Arts (Interpreting and Translation) and a Bachelor of Arts (Community Languages) at the University of Western Sydney with a total of 40 students at UWS across all year levels. The Victoria College had 17 students enrolled in an Arabic major in the Bachelor of Arts (Interpreting and Translating) and also offered Arabic in a combined Bachelor of Arts/Bachelor of Business with an emphasis on overseas trade.

The diversity of these offerings demonstrated what the authors of the Arabic language profile maintained: there was a 'complementary picture of tradition versus innovation' in the tertiary courses in Arabic in both Melbourne and Sydney (Campbell, Dyson, Karim, & Rabie, 1993, p. 20; Leal, 1991b, pp. 30, 96, 147). The authors made several recommendations about the need to expand Arabic programs in universities, and the need for universities to make such programs attractive to non-native speakers of Arabic. They did suggest that a small group of high profile individuals of Arabic-speaking background might assist in ideas for language promotion. Arabic language training for DFAT officers posted to Arabic-speaking countries was also seen as an important priority. In a reference to funding, the overall comment about Arabic language teaching in tertiary institutions was made that 'Arabic is healthy and stable in Sydney and healthy and unstable in Melbourne' (Campbell et al., 1993, pp. i, ii, iv, vi, 20). There was no mention of an advisory council to work on making Arabic more attractive to those of a non-Arabic background which had been proposed in the Leal Report.

What was missing here was some action to impel the States to see Arabic as a language worth promoting in schools in order to access ALLP priority funding. Eventually, an advisory committee was set up comprising university academics, teachers, and business representatives. In 1994 the National Advisory Committee on Arabic and Middle Eastern Studies submitted a report to Simon Crean, the Labor Minister for Employment, Education and Training. That extensive report traced the movement of Arabic and Middle Eastern Studies 'from an older orientalist tradition to an approach based on disciplines such as history, political science, economics and linguistics' (DEET, 1994, p. 6). Other themes explored were Australia's trading relationship with the Middle East, the issue of multiculturalism, funding for the discipline, and the state of Arabic teaching in schools, colleges and universities. In conclusion, the advisory committee argued that 'the present moment is probably the most auspicious in our history to make an investment in Arabic and Middle Eastern Studies' (DEET, 1994, pp. 6, 7).

There is no evidence available that any further development of Arabic and Middle Eastern Studies was supported by the Federal government at that time and another opportunity to promote Arabic as a language of both multiculturalism and trade and strategic importance for Australia was lost. In less than two years the Labor government that had set up the advisory committee was defeated, and the Liberal/National Coalition under John Howard took power. In the years between that report of 1994 and the survey work of Baldauf and White in 2006, it can be seen that the number of institutions offering Arabic language had virtually not changed: five in 1994, four in 1997, four in 2001, five in 2002, 2003, 2004, and 2005. The Universities of Melbourne, Sydney, Western Sydney, and Deakin University offered Arabic in each of the survey years. The University of Adelaide offered it only in 1994 through the auspices of the University of Sydney, and the ANU introduced Arabic in 2002 and offered it for the next four years. Arabic was one of the languages, according to this survey, in which there had been growth in EFTSUs (Equivalent Fulltime Student Units) between 2001 and 2005 nationally rising from 77.6 to 121.4 (Leal, 1991a, p. 173; White & Baldauf, 2006, pp. 13, 54, 55, 57, 58, 59). The authors of this survey did caution the reader, however, to note that estimates of EFTSU were based on incomplete reporting of data.

6.8 Arabic as a Trade Language

Whilst the 1994 DEET Report, with its recommendations for trade, more Arabic language teaching, and appreciation of Arabic history and politics had brought no action, a 2001 House of Representatives Report on Australia's trade relationship with the Middle East (Joint Standing Committee on Foreign Affairs, Defence and Trade) emphasised anew the importance to Australia of this market. Now the Federal government was concerned that 'despite all the trade policy and market development work undertaken by Australian government agencies and private companies, Australia's share of the Middle East market has not increased,' and so Middle East trade became an issue for Australia's national interest (JSCFADT, 2001, p. 135). Much was made of the seven embassies which DFAT had in the Middle East, the four Austrade offices managed by Australian trade commissioners, and the resources which individual states were putting into their efforts for Middle East trade. The Australian Arabic Council had made a submission to this House of Representative's committee for the 'establishment of an Australian Arabic Foundation to oversee the development of closer economic, cultural and political ties'. The Committee endorsed this proposal and noted the significance of other foundations which had been established by DFAT covering countries seen to be 'important to Australia's national interest' (JSCFADT, 2001, p. 137). No mention was made in this Government Report about a need for Arabic language teaching. The Federal government interest in the Middle East now was clearly an economic one. Trade initiatives were to be prioritised although without including the promotion of Arabic language skills for those involved in promoting this trade.

This House of Representatives committee also commended the University of Wollongong for its establishment of a Dubai Campus, which campus in December 1999 had been 'granted a licence by the UAE Ministry for Higher Education and Scientific Research to operate a fully-fledged university campus.' In 2001 this campus offered courses in business and information technology (JSCFADT, 2001, p. 168). There was no mention of Arabic language in the 2001 House of Representatives Report, either in the section on DFAT and Austrade staffing or in the section on the University of Wollongong Dubai Campus. In 2014, the Dubai Campus offered only business, engineering and information technology undergraduate degree courses with English as the language of instruction and a student cohort of many nationalities (University of Wollongong in Dubai, 2014a). Languages courses including Arabic were on offer, but these were non-credit bearing courses, only available in private tuition mode (University of Wollongong in Dubai, 2014b). What was demonstrated by the findings of this Report was that educational ties with the Middle East meant those in-country courses which Australia could market, not the education of Australians in the Arabic language and culture.

Nevertheless, the Council for Australian-Arab Relations (CAAR) had been established by the Australian government through DFAT in 2003 (still in existence at the time of writing) to 'strengthen ties and understanding between Australia and Arab countries', focussing 'primarily on commercial and people-to-people links'

(Downer, 2002, p. 1). Small grants could be sought from CAAR for activities which were relevant to their strategic objectives. Among its educational, cultural and business activities were objectives for the promotion of Arabic language in Australia (CAAR, 2003, p. 3). These were not large sums of money to be spread across a wide range of activities. Despite all the rhetoric about the national interest for Australia of the Arabic-speaking countries, the Government had not matched rhetoric with significant funding to promote Arabic as a language of national importance.

6.9 Waning Support for Arabic in the Universities

In a 2011 report on languages taught in Australian universities, Arabic was still taught at eight universities across four states and territories (Dunne & Pavlyshyn, 2011, p. 18). A subsequent survey by Dunne & Pavlyshyn (2014, p. 16) showed only four universities teaching Arabic. From about 2012 onwards though, there had been declining support for Arabic language teaching with the University of Western Sydney's program being discontinued because of continuing low student numbers. This university had taught Arabic since the early 1980s in one of its previous iterations: the Milperra College of Advanced Education. This course, originally a Bachelor of Arts (Community Languages) continued into the early 2000s. Regardless of the longevity of Arabic teaching, the University of Western Sydney in 2012, decided to discontinue Arabic, and Italian and Spanish as well from 2013 (Callan, 2012, p. 1; Lane, 2012a, Language loss, p. 1). This action was taken despite a funding agreement between the Department of Education, Employment and Workplace Relations and the University of Western Sydney, specified under the Commonwealth Grant Scheme in respect of the 2012 grant year, that Arabic was a Nationally Strategic Language and the University had to consult the Commonwealth government and obtain their approval before closing such a course (Australian Government, 2012, p. 10).

The University of Western Sydney had also been for several years a partner university with the University of Melbourne and Griffith University in the National Centre for Excellence in Islamic Studies. The Centre importantly 'aims to meet the learning needs of aspiring and existing Muslim community leaders, as well as teachers, students and other professionals interested in Islam and Islamic culture' (National Centre for Excellence in Islamic Studies (NCEIS), n.d.). I argue that Arabic at the University of Western Sydney should remain an important priority. Not only has that university a long tradition of teaching Arabic, but it sits in the region of Australia's greatest concentration of Arabic speakers, which should impel the University and the Federal government to take a serious strategic interest in the promotion of Arabic language teaching and understanding of culture, history and politics of the relevant countries. It was reported, in mid-2014, that UWS intended to reintroduce Arabic using the Deakin University curricula and on-campus tutorials. One reason given for this change of decision was that the new vice-chancellor believed that 'the previous decision has not been a felicitous one' (Dunne &

Pavlyshyn, 2014, p. 14). Subsequently Arabic was re-introduced, and new curricula devised in 2016, using Deakin University online materials for consolidation purposes (Chakhachiro, personal communication, 5 February 2018).

6.10 Conclusion

This chapter has demonstrated that the Russian, Korean, and Arabic languages all have significance for the national interest of Australia, although the importance accorded to each has been affected by the prevailing attitudes and priorities of the Federal and State governments of the day. Each of the regions of these three languages continues to have political and strategic significance for Australia in the twenty-first century. Australia's interest in Korea has been, and continues to be, largely one of trade and Korean language certainly had funding prioritisation for a time to enhance trade interests. However, as has been shown, Korean language has not captured enough student interest to compete with the three larger trade languages, Chinese, Japanese and Indonesian.

By contrast Russian and Arabic have never had government funding or promotion to the same extent as the Asian languages. The cachet of Russian language learning for about 40 years in Australia was as a language of great literature. Russian was also important as a scientific language throughout the Cold War as Western Bloc countries sought information on the scientific and technological advances in Russia. As has been described, Russian lost popularity amongst students with the fall of the Soviet Union, but it has remained a significant community language for many migrants. Whilst Arabic had its roots as a scholarly language relating to the history, archaeology and religions of the Middle East, it became a language of significant Australian communities of migration in the latter half of the twentieth century. It is now, with Mandarin and Italian, one of the top three languages spoken at home according to the census of 2011 (Australian Bureau of Statistics, 2011b, p. 9). Unfortunately, although remaining as a government designated Nationally Strategic Language, it has not gathered sufficient and continuous student demand to overcome its vulnerability. The government designation of significance and national importance has shown itself to be unenforceable when tested by declining student demand. I argue that in the light of the current instability in the Middle East and domestic concerns for an objective understanding of Islamic culture and politics in Australia, Arabic remains, quite strongly, a language of national interest to Australia and should be supported and promoted regardless of student numbers.

Text for the Arabic language teaching section of this chapter has been taken from a previously published article. The author acknowledges the permission of Emerald Publishing to reproduce the text taken from the article, The place of Arabic language teaching in Australian universities, *The History of Education Review, 47*(1), pp. 77–86, https://doi.org/10.1108/HER-05-2016-002111

Chapter 7
Languages in the 1990s: The Context and the Changes

> Languages and universities are under siege. (White, Baldauf, & Diller, 1997)

This very forceful statement by White, Baldauf and Diller in their report, *Languages and universities: Under siege,* was presented to the Australian Academy of the Humanities in July 1997. For the university sector this was a time of significant challenge and change, not just with university amalgamations that proceeded in the early 1990s, but also with the shifting priorities and restructuring that affected the curriculum in several institutions, including the teaching of languages. This chapter charts those structural changes across the 1990s. I will show that in the case of languages there was a proliferation of reports and reviews and public debate about language offerings, which affected not only the whole sector generally, but also particular institutions. Some changes led to a greater engagement with Asian languages. Other structural changes were made largely because of increased financial strains within particular institutions that needed to be dealt with in an administratively expedient way. In several universities, structural changes in language departments made languages with smaller enrolments vulnerable, even to the point of extinction. Generally though, there was an increased engagement with not only Asian languages but Asian studies, in both the newer and more established universities.

In 1996, the newly elected conservative Howard government immediately instituted its foreshadowed cuts to university funding (Karmel, 2000, p. 167; Manne, 2001, p. 4), justified by the user pays notion and that 'universities should raise the shortfall in funding from the market' (Singleton, 2000, pp. 4, 5). Whilst some respondents to the survey preceding the 1997 AAH Report, suggested that there was a link (White et al., 1997, p. 21), there is no clear documented evidence of a direct correlation between these funding cuts, and changes to university language teaching. Government funding of universities was obviously significant for operating budgets. Nevertheless, as I will show, there were diverse priorities across the sector. Not all universities had the same organisational structures for the teaching of languages, not all had managed their financial governance to avoid deficits, nor did they set their priorities for languages in the same way.

In 1997, the Coalition Government issued a White Paper, *In the national interest: Australia's foreign and trade policy* (C of A, 1997), stating that 'a country's perception of its national interests is shaped by its geography, history, strategic circumstances and economic profile, as well as by its values' (C of A, 1997, p. 1). Amongst Australia's assets, the Paper trumpeted the cultural diversity of Australia which had come from the immigration of many different cultures (C of A, 1997, p. 35). The White Paper also emphasised the language skills and cultural expertise which this immigration had afforded Australia. It appeared though, that the Government was blind to the ironic contrast between the cuts to universities which obviously affected resources for language teaching along with other areas of teaching, and the above-mentioned linguistic resources of which the Coalition was so proud.

A case study of the University of Melbourne's strategies for languages will be used to guide this exploration of languages instruction in the 1990s. The University of Melbourne's language offerings will firstly be explored, considering why some languages were discontinued whilst others were introduced. I will show that philanthropy had been crucial for the introduction of new languages, but that earlier financial difficulties had led to piecemeal development through a lack of strategic planning. Following is a comparison with other universities, first setting the scene with an overview of universities' language structures in 1991. I argue that the University of Melbourne's changes, implemented in 1992, were unique in Australian universities and led the way with an innovative restructure. The next set of changes to languages at the University of Melbourne in 1998 under the next Vice-Chancellor is then examined, again compared with other universities' language structures to see if the University of Melbourne was setting a trend. Finally, in this chapter I will go behind the structures, examining the actual state of languages in the 1990s: the languages being taught and the number of students enrolled in those languages.

7.1 Comparison of University Languages Structures

By 1991, institutional amalgamations forced by the introduction of the Unified National System, engineered by the Labor Government Minister Dawkins, were nearly complete. Some 46 colleges and institutes and 19 universities were compressed into 36 universities. By 1992 there had been significant increases in university enrolments 'with an accompanying increase in Commonwealth expenditure' (Ryan & Bramston, 2003, p. 193). The Go8 universities were sampled for this comparison, as the University of Melbourne is part of this group which represents nearly all of the oldest established universities in Australia except for the University of Tasmania. As can be seen from Appendix 4, the most common structure for language teaching in 1991 was through a Faculty of Arts or Arts and Social Sciences, with individual departments for each language. That traditional departmental placement of languages within Arts was also common in other institutions at the time

7.1 Comparison of University Languages Structures 163

such as Victoria College (soon to be amalgamated with Deakin University) (VTAC, 1990, p. 119), and Macquarie University (Mansfield & Hutchinson, 1992, p. 183).

Asian languages were sometimes grouped together in a single department such as at the University of Adelaide and Flinders University (Flinders University, n.d.a, Asia Centre). This grouping was the approach used from when Asian languages were first taught at either existing or newly established institutions in the 1970s, and was more likely in those new universities where Asian languages were taught. This may have been a reaction to the encouragement from the 1970 Auchmuty Report of Asian languages and cultures teaching. It may also be due to the long-standing Australian tradition of the teaching of national studies for major European languages. Asian Studies, by contrast, tended to be seen as a single discipline with no clear delineation from the outset of specific national cultures. UWA took a different approach in 1975, teaching Japanese within the Economics department. Mining companies trading with Japan,[1] who had donated funds for Japanese teaching in 1972, wanted that teaching in Japanese linked to 'practical competence in commercial situations rather than the traditional emphasis on literature' (de Garis, 1988, pp. 273, 274).

At ANU, languages were already separated between two faculties, Arts and Asian Studies. This had been the structure since Asian languages, classical and modern, had been first introduced at the CUC in 1952,[2] which was subsumed into the Australian National University in 1960 (Foster & Varghese, 1996, p. 303). It was Griffith University though, where the priority for Asian Studies was reinforced by its establishment of a School of Modern Asian Studies as one of its four foundation Schools with teaching beginning in 1973 (Quirke, 1996, p. 20). Griffith had clearly set its Asian Studies as a distinct 'modern' entity, engaging with contemporary Asia. Indeed, Colin Mackerras, first deputy chair of that School of Modern Asian Studies, paid tribute to Theodore Bray, the first Chancellor, and John Willett, the first Vice-Chancellor, for the foresight they had shown in creating this School at Griffith. Whitlam's China diplomacy, the importance of Japan as a major trading partner and the proximity of Indonesia were all factors in Griffith's decision, illustrated by Chinese, Japanese and Indonesian as the Asian languages first taught. Bray insisted that providing Asian Studies was inescapable logic (Quirke, 1996, p. 20). As Mackerras said, Bray and Willett 'took a pioneering role in introducing Asian and Chinese studies into Griffith University at a time when they were not nearly as fashionable as they are now' (Mackerras, 2006, p. 3). This Asian Studies structure at Griffith was indicative of the structures for languages which had emerged in the new universities.

---

[1] The mining companies were possibly BHP, Hamersley Iron and Rio Tinto which were crucial in that iron ore trade with Japan.

[2] Oriental languages, later Asian languages, were important for the Federal government's push for Asia literacy at the time.

7.2 A Case Study of the University of Melbourne

Since its beginnings, the University of Melbourne has had a rich history of language offerings in modern European, classical, Semitic and Asian languages and the older Germanic languages, Gothic and Old Norse. Dutch, which began in 1942, was the first new language offered as a degree subject in the twentieth century, a language of the European colonialism in the region. Through the next three decades, endowments were crucial for the introduction of new languages (Poynter & Rasmussen, 1996, p. 210; UniMelb, 1942, p. 605, 1946, pp. 707, 708, 1961, p. 614). Both within the University and in the business community, Dutch was seen to be useful for Australia's economic national interests. The Dean of Arts stressed to Vice-Chancellor Medley in July 1941, 'the growing importance of all languages in the Pacific area to Australia's commercial, diplomatic and political relations', and commended the proposal for Dutch 'as one way in which it can serve the long-range interests of Australia' (UMA-Registrar's Correspondence, 1942/201. PB 8/7/41 Item 10. Gibson).

Medley approached Sir Keith Murdoch, a wealthy Melbourne newspaper magnate, in August 1941, for £100 to begin the teaching of Dutch, which Murdoch promptly donated. Murdoch had replied, 'it is vitally important that Australians should make their country better known to their neighbours and know more about their neighbours. This is difficult to achieve because we are so isolated and insulated, but I think you do great work in turning our thoughts that way' (UMA-Registrar's Correspondence, 1942/201. 11/9/41. Murdoch). Some of the refugees from the Dutch East Indies, fleeing the Japanese invasion, joined the small Dutch class in 1942 which had just begun at the University. The irony of the introduction of Dutch was that it was almost irrelevant for Australia's national interest by 1942. The nationalist movement in Indonesia had grown very strong and eventually, in 1949, Indonesia gained its independence. Indonesian was the language of this new nation, not Dutch, although Dutch did continue at the University for another 43 years.

Further expansion of language offerings also came through philanthropy. Ronald Goldman was appointed as Head of Semitic Studies in 1945, a department newly endowed by the Sicree brothers, with funds to support teaching for five years. This endowment was accepted by the University on the understanding that, from 1950 onwards, the University would take on the ongoing funding. Hebrew and Arabic were first taught in 1946, with Aramaic, Ethiopic and Syriac beginning in 1947. Nina Christesen had commented that Goldman fitted well into the intellectual climate of Vice-Chancellor Medley's era at the university (Christesen, 1996, p. 2). Poynter and Rasmussen maintained that Medley had been particularly supportive of the humanities and noted the 'unusually high proportion of … new chairs established between 1943 and 1950' which went to the Faculty of Arts (Poynter & Rasmussen, 1996, p. 79).

Following the 1950 Mills Report which examined the needs of universities (CCNU, 1950, p. 1), a new system of Commonwealth university grants was

7.2 A Case Study of the University of Melbourne

introduced. Unfortunately, the modest increase that the University of Melbourne received was soon outstripped by 'rapidly rising salary rates.' Added to this, there was a loss of income in the value of endowments when interest rates dropped. This was concerning because 'many chairs were completely supported by endowments' (Poynter & Rasmussen, 1996, p. 120). As Poynter said, 'university finances were unpredictable from year to year and developments were funded piecemeal' (Poynter, 2012, p. 2).

A public appeal launched on 13 April 1955, sought funds for capital works, and greater capacity for teaching and research. The appeal brochure, whilst highlighting the university's achievements in the sciences and engineering, made just one mention of languages, noting Melbourne as the only University in Australia and New Zealand teaching Dutch (UniMelb, 1955a). The brochure did not explain, however, why the University felt that Dutch was an important subject in the curriculum. Apart from the Appeal brochure, languages were mentioned in a journal entitled *Discovery* first published in June 1955 to showcase the University's research work (UniMelb, 1955b, p. 3). Chisholm, the Head of the French Department, wrote of the importance of proficiency in foreign languages not just for themselves as an academic discipline, but as an attribute necessary for Australia's national interest: 'apart from the intrinsic interest and value of thought and its expression, our linguistic efficiency, which is a national necessity, depends in the long run on our having people who pursue the study of languages at the most advanced levels' (UniMelb, 1955b, p. 62). More external funding enabled yet another language to be introduced, this time Indonesian, strengthening the cohort of Asian languages taught. As previously mentioned in Chap. 5, that establishment funding had come from the Federal government to the University of Melbourne, the University of Sydney and the Canberra University College in 1955. At the University of Melbourne, a Department of Indonesian and Malayan Studies began with one lecturer in 1956, with a second, appointed at senior lecturer level, in 1959 (UniMelb, 1959, p. 49).

Whilst Italian had been taught in the instructor mode since the 1920s, it was not till the 1950s that a campaign for the teaching of Italian as a degree subject gained momentum, spearheaded by Chisholm and Dr. Soccorso Santoro, a prominent member of the Italian community. Whilst many letters of support were written to The Age newspaper from University staff members, there was also a groundswell of commentary from the Italian community as Santoro mobilised their support (Letters to the Editor- The Melbourne Age, 1956). Eventually in 1959, Italian was approved as a degree subject by the University and was located within the French department where teaching began in 1960 (Chisholm, 1957 p. 9; Griffin, 1988, p. 1; Mayne, 1997, p. 108). The University of Melbourne was not the national leader in the introduction of Italian. The University of Sydney had already taught Italian from 1930 (Turney, Bygott, & Chippendale, 1991, p. 510), and the University of Western Australia had taught Italian from 1929 (UWA, 1929, pp. 138, 155).

This pattern of language development enabled by philanthropy continued. It was a very large donation (eight annual amounts of £8000 each) from the Myer Foundation, which enabled the University of Melbourne to establish a School of Oriental Studies with a professorial chair (UMA-Registrar's Correspondence,

1961/986/107, 108- 12 October, 1960. Myer; UMA-Registrar's Correspondence, 1961/987/26- 5 September, 1961. Simon). Such a School had been discussed by the University as far back as 1941, but the University simply did not have the finances to fund Asian studies. Chinese was first taught from 1962, with Japanese re-introduced as a degree subject in 1965 (UMA-Registrar's Correspondence, 1961/986/21- 28 April, 1941. Gibson; UMA-Registrar's Correspondence, 1961/987/18, 19- 5 September, 1961. Simon). In the University's 1960 Annual Report, the importance of external funds for Asian studies and languages was highlighted. These included the Oriental Studies Chair, the monies provided by the Indian Council for Cultural Relations and the Spalding Trust, Oxford for Indian Studies, and monies provided by the Government of Pakistan and the Spalding Trust for Islamic Studies. 'These new establishments should do much to increase our knowledge and understanding of Middle and Far Eastern peoples and their cultures' said the Vice-Chancellor, George Paton (UniMelb, 1961, p. 600). However, the University of Melbourne had been quite slow to establish Oriental Studies and was merely catching up with the University of Sydney and the Canberra University College where Oriental Studies' departments had been established in 1917 and 1952 respectively.

Whilst Oriental Studies began with much fanfare and considerable funds, another language had quietly been introduced in the Department of Germanic Languages but with more modest external funding. Augustin Lodewyckx, the retired Head of Germanic Languages and his wife Anna, 'donated £6,000 in 1960 as the initial finance to start the teaching of Swedish.' They donated a further '£1000 to the Baillieu Library for Swedish books' (Martin, 2007, p. 17). Swedish was yet another language which had been first taught at the University under the instructorship scheme. Following the Lodewyckxs' donation, a generous grant was received from the Swedish government in 1964 to finance Swedish teaching until 1966. The assumption was that after 1966, the University would take on the financial responsibility for the subject (Martin, 1967, p. 32). Given the linguistic relationship between Swedish and Old Norse, it might be assumed that Swedish was introduced as a modern alternative to Old Norse. However, an examination of the papers of Ian Maxwell, former Professor of English and Old Norse enthusiast and teacher, and discussions with a former student of Old Norse, Chris Wallace-Crabbe, did not lend weight to this notion. Whilst Maxwell did assist in the selection of the first Swedish lecturer, Old Norse and its great medieval literature and sagas stood apart from Swedish (Paton, 1964, p. 1; Wallace-Crabbe, personal communication, 17 March 2014). These Old Norse Honours offerings were eventually discontinued in the late 1980s. Old Norse, which re-emerged in 1985 within an undergraduate subject, Viking Language, Literature and Culture, continued till 2006 when it too was discontinued (UniMelb, 1984, p. 458; UniMelb. (2006). Swedish itself was eventually discontinued in 2012.

So, by the middle of the 1960s, the major languages taught at the University of Melbourne in degree programs were Latin, Ancient Greek, French, Italian, German, Swedish, Dutch, Russian, Hebrew, Indonesian/Malayan, Arabic, Chinese and Japanese (UniMelb, 1964, pp. 55–60). Most of these languages owed their

7.2 A Case Study of the University of Melbourne

beginnings to some form of endowment by private individuals or from government sources. The two exceptions were Russian, introduced in a degree program in 1946, and Italian. The uncertainty which flowed from this type of funding was whether the University itself was prepared to pick up the ongoing funding of a particular language when endowments ceased. Of all these languages, Dutch and Swedish were not taught by any other Australian university (Wykes, 1966, p. 27).

As the University continued to have financial problems in the late 1960s, with the AUC recommending just over 70% of the recurrent funds which the University had sought, the possibility of the University picking up new language funding remained uncertain (Poynter & Rasmussen, 1996, p. 299). At this time also, the Myer Foundation funding for Oriental Studies would have ceased (UMA-Registrar's Correspondence, 1961/987/26- 5 September, 1961. Simon). Asian languages departments at the University of Melbourne were struggling to gain the student interest and numbers they needed to survive. By 1971, the Departments of Oriental Studies and Indonesian and Malayan Studies were amalgamated in what Poynter and Rasmussen called 'an arranged marriage, a sop to throw to the ravening rationalisers' (Poynter & Rasmussen, 1996, p. 373). Whilst Indian Studies was also struggling, and the Bengali major reduced to a terminal first year subject from 1970, it did not join in the departmental marriage of convenience (Poynter & Rasmussen, 1996, p. 373). Hindi, which started in 1976 with just two students, remained as a listed subject,[3] but had no students in the next three years (Hawley, 1982, p. 48).

Whilst Asian languages were struggling to consolidate their student numbers, discussions had begun about the need for a lectureship or chair in Modern Greek at the University of Melbourne. These were prompted by a push for Modern Greek to be introduced as an examinable subject in the Victorian school system in 1966 which required the necessary local academics as external examiners for the Matriculation examinations. Harold Hunt, the Professor of Classical Greek, was an ambivalent advocate for the establishment of Modern Greek. In his memo to the Victorian Universities and Schools Examinations Board (VUSEB) on 11 September 1966, he wrote:

> There is a case for this [the introduction] in that children of Greek origin should have the opportunity to maintain knowledge of their original language. It is also important that Australians should be able to communicate with Greek migrants. One factor of importance is that the study of Modern Greek should not divert students from Classical Greek which is of supreme value for the understanding of Western civilisation, its literature, thought and art. (UMA-Registrar's Correspondence. Policy File No. 13/23/12. 11 September, 1966. Hunt)

Discussions did not proceed quickly. The next correspondence on the subject in the Registrar's Correspondence archives of the University was dated June 1968. Hunt wrote again to the Vice-Chancellor, David Derham:

---

[3] It is possible that Hindi was enabled to continue with such poor numbers given the earlier external funds which had been given in the 1960s, although no evidence had been found to support this contention.

If Modern Greek were established it would be desirable not to have a Chair since the language itself is not of high educational value (although it would be politic not to tell the Greek Community this.) On the other hand, a lectureship held by a thoroughly well-trained academic competent also in classical Greek would be an advantage to either us or to Monash. (UMA-Registrar's Correspondence. Policy File No. 13/23/12. 21 June, 1968. Hunt, p. 1)

Hunt went on to say that the Greek community should be informed of the costs of financing a lectureship, but he also warned the Vice-Chancellor that there were different factions in the Greek community and to be careful with which groups any negotiations were conducted (UMA-Registrar's Correspondence. Policy File No. 13/23/12. 21 June, 1968. Hunt, p. 2). Subsequently, in October 1970, a Modern Greek Lectureship Appeal was launched with Sir Robert Menzies, former Prime Minister, as the patron. In April 1973, Vice-Chancellor Derham issued a press release to announce the establishment of a lectureship in Modern Greek at the University. This had been made possible he said because of the 'many hundreds of individual donations received from members of the Greek community[4] in Victoria, from Melbourne businessmen and from members of the University staff. The Greek Government also gave $35,000 and about one thousand books' (UMA-Registrar's Correspondence. File No. 13-23-12. Part 1. Derham- Press Release, 5/4/1973; UniMelb, 1970).

Contemporaneously with the beginning of a lectureship at the University was the teaching of Modern Greek in Victorian secondary schools. Further money from the University's General Development Grant on the recommendation of the AUC, made the continuation of tertiary teaching possible. Even with this triumph of a public appeal enabling a lectureship in Modern Greek to begin at the University of Melbourne in 1974, the University of Sydney had already secured funding for a Chair. Whilst the public appeal in Melbourne took several years to raise the necessary funds, the University of Sydney had received a single donation of $100,000 in 1968 from Nicholas Laurantus, a financier and grazier, and Greek immigrant, who felt 'that Greek immigrants should know and love their own language and culture' (Michaelides, 2000, p. 2). This generous gift enabled the University of Sydney to establish a Chair of Modern Greek in 1970 with teaching beginning in 1974, although the Chair was not filled till 1983 by Michael Jeffreys, the lecturer who had joined the staff in 1976 (Connell, Sherington, Fletcher, Turney, & Bygott, 1995, p. 135).

During the 1970s when community or migrant languages became more prominent in both secondary school and tertiary sectors, just two new languages had been introduced at the University of Melbourne, Modern Greek in 1974 and Hindi in 1976. Italian, a significant community language, had been taught within a degree program since 1960. Modern Greek flourished, with student numbers rivalling the numbers taking German and Italian by 1980 (Hawley, 1982, p. 48). The Galbally Report was published in May 1978 in English and nine other languages: Arabic,

---

[4] Greek-born Victorians numbered 79,048 according to the 1971 ABS census. There would also have been many more Australians of Greek heritage.

Dutch, German, Greek, Italian, Serbo-Croatian, Spanish, Turkish, and Vietnamese. Of these languages, the University of Melbourne taught Arabic, Dutch, German, Greek and Italian. Indeed, professorial chairs had been created in 1975 for Italian as well as Russian. Modern Greek and Italian were now well represented nationally in the university and advanced education sectors. Hawley's 1974–1981 tertiary statistics showed Italian offered at 11 universities and 14 colleges of advanced education, and Modern Greek at four universities and eight colleges of advanced education (Hawley, 1982, pp. 7, 9, 76, 79).

Given the social and political prominence of migrant languages in the 1970s, it was clearly a time for language offerings to be expanded in the tertiary sector. Even in the institutes and colleges which had embraced the newer migrant languages more readily than the universities, the numbers were small. As for the University of Melbourne, it was not one of the leaders in offering the newer and smaller migrant languages. This was happening in other tertiary institutions. Flinders University, for instance, offered Latvian, Portuguese, Spanish and Romanian, and the University of Wollongong offered Serbo-Croatian and Spanish. Prahran CAE offered Modern Hebrew, Yiddish, and Croatian and Serbian. Melbourne State College offered Maltese, Spanish, Vietnamese and Turkish (Hawley, 1982, pp. 11–13, 64, 66, 69). The University of Melbourne's largest student enrolments in languages in 1980 and 1981 were in French, German, Italian and Modern Greek, with French by far the most popular language. At that time, Spanish was not offered at the University of Melbourne but both Monash and La Trobe Universities were attracting reasonable student numbers for this language (C of A, 1978, pp. 105, 107; Hawley, 1982, pp. 18, 41, 44, 47–49, 65–67, 69, 80; Poynter & Rasmussen, 1996, p. 397).

By 1982, a variety of languages were taught at the University of Melbourne in eight of the 18 departments of the Faculty of Arts, with French and Germanic Studies the largest and oldest modern languages departments (UniMelb, 1982, pp. 36, 38, 39, 40, 41). However, because of 'current financial stringencies and both University and Commonwealth Tertiary Education Commission pressure', and 'pressures on staffing', two restructures took place from 1983: The Department of Russian and the Horwood Language Centre were merged, as were the Departments of Indian Studies and Indonesian and Malayan Studies (UniMelb, 1983, pp. 10, 11). At this juncture in the early 1980s, student numbers for Dutch and Swedish language were faltering. Swedish survived, but Dutch lasted until 1991 when an Arts Faculty vote at the November meeting abruptly terminated the teaching of Dutch without debate, with the concession allowing it to be taught out in 1992. Bruce Donaldson, the Dutch lecturer at the time, recollected that German numbers had risen enormously after the fall of the Berlin Wall and there was no money for additional German staff, so this was a cost-saving measure as he was to be switched from Dutch to German teaching. He claimed 'small languages were easy targets' (UniMelb. Faculty of Arts Minutes, 1991; Donaldson, personal communication, 5 February, 2014).

Nevertheless, the 1984 Arts Faculty Annual Report stated that 'the Faculty is probably the most wide-ranging teacher of foreign languages at the tertiary level in Australia, and therefore has a strong interest in the growing public discussion of the need for a national policy towards the teaching of languages' (UniMelb, 1985, p. 9). There was further restructuring of language departments again in 1988: the new Department of Asian Languages and Anthropology now encompassed Chinese, Japanese, Indonesian and Hindi teaching (UniMelb, 1988a, p. 35). Languages were still not free from mergers of departments. By the end of 1988, a single Department of Classical and Near Eastern Studies had been formed, bringing Ancient Greek, Latin, Modern Greek, Hebrew, Arabic, and the postgraduate Semitic languages, Akkadian, Aramaic, Ethiopic, Ugaritic, and Syriac, into the same structure (UniMelb, 1989a, p. 39, 1991b, p. 19). However, it is important to note that enrolments for these languages were small and that the particular strength of this department was its studies in history, archaeology, culture and religion. Unfortunately, the postgraduate Semitic languages were taught only up until 2003 and then disappeared from the handbook. Syriac and Egyptian were revived as undergraduate units in 2012, with Akkadian taught occasionally in intensive mode (SHAPS. UniMelb, 2014, p. 1).

7.3 A Review of Languages

From the 1988 Dawkins reforms, various amalgamations of institutions were taking place as the Unified National System took shape (Penington, 2010, p. 246; UniMelb, 1989a, p. 5). David Penington had become the Vice-Chancellor at the University of Melbourne from 1 January 1988, succeeding David Caro. Penington was keen that the University have a strategic plan as this had not previously been part of the management strategy. In his first strategic plan entitled *Looking to the future*, objectives for the next three years included a restructure of language programs to be more responsive to 'national needs', a commitment to studies with an international dimension, and an expansion of the teaching of English as a second language. How language programs were to be made more responsive to 'national needs' was not spelled out, although there was reference to the University's interest in Asian languages, and a greater understanding of the place of Australia in the Asian-Pacific region (UniMelb, 1988b, pp. 5, 19; UniMelb, 1991a, p. 3). Penington also wanted the teaching priorities and budgetary requirements for the language departments of the Faculty of Arts reviewed (Penington, personal communication, 6 August 2012). All language teaching was to be reviewed, but this review was set in the context of a greater emphasis on Asian languages. In that sense the University was also turning its attention towards Asia, a symptom of the 1990s.

In his second strategic plan for 1991–1993, Penington's goals included the strengthening of teaching and research in languages other than English, with particular emphasis on Asian languages and Asian studies. Also mentioned in that plan was the review of Asian languages and studies being conducted by Stephen Fitzgerald from the University of New South Wales (UniMelb, 1991a, pp. 9, 19,

7.3 A Review of Languages

1992c, p. 20). As Penington recollected about this time: 'We needed to be preparing our students for careers in the world not just in local professions and that involved a review of our relationship with Asia which was starting to develop as an important area, but also other languages which would interface with Europe. It was broader than just language; it was a whole cultural interface with Asia that became part of our commitment as a university' (Penington, personal communication, 6 August 2012).

Fitzgerald submitted his report entitled *Asia in the University of Melbourne: a review* to the University's Joint Committee on Policy (JCP) in December 1991 (UniMelb, 1992a, pp. 838–873). Whilst Asian studies and languages had been the main brief for this report, Fitzgerald also commented on languages other than English in general, and the 'fragmented nature of language organisation at the University' (UniMelb, 1992b, p. 710). The Review's recommendation was

> that there should be a School of Modern Languages in the Faculty of Arts embracing both modern Asian languages and modern European languages and the applied elements of Linguistics. The rationale for this is not to use the strong to buttress the weak, but to re-establish foreign languages as central to the humanities in the University, for intellectual and cultural and social science, and science and professional and communicative reasons and not immediately for utilitarian purposes. (UniMelb, 1992d, p. 858)

This recommendation, said Fitzgerald, was made on the basis that 'there are sufficient elements in common in learning and teaching a foreign language to warrant treating modern languages as a discipline' (UniMelb, 1992d, p. 858). This was an important point of pedagogy for bringing all modern languages studies together under the one structure.

At its October 1992 meeting, the Joint Committee agreed that 'the School of Languages be established within the Faculty of Arts with an earmarked budget for a period of five years' (UniMelb, 1992b, p. 693). The JCP stressed the national and economic imperatives for languages noting that 'there is an urgent national need to improve the quality and quantity of LOTE acquisition. Australia's future depends largely on the quality of its involvement with the global economy, and its capacity to communicate across cultures - particularly those of the region' (UniMelb, 1992a, p. 711). The JCP adopted the organising principle of 'mainstreaming' all languages, to make them accessible to students across all faculties. They encouraged the development of Asian studies and research across the University, acknowledging also a major new initiative, the Asia Education Foundation to be established to 'spearhead developments in the school system' (UniMelb, 1992b, p. 692). They reiterated that to be a major international university in a new century, an Australian university must be literate in many ways, and encompass not just Britain and Europe, but Asia (UniMelb, 1992d, p. 844).

From the minuted JCP discussions, it was clear that the University of Melbourne was reiterating its position as a quality university committed to internationalisation. Whilst reviewing the quality of teaching and pedagogy and administrative structures for languages other than English, the review was also looking outwards to the place of the University nationally and internationally. All this was very much in line with the goals of the 1991 strategic plan, *A Commitment to Quality* (UniMelb, 1991a, p. 9). The University intended 'to enhance the international reputation of the University through the quality of its educational and research programmes, by continuing to provide international educational opportunities for overseas and local students, and by strengthening teaching and research in languages other than English, with particular emphasis on Asian languages and Asian studies' (UniMelb, 1991a, p. 9; UniMelb, 1992a, p. 17). The University's major shift was the Asian languages emphasis.

This review of, and commitment to, languages at the University of Melbourne coincided with the introduction of the new Victorian Certificate of Education (VCE) in Victoria. Over a period of some four years, the certificate awarded for completion of Year 12 transitioned from a one-year Higher School Certificate to a two-year Victorian Certificate of Education awarded for the first time for the year 1992 (VTAC, 1989, p. 2, 1991, p. 4, 1992, p. 5). As Penington recollected, the universities had begun joint discussions about selection processes encompassing student results of the VCE: 'we wanted recognition of languages other than English as an important subject. …We began to have discussions within the university late 1991 and early 1992 about how we would give recognition for people taking a second language. … My memory is that we got that through by the end of 1992 for selection into the university for 1993' (Penington, personal communication, 6 August 2012). That recognition took the form of 'a bonus of 10% of the maximum possible score… awarded to an applicant who obtains a grade average of at least D[5] for a language other than English study in the Victorian Certificate of Education or equivalent qualification' (UniMelb Council Minutes, 1992, meeting no. 3, 4 May, Item 2.2.11).

Whilst Penington was speaking particularly about internal discussions, these bonus points for languages were decided upon jointly by all Victorian universities and administered in the selection process by the Victorian Tertiary Admissions Centre. Such a joint decision was a commitment by them all to the importance of languages other than English (LOTE). This commitment to languages thus extended into the secondary school system by means of the bonus points allocated in tertiary selection. The first manifestation of this bonus for languages happened in selection for the 1993 academic year. Although there was considerable statistical analysis of VCE student results for the 1993 selection year, there was however, no mention of the efficacy of the LOTE bonus for selection in the minutes of subsequent Selection Procedures Committee meetings for the whole of 1993 (UniMelb, 1993, p. 3). Given the importance accorded to the bonus points for LOTE decision, it would have been expected that some evaluation might have been sought about the effect of the language bonus points.

---

[5] The scale used was the letter grades A, B, C, D, E.

7.4 The New School of Languages at the University of Melbourne

The languages now available through this new School were Arabic, Indonesian, Russian, German, Swedish, French, Italian, Japanese and Chinese. Dutch had been discontinued in 1992 (UniMelb, 1993, pp. 41, 43, 46). Ivan Barko, a language academic who had held Chairs previously at Monash and Sydney Universities, was the foundation head of the School of Languages. He came out of retirement to undertake this role in 1993, for initially 12 months which was extended to 18 months. Barko recollected: 'I was tempted by the challenge and more specifically by the assurance that the Vice-Chancellor was determined to support the revival of languages. …This was an unusual, indeed a unique position: languages are usually just tolerated by universities rather than actively promoted' (Barko, personal communication, 11 March, 2013). In his farewell lecture in June 1994, he commented: 'The University's recent commitment to languages also brought with it increased resources and needs-based rather than formula-based funding for a period of protected growth during which the School will have to prove its viability' (Barko, 1994, p. 17). Barko was reiterating that funding was a crucial part of the implementation of the new School, a point which Fitzgerald had made in his review:

> If the University is committed to change, and accepts the broad direction of the recommendations of this review, the funding mechanisms in the faculties, particularly but not only in the Faculty of Arts, and the tyranny of student demand which inhibits the extent to which it is possible to move in the advance of demand, requires that the central administration provided earmarked funds. (UniMelb, 1992a, p. 12)

This new School was therefore not primarily a cost-cutting measure. By its foundation the University had demonstrated not only a commitment to the place of languages but to the adequate funding of languages. Barko went on to say: 'it is a federation of language departments each with a fair measure of autonomy and a federal management structure of a consultative and democratic style' (Barko, 1994, p. 17). The School of Languages 'was called upon to play its part in the internationalisation of the campus, and mainstreaming language programs across the University was one of the aims of the enterprise. Offering concurrent language diplomas to students enrolled in other faculties is the means we have chosen to achieve our objective' (Barko, 1994, pp. 17, 18). The University of Melbourne had its first intake of students in the Diploma of Modern Languages in 1995 (UniMelb, 1995, p. 3). Other universities around the country followed suit: the University of Sydney in 1996 (UniSyd, 1996, pp. 180, 232), the University of Adelaide in 1998 (University of Adelaide, 1998, p. 241), and Monash University and the University of Western Australia by 1999 (Monash University, 1998, p. 25; UWA, 1998, p. 28).

In his third and last strategic plan, for 1994–1996, Penington reiterated again the importance of 'languages other than English and the study of foreign cultures' as core parts 'of the creation of an international university' (UniMelb, 1994, p. 8). Recollecting that time of change in the School of Languages, Penington said, 'I was thrilled by the completely changed culture and commitment to students and good outcomes in language teaching and the fact that it was attracting students from many different faculties in their Diploma in Modern Languages (Penington, personal communication, 6 August 2012). Colin Nettelbeck, who had come to the University of Melbourne as the Professor of French and Head of French and Italian Studies in 1994 (becoming the Head of the School of Languages in 2000), commented on the way the School of Languages had been created:

> we talked at the time of mainstreaming languages which was putting languages in the University in a place where they would be available for all students hence the creation of the Diploma of Languages. The other key factor at the time (there were several underpinning axioms or beliefs at the time the School was created), is for any language to do well, all languages need to do well. When all languages thrive, Asian languages thrive. For the first time in my memory languages were not under threat, they were the flavour of the month and for three or four years that lasted. (Nettelbeck, personal communication, 13 October 2011)

Penington had been a real supporter of all languages for the University throughout his term as vice-chancellor. As Nettelbeck said of the creation of the School of Languages, 'it was a brave and a bold move, and a correct move.' But, as Nettelbeck further signalled in his recollections, the solidarity of that federation of language departments into a School did not last (Nettelbeck, personal communication, 13 October, 2011).

The vision of the new Vice-Chancellor, Alan Gilbert, was rather different to that of Penington. In late December 1997 (Stephens, personal communication, 19 September 2013), Gilbert decided that Asian languages and societies needed to have 'more visible focus and prominence', and needed to be placed 'on a sound long-term financial footing' (UniMelb. Executive Committee Minutes, 1/97, Item 3.6.3 (tabled) p. 139). His intention was to create an Institute of Asian Languages and Societies located within the Faculty of Arts together with the School of Languages. This Institute would 'enhance the reputation of the capacity of the University of Melbourne in these fields' of Asian languages and societies. However, the Institute was to be provided with 'the necessary budgetary and structural autonomy to provide a focus for developments across the relevant faculties of the University as a whole' (UniMelb. Executive Committee Minutes, 1/97, Item 3.6.3 (tabled) p. 140). This action, of emphasising Asian languages and culture and internationalisation, which changed language structures again at the University, was symptomatic of much of the 1990s.

This decision had not been signalled in Gilbert's strategic plan of 1997–2001, despite the statement in that plan that 'changing the educational profile and functional obligations of a university (therefore) involves considerable forward planning' (UniMelb, 1997, p. 2). Although not spelled out in Council meeting minutes, there was also consequent general budgetary savings with the reduction of the number of individual budgetary units. The University nevertheless did not fund these new measures alone. Philanthropic support was obtained from the Myer Foundation which had already supported the Chair of Oriental Studies at the University back in 1960. The Sidney Myer Asia Centre, a new building in a prominent position, begun in 1999, was an excellent marketing backdrop to this new approach to Asian languages and societies (UniMelb, 1999a, p. 27).

The Executive Committee noted the Gilbert proposals on 22 December 1997, with a subsequent announcement in the Vice-Chancellor's Report to Council in March 1998, that the Melbourne Institute of Asian Languages and Societies (MIALS) had been established on behalf of Council from 1 February 1998 (UniMelb Council Minutes, Meeting no. 1/1998, Item 7). Under the interim director, Boris Schedvin, MIALS' teaching of Arabic, Chinese, Indonesian, Japanese, and related cultural subjects, began in October 1998 (UniMelb, 1998a, p. 102). As can be seen by the short period of time between the proposal coming before Council, and the actual announcement of the new Institute, there was a paucity of planning leading up to this decision to create MIALS. Nevertheless, the Gilbert plan of 1997–2001 was certainly couched in terms of international positioning, the need to encourage international engagement, and the need for the University to 'persuade Government and informed public opinion that world class higher education is imperative in the national interest' (UniMelb, 1997, pp. 5, 10). However, unlike Penington's strategic plans of 1988 and 1991, stressing a greater commitment to foreign languages (UniMelb, 1988b, p. 5), the international dimension, and a major review of the University's Asian languages and studies, Gilbert's 1997–2001 strategic plan spoke only of 'encouraging the study of languages other than English' (UniMelb, 1997, p. 10).

Whilst these structural changes were occurring at the University of Melbourne, the commissioned 1997 AAH Report had signalled by its title the belief that universities and languages were under siege. This came from a perception of most the respondents surveyed that they were under threat because of reduced funding (White et al., 1997, p. 21). This did not seem to be the case at the University of Melbourne as funding had not been reduced for languages. Whilst Asian languages were being promoted, the teaching of another European language, Russian, had closed at the University of Melbourne in 1998. The uncertainty for, and vulnerability of, this language was illustrated by the fact that, for the next three years, Russian at Melbourne was taught to a very small student cohort, through a collaborative arrangement, by Monash staff. Then, in 2002, Melbourne again re-introduced Russian, with the influence of Nettelbeck, the then Head of the School of Languages, aided by a large bequest (Lagerberg, personal communication, 23 February 2014).

7.5 Other Universities' Languages Structures in 1999

By 1999, when the University of Melbourne had created the MIALS, there were changes in other universities' structures. Some universities had initiated change in the late 1990s for pedagogical reasons, also citing academic rigour and administrative efficiency as being of prime importance. Whilst University of Melbourne's stated reason for its 1998 changes was the need to give greater prominence and focus to Asian languages, in other universities it was for financial reasons that change occurred: citing budget deficits and government funding cuts and that Asian languages had not, by contrast been given greater prominence. Appendix 5 shows language department structures in major universities in 1999.

An investigation of these 1999 structures does not, however, point to an emulation of the Melbourne model of MIALS by other universities, although both Monash University and the University of Sydney had instituted major structural changes. At Monash University in June 1998, Vice-Chancellor David Robinson instituted a review of the Faculty of Arts with subsequent drastic downsizing, given the desired model was a tighter structure of departments which, of course, had significant financial savings. By 1999, Monash Arts had a faculty structure of ten schools as opposed to the 14 departments of the early 1990s (Monash University, 1992, p. 1, 1998, p. 3, 1999, p. 24). The then Dean of Arts at Monash, Marian Quarterly, in recollecting this very difficult and stressful time for Arts Faculty staff, said that, whilst they at Monash were aware of the changes for languages at the University of Melbourne, these were not an influence on what happened at Monash (Quarterly, personal communication, 18 September 2013). At Monash, language teaching was caught up in the push for downsizing. Quarterly herself felt strongly that the most appropriate model was two separate Schools for Asian and European languages, and this was the structure kept in place for another few years. Unfortunately, in the downsizing push, several smaller languages were closed when the enrolled student numbers did not meet the mandated minimum class size. A 2006 retrospective survey on language offerings showed that by the late 1990s, Monash no longer offered Hindi, Khmer, Polish, Russian, Sanskrit, Serbo-Croatian or Vietnamese (White & Baldauf, 2006, p. 56). However by 2002, under a new Dean, the Faculty had to capitulate to the Vice-Chancellor's wish for a single School of Languages, Cultures and Linguistics where all languages were taught, Asian, Classical and Modern European, which was the structure adopted at the University of Sydney (Quarterly, personal communication, 18 September 2013).

According to Tony Stephens, who became the Foundation Head of the School of European, Asian and Middle Eastern Languages and Studies at the University of Sydney in 2000, the change in the Faculty of Arts from some 17 schools/departments, with their own heads and general staff, to four Schools with one head of each, was principally a financial decision. Stephens claimed that, in the preceding review of the Faculty's finances, it was felt that a new structure was required to deal with a large deficit. Considerable savings were achieved in that restructure when senior academic staff were replaced, if at all, with academic staff with lower classifications (Stephens, personal communication, 19 September 2013). Stephen Garton, the Pro-Dean of Arts in 1999, recalled that a fundamental reason for the restructure was to resolve a decade of annual budget deficits. Too many unconnected small departments had 'created administrative complexity and chaos'. The creation of schools and thus larger organisational units facilitated tighter budget oversight.

Garton went on to say that financially the new structure proved to be an important contributing factor in eradicating the deficit (Garton, personal communication,

7.5 Other Universities' Languages Structures in 1999

14 October 2013). Whilst this new structure for languages at the University of Sydney brought about in 1999, was almost identical to that of the University of Melbourne's School of Languages created in 1992, the reasons for each university's actions were quite different. Sydney's 1999 language restructure was couched in terms of financial restraint, rather than as a positive promotion of languages which Melbourne had achieved in 1992. The University of Sydney did, in its strategic plan of 1999–2004, speak of the importance of internationalisation, but there was no reference to languages as an integral part (UniSyd, 2000, p. 23). This was in stark contrast to the University of Melbourne's 1991 strategic plan where a commitment to languages was part of the push for greater internationalisation of the University (UniMelb, 1991a, p. 9).

The 1999 structures for languages at the Australian National University had not changed since 1991, with Asian languages in the Faculty of Asian Studies and all other languages in Arts. Nevertheless, the impetus for restructuring in Arts was, said Dean Paul Thom in March 1998, that the budget deficit had to be reduced. One of the proposals circulated for discussion by Thom, was that no 'European languages would be taught at degree level.' He said that he was forced to assess the place of language teaching within the faculty because of government funding cuts and a need to find budget savings. He also commented that he had been challenged by non-languages members of the Arts Faculty as to whether 'language teaching, particularly *ab initio* has any place in a university arts faculty' (Thom in Harvey, 1998, p. 37). There was an outcry from staff and students about the cuts in general, and the driving down of numbers in Russian specifically, by the University (Thom in Harvey, 1998, p. 37; Windle, 1998, p. 1). Thom, in his final decision, chose less drastic options. Although the net result was fewer staff redundancies, Russian teaching was still to be closed down, and there was to be some reduction of other language majors (Office of the Vice-Chancellor, ANU, 1998, pp. 1, 2). Nonetheless, according to one ANU language academic, modern languages were decimated by staff cuts and program closures at that time (Martin, M. 2005, p. 70).

Following this discussion of other universities' languages structures, this analysis returns to what the University of Melbourne had achieved. The case study of the University of Melbourne's history of language offerings up to 1992 has shown the importance of endowments from influential citizens, the commitment of academics to languages, but also the slowness to embrace the community languages notwithstanding the push from various ethnic communities. What is also obvious is that, in this institution, the commitment of the vice-chancellor to review and change was very powerful in bringing about that subsequent change. This was apparent in: the choice of the academic to review the University's languages, the ability of the vice-chancellor to 'bring others along' with him in that strategy, the commitment of the necessary financial resources and the choice of an external and very experienced academic to lead the newly-formed School of Languages. However it is also apparent that another vice-chancellor, Gilbert, with a rather different focus was able to institute, albeit rather swiftly, another substantial change.

Elsewhere in the sector in the latter half of the 1990s, there were financial challenges, which simply did not allow for new and innovative structures for languages amongst their priorities. In the case of the University of Sydney, the vice-chancellor decided to meet those financial challenges. The resulting structures, however, were a reaction to the critical financial situation in which they found themselves, rather than a positive initiative. In the case of Monash, the changes were mooted as tightening up administration and reporting, but an undeniable outcome was the financial savings.

7.6 Political Implications for Languages

As Thom at ANU had stated, there were funding cuts for universities when the Coalition government took government in March 1996 after 13 years of Labor government. Higher education matters were still under the Employment, Education and Training portfolio which had Youth Affairs added (Wettenhall, 2000, p. 88). Amanda Vanstone, the first minister of this DEETYA portfolio, angered vice-chancellors when, in May 1996, she hinted at very large budget cuts for universities (Armitage, 1996, p. 2). In the first Coalition budget in August 1996, universities suffered 'severe' funding cuts (Cater, 2006, p. 220; Manne, 2001, p. 4). Prime Minister Howard and Treasurer Peter Costello maintained that their government would work towards budget surpluses and become defined as a 'surplus strategy government' (Kelly, 2008, p. 4). These funding cuts hit the social and pure sciences, and the humanities where languages were usually located. A 2000 AAH survey, *Subjects of small enrolment in the humanities: Enhancing their future,* summed up the decade, reporting a loss of 88 language teaching positions and extrapolating that the loss would be 'at least 100 language teaching positions in the four years 1996–1999, and with some more to come' (AAH, 2000, p. 43). They also reported a consequent loss of the number of languages being taught in Australian universities, from 66 down to 53 (AAH, 2000, p. 44; White et al., 1997). Unfortunately, these cuts coincided with the Asian financial crisis so that, as the languages researcher Mario Martin contended, 'even the instrumental reasons that maintained the teaching of Asian languages lost ground' (Martin, M. 2005, p. 69). The 2000 AAH Report also commented on the 'volatility in the take-up of some of the Asian languages which are important for strategic and commercial purposes' (AAH, 2000, pp. 41, 42).

The Government had stressed the need for proficiency in Asian languages in its 1997 White Paper as an important element in Australia's engagement with Asia and understanding of Asia (C of A, 1997, p. 80). The NALSAS (National Asian Languages and Studies in Australian Schools) program beginning in 1995 had distributed funding for government and non-government schools for Asian languages. Nevertheless, there were no financial incentives for any other languages in the university sector, let alone Asian languages, despite the rhetoric of the 1997 White Paper.

7.7 Reports from the Academic Sector

Whilst the Federal Government had not taken any financial interest in languages other than English in the university sector, the sector itself, particularly those committed to, and concerned about, the state of languages, had a lot to say in several reports in the latter years of the 1990s. The AAH had commissioned a report in May 1997 specifically as part of their submission to the West review on higher education, financing and policy. The West review aimed to produce a policy and financing framework to enable the sector to meet Australia's future economic and social needs (Higher Education Financing & Policy Review Committee. (HEFPRC), 1998, p.1).

The in-house working title for this AAH Report was 'Tertiary Languages in the National Interest: New Imperatives for Planning'. The data-based Report submitted by the consultants to AAH was formally published under the title of *Languages and Universities: Under Siege* (White et al., 1997), then submitted to the West review. The consultants undertaking the study sought to examine hypotheses 'related to program change and the impact of that change on the teaching of languages' (White et al., 1997, p. 2). The first hypothesis they wished to test was, 'that the changes occurring in language programs were threatening the capacity to teach some languages at all, or to maintain the quality of language programs.' The second hypothesis was 'that there was a need for restructuring and that the changes occurring were not having a significant impact on languages' (White et al., 1997, p. 2).

In their conclusions, the consultants pointed out that, a casual glance at the table of language offerings for 1997 in their Report, could suggest a healthy climate for languages. However, they cautioned that their findings in the rest of their Report showed 'languages in a somewhat parlous state,' and that added weight to their first hypothesis (White et al., 1997, p. 25). They cited instances of language losses in the European and classical languages, and the greater costs of running many of the European language departments as they tended to have more senior staff. They contrasted these costs with the lower costs of the newer Asian programs often staffed with contractual staff on lower academic levels.

Substantial staff attrition, the consultants said, was particularly serious, citing instances of senior staff retiring or being made redundant, being replaced by fewer staff, part-time or casual staff, or not being replaced at all. Underlying all of this was the concern that languages were often held in 'low esteem' by university administrators and that there was a 'lack of understanding of the complexity involved in providing sound pedagogical language teaching'. There was though, no evidence given in the Report for their contention about low esteem and lack of understanding. The consultants further maintained that there was a 'lack of understanding by the community at large of the value of languages' which, they argued, was 'also a problem for governments with their sole emphasis' in cost cutting (White et al., 1997, pp. 25, 26).

This AAH survey was followed in April 1998, by the two volume report, *Knowing ourselves and others: the humanities in Australia into the 21st century*, prepared by an AAH Reference Group, further reinforcing the plight of languages. This Report cited government funding cuts since 1996, resulting in 'a serious contraction of funding for universities' since the reforms of the 1950s–1960s through the Murray and Martin Reports instigated by Prime Minister Menzies (AAH, 1998, p. 45). They went on to say that 'the impetus of the language revival of the late 1980s and early 1990s appears indeed to have been lost, even though the policy [National Policy on Languages] has not been formally repudiated. The country's universities have been cutting their language offerings in the face of low funding levels' (AAH, 1998, p. 47). They stressed the importance of languages to Australia in diverse areas such as economic exchanges, diplomatic and political relations, tourism, international events, the arts and the media. The learning of second languages and their social and cultural background

> has become an essential requirement at virtually all levels of education and when Australian universities themselves have unanimously embraced policies of internationalisation, the nation's capacity to sustain serious languages programs and specially to train researchers, area specialists and teachers is being seriously jeopardised. (AAH, 1998, pp. 47, 69)

It was only a few years earlier in 1994 that Elizabeth Dines, Academic Registrar of the University of Adelaide had made a provocative comment at a linguistics conference about the rationalisation of languages across universities: 'While [languages offerings rationalisation is] superficially appealing in a climate of fiscal restraint, I find it strange that no one suggests that comparable rationalisation should take place in, say, history or maths. It is important for us to keep abreast of moves to rationalisation, to ensure that they are not in fact moves towards annihilation' (Dines, 1994, p. 14). Coincidentally, the West review issued its final report in April 1998, the same month as the AAH Report. There was only one reference to languages in the West review under the heading of 'significant but low demand disciplines' (HEFPRC, 1998, p. 145), with recommendations that

> the Government should provide special-purpose support for significant but low demand disciplines on a case-by-case basis, using competitive tendering as the vehicle for distributing any funding, and with funding being provided *only* (my emphasis) when it is in the public interest and when all other options for preserving the discipline without special-purpose funding have been exhausted. (HEFPRC, 1998, p. 146)

How it would be determined what was 'in the public interest' to warrant funding was not specified. In any case, special funding on a last resort basis would have been no comfort to the AAH. That sort of remedy added weight to the concerns about lack of understanding, and low esteem mentioned in the 1997 AAH Report, and did nothing for the 'under-funding, under-staffing, and under-resourcing' which was cited in that AAH Report as 'the lot of most language departments in 1997' (White et al., 1997, p. 26).

The warnings and concerns for languages spelled out by the AAH in its *Languages and Universities: Under Siege* Report of 1997, its 1998 publication, *Knowing Ourselves and Others*, and its 2000 Report, *Subjects of small enrolment in the Humanities* (AAH, 2000), did not prompt the Federal government to pump more funds into universities specifically for languages. It can be argued that whatever structural arrangements might have been put in place in various universities, these structures hid the actual health of the state of languages nationally leading up to the end of the twentieth century. Increased financial support of universities' language programs was not forthcoming from the Federal government. Language departments were vulnerable within their own institutions when budget cuts were decided. Despite the policies for internationalisation in most universities, as previously mentioned, this rhetoric was not matched by funding the language offerings which could underpin this internationalisation. Despite too the rhetoric about languages being in Australia's national interest, funding was not forthcoming from the then Coalition government to support this stated aim.

There was, and is, an additional issue to be considered, that of differential funding for language subjects in contrast to other humanities subjects.[6] This differential funding, illustrated by the quite complex table of contributions for Commonwealth-supported places cited by the Grattan Institute in its mapping of Australian higher education, recognises different teaching costs for different courses. In the case of languages, the greater cost of provision through smaller classes and more teaching hours is recognised also (Norton, 2013, p. 52). However, according to the Higher Education Support Group of the Commonwealth Department of Education, 'whilst the amount for each funding cluster/band reflects the costs associated with providing the unit of study, universities are able to adopt their own internal resource allocation methods to allocate these funds to particular faculties or course' (Higher Education Support Group, personal communication, 24 February 2014). This is a particularly complex issue which is worthy of further investigation.

So where did the responsibility lie for the precarious state of languages in the Australian tertiary sector at the turn of the century? Universities can speak of government funding cuts, and these were real enough. However, it was argued by Macintyre and Marginson in 2000 that

> government no longer understands the universities as instruments for nation-building. Continued public funding is seen more as a cost than an investment. The university is now expected to serve national objectives in new ways: as a teaching institution engaged in vocational training of a far more direct and systematic nature, as a place of research where the production of knowledge is much more closely linked to practical and commercial uses, and as a business with the potential to generate foreign income. (Macintyre & Marginson, 2000, p. 67)

Whilst Macintyre and Marginson sheeted home blame to government for not adequately funding universities, they also chided university administrators for capitulating to government, for accepting chronic 'fiscal constraints' and becoming more like the corporate sector in their competitiveness and marketing (Macintyre & Marginson, 2000, p. 68). And they were not alone in their criticisms. The ANU historian John Molony argued that as universities are beholden to governments for funding, their accountability for those funds 'includes the university's readiness to serve "the national interest"' (Molony, 2000, p. 76). Molony went on to question just what is 'the national interest, and who decides what it is, and how it is to be achieved

---

[6] Anecdotal evidence suggests that differential funding for languages began around the mid-1970s. The Commonwealth Parliamentary Librarian was unable to supply any information. Additional investigation would be required.

and what universities have to do with it.' He questioned too, senior university administrators not taking responsibility for decisions made about areas no longer to be taught, and disciplines no longer deemed useful to the university. Such decisions, he said, are usually explained by the government cutbacks, rather than being explained by the priorities they, the senior university administrators, have settled on (Molony, 2000, pp. 79, 84). The further question here is how do they set their priorities? Are they constrained by internal financial policies and who has the ultimate responsibility in any university to make that decision? There is no one answer to this question as the circumstances will depend on the individual university.

The assumption here was that national interest or the national objectives, of which Macintyre and Marginson spoke, was the spectre which could be used to justify financial decisions. However, it is a concept not easily defined. I agree with Ashton Calvert, a former Secretary of DFAT, when he said in 2003 that 'the national interest is not static' (Calvert, 2003, p. 1). It follows therefore that successive governments, politicians, influential speakers and writers will expound on what they believe is the national interest. Such an elusive concept as national interest will continue to be used, re-shaped, and reinterpreted by governments to justify their political decisions.

7.8 Conclusion

In this chapter I have shown that the term national interest can be interpreted in many ways and those interpretations are influenced by the existing values and priorities of those making decisions and the context in which decisions are made. This has been particularly relevant in the period of the development of universities through the 1990s. For instance, meeting the Federal government's national objectives and accountability requirements can be used by university administrators as a justification in their financial decisions, for as Lo Bianco remarked, 'universities are also businesses' (Lo Bianco, 1998, p. 1). What I have also shown is, in a time of considerable structural change for language teaching in universities, there was a move towards a greater emphasis on Asian languages and Asian studies couched in terms of Australia's economic and strategic interests. Having explored this segment of university history where there was significant change for languages, it is clear that the battle for the relevance of language learning was still being fought at the beginning of the twenty-first century. What was needed was to reframe the attitudes of government, the general community and university administrators to embrace language learning as essential and central to a university which proclaims itself as international.

Chapter 8
The Asian or Global Century?

> As a nation we need to broaden and deepen our understanding of Asian cultures and languages, to become more Asia literate. (National Library of Australia (NLA), n.d.. Australia in the Asian Century, p. 2). Labor government's Asian Century White Paper

This was the message of the *Australia in the Asian Century* White Paper released, with much fanfare in October 2012, by the Labor government of Julia Gillard. This White Paper traced the economic rise of Asia and the likely outlook to 2025 and, as the Terms of Reference indicated, was to devise a series of national objectives and pathways for Australia towards 2025 (Australian Government, 2011, p. 3). It proclaimed that 'the Asian century is an Australian opportunity and that 'as the global centre of gravity shifts to our region, Australia is located in the right place at the right time – in the Asian region in the Asian century' (NLA, n.d., p. 1). 'It is in the interests of all Australians – and therefore in the national interest – to develop' Asian capabilities and connections (NLA, n.d., p. 3).

Commentary in the press was massive in its volume, variously positive, negative and/or cautionary. The White Paper, said Tim Lindsey, professor of Asian law at the University of Melbourne, was 'an eloquent statement of the critical importance of the Asian region for Australia's future', although he warned that it 'sets some enormous, and probably expensive, challenges for Australian governments. The question is', he said, 'whether government is prepared to invest significant funds to salvage Asian studies in Australia before time runs out' (Lindsey, 2012, p. 7). The professor of Asian policy at Swinburne University of Technology, Kenneth Chern, whilst welcoming the proposal for Asian language studies, echoed Lindsey's warnings: the 'plan to allow all students the opportunity to study an Asian language would cost billions of dollars' (Chern in Preiss, 2012, p. 2). Despite the largely positive reception to this White Paper, this 'strong Asian narrative' (A strong Asian narrative, 2012, p. 13) went no further as the Labor Party lost government less than

© Springer Nature Switzerland AG 2019
J. J. Baldwin, *Languages other than English in Australian Higher Education*,
Language Policy 17, https://doi.org/10.1007/978-3-030-05795-4_8

a year later.[1] The incoming Coalition government took up its own rather different policy of the *New Colombo Plan* (DFAT, 2013b) as a way of engaging with Asia.

This chapter takes a national view of languages in universities from the late 1990s into the 2000s by firstly exploring the attitudes of various governments to languages: the Howard Coalition government of 1996–2007, the Labor governments of 2007–2013, followed by the Abbott Coalition government from September 2013. The commitment of universities to languages across the same period is explored through their language offerings. Most universities by this time embraced internationalisation, as an important aspect of their mission. Internationalisation, according to Jane Knight, a Canadian higher education researcher, is the integration into curriculum of an international or global dimension (Knight, 2004, p. 11). However, as will be shown, the value of languages other than English as an essential tenet of internationalisation was not common across universities. This period was also marked by a series of events as academics continued to drive the debate about the importance of languages: the 'Marking Our Difference' conference in 2003, the Go8 universities Report of 2007, a national languages colloquium held in February 2009, and the formation in 2011 of LCNAU, the Languages and Cultures Network for Australian Universities.

This chapter explores current issues for languages education and innovations to reinforce opportunities for languages learning in the university sector. The question of the linkage between Australia's trade in the twenty-first century and languages of economic national interest as specified by government is discussed. A global perspective is explored, considering whether other English-speaking countries grappled with the same language offerings issues as Australia. This chapter concludes with the premise that a commitment by successive governments to languages for the national interest, whether Asian or non-Asian languages, has not been forthcoming. The current stance has been rather a commitment to international, particularly Asian, experiences for students, not necessarily involving language proficiency. An underlying monolingualism still exists.

8.1 Government Languages Policy from Mid 1990s to Early 2000s

The era of 11 years of the Howard government has been considered by many observers a negative period for languages. Clyne wrote of the disabling changes after the important enabling changes for languages of the 1970s and 1980s (Clyne, 2005, p. 158). Bradshaw and her colleagues contended that, 'national language policy making foundered', there was 'a general lack of activity at the Federal level' and 'funding stringencies' forced the closure of many university language programs'

---

[1] After the Labor government lost power and the Coalition government took over, the White Paper was consigned from the Department of Prime Minister and Cabinet's website to the archives website of the National Library of Australia.

(Bradshaw, Deumart, & Burridge, 2008, p. 22). Liddicoat and Scarino were even more critical, citing '10 years of relative neglect from the mid-1990s at both Commonwealth and State and Territory levels' (Liddicoat & Scarino, 2010, p. 1). There was, in 2006, a national seminar on languages education held in Canberra, although almost solely focussed on the school sector. Its goals were less action-oriented and more about encouraging language learning and sharing best practice (DEST, 2006, p. 2). Nevertheless, in the early 2000s, university language academics continued to be very concerned about the deteriorating situation for languages, particularly in the tertiary sector. They also felt that a significant part of the responsibility for the advancement of the importance of languages rested with them, both in the teaching of languages and cultural knowledge, and also in training the next generation of teachers (LCNAU, n.d., Background).

In May 2007, the Go8 universities' Report, *Languages in crisis: A rescue plan for Australia* (Go8, 2007), claimed that the declining interest and enrolments in languages in both school and university sectors was the fault of the Australian government. Governments are 'failing current and future generations of students as well as the future of the Australian economy if they do not work with schools and universities to address the languages crisis in our education system' (Go8, 2007, p. 8). This crisis, they said, which affected both Asian and non-Asian languages, had deepened since 1997, when 66 languages were offered at Australian universities. In 2007, they reported just 29 languages on offer (Go8, 2007, p. 4).

In late November 2007, after 11 years of Coalition government, a Labor government was elected which lasted six years. In September 2013, the electorate swung back to the Liberal/National Coalition. Whilst the settling in of a new government may have diverted attention away from possible university budget cuts, commentators warned universities that in the light of announcements by the Coalition thus far, those 'in the humanities, arts, and social sciences … might be entering a difficult period' (Shiel, 2013, p. 2). It was too early to know exactly how cuts to universities might impinge on subject offerings across the board, let alone languages.

To capture the situation for languages in 2013, Go8[2] universities' languages offerings from their 2013 websites are summarised in Appendix 6. As student demand can be critical for the continuation of language offerings, information was collated from the same websites to show, in Appendix 7, how universities promoted to prospective students the value of languages learning and the personal and career benefits which might accrue from language proficiency. As the researchers Dunne and Pavlyshyn indicated in their 2011 survey, 'student choice is the determining factor rather than considerations such as ensuring that a range of languages is offered across the country as a whole' (Dunne & Pavlyshyn, 2011, p. 11). Most universities indicated that they taught languages in a broad context with culture, literature, art, history, politics and society essential in this teaching. As the University of Adelaide put it, languages cannot be taught in a vacuum. The University of Queensland stressed intercultural communication and sensitivity as well as

---

[2] Go8 universities were sampled as it is often from the Go8, that regular reports and submissions relevant to the national scene for higher education generally and languages specifically, emanate.

scholarship. Most universities commended the study of modern European languages in terms of their cultural, political and literary value. French, for instance, was important as a very widely spoken language, a language of the United Nations and European Union. German was valued not only as a major world language but one important in philosophy, literature, medicine, science and engineering. The links between Australia and Italy with economic and cultural benefits accruing were mentioned. Classical languages were promoted for the understanding of the classical cultural contributions to the modern world. Spanish was promoted not only as the second mostly widely spoken language, but also as a language with employment possibilities in newly flourishing economies in Latin and South America. There were broad career possibilities mentioned for modern European languages such as international relations and diplomacy, the arts, publishing, the media, teaching the public service, and opportunities in the corporate world (ANU, 2013a, b, c, d; Monash University, 2013; University of Adelaide, 2013a, b, c, d, e, f; UniMelb, 2013a, b, c, d, e, f, g, h, i; UNSW, 2013; University of Queensland, 2013; UniSyd, 2013; UWA, 2013a, b, c).

It was with Asian and Middle Eastern languages, however, where more utilitarian prospects were suggested. UWA stressed the importance of Asia for Australia's future prosperity and career prospects in government departments such as immigration, defence and foreign affairs and trade as well as tourism, commerce and teaching. The University of Sydney suggested good prospects with multinational corporations, tourism and in education. The University of Melbourne promoted Indonesian as the language of a country of geographical and strategic importance to Australia, and noted Arabic as a priority language of strategic importance to Australia's national interests. The ANU promoted their focus on the commercial, scientific and industrial ties with countries where the languages Arabic, Persian and Turkish were spoken. With all these suggestions and promotions from other Go8 universities, the University of NSW stood out as not using its website a marketing tool for its language offerings, with quite briefly stated material (ANU, 2013a, b, c, d; Monash University, 2013; University of Adelaide, 2013a, b, c, d, e, f; UniMelb, 2013a, b, c, d, e, f, g, h, i; UNSW, 2013; University of Queensland, 2013; UniSyd, 2013; UWA, 2013a, b, c).

An additional vehicle for understanding the depth and breadth of language offerings in Australian universities came from the 2011 Dunne and Pavlyshyn survey. Their survey results showed which languages were offered as majors, minors, or individual subjects. An abbreviated version of their table, showing the ten universities with the largest number of language offerings in 2011, the Go8 universities plus La Trobe and Macquarie Universities, appears in Appendix 8. This table shows that seven languages, French, German, Indonesian, Italian, Japanese, Mandarin and Spanish, were widely taught across the university sector, a fairly even mix of European and Asian languages. It also shows however, that the majority of those languages less commonly taught were offered by one institution: the ANU. ANU in fact in 2011, was the university with the largest number of language offerings as a result of a particular local initiative to provide access to a range of Asian languages. The then vice-chancellor, Ian Chubb was hugely supportive of language initiatives, according to Kent Anderson, then then Dean of Asian Studies.[3] What this 2011 survey indicated were the difficulties in obtaining accurate data from websites. There is no doubt, as Dunne and Pavlyshyn have said, that what is needed is a 'truly comprehensive picture of current language teaching at the tertiary level,' as such a survey has not been undertaken since the Leal Report of 1991 (Dunne & Pavlyshyn, 2011, p. 15). Dunne and Pavlyshyn's (2014) report on languages, particularly those less commonly taught (LCTLS), did not show any appreciable difference in the languages landscape. They concluded that report with a challenge to the government: 'We believe LCTLS are a matter of national importance and it is the role of government to ensure that they are effectively represented in the institutional framework of Australian higher education' (Dunne & Pavlyshyn, 2014, pp. 10, 14).

8.2 Internationalisation

As mentioned earlier, internationalism was now a catchcry for universities. Internationalisation, according to researchers Fazal Rizvi and Lucas Walsh, had become mainstream by the late 1990s (Rizvi & Walsh, 1998, p. 7). Numbers of researchers sought to show the importance of this concept in contemporary universities. A 1995 survey by IDP Education showed that 'over 70% of universities had strategies for the internationalisation of form and content of their curricula' (Rizvi & Walsh, 1998, p. 7). Then, by 2001, according to a joint RMIT/Monash study: 'all Australian universities [evoked] internationalisation as central to their mission' (Clyne, Marginson, & Woock, 2001, p. 112). Some 11 years later in 2012, Lynne Li of RMIT echoed the 2001 findings about the universality of the concept of internationalisation of the university curriculum as seen in university websites (Li, 2012, p. 50). In 2012, Sophie Arkoudis (from the University of Melbourne's Centre for the Study of Higher Education (CSHE)) and her colleagues, in their research work on internationalising the student experience (Arkoudis, Baik, Marginson, & Cassidy, 2012), examined the mission statements, goals and values on university websites, discovering that internationalisation as a term was universally used by universities. However, they said, internationalisation was used mostly to refer to the diversity in the student body with study abroad or international exchange programs given as examples of the internationalisation of a university campus (Arkoudis et al., 2012, pp. 6–7). Arkoudis and her colleagues had drawn on Jane Knight's definition of internationalisation, previously mentioned: 'the process of integrating an international, intercultural or global dimension into the purpose, functions or delivery of post-secondary education' (Knight, 2004, p. 11).

What Arkoudis and her colleagues argued was that internationalisation needed to involve all students, both international and domestic, pointing out the great diversity of student background. Most importantly, they said, there are both differing language

---

[3] The range of measures undertaken at ANU included exchange lectures and tutorials from overseas universities, in-country electives, and video links to other Australian universities.

capacities of students, whether monolingual, bilingual or multilingual, and differing cultural and socio-economic backgrounds. This diversity was why, they contended, 'all students must be included in internationalising the student experience.' It was significant also in the national fora which the researchers conducted, that the proportion of English-speaking students taking LOTE studies was tabled by participants as an indicator of internationalisation in an institution (Arkoudis et al., 2012, pp. 5, 7, 13).

Chi Baik, also from the CSHE, also stressed learning a foreign language as a vital part of the genuine internationalised student experience particularly for students who might never leave their home country (Baik, 2013, p. 137; Wächter, 2003, pp. 5, 10). Opportunities for study abroad, a curriculum with 'relevant international content,' building 'cross-cultural skills and awareness' through 'interaction among diverse students' were all cited as important components of this student experience. Baik conceded that foreign language learning was not readily acknowledged as an essential part of internationalisation within institutions and strongly encouraged universities to make languages a core component of curricula as they are in many institutions worldwide (Baik, 2013, pp. 135, 137). She stressed the declining foreign language learning in Australia, and urged universities to take steps to increase students' awareness of the benefits of learning a foreign language (Baik, 2013, p. 137) Dennis Murray, from the University of Melbourne, also picked up this issue, arguing that

> politicians frequently mistake attracting large numbers of international students to Australia for the alpha and omega of internationalisation of Australian education. There is little appreciation of the role played by the international mobility of teaching and research… Australian education institutions do not share this narrow view and therein lies a problem. (Murray, 2013, p. 114)

It was a sobering reflection on universities' values that, as far as the overview of universities' 2013 websites showed, none of the languages websites related language offerings directly to the concept of internationalisation so prevalent in universities' mission statement and values rhetoric.

8.3 Differing Understanding of the Role of Languages

The problem of which Murray spoke was the differing views of politicians who control university resources, and academics, who through their training and research, have clear ideas of the role and importance of the learning of languages in Australia. This concern about declining LOTE learning in a time of increasing internationalisation in universities was emphasised in a conference on language education in Australian and New Zealand Universities, *Marking our Difference*, held at the University of Melbourne in October 2003. This conference, driven by Colin Nettelbeck, the then Head of the School of Languages at the University of Melbourne, aimed to bring language teachers and specialists together to showcase

8.3 Differing Understanding of the Role of Languages

their work, their goals and methodologies, strengthen their networks, and gain publicity by highlighting their concerns in an international forum. The organisers intended that the conference findings would also gain publicity 'in the wider community, where monolingualism in English is often considered the norm' (Wigglesworth, 2003, p. 3). In her paper at that conference, Anne Pauwels, from the University of Western Australia, detailed three factors which she believed had contributed to the current situation for languages. She argued that whilst values such as intercultural understanding, linguistic tolerance and diversity have some airing, public discourse has favoured the 'utilitarian aspects of language study such as its value for trade, business and increasingly national security' (Pauwels, 2003, p. 10).

She argued that the 'more moderate form of instrumentalism' prevailed in most of the sector. It was due to this attitude, she said, that subjects and courses with small enrolments (including many languages) were considered economically unviable, then were downsized, closed or transferred to a cross-institutional teaching mode (Pauwels, 2003, p. 10). Secondly, whilst Pauwels acknowledged that languages notionally receive a higher funding weighting than other related disciplines, she also noted 'universities can internally adjust the weights of disciplines and courses to suit their needs.' If universities adjusted language weightings downwards, as had often happened, language departments were subject to additional pressures (Pauwels, 2003, p. 13). A third downward trend was the significant reduction of professorial chairs in languages. Chairs give status to a discipline, she contended, and allow such language professors opportunity to argue for the importance of languages in high-level management committees of the university (Pauwels, 2003, p. 15). These sentiments were reinforced by Nettelbeck, Hajek and Woods in their 2012 paper, *Re-professionalizing the profession*, where they described the 'marked erosion of senior leadership' in languages departments. Language academics at the Level E Professors position 'have the authority and the power to speak effectively for their fields at those levels of the university where key budgeting, staffing and curricular decisions are made' (Nettelbeck, Hajek, & Woods, 2012, p. 63).

The issue of declining interest and enrolments in languages had been raised by the Group of eight universities in their 2007 Report, *Languages in Crisis*, where they laid the blame for the parlous situation squarely at the feet of both state and federal governments (Go8, 2007, p. 8). From the momentum generated by this Go8 Report, a national languages colloquium, supported by the Australian Academy of the Humanities, was held in Melbourne in February 2009 entitled, 'Beyond the Crisis'. This colloquium was led by Joseph Lo Bianco who was president of AAH at the time and Colin Nettelbeck, the Head of the School of Languages at the University of Melbourne. From this colloquium where possible actions to advance the debate were discussed, the creation for a national network emerged as a way forward. Funds, for a project to set up this network, were sought and obtained from the then Australian Learning and Teaching Council (ALTC), now the Office for Learning and Teaching (OLT). This office was an Australian government initiative begun in November 2011 to promote and support 'change in higher education institutions for the enhancement of learning and teaching' (Office for Learning and

Teaching, n.d.). The culmination of this project work was the creation of the Languages and Cultures Network for Australian Universities (LCNAU, n.d., Background). The aim of the LCNAU Project was to 'develop a coordinated national approach to language education and scholarship in Australian universities by building strategic leadership across disciplines and institutions through an improvement-oriented network' (LCNAU, 2011, p. 2). Their focus was to be especially in the tertiary sector but also to extend across the broader languages and cultures education network.

8.4 Australia in the Asian Century

Whilst LCNAU was working to 'raise the profile of language educators and public awareness of the cultural, strategic and economic importance of language education for Australia' (LCNAU, 2011, p. 2) the Gillard Labor government mounted a significant national review as described at the beginning of this chapter. This was to be a 'comprehensive review of economic and strategic change in Asia and its implications and opportunities for Australia' (Australian Government, 2011, p. 1). The White Paper, *Australia in the Asian Century* was to be 'a roadmap to guide Australia to become a more prosperous and resilient nation, fully part of the region and open to the world' (NLA, n.d.). The importance of the Asian region was emphasised as 'in the interests of all Australians and therefore in the national interest'. Australia therefore needed to broaden and deepen its understanding of Asian cultures and languages (NLA, n.d., pp. 2, 3). The priority languages were to be Mandarin Chinese, Hindi, Indonesian and Japanese. Korean had now been dropped from its earlier Labor prioritisation in the 1990s (NLA, n.d., p. 16). Nevertheless, as Lo Bianco and Aliani pointed out, the rhetoric of the White Paper was that all students were to have 'access' to these four languages, a rather vague statement that did 'little to foster optimism in realistic language planning' (Lo Bianco & Aliani, 2013, p. 130).

Following the White Paper, the Government published a series of Country Strategies on which they sought submissions by May 2013. Two hundred and fifty submissions were received from a wide range of organisations and individuals, many from within the university and business sectors. Most submissions commented on the specific countries for which strategies had been written: China, Japan, South Korea, Indonesia and India, although LCNAU commented on the need for a policy which promoted all languages (DFAT, 2013c). The LCNAU submission of March 4, 2012, responding to the previous Issues Paper: *Australia in the Asian Century*, also had a much broader focus. Whilst welcoming the initiative in the renewed attention to Asia, they also said that as an organisation LCNAU was 'dedicated to supporting all languages and cultures – Asian or otherwise – in Australia's university system.' They cautioned an approach which focused too heavily on just Asian linguistic and cultural skills with the commanding statement: 'This is not just the Asian century – it is the global century'. LCNAU went on to point out that other parts of the world were growing as fast as parts of Asia. The so-called BRICS nations – Brazil, Russia, India, China and South Africa – which cross four different continents, are leading economic development in the developing world. 'Our students need not only to be Asia-literate and ready. They need to be world-literate and ready' (LCNAU, 2012, p. 1).

8.5 The New Colombo Plan

Whatever was thought of the Asian Century White Paper and Country Strategies, these initiatives had no chance for implementation. The new Coalition government had its own policy for Australia's relationship with Asia. This was a very different policy which did not highlight languages as the Labor government's policy had done. The New Colombo Plan picked up the historical precedent of the original Colombo Plan which, as previously mentioned in Chap. 3, stemmed from a conference of Commonwealth Foreign Ministers in Colombo, Ceylon in 1950 (Blackton, 1951, p. 28). Whilst appropriating the name and 'inheriting the favourable brand recognition of its predecessor' (Gothard, 2013, p. 2), the New Colombo Plan was not about aid and training for Asian countries as the original Plan was, but aimed 'to lift knowledge of the Asia Pacific in Australia and strengthen …relationships, through study and internships undertaken by Australian undergraduate students in the region' (DFAT, 2013a, p. 1). There was no reference to the learning of languages at the launch by Minister Julie Bishop (Bishop, 2013). The emphasis on the DFAT website was the internship or mentorship experience, 'ensuring Australian students are work ready and have professional connections in the region.' The four countries involved in the 2014 pilot phase were Hong Kong, Indonesia, Japan and Singapore (DFAT, 2013b, p. 1). Significantly, Hong Kong and Singapore are English-speaking countries where students would not need a language other than English to undertake their placement.

Minister Bishop, in her launch speech, put her personal stamp on the importance of the Plan, saying, 'I was convinced of the need for Australia to ensure that more of our students not only studied overseas, but studied in our region. And the idea came to me that we needed to reverse the original Colombo Plan in order to achieve that outcome.' It will be a means to 'transform Australia's engagement in our region' as 'the educational experience of young Australian undergraduates' is also transformed (Bishop, 2013, p. 1). The telling point about the underlying national purpose of the New Colombo Plan was Bishop's emphasis that the Plan was an initiative of the DFAT, not the Department of Education (Bishop, 2013, p. 2).

It was claimed that the Plan would ensure 'a growing two-way exchange in the region', with Australian students going to study in the Asian regions, complementing 'the thousands of students from the region coming to study in Australia each year' (DFAT, n.d., New Colombo Plan pilot program, 2013b, p. 1). Nevertheless, it was clear in a report of a speech by the parliamentary secretary to the Minister for Foreign Affairs, Senator Brett Mason, in Melbourne in March 2014, that Asian language proficiency was not an essential part of the New Colombo Plan. He said: 'getting students to work and study in Asia was the best way to encourage them to take up studying languages rather than "artificially" stoking demand for languages' (Trounson, 2014, p. 28). The danger of such a statement is a slide back to the monolingual mindset of the twentieth century discussed so eloquently by Clyne in his 2005 publication *Australia's language potential* (Clyne, 2005). I argue however that the monolingual mindset, which suggests that in this age of globalisation English alone is sufficient, has never completely disappeared in Australia. I agree with the many commentators who have maintained that a major deficiency in the New Colombo Plan is the concentration on one region – the Asian region. This too was a deficiency of the Asian Century White Paper of the former Labor government – to concentrate on Asian languages alone, and not formulate a policy to promote other significant languages.

There is a chronic problem between the various stakeholders as to which languages should be supported. There is a lack of synergy between what successive Federal governments have promoted, what language academics insist is necessary, what universities through senior management are prepared to fund, and what languages students might want to take, for instance, their current enthusiasm for European languages. Governments are well known for their short-term policies lasting from one election to the next, and have repeatedly shown an economic rationalist approach to other languages.[4] Universities, on the other hand, must have longer term policies and funding certainties to properly support the teaching of languages. Mariel Tisdell, a language policy researcher from the University of Queensland, argued for the importance of language policies formulated by governments to establish the language needs of a society (Tisdell, 1998, p. 135). She further maintained that Australia still had a monolingual attitude holding back its social justice and economic development:

> until a broader base of competent foreign languages speakers has been trained who are competently and confidently using their 'other' languages, Australia will remain one of the very few industrial countries where expediency and preoccupation with monolingualism as a confirmation of national identity, overrides concerns for social justice and economic survival. (Tisdell, 1998, p. 143)

Whilst Tisdell expressed these views in 1998, numbers of commentators suggested that a revision of national language policy was needed. Clyne had strongly advocated in 1997 for such a review (Clyne, 1997, p. 69), the Go8 universities cited the need for a national policy in 2007 (Go8, 2007, p. 8). No government, since the NPL of 1987 and the ALLP of 1991, had sought to formulate a new language policy.

Whilst Federal governments were not formulating the updated national language policy that commentators sought, the Go8 universities gave their considerable voice and influence to the need for more language teaching resources with their August 2011 statement: 'Learning to speak a Language Other Than English (LOTE) is

---

[4] The 1991 ALLP and the 1994 Rudd Report were both in this vein.

increasingly important for effective participation in a globalised world'; and 'Group of Eight (Go8) universities play a vital role in the delivery and support of languages education in Australia.' The statement[5] went on to detail the LOTE Incentive Schemes for entry to university for Year 12 languages students, and bonuses awarded for LOTEs by each Go8 university (Go8, 2011a). However, disappointingly, there was no mention of languages in the Go8 strategic plan for 2011–2014. This would have been a perfect opportunity to voice such concerns and reiterate a precise vision for the significance of languages (Go8, 2011b).

8.6 The Languages Component of the Australian Curriculum

In the meantime, in the secondary school sector, the Australian Curriculum (often referred to by the Coalition government as the National Curriculum) was being rolled out through the auspices of the Australian Curriculum, Assessment and Report Authority (ACARA). The Languages component of this curriculum was designed 'to enable all students to engage in learning a language in addition to English' (ACARA, n.d., Languages, p. 1). Work on the languages component began in 2009, with the writing phase completed in December 2013, for implementation proposed from May 2014. The languages in this phase[6] were Arabic, Vietnamese, French, German, Indonesian, Italian, Japanese, Korean, Modern Greek, Spanish and Chinese (ACARA, n.d., p. 1). Lo Bianco and Aliani commended the broadness of the approach to languages in the Australian Curriculum: 'in the planning for the national curriculum, languages, and not exclusively Asian languages have been declared a priority discipline' (Lo Bianco & Aliani, 2013, p. 19).

ACARA's plan for the May 2014 rollout was turned upside down by the Coalition government's January 2014 announcement of a review of the Australian Curriculum with recommendations expected by June 2014 (Liberal Party, 2014, Review of National Curriculum). A group of prominent educators, professors, lecturers, and teachers voiced their concerns, commenting that to suggest recommended changes would be ready for the 2015 school year demonstrated a lack of understanding of the planning processes for classroom implementation (Tovey, 2014). ACARA then made four languages, Chinese, French, Indonesian and Italian available for use in July 2014 (ACARA, 2014a, Media release), to assist schools in forward planning although the completed curriculum review was not due for discussion until December 2014 (ACARA, Message from the Chairman). This was another example of new policies and reviews being announced by a new government with the potential to change existing priorities. The review had come at a time when schools would

---

[5] The identical statement was reiterated in August 2014.

[6] Aboriginal and Torres Strait Islander Languages were also part of this phase but have not been part of the research for this book.

have been expecting a period of implementation and stability not a continued state of flux.

The review recommendations were referred to ACARA for advice in early 2015 (Barrett, 2014, National curriculum changes). Subsequently the languages Arabic, Chinese, French, German, Indonesian, Italian, Japanese, Korean, Modern Greek, Spanish and Vietnamese were endorsed by ACARA in September 2015 (ACARA, n.d., Languages). It is true to say that the teaching of languages in schools and the language offerings in the university sector are interdependent and this had been acknowledged as far back as the Kramer report of 1975 (AUC, 1975a, p. 17). It would be expected therefore that the broad promotion of languages in the Australian Curriculum might in time, influence the language offerings in the university sector and indeed the student take-up of university languages. However, given the existing cross-state differences in school language offerings, and the findings of the review, the rollout of the Curriculum could take longer than expected to settle down and thus the effect on university offerings may be much further into the future. Lo Bianco has argued that 'the upper secondary and university level should, ideally, offer articulated continuation...linked closely to disciplines, including of language itself' (Lo Bianco, 2009, p. 60). He went on to say that not only should schools' language teaching be linked to university language teaching, but that well trained and supported language teachers are a crucial element in this equation (Lo Bianco, 2009, p. 64).

Certainly, this relationship between the school and university sectors can be seen in the languages component of the Australian Curriculum, both through the broad range of submissions in the consultation phase, and also through the range of university academics involved in the shaping and writing phases (ACARA, n.d., p. 1). However, it is possible that these people were not of sufficient seniority in the university sector to influence the decision making about language offerings. Pauwels, in her foreword to the publication by Joanne Winter about collaborative models for languages teaching (Winter, 2009), commented that it is Deans and Pro Vice-Chancellors in Faculties of Arts, Humanities and Social Sciences, who generally have the responsibility for managing and making decisions about 'the volatility around the position of languages in universities'. She went on to say that 'without the informed support of such senior staff, suggestions about changes and 'initiatives will often not be sustainable.' It is also at this senior level, she contended, that discussions take place about 'maintaining, introducing and /or phasing out language programs' (Winter, 2009, p. iii). However, as Dunne and Pavlyshyn have argued, 'university business models require universities to make a profit or at least break even', and that 'in such a climate, university administrators are not inclined to invest in staffing [languages] to enhance the intellectual capital of the country' (Dunn & Pavlyshyn, 2011, p. 11).

8.7 The Stakeholders for Languages

Whilst the funding of languages is a matter of university budgets, it must not be forgotten that students will make choices about what they believe are, as King and James put it, 'the skill sets they need for the future,' and whether language proficiency is a part of such a future skill set (ACARA, n.d., p. 1). Universities Australia, in their representation of all Australian university vice-chancellors, agreed that 'the student demand-driven system means that the allocation of places to different fields is determined mostly by students rather than by institutions or governments' (Universities Australia, 2013, p. 17). Languages could be seen a part of a much broader skill set that students might choose to forge their future because, as Lo Bianco maintained,

> deep and rapid globalisation over recent years has added some pragmatic or utilitarian justifications for language study. But this is not the main reason for teaching languages. We must not forget 'the deepest purposes of education itself, to instil knowledge, to deepen understand, to stimulate reflection and to foster skills. Languages are intimately linked to the essentially humanistic, cultural and intellectual reasons for making education compulsory. (Lo Bianco, 2009, p. 64)

Not only was it crucial to get the message through to students about the importance of languages but a significant challenge was to put in place guaranteed mechanisms for easy ongoing access to languages through different degrees. As Nettelbeck and his colleagues pointed out, 'where universities have introduced mechanisms to facilitate access to languages study, enrolments have increased (Nettelbeck et al., 2012, p. 62).

There have been then conflicting purposes about the value of languages amongst the stakeholders of higher education. The 1987 National Policy on Languages stated amongst its general principles that the 'language pluralism of Australia is regarded as a valuable resource enhancing and enriching cultural and intellectual life' (Lo Bianco, 1987, p. 6). However, the bias of successive governments has been to see the acquisition of languages as important for utilitarian purposes, and how they might further the national interest of Australia in trade and commerce, defence and national security. Universities, whilst holding to the intellectual and cultural reasons for languages as part of higher education, have been shackled by the economic imperatives of offering subjects attracting sufficient student numbers to be economically viable. And then ultimately, there have been the student participants in the whole university environment who have chosen what they want to study, for how long, and at what level. In 2015 students could choose not to study languages at all, unlike the pre-1960s era when most universities required a pass in a language as part of the requirements for an Arts degree. If a particular degree, and these were relatively unusual, had a compulsory language component such as the Bachelor of Asia-Pacific Studies at the ANU, the student could choose whether or not to apply for this degree (Australian National University, 2013a, b, c, d). It could be the fate of such degrees however to have to capitulate to pressure to loosen the language requirements to allow more students access to the contemporary economic, political and global non-language content offered.

However as has been shown, governments often seek to prompt or force student choices by targeted funding for specific languages, scholarships, or tied internships, or by promoting the economic benefits to students of certain language choices. The languages of the Asian Century White Paper, Chinese, Japanese, Indonesian and Hindi, prioritised but not with preferential funding, were an example of such government strategies. Korean, which had in earlier Labor strategies been a priority language, was not in the original Asian Century White Paper languages, but was later reinstated. The previous Labor government had chosen to focus on the Asia-Pacific region as had the Coalition government elected in September 2013, although the Coalition government did not focus on languages. By this emphasis, both Federal governments gave weight to the premise for Australia's Asian century rather than Australia's global century.

8.8 Current Issues: Collaborative Arrangements

Regardless of the frustrations of underfunding of languages and differing priorities between those who allocate the funds and those who teach languages, the work of committed language educators has been seen in the innovative ways of offerings languages. These innovations have been useful in enabling a wider range of LOTEs to be offered to a wider range of students, especially the smaller languages, in what has been a chronically tight economic scene for universities. Collaborative teaching arrangements have been in place across various institutions for numbers of years and much work has been done to document the history and effectiveness of these arrangements (Hajek, Slaughter, & Stevens, 2008; White & Baldauf, 2006). One example, still current in 2018, was the Brisbane Universities Alliance known as BULA, a collaborative framework for university languages provision in South-East Queensland of the city-based type. The setting up of this Alliance was enabled by substantial funding ($2,271,000) from DEEWR's Diversity and Structural Reform Grant program (Levy & Steel, 2011, p. 110). Three universities were involved: the University of Queensland offering Chinese, Japanese, Spanish, French and German; Griffith University offering Chinese, Japanese, Spanish and Italian and Queensland University of Technology (QUT) offering Chinese only. The initial agreement was signed in 2009, with a further agreement for 2014–2016 focussing on both academic and administration collaborations. In their first report, Mike Levy and Caroline Steel cited the importance, for this BULA alliance, of collaboration in languages provision. This bore out White and Baldauf's contention that such collaborative arrangements are a way of 'maintaining language teaching vitality' given 'the current financial and structural pressures on languages' (White & Baldauf, 2006, p. 3).

8.8 Current Issues: Collaborative Arrangements

Levy and Steel indicated that the BULA project had enabled these three Queensland universities to 'provide tertiary language learning to a larger pool of students from several universities' (Levy & Steel, 2011, p. 118). Hajek, Slaughter and Stevens in their evaluation of city-based collaborative models noted the difficulties of the compatibility of course structures and programs and the complications of different enrolment systems in the institutions they surveyed (Hajek et al., 2008, pp. 34, 35). Levy and Steel had indeed indicated in their paper that early challenges had been to deal with program differences between the three institutions and the sheer complexity of the administration, given differences in enrolment procedures, credit transfer, fee structures and GPA calculation. Despite these very time-consuming issues, they indicated that 'duplication had been reduced and efficiencies achieved in their offerings' (Levy & Steel, 2011, pp. 112, 113, 118). In a more recent discussion, Levy commented that the administrative arrangements, which were particularly complex in the beginning, were now well established as were the teaching relationships between the academics of the three universities. A particular boost to these arrangements had been substantial grants for the scholarship of teaching across these universities (Levy, personal communication, 3 March 2014). Levy and Steel (2011, p. 118) had reported that further collaborative research was planned to investigate matters such as student transition, engagement and retention. However no data is publicly available on the results of this proposed research.

Whilst the BULA arrangement continues, mention must be made a forerunner program in Adelaide developed during the 1980s, which eventually failed. The Outreach Programme, as it was called, was a collaboration between the University of Adelaide and Flinders University. These arrangements greatly benefited students who were now able to study languages not available at their home institution. However, over time, the student numbers reciprocally taught across the institutions, became unbalanced and issues emerged such as student fees and library privileges and pressures on staff who were travelling between institutions. Added to this was the entry of a third university, the University of South Australia, 'into the language market-place' (Fornasiero & West-Sooby, 2003, pp. 2, 3, 8). As the architects of this program said: 'never has this kind of cross-institutional co-operation been more necessary, but never has it been more difficult to sustain' (Fornasiero & West-Sooby, 2003, p. 10).

A third cross-institutional arrangement between the Australian National University and the University of Canberra began in 2011, when the University of Canberra decided to close its Japanese language program. A cross-institutional arrangement was put in place with the ANU where students travelled between the two institutions (Kinoshita, 2018, pp. 3, 4). This was less of a collaboration but rather a 'unidirectional relationship', poorly implemented, argued Kinoshita, 2003, pp. 11, 13). The result of these arrangements was a very large loss of numbers of languages students at the University of Canberra and in the region generally.

The continuation of the BULA arrangements bore out the conclusions of Hajek, Slaughter and Stevens' analysis as to what worked in collaborative arrangements: arrangements which were long-term, and where there were excellent relationships between the various teaching and administrative staff (Hajek et al., 2008, p. 59). To this should be added the need for arrangements to be carefully balanced between institutions so that each institution will benefit. Nevertheless, as Hajek and his colleagues concluded, 'the high cost of language teaching has been a major issue for the Australian tertiary sector for many years, and has been the major driver, along with changing patterns of student demand, in reducing and closing down language programs and offerings around the country.' They noted also that the strength of the collaborative arrangements was to 'offer much lower overall costs of provision for a specific language in a given city – since it required the maintenance of fewer programs.' Such arrangements could be particularly appropriate for smaller languages (Hajek et al., 2008, pp. 22, 56, 57). There were downsides, however, in the measures needed to lower costs: lowering of institutional profile, loss of staff, and downgrading of staff to teaching only and sessional status. Hajek and his colleagues suggested that a future innovation which would assist would be national leadership for collaborative arrangements, which could include 'explicit promotion of collaborative programs for smaller languages and their importance for tertiary level language provision'. In order to achieve this goal, such promotion could piggyback on the 'language of the dominant government rhetoric, for Australia's economic future' (Hajek et al., 2008, p. 61). Such a tactic may well be the way to persuade governments that the financial outlay for more consistent funding of languages is important for Australia's national interest.

8.9 New Models: University of Melbourne and UWA

Yet another innovation which has advantaged the university languages sector was the advent of breadth subjects. Whilst the Melbourne Model (or the Melbourne Curriculum) instituted in 2008 at the University of Melbourne restructured undergraduate courses, it was the introduction of 'breadth' subjects in all undergraduate degrees, which had a positive effect on language enrolments (Lane, 2012b, 1 August. Languages soar). This enabled students to take most subjects, outside of their main fields of study within their home faculty, as breadth subjects (UniMelb, n.d., Learn more about breadth, p. 2). Bernard Lane reported the cautionary comments of the LCNAU project manager, Anya Woods: 'the Melbourne Model seems to show that the non-take-up of languages in many institutions may not be a matter of student demand, but of structural impediments' (Lane, 1 August). Nettelbeck and his colleagues too, have noted though that structural barriers, such as severe limits on subjects taken outside the home faculty, have often impeded a clear access for languages being taken through different degrees. Faculties other than where languages are taught have often treated languages as electives with very limited access, 'to be tolerated rather than actively encouraged' (Nettelbeck et al., 2007, p. 17, 2009, p. 11).

The University of Western Australia (UWA) instituted new degree structures in 2012, called New Courses, containing what were designated as broadening units. These initiatives were generally very similar to those instituted by the University of

8.9 New Models: University of Melbourne and UWA

Table 8.1 Enrolments on first beginners' language unit, by language- UWA

Languages available	Number enrolled in 2011	Number enrolled in 2012	Number enrolled in 2013	Overall % increase since 2011	% increase from 2011 to 2012	% increase from 2012 to 2013
Chinese	88	169	208	136	92	23
Indonesian	20	49	56	180	145	14
Japanese	119	229	292	145	92	28
Korean	89	143	195	119	61	36
French	200	459	494	147	130	8
German	73	159	212	190	118	33
Italian	108	206	196	81	91	−5
Latin	52	128	207	298	146	62
Total	749	1542	1860	148	106	21

Languages growth: Asian 138%; European: 137%; Classical (Latin): 298%
Figures for 2013 are as at 13 March, reproduced from data supplied by Dr. Josh Brown (UWA) from Brown & Caruso, 2014, pp. 40, 41

Melbourne. UWA's changes were very much driven by the then vice-chancellor who insisted that all new degrees should provide unhindered access to languages. The aim of these broadening units was to allow students the time and flexibility to acquire a broader general knowledge in their preparation for employment. In 2011 a 10% LOTE bonus for university entrance for Year 12 students, similar to that existing in some other states, was introduced, aiming to counter the decline in the number of students taking a secondary school LOTE. As for the broadening units at UWA, these proved attractive to students with significantly increased enrolments in all languages (Brown & Caruso, 2014, pp. 40, 41, 48). Table 8.1 indicates the percentage increases in student enrolments in the 1st year beginners' course.

When comparing the breadth subjects of the University of Melbourne, with the UWA broadening units, the UWA innovation stood out as much more flexible for two reasons. Firstly, UWA students had unfettered access to broadening units across the faculties and, unusually, an Arts student, for instance, was able to take language units as broadening units despite those units being from the same faculty, as languages had special dispensation in this regard (Brown & Caruso, 2014, p. 40). At the University of Melbourne by contrast, students could still be required to take subjects from other faculties. In addition, the breadth requirements had been reduced from a maximum of 75 points to a maximum of 50 points. Whilst Arts students might not, according to the rules, take languages units as breadth, this was allowed since 2014 for Asian languages only (UniMelb, n.d., Learn more about breadth, p. 2). These were but two examples of institutions which instituted measures to clear the way through institutional and faculty structures enabling languages to be taken across different degrees. Given the success of these measures, it is surely an issue which should be taken up widely within universities to facilitate as much as possible students' access to languages regardless of what degrees they are enrolled in.

The Diploma in Languages was another curricular arrangement, widely offered in Australian universities and previously mentioned in Chap. 7, which allowed greater flexibility for students wishing to take a sequence of language studies concurrently with their undergraduate degree studies. However, one such proposed program at RMIT University required considerable additional documentation to meet regulations when the planning for their Diploma in Languages began in 2012. At about this time the Tertiary Education Quality and Standards Agency (TEQSA) established in 2009, was refining its regulations which included the existing Australian Qualifications Framework (AQF). The AQF 'underpins the national system of qualifications in Australia encompassing higher education, vocational education and training and schools' (Australian Government, 2014). In January 2013, the AQF issued a revision of its regulations. In order to comply with AQF regulations, RMIT mapped the student learning objectives of their Diploma for certain graduate attributes and learning outcomes to meet a particular AQF level and, in that way, were enabled to implement this Diploma of Language at RMIT (Mullan & Seaman, 2014, pp. 72, 78). The issue at stake here was where an existing education authority revised its policies which then did not fit the spirit of existing or proposed programs. TEQSA procedures for program compliance used new threshold standards and frameworks different to the former 'fitness for purpose' regulations. It could be argued, that with the re-accreditation of existing Diplomas of/in Languages, there might be difficulties meeting TEQSA requirements, a body which did not exist when those Diplomas were originally accredited.

8.10 New Countries (and Languages) of National Interest?

Whilst, as has been shown throughout this research, the Australian government focusses on what might advantage Australia's economic future and national interest, there was the issue of the major emerging market countries and their languages, what one might call languages of emerging national interest. The major emerging market countries were suggested as the so-called BRICS countries (LCNAU, 2012, p. 1): initially in 2008, Brazil, Russia, India and China, joined by South Africa after 2011. Significant trade already existed between Australia and both China and India. One might have expected that the Government would have considered these BRICS countries in terms of maximising trade opportunities and establishing educational relationships, study abroad schemes, mentoring and internship programs as was announced through the New Colombo Plan. There was, however, no government rhetoric to suggest such measures. It was encouraging, nevertheless, that China and India became part of the Plan in 2015 along with Pakistan and Vietnam and many Pacific island locations. It could also be argued that Brazil, as a country with whom Australia signed a strategic partnership in 2012, would be an obvious regional partner. Not only did the agenda of that strategic partnership detail growing trade and investment links, but it was agreed that 'the institutions and peak bodies of the respective universities and vocational educational systems should cooperate even more closely' (Gillard, n.d., Brazil-Australia). However, as this partnership was forged under a previous Labor government, the Coalition government would likely seek its own unique relationship with Brazil, before any of previous partnerships were progressed.

As has been mentioned in earlier chapters, philanthropic donations for languages have often been important for the introduction of, and the sustaining, of tertiary languages. The ANU received a significant anonymous donation for Russian and Portuguese (languages of two of the BRICS countries) in November 2013. In announcing the $200,000 given for each language, the Vice-Chancellor of the ANU, Ian Young, said 'the teaching of languages is so important and as Australia's national university we have a responsibility to uphold areas of national significance' (Macdonald, 2013, ANU gets $1m gift). However, it appeared that this money was to shore up the teaching of Russian and Portuguese which were already being offered as minor sequences (Dunne & Pavlyshyn, 2011, p. 19). (Portuguese of course would be very significant for Australia's relationship with Brazil, quite apart from other countries where Portuguese is spoken.) It was also not clear from this ANU announcement whether this was a one-off donation, or whether other funds were forthcoming. As it stood, it would not have been sufficient to cover a couple of lecturing positions for a year. It was certainly significant that a philanthropic individual put forward the funds for these languages for his/her own private reasons rather than the university or government. However, as has been shown in the past, when initial philanthropic funds run out, it is the university to whom the funds were given which has to decide whether to continue the ongoing funding of the language. This depended on whether the language had commanded sufficient student enrolments to justify its continuance or whether the language offerings were simply not economically viable.

Whilst philanthropy is given much media attention, what is perhaps not commonly known is that a lot more crucial financial support for languages comes from external sources such as foreign governments year by year in cash or kind. The Cassamarca Foundation, for instance, an Italian philanthropic body, has partially funded 14 Italian studies positions in Australian universities for many years (Australian Centre for Italian Studies, n.d.). The Sultan of Oman Endowed Chair in Arab and Islamic studies at the University of Melbourne has existed since 2003 (UniMelb. Asia Institute, n.d.). The Japan Foundation, a Japanese public organisation, has operated a program of Japanese language education for more than 30 years, providing, amongst other endeavours, funding for individuals and organisations involved in the field of Japanese studies (Japan Foundation, n.d.).

8.11 The Global Perspective: Languages Elsewhere in the English-Speaking World

In the context of globalisation, similar trends and challenges for language learning to those identified for Australia have been noted in other English-speaking countries. In October 2013, a joint gathering of UK and US professors, researchers, policymakers and public servants organised by the British Academy and various US bodies such as the American Council on the Teaching of Foreign Languages, was hosted by the University of Maryland to discuss the state of languages in their respective countries. The message was that 'Britain and the United States must rapidly increase their number of competent foreign language speakers if they are to compete in the global jobs and services markets of the future' (Helmore, 2013. Policy needs to change. pp. 1, 2). Richard Brecht, the director of language policy at the University of Maryland, authored the paper *Languages for all?* presented at the October forum. The paper was offered as a 'basis for a national and international dialogue on language in the United States and other English-speaking countries'. It posed the question of a national educational dilemma that language study was not given the resources to make such study 'an essential part of preparation for life' in the twenty-first century (Brecht, 2013, pp. 3, 4, 6). As Brecht said: 'We're so far behind because we've been religiously monolingual and we've got (sic) away with that-till now; now there's a global war for talent and we can't compete in that market' (Helmore, 2013, p. 3).

Concern about falling numbers of students taking foreign languages in the UK was not a new issue. The recommendations of a 2009 report by the Higher Education Funding Council for England reiterated many of the issues which have been argued for in the Australian context: encourage language departments and centres to work together 'to promote a clear and compelling identity for modern foreign languages' within humanities; encourage vice-chancellors and other senior managers to 'understand that languages have more than one function' in a university and should be located 'within the context of internationalisation ambitions and the university's strategic mission' (Worton, 2009, p. 36). The British Academy published a report in November 2013 which argued for increased language capacity within government in the interests of the UK's future security and capacity for global influence. The Chair of the Foreign Affairs Select Committee, Richard Ottaway, said at the launch of the report: 'It's a point that my Committee has highlighted time and time again in almost every single enquiry we've undertaken since 2010. The language problem is not just a problem for the government – it needs to be tackled all the way from schools and universities across to business too' (British Academy, 2013. Lost for words).

New Zealand and Canada are very pertinent examples of countries which have similar migration and settlement histories to Australia beginning with their origins as colonies of Great Britain. Both countries have also grappled with the issues of multiculturalism and both also have an indigenous population but with vastly different emphases on the teaching of those indigenous languages.[7]

New Zealand's unique language position includes Maori as an official language as well as English. A paper produced by the Royal Society of New Zealand in March 2013 decried the ongoing lack of a national languages policy which had been

---

[7] As previously indicated the research for this book did not included the indigenous languages of Australia. Valuable future research could be undertaken examining indigenous language policies of Australia, Canada and New Zealand.

8.11 The Global Perspective: Languages Elsewhere in the English-Speaking World

first framed since 1992. The writers argued the need for language learning to facilitate 'the development of global links and the internationalisation of the population.' Their approach was not simply an economic one but one which argued that languages played a central role in the development of the country: in a variety of areas including education, social and economic mobility, identity building and cultural maintenance. They cited the 1987 Australian National Policy on Languages as a policy which described all the aspects which the Royal Society thought important. They also raised the problem of monolingualism as a communication barrier to trade. The lack of clear articulation between secondary and tertiary language offerings was noted, as were the funding pressures which language departments in tertiary institutions often faced (Royal Society of New Zealand, 2013, *Aotearoa New Zealand*, pp. 6, 7).

Sharon Harvey (one of the writers of the Royal Society of NZ paper) again raised the issue of New Zealand's multicultural and multilingual society in her 2015 conference paper *Superdiversity, language and policy*. She pointed out the decline in learning of languages and entrenched public monolingualism and the need to embrace the language heritage of New Zealand people in an enabling not constraining policy (Harvey, 2015). These issues of monolingualism and the value of a language policy for all people of a particular society are all too familiar in Australia.

Canada is another example of a former British colonial society where language policy issues have been ongoing for some decades and where the issues involve not only the official languages, but aboriginal languages and immigrant or heritage languages. Here there is not one pan-Canada language policy, but rather thirteen policies, one for each of the ten provinces, two for two of the territories and one for the federal government. The unique situation in Canada was encapsulated by their Official Languages Act on 1969 enshrining English and French as the official languages. This Act was subsequently reviewed culminating in a new Official Languages Act in 1988 (Mackey, 2010, p. 49). However, heritage languages and Aboriginal languages have not received the same fiscal recognition as the two official languages (Burnaby, 2008, pp. 3, 14; Morris, 2010, p. xi). As Burnaby remarked: 'the focus on the French/English debate has drawn attention away from other languages in the country and their value (Burnaby, 1996, pp. 217–218). Haque critiqued the 1988 Act as outlining a hierarchy of languages rendering 'the language resources that newcomers bring with them simply a cultural trait' (Haque, 2010, p. 293).

These brief examples of the languages issues for other English-speaking countries, particularly in the USA, New Zealand and the United Kingdom, highlight the similarities of the challenges which Australia also faced: the complacency of English language monolingualism, the need to ensure that senior management in universities understood the need to provide sufficient funding for languages (Worton, 2009, p. 36); the need for language academics to have developed strategies collaboratively; the need for dialogue between language educators, university leaders and government about current and future challenges for language education (Worton, 2009, p. 38); and the imperative that students needed to be prepared for global careers by being both culturally and linguistically competent. As Brecht had put it: 'a second language is crucial in the job market- they can't be a whole global citizen without one' (Helmore, 2013, p. 3). The issue about management in universities understanding the need for sufficient funding and profile for languages raised by the Higher Education Funding Council for the English context was particularly pertinent at the University of Melbourne in mid-2014. A draft strategy paper for discussion was released entitled *Growing Esteem: 2014* (UniMelb, 2014). As LCNAU pointed out to its members at that university, the glaring omission in this paper was a commitment to languages and cultures as a central element in the University's plans for the future.

As was shown in the case of the United States and the United Kingdom, it was crucially important that the debate for the relevance and adequate funding of languages, was continually raised by academic societies and bodies of language educators. A significant report from the Academies of the Humanities and the Social Sciences in Australia was launched in October 2014 with an accompanying analysis of university statistics 2002–2011 (Dobson, 2013; Turner & Brass, 2014). Amongst the very comprehensive information of what the humanities, arts and social sciences sector was currently delivering, was data about the state of languages. An increase in just over 4000 EFTSL language enrolments (Dobson, 2013, p. 25) was certainly a positive sign for student interest in languages. However, what was not available was whether language study had increased as a percentage of total EFTSL enrolments for the same period.

A notable innovation, developed by three universities, the ANU, Macquarie University and the University of Melbourne, in partnership with LCNAU, has been a national language studies portal for Australian universities. This project, a single online location, which aims to improve access to languages at tertiary level for all students in Australia, was funded by an Office for Learning and Teaching grant (LCNAU, 2014a. Media release, LCNAU, 2016. University languages portal). Such an innovation highlighted the significance of the organisation, LCNAU, the Languages & Cultures Network for Australian Universities. I argue that, in Australia, LCNAU is a vitally important organisation for four reasons. Firstly, LCNAU provides a focus and a network, and is a national body able to speak authoritatively on behalf of language educators and academics to vice-chancellors and senior university administrators. It can also be a body which can work with governments both State and Federal, and lobby for necessary changes. Secondly, LCNAU provides a national forum for dissemination of knowledge and continuity and accumulation of experience to members, enabling them to be readily informed about what is happening across the sector. Thirdly, LCNAU aims to encourage and enable university research on and through languages other than English. Finally, and perhaps the most important one, is the aim of LCNAU to provide the next generation of leadership for language education in Australian higher education (Hajek, Nettelbeck & Woods, 2013, pp. 11, 12; LCNAU, n.d., Background).

8.12 Conclusion

As this chapter has shown, the environment for tertiary languages teaching in Australia had continued to be mixed and often uncertain. This environment was variously affected from two angles: the often short-term vagaries of government priorities for languages which they deem to be in the national interest, and the priorities of senior university management as to what were deemed to be languages worthy of sustaining, whilst always keeping a weather eye on funding. Underlying much of the debate was the salient point that trade was a driver for languages everywhere. The pressing issues for language educators and academics in Australia clearly had a global dimension. However, in the Australian scene, the attitude of monolingualism that English alone, being a global language, was sufficient, needed to be countered as other languages such as Chinese, Spanish and Hindi have grown as global languages. Organisations such as the languages lobby group LCNAU remained crucial in advancing the importance of languages in the national interest.

Chapter 9
Conclusion

This book has examined the development of language offerings in the Australian tertiary sector from the colonial period up to the current time. In order to understand trends across this period, an analysis of influences driving the development of tertiary language education highlights whether the impetus came from within the institutions themselves, from government initiatives, or from other sources such as private individuals. From the fairly autonomous beginnings of universities, governments later sought to make universities more accountable for their funding and to justify the economic viability of their courses including language teaching. Governments took more control when they began to tie funding for university courses to political imperatives whether for economic, defence or strategic reasons. It is at this point that perceptions of what was in the national interest became influencing factors in funding and support. There was a shift away from the traditional notion of a focus on classical languages, towards a more utilitarian understanding of the value of languages. National interest ideas moved away from what was important just for the leadership of the nation towards what was important for the whole of society and the economic future of the country.

I have argued that the study of languages was important right from the establishment of universities in the Australian colonies. This education, modelled on the elite universities of Britain, signalled not only Australia's position as part of the British Empire, but also the strength of that British educational influence. This liberal education, according to Woolley, first Classics professor at the University of Sydney, enabled the development of independent thinking and intellectual enquiry through the study of mathematics and the classics as the key to understanding the great ideas of Western civilisation (UniSyd, 1853, pp. 53, 54, 55). The classics required the study of Latin and Ancient Greek, the languages first taught as the first university was founded in each colony, or, after 1901, state. As French and German were also part of this inherited liberal education, these modern languages were also taught in Australia's universities. This liberal education was seen as important for Australia's future leaders, statesmen, businessmen, and professionals such as doctors and lawyers in exercising their professional and civic responsibilities. Languages were an essential part of the emerging Australian national identity.

After Federation in 1901, when Australia as a nation was becoming more involved in international affairs, the Federal government intervened to influence the teaching of a particular language. The Department of Defence provided the funds for Japanese to be introduced at the University of Sydney in 1917, and concurrently at Duntroon Military College. Australia needed to know about Japan's military intentions and gleaned this through the Japanese lecturer's annual reports of his trips to Japan. This was a very strategic and carefully crafted arrangement for the government's interests.

This study demonstrates that the terms national interest, the national need, the national importance, have been frequent key signposts in the rhetoric used by governments, individuals and institutions to justify decisions made about languages offered, funding sought and allocated for languages to be taught. What has been shown, however, is that these terms have been used differently at various times by different groups and governments. The national interest of the middle nineteenth century, to establish fine leadership in the British mould in Australian colonies, was of a different order to that of the early twentieth century when Australia was beginning to be part of the new world order. Those early twentieth century interests meant Australia's developing national identity and defence interests through two world wars. It was different again to the national interest of the early twenty-first century which concentrated on Australia's economic future and geopolitical interests in the wider world, specifically with Asian countries.

Whilst governments have been the key agents of funding for Australian universities and their courses, including languages, it has also been demonstrated that there has been a long history of philanthropic support for languages with numerous individuals and communities giving funds to universities to support particular languages. One such example was the funds given by several businessmen, principally Keith Murdoch, to establish the teaching of Dutch at the University of Melbourne in 1942. He felt it would be useful for Australia's relationship with the Dutch East Indies. It was ironic that after World War II the Dutch could not regain the Dutch East Indies and the language which would become significant in that region in the second half of the twentieth century was Indonesian. The defence and security implications for a particular language were again evident when the Federal government granted funding for the teaching of Indonesian in the university sector from 1956, as the newly independent Indonesia was strategically important to Australia. The defence and security issues behind funding were evident again in the involvement of the Federal government in the creation of the Oriental Languages Department of the Canberra University College in 1952, where Chinese was taught, from 1953, for the first time in an Australian university. It was very timely to promote such studies given the Chinese involvement in the Korean War and Australia's security and defence concerns about the spread of communism throughout South-East Asia. In this context, in another philanthropic gesture, the Myer Foundation gave significant funds for the founding of a Department of Oriental Studies at the University of Melbourne in 1960. Kenneth Myer believed that Australians should know about the great historical cultures of China and Japan, their languages and their current aims and aspirations (UMA-Registrar's Correspondence. 1961/986. 12 October 1960. Turnbull).

By the mid-1950s, the university sector had changed from its elite status to one of a much wider democratic intake and government was becoming more involved in universities' affairs, wanting universities to work collaboratively to produce plans for financial and course needs. Academics, through the Australian Humanities Research Council, concerned about the dearth of information about the state of languages in Australia commissioned a report. The 1966 Wykes Report deemed all languages as crucial, having both educational and cultural importance. They also looked beyond the traditional classical and modern European languages curricula which held sway in Australia's universities, reinforcing the need for more attention to Asian languages.

Growing links between Australia and Asia based on trade, prompted the Federal government in 1969 to commission a report on the teaching of Asian languages and cultures in Australia. Indeed that 1970 Auchmuty Report recommended an increase in the teaching of Asian languages and cultures, mentioning all the issues, trade and political and economic which the government had cited as important (C of A, 1970, p. 89). Greater awareness of Asian philosophies, customs and outlook was crucial (C of A, 1970, pp. 63, 89). This stance was very clear and decisive about which languages were in Australia's economic interests. Australia needed to redefine its trade interests towards Asian markets because its traditional British markets were declining as Britain turned towards the European Economic Community. This turning towards Asia was demonstrated in the language offerings of newly established universities of the 1970s, particularly Griffith University, responding to the proximity of Asia and the national imperative to be more familiar with Asian languages and cultures. When Griffith began teaching in 1975, it was the first university to establish a School of Modern Asian Studies with a brief towards commercial, industrial and cultural contacts with Asia. Such transformed national sentiments showed how far Australia's focus and self-identity had changed from its early colonial days, its British university inheritance and its place in the British Empire.

Through the large-scale migration program post-World War II, Australia could not ignore the fact that, in the ensuing years, the population had become more multicultural and thus multilingual. However, some migrants were finding settling into Australia very challenging. The 1978 Galbally Report commissioned by the Federal government to investigate post-arrival migrant services and programs, was clear in its understanding: 'We believe Australia is at a critical stage in the development of a cohesive, united multicultural nation.' (C of A, 1978, p. 3). That the Galbally Report was published in nine community languages as well as English, was certainly acknowledgement of that diversity of ethnic cultures and languages in Australia. I argue that it was a genuine move to communicate with the major migrant groups through their own languages to show the goodwill of government 'to encourage multiculturalism' (C of A, 1978, pp. 3–4). The Federal government needed to heed the calls from migrant communities for their languages to be valued and taught in the school and university sectors. There was a period of some 20 years or so when government funding for migrant languages was forthcoming, but such funding was not sustained as government priorities for languages shifted as economic interests in Asia expanded.

I have shown that it was community philanthropy which was crucial at various times from the middle twentieth century for the introduction of additional languages at the university level, which might not otherwise have been introduced. Such philanthropic endowment was significant for migrant and community languages in the 1970s and 1980s onwards. The reality was however, that where student demand for such languages declined and community funds ceased, the languages were often discontinued. There are significant examples cited in this book where community philanthropy was the only funding which enabled the continued teaching of relatively small languages.

As has been demonstrated, the 1987 National Policy on Languages was a further commitment from the Federal government to the diverse languages of Australia's population with the important distinction of prioritising languages for the first time. Whilst maintenance of mother tongues was deemed essential, a group of nine languages of wider teaching were recommended as important for Australia's economic, national and external policy goals, or, in other words, Australia's national interest. That group of languages encompassed both European and Asian languages but did not have the spread of migrant languages highlighted in the Galbally Report. Now the national interest required a truly international focus. Crucially for the growth of languages, the budgetary recommendations of this policy were mostly accepted by the Federal government.

This analysis of influences on Australian tertiary languages and what was deemed in the national interest has been shown to be quite dynamic, with priorities often shifting when Federal and State governments changed. The 1991 Australian Literacy and Language Policy (ALLP) had its own emphasis on what was now understood to be of national importance. The title said it all: literacy in English was of primary importance. Whilst there was some emphasis for languages of broader national interest relating to Australia's patterns of overseas trade and geopolitical position in the Asia-Pacific, the new list of priority languages now included three more Asian languages: Korean, Thai and Vietnamese, signalling a still greater focus on Australia's trade interests in Asia. Nevertheless, the dominant factor in the ALLP was literacy in English, characterising what that Coalition government believed was the greatest priority for the nation.

Nevertheless, universities' language priorities had not been solely driven by governments' policies and stated priorities. The University of Melbourne case study has demonstrated the significant structural change and focus on languages teaching instituted there in the early 1990s. As Australia's economic and strategic focus was slanted even more decidedly towards Asia, Asian languages were prioritised strongly in the 1994 Rudd Report. Four languages, Mandarin Chinese, Japanese, Indonesian and Korean, were linked in importance to Australia's international and regional economic performance (NALCWG, 1994, pp. iii, v). Whilst Australia was clearly aligning its economic national interest to Asia, prioritising certain Asian languages along the way, there was no official government interest in other languages, such as

9 Conclusion

the modern European languages. Significantly too, the languages' emphasis of the Rudd Report and the funding recommendations accepted by the Labor government were for the school sector only, not for universities (NALCWG, 1994, pp. xviii, 43).

Again, when in 1996 a new Coalition government took power, there were new political priorities. Seeking to reduce the deficit, the Government implemented university funding cuts. Languages, always vulnerable to changes in funding, were caught up in these cuts with a consequent decline in the number of languages taught. The Academy of the Humanities sought to highlight the perilous state of languages in the university sector. Through the late 1990s into the middle 2000s it was generally agreed in academic circles that for language policy 'there was a general lack of activity at the Federal level and reduced activity at the state and territory level' (Bradshaw, Deumart, & Burridge, 2008, p. 22). However, universities across this period showed again a period of structural change for languages: for instance, an increased profile for Asian languages at the University of Melbourne but restructuring into a single languages school because of downsizing at Monash University and for financial reasons at the University of Sydney. As far as perceptions of the standing of languages and the importance of their funding were concerned, it has been shown that there was a divide between the attitudes of university academics, senior university administrators and governments holding the purse strings.

By the twenty-first century, universities for the most part, shaped their courses in a global context, a context which promoted languages as giving enhanced graduate employment prospects both domestically and internationally, appealing to students' self-interest. The advent, in 2011, of a national organisation of language academics, Languages and Cultures Network for Australian Universities (LCNAU), was an important step to raise the national profile of languages teaching and research. This organisation carefully and shrewdly couched its principles about its aims and activities in the government rhetoric of national interest, citing 'the strategic importance of linguistic and cultural diversity within institutions and for Australia as a nation' (LCNAU, 2014a).

With the change of Federal government in 2013, Australia again experienced a shift of focus as to what the new government believed should be Australia's international priority, what regions needed attention to ensure Australia's economic future, and what priorities were given to languages. The 2011 Asian Century White Paper of the previous Labor government had linked engagement with the Asia-Pacific region with specific languages to be prioritised. Nevertheless, these priorities were never implemented as the new Coalition government had a new focus and new priorities. Employment outcomes stimulated by internships in Asia, rather than language proficiency, became the catchcry for the next iteration of what was deemed to be in Australia's national interest. Throughout this study the evidence has shown that shifting priorities of governments have affected sustained and consistent funding of languages. In such an environment, I argue that consensus on which languages should be taught for Australia's national interest would be difficult to achieve.

This book has shown that, despite the vagaries and uncertainties of government policies, of university priorities and of student demand for languages, university language educators have continued to develop and implement new and innovative ways of language teaching and curricula. Such innovations, which have been discussed in specific contexts in this book, included various forms of collaborative teaching, breadth or broadening units, and separate diplomas in languages enabling more students to access languages in their tertiary studies. Such measures have enhanced and strengthened the significance of languages in Australia's need for a linguistically competent population. Future research into student motivation and satisfaction regarding language learning would aid the consolidation of existing modes of access to languages, and perhaps introduce more innovations. I argue that such innovation and continuous improvement has been and is the strength of languages education for Australia.

It has also been shown that the challenges for language learning in Australia are not dissimilar to those faced in other English-speaking countries. A key example is the persistent monolingual mindset of many decision-makers and for Australians more generally that, despite official rhetoric, English is the only language Australia needs for its global engagement. Clyne had argued that this complacent attitude was an impediment to Australia's economic development and communications with other countries (Clyne, 2005, pp. xi, xii; Hajek & Slaughter, 2015). This study has also shown that secondary school language teaching has always been an important factor to languages in the tertiary sector, both in shaping student interest in languages and feeding students into further language learning in the universities. I have also shown that language teaching in universities has been driven by the availability of adequate finances as government funding for languages in universities has not been consistently sustained. Indeed, governments have clearly shown their priorities as the only comprehensive language program in Australia that has been funded federally over the last 20 years or so has been for the teaching of Asian languages in the school sector.

I have argued that the evidence shows that funding for languages was only prioritised by governments when particular government policies, deemed to be of national importance, highlighted the value of language proficiency. However, it has also been demonstrated that there has been a long thread of community and individual philanthropy for language teaching across the twentieth and into the twenty-first centuries. Trends and evidence examined here suggest that whilst such benefaction cannot be anticipated, coupled with ongoing and fundamental support from foreign governments, substantial philanthropy may well be the way that the health of university languages teaching in Australia is bolstered in years to come.

Appendices

Appendix 1

Countries of last residence of settler arrivals in Australia 1949–1954

Country of last residence of settler arrivals 1949–1954	Number of people	%
UK & Ireland	227,286	34.9
Germany	122,890	18.9
Italy	96,563	14.8
Netherlands	51,355	7.9
Malta	17,533	2.7
New Zealand	13,844	2.1
Austria	13,603	2.1
Greece	12,445	1.9
USA	7205	1.1
Egypt	6489	1.0
Poland	6194	1.0
Cyprus	4441	0.7
China	4327	0.7
Indonesia	3943	0.6
Papua New Guinea	3736	0.6
India	3650	0.6

(continued)

© Springer Nature Switzerland AG 2019
J. J. Baldwin, *Languages other than English in Australian Higher Education*,
Language Policy 17, https://doi.org/10.1007/978-3-030-05795-4

Country of last residence of settler arrivals 1949–1954	Number of people	%
Yugoslavia	3534	0.5
Malaysia	3188	0.5
Hong Kong	3132	0.5
Canada	2399	0.4
Lebanon	2216	0.3
South Africa	2059	0.3
Singapore	1801	0.3
Sri Lanka	1673	0.3
Fiji	1205	0.2
Denmark	1125	0.2
Sweden	720	0.1
USSR	668	0.1
Hungary	489	0.1
Philippines	467	0.1
Turkey	135	0.02
Other	28,593[a]	4.4
Total	**650,999**	**100.00**

Source: Department of Immigration and Multicultural Affairs. (2001). p. 26
[a]Numbers from individual countries not large enough to warrant a separate entry
NB:DIMA cautions interpretation of this data as settler arrivals by birthplace data are not available for this period and, 'in the period immediately after World War II, there were large numbers of displaced persons whose country of last residence was not necessarily the same as their birthplace'

Appendix 2

Birthplace of the Australian population for the 1954 census

Country of birth from 1954 census	Number of people	% overseas born
Australia	7,700,064	–
United Kingdom	626,035	48.7
Italy	119,897	9.3
Germany	65,422	5.1
Poland	56,594	4.4
Netherlands	52,035	4.0
New Zealand	43,350	3.4
Ireland	38,170	3.0
Greece	25,862	2.0
Yugoslavia	22,856	1.8
Malta	19,988	1.6
Hungary	14,602	1.1
India	11,955	0.9
China	10,277	0.8
USA	8289	0.6
Egypt	8150	0.6
South Africa	5971	0.5
Lebanon	3861	0.3
Denmark	2954	0.2
Malaysia	2279	0.2
Sweden	2191	0.2
Sri Lanka	1961	0.2
Hong Kong	1554	0.1
Philippines	217	0.002
Other overseas	14,996[a]	11.0
Total	**8,986,530**	**100.00**

Source: Department of Immigration and Multicultural Affairs. (2001). p. 18
[a] Numbers from individual countries not large enough to warrant a separate entry

Appendix 3

Community languages taught in the tertiary sector 1974–2013

Kramer 1975: key migrant languages in Aust. which should be taught (according to country)	Hawley 1982 survey: languages taught 1974–1981	White and Baldauf data 1981	Under-represented or new community languages started with TEC grants for 1982–1984 trie&$$$;	White and Baldauf data 1988	White and Baldauf data 1990	White and Baldauf data 1994	Dunne and Pavlyshyn data 2011	Dunne and Pavlyshyn data 2013
Lebanon (Arabic)	Arabic (modern)	Arabic (modern)	Arabic	Arabic (modern)	Arabic (modern)	Arabic (modern)	Arabic (modern)	Arabic (modern)
Czechoslovakia	X = not offered	X	X	X	Czech	X	X	X
	Greek (modern)	Greek (modern)	Greek (modern)	Greek (modern)	Greek (modern)	Greek (modern)	Greek (modern)	Greek (modern)
	Hebrew (modern)	Hebrew (modern)		Hebrew (modern)	Hebrew (modern)	Hebrew (modern)	Hebrew	Hebrew (classical & modern)
	Italian	Italian		Italian	Italian	Italian	Italian	Italian
Hungary	X	X	X	X	X	X	X	X
Latvia	Latvian	Latvian	X	Latvian	X	Latvian	X	X

Appendices

Lithuania	X	X	X	Lithuanian	Lithuanian	X	X
	X	X	Macedonian	Macedonian	Macedonian	X	X
Malta	Maltese	Maltese	Maltese	Maltese	X	X	X
Poland	Polish	Polish	Polish	Polish	Polish	Polish	Polish
	Portuguese	Portuguese	Portuguese	Portuguese	Portuguese	Portuguese	Portuguese
	Russian	Russian		Russian	Russian	Russian	Russian
Turkey	Turkish	Turkish	Turkish	Turkish	Turkish	Turkish	Turkish
	Spanish	Spanish		Spanish	Spanish	Spanish	Spanish
	Vietnamese	Vietnamese	Vietnamese	Vietnamese	Vietnamese	Vietnamese	Vietnamese
		X		Ukrainian	Ukrainian	Ukrainian	Ukrainian
Yugoslavia	Serbo-Croatian	Croatian	Croatian, Serbian	Croatian Serbo-Croatian	Croatian	Croatian	Croatian
					Serbian		
	Yiddish	Yiddish		X	X	Yiddish	Yiddish

Source: Dunne & Pavlyshyn, Hawley, Leal, Kramer, White & Baldauf

Appendix 4

Language department structures in major universities in 1991

University	Language department structures
Adelaide	Asian, Classical & European languages in Faculty of Arts; individual language departments, except Asian languages in the Centre for Asian Studies within Arts
ANU	Department of Classical and Modern European languages in Faculty of Arts; Asian languages through Faculty of Asian Studies
Monash	All languages in individual departments taught through Faculty of Arts
Melbourne	Languages taught in departments of Faculty of Arts: Classics and Near Eastern Studies, French and Italian Studies, Asian Languages, Germanic Studies and Russian.
UNSW	All languages in individual departments of Faculty of Arts & Social Sciences
UQ	Asian, Classical and Modern European languages taught in individual departments in Arts Faculty.
Sydney	Classical, European and Asian languages taught in individual departments in Faculty of Arts
UWA	Individual language departments for all languages in Faculty of Arts, except Japanese taught through the Department of Economics in the Faculty of Arts

Source: University of Adelaide, ANU, Monash University, University of Melbourne, University of NSW, University of Queensland, University of Sydney, University of Western Australia Handbooks and Calendars of 1991

Appendix 5

Language department structures in major universities in 1999

University	Language department structures
Adelaide	Humanities and Social Sciences (formerly Arts); still individual language departments with Asian languages in The Centre for Asian Studies in Humanities and Social Sciences
ANU	Department of Classical and Modern European languages in Faculty of Arts; Asian languages through Faculty of Asian Studies (unchanged from 1991)
Monash	Arts Faculty restructured into Schools: School of Asian Languages and Studies now separate from School of European Languages and Cultures.
University of Melbourne	School of Languages: Ancient & Classical languages; modern European languages; Hebrew Studies
	Asian languages now separate in MIALS: Arabic, Chinese, Indonesian, Japanese
UNSW	In 1999, a School of Modern Language Studies in Faculty of Arts was still the structure (created in 1995), unifying individual language departments (Chinese located in Arts); In 1995, School of Asian Business and Language Studies created within Faculty of Commerce & Economics becoming in 1998, the School of International Business. Japanese and Korean in Asian languages till 1998 when they moved into Arts- no explanation available for decisions of 1995 or 1998. (records closed for 30 years)

(continued)

University	Language department structures
University of Queensland	4 Arts departments: Asian Languages, Classics, German & Russian Studies, Romance Languages
University of Sydney	School structure created in 1999: all languages in School of European, Asian and Middle Eastern Languages and Studies
UWA	All languages taught in Faculty of Arts; Asian languages in School of Asian Studies; Classical languages in Department of Classics; Modern European Languages in School of European Languages

Source: University of Adelaide, ANU, Monash University, University of Melbourne, University of NSW, University of Queensland, University of Sydney, University of Western Australia Handbooks and Calendars of 1999

Appendix 6

Go8 universities' languages offerings websites for 2013

Go8 Uni	Summary comments from their 2013 websites re languages
ANU	Modern European and Classical languages in the **School of Language Studies in the ANU College of Arts & Social Sciences: Centre for Arab & Islamic Studies in College of Arts & Social Sciences**: Arabic, Persian and Turkish- **Faculty of Asian Studies**: Arabic, Chinese, Hindi, Indonesian, Japanese, Korean, Sanskrit, Thai & Lao, Urdu & Persian, Vietnamese.
U of Q	Offered in Arts faculty in the **School of Languages and Comparative Cultural Studies**: Chinese, Classical languages, French, German, Indonesian, Italian, Japanese, Korean, Russian and Spanish.
UniSyd	**Faculty of Arts & Social Sciences, School of Languages and Cultures.**
	Arabic, Chinese: French: German, Hebrew (Modern), Hebrew (Classical), Sanskrit
	Indonesian, Italian, Japanese, Korean, Greek (ancient and modern) Spanish
	Faculty of Arts, School of Philosophical and Historical Inquiry, Department of Classics and Ancient History: Latin, Ancient Greek
Monash	**Faculty of Arts, School of Languages, Cultures and Linguistics:** Ancient Greek, Chinese, French, German, Indonesian, Italian, Japanese, Korean, Latin, Spanish, Ukrainian
Uni of Adelaide	**Classics & European Languages in School of Humanities:** Ancient Greek, French, German, Latin, Spanish; **Asian Languages in School of Social Sciences:** Chinese, Japanese
UNSW	**Languages in Faculty of Arts and Social Sciences within the School of Humanities and Languages:** French, Italian, Spanish, Greek, Japanese, Chinese, Indonesian, Korean
UWA	**School of Humanities, Classics, European Languages and Studies:** Ancient Greek, French, German, Italian, Latin
	School of Social Sciences, Asian Languages: Chinese, Indonesian, Japanese, Korean.

(continued)

Go8 Uni	Summary comments from their 2013 websites re languages
UniMelb	**Faculty of Arts: School of Languages and Linguistics:** French, German, Italian, Russian, Spanish.
	Faculty of Arts: Asia Institute: Arabic, Chinese, Indonesian, Japanese.

Source: University of Adelaide, ANU, Monash University, University of Melbourne, University of NSW, University of Queensland, University of Sydney, University of Western Australia 2013 websites

Appendix 7

Universities' statements of students' personal and career benefits of language learning

University	Benefits of language learning
ANU	Focus on language in the broadest sense-the social context of language, the culture, literature, art, history, politics, and society.
	Focus on issues pertinent to Australia's interest in, and the development of its commercial, scientific and industrial ties with its areas of coverage.
	ANU major world centre for teaching and research on Asia, the leading centre for Asian studies in Australia; offers the widest range of Asian Studies available in Australia:
UQ	Languages taught in the interests of scholarship, promoting languages other than English, developing linguistic skills relevant to students' personal and professional goals. Intercultural communication, intercultural sensitivity important. Actively promote the knowledge and study of languages and cultures in the wider community. Importance of a LOTE in the global economy.
UniSyd	Arabic: major language of the Middle East and North Africa; language of Islam; insights into history, civilisation and current culture and media of the Arab world.
	Chinese: the language of the future; can lead to careers in international relations, multinational corporations, tourism, education, NGOs.
	French: major world language; key language of UN and European Union; can lead to careers as diplomats, interpreters, translators, teachers, TV presenters, lawyers, journalists.
	German: important in science, music, philosophy, literature.
	Hebrew: (Modern) important for contemporary Israeli culture and society; (Classical) important as language of the Bible and for study of ancient texts.
	Sanskrit: important classical language of the Indian subcontinent.
	Indonesian can lead to careers in research, education, government and the arts
	Italian: both contemporary and historical Italy covered; learnt for many and varied reasons, can be used in many different careers
	Japanese: a rich variety of language, history and cultural units.

(continued)

University	Benefits of language learning
Monash	(Korean, although no longer prioritised in the Asian Century White Paper, is still a language to which Monash is committed.)
	Acquire and develop language skills but also gain access to the worlds of culture that each new language unlocks. Graduates- international relations and diplomacy, international trade and banking, business, the arts, publishing, the media, law, medicine and engineering, scientific research, teaching, public service, the corporate world.
	The Centre for Southeast Asian Studies at Monash is for postgraduate research, not the teaching of languages.
Uni of Adelaide	Committed to the pedagogical principle that languages cannot be taught in a vacuum, isolated from their cultural, social and historical context.
	The significance of Asia for Australia's future is widely recognised in the community, in the schools system and by government. Increasing number of employment opportunities opening up for graduates with expertise in the area.
	Why study German? An important language in science, the arts, trade and technology; German speaking countries of Europe together are Aust's third most important trading partners. A heritage language in SA; career prospects in education, media, public service, libraries, diplomatic service, tourism and business, increasingly in international legal firms.
	Why Hispanic Studies? Spanish second most widely spoken language in the world. Spanish speakers in 5 continents and more than 20 countries. Work possibilities with new economies flourishing in Latin America.
	Why study French? One of the most widely spoken languages in the world; still a key diplomatic language; French language and culture (writers, artists, philosophers) a great influence on the world.
	Why study Classics? To learn about the origins of European culture: its art,
UNSW	[very little marketing of languages on this website]
UWA	Classics and the contributions these cultures have made to the modern world; Acceptable background for teaching, diplomatic service, librarianship, public service and industry; European languages- contemporary and historical perspectives facilitate a high level of cultural competence and international outlook, vital knowledge and skills to be effective global citizens in the twenty-first century. Asia is an economic powerhouse vital to Australia's future prosperity and security. Asian languages for careers in Govt. depts. e.g. Defence, Immigration, DFAT, commerce, tourism, cultural organisations, NGOs, academia, teaching.
	European languages for careers in the diplomatic services, teaching and training, interpreting and translating, travel, hospitality, publishing, theatre, commerce, manufacturing, law and international relations. Useful for international banking, journalism and communications, medical areas, music and the arts, the public service.

(continued)

University	Benefits of language learning
UniMelb.	French: one of the world's major international languages; may enhance career prospects in international relations and development studies, business, sciences, the arts.
	German a major world language. Used extensively throughout Europe in business and commerce. third most popular foreign language worldwide, German in philosophy, literature, medicine, chemistry and engineering.
	Italian: many links between Australia and Italy- many opportunities for economic and cultural development
	Spanish: a global language spoken by nearly 500 million in 5 continents; official language in 22 countries; second most widely spoken language by native speakers; an official language of many international organisations.
	Indonesia: of geographical and strategic importance to Australia; fourth most populous country in the world; the most influential ASEAN member; Indonesian studies can enhance employment opportunities in commerce, education, government and cultural affairs.
	Arabic: a priority language of strategic importance to Australia's national interests.
	Japanese: a language which contributes to wider understanding of the complex cultural, historical, political and economic flows in Asia.

Source: University of Adelaide, ANU, Monash University, University of Melbourne, University of NSW, University of Queensland, University of Sydney, University of Western Australia 2013 websites

Appendix 8

Language offerings in Australian universities 2011

Uni	UAdel	ANU	UMelb	LaT	Macq	Mon	USyd	UNSW	UQ	UWA
Akkadian							E			
Arabic		M	M			E_x	M			M_+
Aramaic							E			
Burmese		E								
Cantonese		E								
Catalan				E						
Croatian						M				
Egyptian (ancient)						E				
French	M	M	M	M	M	M	M		M	M
German	M	M	M		M	M	M	M	M	M
Greek (ancient)	M	M	M	E		E				M
Greek (modern)	M			M	M	E	M		m	
Hebrew			M				M			
Hindi		E		m; sc						
Indonesian	M	M	M	M		M	M	M	M	M

(continued)

Appendices

Uni	UAdel	ANU	UMelb	LaT	Macq	Mon	USyd	UNSW	UQ	UWA
Italian	M	M	M	M	M	M	M			M
Japanese	M	M	M	M	M	M	M		M	M
Javanese		E								
Korean		M				M	M	M	M	M∂
Latin	E	M	M			M				M
Lao		E								
Malay		E				?E				
Mandarin	M	M	M	M; sc	M	M	M		M	M
Mongolian		m								
Pali							E			
Persian		M								
Polish				M						
Portuguese		M		M					m; E	
Russian		M	M		M			M	M	
Sanskrit		M		M			M			
Spanish	M	M	M	M	M	M	M	M	M	
Swedish			M							
Syriac							E			
Tetum		E								
Thai		M								
Turkish		M								
Ukrainian						M				
Urdu		M								
Vietnamese		M								
Yiddish						M				

Modified from Dunne and Pavlyshyn 2011, pp. 18–19
Key: x possibly in 2012
+ from 2012
∂ staggered introduction from 2012
sc short course
M major
m minor
E individual U/G subject(s)

Bibliography

Primary

Government Reports, Records and Legislation

Asian Studies Council. (1988). *A national strategy for the study of Asia in Australia*. Canberra, Australia: Australian Government Publishing Service.

Australia Korea Foundation. (1993). *Australia-Korean Foundation: Annual report 1992–93*. Canberra, Australia: Australian Government Publishing Service.

Australian Advisory Council on Languages and Multicultural Education (AACLAME). (1990). *The national policy on languages: December 1987–March 1990: Report to the minister for employment, education and training*. Canberra, Australia: Australian Advisory Council on Languages and Multicultural Education.

Australian Bureau of Statistics (ABS). (1986). *Census 86 – Australia in profile: A summary of major findings: Catalogue no. 2502.0*. Accessed from http://www.ausstats.abs.gov.au/ausstats/free.nsf/0/0D42204C00A51765CA2574CE0015DD7C/$File/25020_1986_Australia_in_Profile.pdf on 8 Feb 2015.

Australian Bureau of Statistics. (1996). *1996 Census of population and housing Australia- language spoken at home*. Accessed from http://www.abs.gov.au/websitedbs/D3110124.NSF/4a3fed835c77efdd4a2564d4001de2e5/a10306e7286229884a2564d400286577!OpenDocument on 8 Feb 2015.

Australian Bureau of Statistics. (2011a). *2011 Census shows Asian languages on the rise in Australian households*. Accessed from http://www.abs.gov.au/websitedbs/censushome.nsf/home/CO-60 on 4 July 2014.

Australian Bureau of Statistics. (2011b). *2071.0 – Reflecting a nation: Stories from the 2011 census, 2012–2013*. Accessed from http://www.abs.gov.au/ausstats/abs@.nsf/Lookup/2071.0main+features902012-2013 on 4 July 2014.

Australian Bureau of Statistics. (2011c). *4102.0 – Australian Social Trends, Dec 2011: International students*. Accessed from http://www.abs.gov.au/AUSSTATS/abs@.nsf/Lookup/4102.0Main+Features20Dec+2011#WHEREENROLMENT on 18 Feb 2015.

Australian Citizenship Convention. (1958). *Digest: Report of proceedings of the Australian citizenship convention*. Braddon, Australia: Department of Immigration.

Australian Council on Population and Ethnic Affairs (ACPEA). (1982). *Multiculturalism for all Australians: Our developing nationhood*. Canberra, Australia: Australian Government Publishing Service.

Australian Curriculum, Assessment and Reporting Authority (ACARA). (n.d.). *Languages*. Accessed from http://www.acara.edu.au/languages.html on 1 Feb 2018.

Australian Curriculum, Assessment and Reporting Authority. (2014a). *Media release*. Accessed from http://www.acara.edu.au/verve/_resources/20140721_Four_languages_curricula_release.pdf on 1 Dec 2014.

Australian Curriculum, Assessment and Reporting Authority. (2014b). *Message from Chairman*. Accessed from http://www.acara.edu.au/default.asp on 1 Dec 2014.

Australian Electoral Commission. (2000). *Minute: Naming of the new WA electoral division*. Accessed from http://www.aec.gov.au/Electorates/Redistributions/files/2000/wa/suggestions/stringall.pdf on 8 Sept 2011.

Australian Government. (2011). *Terms of reference. Australia in the Asian century issues paper*. Accessed from http://www.corrs.com.au/assets/thinking/downloads/Australia-in-Asian-Century-Issues-Paper.pdf on 5 Jan 2015.

Australian Government. (2012). *Funding agreement between the commonwealth of Australia and University of Western Sydney regarding funding under the commonwealth grant scheme in respect of the 2012 grant year*. Accessed from http://www.innovation.gov.au/HigherEducation/Funding/CommonwealthGrantScheme/Documents/CGS/UWS.pdf on 12 Feb 2013.

Australian Government. (2014). *Tertiary education standards and quality agency. TEQSA glossary of terms*. Accessed from http://www.teqsa.gov.au/glossary on 11 Mar 2014.

Australian Government. (2017). *2017 Foreign policy white paper*. Accessed from https://www.fpwhitepaper.gov.au/foreign-policy-white-paper on 26 Feb 2018.

Australian Institute of Multicultural Affairs (AIMA). (1980). *Review of multicultural and migrant education*. Canberra, Australia: AIMA.

Australian National University. (1946). *Australian National University Act 1946*. Accessed from http://www.comlaw.gov.au/Details/C2004C02218 on 8 Sept 2011.

Australian Universities Commission (AUC). (1963). *Second report of the Australian Universities Commission, Australian universities 1961–1966*. Canberra, Australia: Commonwealth Government Printer.

Australian Universities Commission. (1972). *Fifth report of the Australian Universities Commission*. Canberra, Australia: Australian Government Publishing Service.

Australian Universities Commission. (1975a). *Languages and linguistics in Australian universities: Report of the working party on languages and linguistics to the Universities commission*. (known as the Kramer Report). Canberra, Australia: Australian Government Publishing Service.

Australian Universities Commission. (1975b). *Sixth report of the Australian Universities Commission*. Canberra, Australia: Australian Government Publishing Service.

Australian Universities Commission. (1976). *Report for 1977–79 triennium*. Canberra, Australia: Australian Government Publishing Service.

Australian War Memorial. (n.d.). *Indonesian confrontation 1963–66*. Accessed from http://www.awm.gov.au/atwar/confrontation.asp on 14 Sept 2012.

Bishop, J. (2013). *Address to New Colombo Plan launch*. Accessed from http://foreignminister.gov.au/speeches/2013/jb_sp_131210a.html on 4 Feb 2014.

Commission of Inquiry into Poverty. (1975). *Poverty in Australia: First main report, April 1975 volume 1*. (known as the Henderson Inquiry). Canberra, Australia: Australian Government Publishing Service.

Commonwealth Committee on Needs of Universities (CCNU). (1950). *Interim report of the commonwealth committee on needs of universities*. (known as the Mills Report). Canberra, Australia: Commonwealth Committee.

Commonwealth Department of Education. (1982). *Towards a national language policy*. Canberra, Australia: Australian Government Publishing Service.

Commonwealth Immigration Advisory Council. (1960). *The progress and assimilation of migrant children in Australia*. Canberra, Australia: Commonwealth Government.

Commonwealth of Australia. (1901). *Immigration restriction act 1901*. Accessed from foundingdocs.gov.au/scan-sid.144.html and foundingdocs.gov.au/item-did-16.html on 23 June 2013.

Bibliography

Commonwealth of Australia. (1911). *Census of the commonwealth of Australia taken for the night between the 2nd and 3rd April 1911. Volume II, Part II-birthplaces*. Melbourne, Australia: Commonwealth of Australia.

Commonwealth of Australia. (1917). *Historical records of Australia: Series I- despatches to and from Sir Thomas Brisbane, volume XI, January 1823–November 1825*. Canberra, Australia: The library committee of the Commonwealth Parliament.

Commonwealth of Australia. (1957). *Report of the committee on Australian universities*. (known as the Murray Report). Canberra, Australia: Commonwealth Government Printer.

Commonwealth of Australia. (1964). *Tertiary education in Australia: Report of the committee on the future of tertiary education in Australia to the Australian Universities Commission*. (known as the Martin Report) (Vol. I & II). Canberra, Australia: Commonwealth Government Printer.

Commonwealth of Australia. (1965). *Tertiary education in Australia: Report of the committee on the future of tertiary education in Australia to the Australian Universities Commission*. (known as the Martin Report) (Vol. Volume III). Canberra, Australia: Commonwealth Government Printer.

Commonwealth of Australia. (1970). *The teaching of Asian languages and cultures in Australia*. Report by the Commonwealth Advisory Committee on the Teaching of Asian Languages and Cultures in Australia (known as the Auchmuty Report). Canberra, Australia: Commonwealth of Australia.

Commonwealth of Australia. (1978). *Migrant services and programs: Report of the review of post-arrival programs and services for migrants*. (known as the Galbally Report). Canberra, Australia: Australian Government Publishing Service.

Commonwealth of Australia. (1997). *In the national interest: Australia's foreign and trade policy white paper*. Canberra, Australia: Department of Foreign Affairs and Trade.

Commonwealth of Australia. (2003). *Advancing the national interest: Australia's foreign and trade policy white paper*. Accessed from http://australianpolitics.com/foreign/elements/2003_whitepaper.pdf on 7 Feb 2013.

Commonwealth of Australia. (2010). *The current state of Chinese, Indonesian, Japanese and Korean language education in Australian schools*. Carlton South, Australia: Education Services Australia.

Commonwealth Schools Commission. (1984). *Review of the commonwealth multicultural education program: Volume one- report and conclusions*. Canberra, Australia: Commonwealth Schools Commission.

Council for Australian-Arab Relations (CAAR). (2003). *Strategic plan 2003–2005*. Accessed from www.dfat.gov.au/caar//strategic_plan_2003-5.html on 20 Aug 2013.

Council of Australian Governments (COAG). (1992). *Asian language development. Council of Australian Governments' communiqué 7 December*. Accessed from http://archive.coag.gov.au/coag_meeting_outcomes/1992-12-07/index.cfm#language on 21 Aug 2013.

Department of Education. (1976). *Report of the committee on the teaching of migrant languages in schools*. Canberra, Australia: Australian Government Publishing Service.

Department of Education. (1979). *Discussion paper on education in a multicultural Australia*. Canberra, Australia: Department of Education.

Department of Education, Science and Training (DEST). (1994). *About NALSAS*. Accessed from www1.curriculum.edu.au/nalsas/about.htm on 10 Jan 2012.

Department of Education, Science and Training. (2006). *Maximising the opportunity: A report on the national seminar on languages education, Canberra, 30–31 October 2006*. Accessed from http://www.asiaeducation.edu.au/verve/_resources/languages_education.pdf on 12 Nov 2013.

Department of Employment, Education and Training (DEET). (1988). *Higher education: A policy statement*. Canberra, Australia: Australian Government Publishing Service.

Department of Employment, Education and Training. (1991a). *Australia's language: The Australian language and literacy policy*. Canberra, Australia: Australian Government Publishing Service.

Department of Employment, Education and Training. (1991b). *Australia's language: The Australian language and literacy policy. Companion volume to the policy information paper.* Canberra, Australia: Australian Government Publishing Service.

Department of Employment, Education and Training. (1994). *Report to the minister for employment, education and training, the Honourable Simon Crean MP, on Arabic and Middle Eastern studies April 1994.* Canberra, Australia: Department of Employment Education and Training.

Department of Foreign Affairs and Trade. (n.d.). *New Colombo Plan pilot program fact sheet.* Accessed from http://dfat.gov.au/new-colombo-plan/pilot-program-fact-sheet.html on 4 Feb 2014.

Department of Foreign Affairs and Trade. (2005). *Australia and the Colombo Plan 1949–1957.* Accessed from https://www.dfat.gov.au/publications/colombo_plan/ on 8 Nov 2013.

Department of Foreign Affairs and Trade. (2013a). *Brazil country brief.* Accessed from www.dfat.gov.au/geo/brazil/brazil_brief.html on 10 July 2013.

Department of Foreign Affairs and Trade. (2013b). *New Colombo Plan.* Accessed from http://www.dfat.gov.au/new-colombo-plan/ on 8 Nov 2013.

Department of Foreign Affairs and Trade. (2013c). *Asian century country strategies submissions.* Accessed from www.dfat.gov.au/issues/asian-century/submissions on 24 Oct 2013.

Department of Foreign Affairs and Trade. (2014). *China country brief.* Accessed from http://www.dfat.gov.au/geo/china/Pages/china-country-brief.aspx on 20 Feb 2015.

Department of Home Affairs. (n.d.) *Migration statistics.* Accessed from https://www.homeaffairs.gov.au/about/reports-publications/research-statistics/statistics/live-in-australia/historical-migration-statistics on 5 Feb 2018.

Department of Immigration and Citizenship. (n.d.). *Muslims in Australia – A snapshot.* Accessed from https://www.dss.gov.au/sites/default/files/files/settle/multicultural_australia/Muslims_in_Australia_snapshot.pdf on 17 Oct 2014.

Department of Immigration and Citizenship. (2008).*The people of Australia: Statistics from the 2006 census.* Accessed from http://www.immi.gov.au/media/publications/statistics/immigration-update/people-australia-2008-statistics.pdf on 10 Oct 2014.

Department of Immigration and Multicultural Affairs (DIMA). (2001). *Immigration: Federation to century's end 1901–2000.* Accessed from http://www.immi.gov.au/media/publications/statistics/federation/federation.pdf on 25 June 2013.

Department of Immigration and Multicultural and Indigenous Affairs (DIMIA). (2003). *Report of the review of settlement services for migrants and humanitarian entrants.* Canberra, Australia: DIMIA.

Downer, A. (2002). *Council for Australian-Arab Relations: Joint media release from the Minister for Foreign Affairs and the Minister for Trade Mark Vaile.* Accessed from www.foreignminister.gov.au/releases/2002/joint_arabcouncil.html on 20 Aug 2013.

Fadden, A. (1950). Australia's expanding prosperity. In F. Crowley (Ed.)., (1973) *Modern Australia in documents 1939–1970, Volume 2* (pp. 229–231). Melbourne, Australia: Wren Publishing.

Garnaut, R. (1989). *Australia and the Northeast Asian ascendancy.* Canberra, Australia: Australian Government Publishing Service.

Grassby, A. (1973). *A multi-cultural society for the future.* Canberra, Australia: Australian Government Publishing Service.

Higher Education Financing and Policy Review Committee (HEFPRC). (Australia). (1998). *Learning for life: Final report: Review of higher education, financing and policy.* (known as the West review). Canberra, Australia: Department of Employment, Education Training and Youth Affairs.

Historical Documents Branch, Department of Foreign Affairs and Trade. (1996). *John Rowland 1925–1996.* Canberra, Australia: Department of Foreign Affairs and Trade.

Joint Standing Committee on Foreign Affairs, Defence and Trade (JSCFADT). (1993). *Australia's relations with Indonesia.* Canberra, Australia: Australian Government Publishing Service.

Bibliography

Joint Standing Committee on Foreign Affairs, Defence and Trade. (2001). *Australia's trade relationship with the region*. Canberra, Australia: The Parliament of the Commonwealth of Australia.

Leal, B. (1991a). *Widening our horizons: Report of the review of the teaching of modern languages in higher education, Volume I*. (known as the Leal Report). Canberra, Australia: Australian Government Publishing Service.

Leal, B. (1991b). *Widening our horizons: Report of the review of the teaching of modern languages in higher education, Volume II*. (known as the Leal Report). Canberra, Australia: Australian Government Publishing Service.

Liberal Party. (2014). *Review of national curriculum to put students first*. Accessed from https://www.liberal.org.au/latest-news/2014/01/10/review-national-curriculum-put-students-first on 11 Mar 2014.

Lo Bianco, J. (1987). *National policy on languages*. Canberra, Australia: Australian Government Publishing Service.

National Asian Languages & Cultures Working Group (NALCWG). (1994). *Asian languages and Australia's economic future*. A report prepared for the Council of Australian Governments on a proposed national Asian languages/studies strategy for Australian schools. (known as the Rudd Report). Brisbane, Australia: Queensland Government Printer.

National Graduate. (2000). *"Nugget" Coombs – A special Australian*. Accessed from http://www.anu.edu.au/pad/alumni/natgrad/nugget.html on 8 Sept 2011.

National Library of Australia (NLA). (n.d.). *Australia in the Asian Century white paper*, Accessed from http://pandora.nla.gov.au/pan/133850/20130914-0122/asiancentury.dpmc.gov.au/index.html on 8 Nov 2013.

NSW Committee appointed to survey secondary education. (1957). *Report of the committee appointed to survey secondary education in New South Wales*. Sydney, Australia: V.C.N. Blight, Government Printer.

NSW Government Courts and Tribunals Services. (n.d.). *History of NSW courts and tribunals*. Accessed from http://www.courts.lawlink.nsw.gov.au/cats/history.html on 10 July 2014.

Office for Learning and Teaching. (n.d.). *About the Office for Learning and Teaching*. Accessed from http://www.olt.gov.au/about-olt on 7 Nov 2013.

Parliament of Australia. (1973). *Final report of the inquiry into the departure of settlers from Australia July 1973: The immigration advisory council committee on social patterns, parliamentary paper no. 226*. Canberra, Australia: Parliament of Australia.

Parliament of Australia. (2009). *Australian citizenship: A chronology of major developments in policy and law*. Accessed from http://www.citizenship.gov.au/_pdf/cit_chron_policy_law.pdf on 25 June 2013.

Pearson, C. (1878). *Public education: Royal commission of enquiry. Report on the state of public education in Victoria and suggestions as to the best means of improving it*. Melbourne, Australia: John Ferres, Government Printer.

Prime Minister-Gillard, J. (n.d.). *Brazil-Australia strategic partnership 2012*. Accessed from http://pmtranscripts.dpmc.gov.au/browse.php?did=18645 on 23 Apr 2014.

Senate Standing Committee on Education and the Arts. (1984). *Report on a national language policy*. Canberra, Australia: The Parliament of the Commonwealth of Australia, Australian Government Publishing Service.

Stanley, J., Ingram, D., & Chittick, G. (1990). *The Relationship between international trade and linguistic competence*. (Report to the Australian advisory council on languages and multicultural education). Canberra, Australia: Australian Government Publishing Service.

Tertiary Education Commission (TEC). (1977). *Recommendations for 1978*. Canberra, Australia: Australian Government Publishing Service.

Tertiary Education Commission. (1981). *Report for the 1982–84 triennium, Volume 1, Part 1: Recommendations on guidelines*. Canberra, Australia: Australian Government Publishing Service.

Academic Reports and Surveys, Conference Proceedings

Arkoudis, S., Baik, C., Marginson, S., & Cassidy, E. (2012). *Internationalising the student experience in Australian tertiary education: Developing criteria and indicators*. Parkville, Australia: Centre for the Study of Higher Education (CSHE), University of Melbourne.

Australian Academy of the Humanities (AAH). (1975). *Survey of foreign language teaching in the Australian universities (1965–1973)*. Canberra, Australia: AAH.

Australian Academy of the Humanities. (1998). *Knowing ourselves and others: The humanities in Australia into the 21st century*. Canberra, Australia: AAH.

Australian Academy of the Humanities. (2000). *Subjects of small enrolment in the humanities: Enhancing their future*. Canberra, Australia: AAH.

Australian Vice-Chancellors' Committee (AVCC). (1952). *A crisis in the finances and development of the Australian universities*. Canberra, Australia: AVCC.

Baik, C. (2013). Internationalising the student experience. In S. Marginson (Ed.), *Tertiary education policy in Australia* (pp. 131–138). Melbourne, Australia: CSHE, University of Melbourne.

Baldauf, R., Jr. (1995). *Viability of low candidature LOTE courses in universities*. Canberra, Australia: Department of Employment, Education and Training.

Borrie, W., & Rodgers, R. (1961). *Australian population projections 1960–75: A study of changing population structure*. Canberra, Australia: The Department of Demography, Institute of Advanced Studies, Australian National University.

Brecht, R. (2013). *Languages for all? The Anglophone challenge*. Accessed from www.casl.umd.edu/sites/default/files/LFA_WhitePaper_fnl.pdf on 25 Mar 2014.

British Academy for the humanities and social sciences (Britac). (2009). *Language matters: A position paper*. Accessed from http://www.britac.ac.uk/policy/languages-matters.cfm on 24 Mar 2014.

British Academy for the humanities and social sciences (Britac). (2013). *Languages: The state of the nation*. London: The British Academy.

Brown, J., & Caruso, M. (2014). New courses 2012: The impact on enrolments in Italian at the University of Western Australia. In C. Travis, J. Hajek, C. Nettelbeck, Beckmann, & A. Lloyd-Smith (Eds.), *Practices and policies: Current research in languages and cultures education. Selected proceedings of the LCNAU colloquium 2013* (pp. 39–53). Melbourne, Australia: LCNAU.

Committee on the teaching of modern languages in the secondary school. Australian Council for Educational Research. (1940). *Modern languages in the secondary school*. Melbourne, Australia: Melbourne University Press in association with Oxford University Press.

Dobson, I. (2013). *Mapping the humanities and social sciences: Analysis of university statistics 2002–2011*. Canberra, Australia: Australian Academy of the Humanities.

Dunne, K., & Pavlyshyn, M. (2011). *Swings and roundabouts: Changes in language offerings at Australian universities 2005–2011*. Accessed from www.lcnau.org/pdfs/lcnau_2011_dunne_pavlyshyn.pdf on 10 Oct 2013.

Dunne, K., & Pavlyshyn, M. (2014). Less commonly taught languages in Australian higher education in 2013: Plus ça change…. In C. Travis, J. Hajek, C. Nettelbeck, Beckmann, & A. Lloyd-Smith (Eds.), *Practices and policies: Current research in languages and cultures education. Selected proceedings of the LCNAU colloquium 2013* (pp. 9–17). Melbourne, Australia: LCNAU.

Group of Eight. (n.d.). *Agreements*. Accessed from https://go8.edu.au/programs-and-fellowships-type/agreements on 23 Sept 2014.

Group of Eight. (2011a). *Go8 LOTE incentive schemes*. Accessed from http://www.go8.edu.au/_documents/university-staff/agreements/lote_august2011-.pdf on 24 Sept 2013.

Group of Eight. (2011b). *Go8 strategic plan*. Accessed from http://www.go8.edu.au/_documents/about/-go8/strat_plan_2011-14-updated090511.pdf on 24 Sept 2013.

Group of Eight (Go8). (n.d.). *Go8 indicators*. Accessed from https://go8.edu.au/page/go8-indicators on 17 June 2014.

Group of Eight (Go8). (2007). *Languages in crisis: A rescue plan for Australia.* Accessed from www.go8.edu.au/__documents/university-staff/agreements/go8-languages-in-crisis-discussion-paper.pdf on 7 Nov 2013.

Hajek, J., Nettelbeck, C., Woods, A. (2013). *Leadership for future generations: A national network for university languages final report.* Office for Learning and Teaching. Accessed from http://www.lcnau.org/resources/publications on 22 May 2014.

Hajek, J., Slaughter, Y., & Stevens, M. (2008). *Innovative approaches in the provision of languages other than English in Australian higher education evaluation of model 2: Collaborative city-based model.* Melbourne, Australia: Research Unit for Multilingualism and Cross-Cultural Communication, University of Melbourne.

Hawley, D. (1982). *Foreign language study in Australian tertiary institutions 1974–1981.* Wollongong, Australia: University of Wollongong.

Hill, D. (2012). *Indonesian language in Australian universities: Strategies for a stronger future.* Australian Learning and Teaching Council National Teaching Fellowship Final Report. Perth, Australia: Murdoch University.

Jackson, R. (1968). Foreign languages in the Australian schools and universities. In Australian Humanities Research Council (Ed.), *The place of foreign languages and literatures in Australian universities: Summary of papers read at a symposium at the Annual General Meeting of the Australian Humanities Research Council, Canberra, 7 November 1967* (pp. 3–6). Sydney, Australia: Sydney University Press.

King, C., & James, R. (2013). Creating a demand-driven system. In S. Marginson (Ed.), *Tertiary education policy in Australia* (pp. 11–19). Melbourne, Australia: CSHE, University of Melbourne.

Languages and Cultures Network for Australian Universities (LCNAU). (n.d.). *Background – Languages in crisis.* Accessed from http://www.lcnau.org/background/ on 7 Nov 2013.

LCNAU. (2011). *The next step: Introducing the languages and cultures network for Australian universities – LCNAU's National Colloquium 2011.* Parkville, Australia: LCNAU.

LCNAU. (2012). *Submission by LCNAU to the issues paper: Australia in the Asian Century.* Accessed from http://asiancentury.dpmc.gov.au/sites/default/files/public-submissions/LCNAU.pdf on 24 Sept 2013.

LCNAU. (2013). *Submission by LCNAU to Australia in the Asian century country strategies.* Accessed from www.dfat.gov.au/issues/asian-century/submissions on 24 Oct 2013.

LCNAU. (2014a). *About LCNAU. Point 2.* Accessed from http://www.lcnau.org/about/ on 11 Mar 2014.

LCNAU. (2014b). *Media release – A national languages studies portal.* Accessed from https://www.lcnau.org/pdfs/LCNAU_LP_PressRelease_07May2014_web.pdf on 1 Feb 2018.

LCNAU. (2016). *University languages portal Australia.* Accessed from http://www.lcnau.org/university-languages-portal-australia-ulpa/ on 20 Mar 2016.

Levy, M. & Steel, C. (2011). The Brisbane Universities languages Alliance (BULA): A collaborative framework for university languages provision in South-East Queensland. *Selected proceedings of the inaugural LCNAU colloquium 2011.* Accessed from www.lcnau.org/pdfs/lcnau_2011_levy_steel.pdf on 10 Oct 2013.

Lo Bianco, J., & Gvozdenko, I. (2006). *Collaboration and innovation in the provision of languages other than English in Australian universities.* Melbourne, Australia: Faculty of Education, University of Melbourne.

McLaren, A. (2011). *Asian language enrolments in Australian higher education 2008–2009.* Melbourne, Australia: Asian Studies Association of Australia.

Mullan, K., & Seaman, M. (2014). The diploma of languages meets AQF 'compliance'. In C. Travis, J. Hajek, C. Nettelbeck, Beckmann, & A. Lloyd-Smith (Eds.), *Practices and policies: Current research in languages and cultures education. Selected Proceedings of the Second National LCNAU Colloquium Canberra, 3–5 July 2013* (pp. 71–84). Melbourne, Australia: LCNAU.

Nettelbeck, C., Byron, J., Clyne, M., Dunne, K., Hajek, J., Levy, M., Lo Bianco, J., McLaren, A., Möllering, M., & Wigglesworth, G. (2009). *An analysis of retention strategies and technology enhanced learning in beginners' languages other than English (LOTE) at Australian universities*. Canberra, Australia: The Australian Academy of the Humanities.

Nettelbeck, C., Byron, J., Clyne, M., Hajek, J., Lo Bianco, J., & McLaren, A. (2007). *Beginners' LOTE (languages other than English) in Australian universities: An audit survey and analysis*. Canberra, Australia: The Australian Academy of the Humanities.

Nettelbeck, C., Hajek, J., & Woods, A. (2012). Re-professionalizing the profession: Countering juniorization and casualization in the tertiary languages sector. *Local-Global Journal, 9*, 60–75.

Pauwels, A. (2003). Strengthening scholarship in language study in Australian universities. In G. Wigglesworth (Ed.), *Proceedings of the marking our difference conference 2003* (pp. 9–21). Parkville, Australia: School of Languages, University of Melbourne.

Royal Society of New Zealand. (2013). *Languages in Aotearoa New Zealand*. Accessed from http://royalsociety.org.nz/assets/Uploads/Languages-in-Aotearoa-New-Zealand.pdf on 1 Mar 2018.

Turner, G., & Brass, K. (2014). *Mapping the humanities, arts and social sciences in Australia*. Canberra, Australia: Australian Academy of Humanities.

Universities Australia. (2013). *An agenda for Australian higher education 2013–2016: A smarter Australia*. Canberra, Australia: Universities Australia.

White, F. (1979). *Robert Gordon Menzies 1894–1978*. Biographical Memoirs of Deceased Fellows. Australian Academy of Science, (revised 1998). Accessed from http://www.asap.unimelb.edu.au/bsparcs/aasmemoirs/menzies.htm on 22 Jul 2011.

White, P., & Baldauf, R., Jr. (2006). *Re-examining Australia's tertiary language programs: A five year retrospective on teaching and collaboration*. Brisbane, Australia: Report to the Deans of Arts, Social Sciences and Humanities (DASH).

White, P., Baldauf Jr., R., & Diller, A. (1997). *Languages and universities: Under siege*. Canberra, Australia: AAH.

Wigglesworth, G. (2003). Introduction. In G. Wigglesworth (Ed.), *Proceedings of the marking our difference conference 2003* (pp. 3–6). Parkville, Australia: School of Languages, University of Melbourne.

Worton, M. (2009). *Review of modern foreign languages provision in higher education in England*. Accessed from http://www.hefce.ac.uk/pubs/year/2009/200941/ on 24 Mar 2014.

Wykes, O. (1966). *Survey of foreign language teaching in the Australian universities*. Canberra, Australia: Australian Humanities Research Council.

Wykes, O., & King, M. (1968). *Teaching of foreign languages in Australia*. Melbourne, Australia: Australian Council for Educational Research.

University Records and Official Publications

Australian National University (ANU). (n.d.). *ANU history – Information services @ ANU*. Accessed from http://information.anu.edu.au/daisy/infoservices/273.html on 17 Jan 2011.

Australian National University. (1991). *1991 ANU handbook*. Canberra, Australia: Australian National University.

Australian National University. (1999). *1999 ANU handbook*. Canberra, Australia: Australian National University.

Australian National University. (2013a). Study at ANU 2013. Introduction. Academic programs. Accessed from https://studyat.anu.edu.au/2013/college_introductions/cap.html on 4 Feb 2014.

Australian National University. (2013b). *Home- School of language studies-ANU*. Accessed from http://www.languages.anu.edu.au on 17 Oct 2013.

Australian National University. (2013c). *Centre for Arab & Islamic studies-undergraduate studies*. Accessed from http://cais.anu.edu.au/programs/undergraduate-study on 20 Sept 2013.

Bibliography

Australian National University. (2013d). *Undergraduate Asian languages*. Accessed from https://studyat.anu.edu.au/2013/undergraduate/AsianLang.html on 17 Oct 2013.

Flinders University. (n.d.-a). *Flinders Asia Centre*. Accessed from http://www.flinders.edu.au/sabs/fac on 17 Nov 2014.

Flinders University. (n.d. -b). *Flinders University established*. Accessed from https://www.flinders.edu.au/about/history/flinders-timeline on 17 December 2018.

Macquarie University. (n.d.). *Russian Studies – Macquarie University*. Accessed from http://www.mq.edu.au/about_us/faculties_and_departments/faculty_of_arts/department_of_ international_studies/european_languages_and_cultures/russian studies/ on 22 Jan 2013.

Monash University. (n.d.). *Yiddish Melbourne – Statistics*. Accessed from http://www.arts.monash.edu.au/yiddish-melbourne/statistics/ on 13 Oct 2014.

Monash University. (1963). In Monash University (Ed.), *Monash University general information for students for 1963*. Clayton, Australia.

Monash University. (1991). In Monash University (Ed.), *Arts faculty handbook 1992*. Clayton, Australia.

Monash University. (1992). In Monash University (Ed.), *Arts faculty handbook 1993*. Clayton, Australia.

Monash University. (1998). In Monash University (Ed.), *Arts undergraduate handbook 1999*. Clayton, Australia.

Monash University. (1999). In Monash University (Ed.), *Monash University undergraduate 2000 guide to courses and subjects*. Clayton, Australia.

Monash University. (2013). *Why study languages at Monash?* Accessed from https://www.artsonline.monash.edu.au/lcl/why-study-languages-at-monash/ on 17 Oct 2013.

Monash University. (2014). *Victor and Maria Rudewych donate $1.52 million to support Ukrainian studies*. Accessed from http://artsonline.monash.edu.au/ukrainian/victor-and-maria-rudewych-donate-1-52-million-to-support-ukrainian-studies/ on 14 Aug 2014.

National Centre for Excellence in Islamic Studies. (n.d.). *National Centre for Excellence in Islamic Studies*. Accessed from http://nceis.unimelb.edu.au/ on 30 Sept 2014.

Office of the Vice-Chancellor, ANU. (1998). *Need for Arts faculty redundancies reduced*. Accessed from http://www.info.anu.edu.au/ovc/media/Media_Releases/1998/artsccuts.html on 15 Oct 2013.

Paton. (1964). *My dear Ambassador*. Ian Maxwell Papers. UMA.

SHAPS, Faculty of Arts, University of Melbourne. (2014). *Ancient world studies and classics subjects*. Accessed from http://shaps.unimelb.edu.au/students/subjects/subjects-classics.html on 18 Feb 2014.

Sussex, R. (1980). *Slavonic and East European languages: Opportunities for study in Victorian universities and colleges of advanced education*. Parkville, Australia: Department of Russian Language & Literature, University of Melbourne.

Swinburne College of Technology. (1970). *Diploma schools handbook*. Hawthorn, Australia: Swinburne College of Technology.

Swinburne Institute of Technology. (1992). *Swinburne institute of technology handbook 1992*. Hawthorn, Australia: Swinburne Institute of Technology.

Swinburne University of Technology. (1997). *SUT handbook 1997*. Hawthorn, Australia: Swinburne University Press.

The University of Melbourne Handbooks of Public and Matriculation Examinations 1944 to 1963 (n.d.).

The University of Melbourne Matriculation Rolls and Handbooks of Public Examinations 1906 to 1943 (n.d.).

University of Adelaide. (n.d.). *Seek light: South Australia's first university and Adelaide's first vice-chancellor*. Accessed from http://www.adelaide.edu.au/seek-light/stories/augustus-short.html on 19 Jul 2014.

University of Adelaide. (1882). *The Adelaide University calendar for the academical year 1882*. Adelaide, Australia: W. K. Thomas & Co.

University of Adelaide. (1889). *The Adelaide University calendar for the academical year* (p. 1889). Adelaide, Australia: W. K. Thomas & Co.
University of Adelaide. (1898). *The Adelaide University calendar for the academical year* (p. 1898). Adelaide, Australia: W. K. Thomas & Co.
University of Adelaide. (1990). *University of Adelaide 1991 calendar Volume 2, part A*. Adelaide, Australia: University of Adelaide.
University of Adelaide. (1998). *University of Adelaide 1999 calendar Volume 2, handbook of courses*. Adelaide, Australia: University of Adelaide.
University of Adelaide. (2013a). *Asian studies*. Accessed from www.hss.adelaide.edu.au/asian/ on 20 Sept 2013.
University of Adelaide. (2013b). *Faculty of Humanities and Social Sciences*. Accessed from www.hss.adelaide.edu.au/about/schools on 20 Sept 2013.
University of Adelaide. (2013c). *Why study classics?* Accessed from www.hss.adelaide.edu.au/classics on 17 Oct 2013.
University of Adelaide. (2013d). *Why study French?* Accessed from www.hss.adelaide.edu.au/french/whystudy/ on 17 Oct 2013.
University of Adelaide. (2013e). *Why study German?* Accessed from www.hss.adelaide.edu.au/german/whystudy/ on 17 Oct 2013.
University of Adelaide. (2013f). *Why study Hispanic studies?* Accessed from www.hss.adelaide.edu.au/spanish/whystudy/ on 17 Oct 2013.
University of Adelaide staff records. (n.d.). Crampton, H. & Crampton, J., staff records. Adelaide: University of Adelaide Archives.
University of Melbourne (UniMelb). (n.d.). *Learn more about breadth*. Accessed from http://breadth.unimelb.edu.au/breadth/info.index.html on 10 Mar 2014.
University of Melbourne. (1881). *The Melbourne University calendar for the academic years 1881–1882*. Melbourne, Australia: University of Melbourne.
University of Melbourne. (1883). *The Melbourne University calendar for the academic years 1882–1883*. Melbourne, Australia: University of Melbourne.
University of Melbourne. (1884). *The Melbourne University calendar for the academic years 1883–1884*. Melbourne, Australia: University of Melbourne.
University of Melbourne. (1887). *The Melbourne University calendar 1887*. Melbourne, Australia: Samuel Mullen and George Robertson & Co.
University of Melbourne. (1902). *The Melbourne University calendar 1902*. Melbourne, Australia: Melville & Mullen.
University of Melbourne. (1903). *The Melbourne University calendar 1903*. Melbourne, Australia: Melville & Mullen.
University of Melbourne. (1904). *The Melbourne University calendar 1904*. Melbourne, Australia: Melville & Mullen.
University of Melbourne. (1914). *The Melbourne University calendar 1915*. Melbourne, Australia: Ford & Son.
University of Melbourne. (1915). *The Melbourne University calendar 1916*. Melbourne, Australia: Ford & Son.
University of Melbourne. (1916a). *Council minutes, 3 July 1916*.
University of Melbourne. (1916b). *Council minutes, 24 July 1916*.
University of Melbourne. (1917a). *Council minutes 5 November 1917*.
University of Melbourne. (1917b). *The Melbourne University calendar 1918*. Melbourne, Australia: Ford & Son.
University of Melbourne. (1919). *The Melbourne University calendar 1919*. Melbourne, Australia: Ford & Son.
University of Melbourne. (1920). *The Melbourne University calendar 1920*. Melbourne, Australia: Ford & Son.
University of Melbourne. (1942). *The University of Melbourne calendar 1942*. Melbourne, Australia: Melbourne University Press.

Bibliography

University of Melbourne. (1946). *The University of Melbourne calendar 1946*. Melbourne, Australia: Melbourne University Press.
University of Melbourne. (1955a). In University of Melbourne (Ed.), *University of Melbourne appeal brochure*. Parkville, Australia.
University of Melbourne. (1955b). *Discovery* (Vol. 1, 3). Parkville, Australia: Melbourne University Press.
University of Melbourne. (1959). In University of Melbourne (Ed.), *The University of Melbourne calendar 1961*. Parkville, Australia.
University of Melbourne. (1961). Annual Report of the Proceedings of the University for the year ended 31st December, 1960. In *University of Melbourne calendar 1961*. Parkville, Australia: Melbourne University Press.
University of Melbourne. (1964). *University of Melbourne calendar 1964*. Parkville, Australia: Melbourne University Press.
University of Melbourne. (1967). *University of Melbourne calendar 1967/1968*. Parkville, Australia: Melbourne University Press.
University of Melbourne. (1970). *Modern Greek lectureship appeal brochure*. Parkville, Australia: University of Melbourne.
University of Melbourne. (1976). *University of Melbourne calendar- annual report*. Melbourne, Australia: Melbourne University Press.
University of Melbourne. (1982). *University of Melbourne calendar 1982*. Parkville, Australia: Melbourne University Press.
University of Melbourne. (1983). Annual report of the proceedings of the University for the year ended 31st December, 1982. In *University of Melbourne calendar 1983*. Parkville, Australia: Melbourne University Press.
University of Melbourne. (1984). *1985 arts faculty handbook*. Parkville, Australia: Melbourne University Press.
University of Melbourne. (1985). Annual report of the proceedings of the University for the year ended 31st December, 1984. In *University of Melbourne calendar 1985*. Parkville, Australia: Melbourne University Press.
University of Melbourne. (1988a). *University of Melbourne calendar 1988*. Parkville, Australia: Melbourne University Press.
University of Melbourne. (1988b). In University of Melbourne (Ed.), *Looking to the future: The strategic plan for the University of Melbourne*. Parkville, Australia.
University of Melbourne. (1989a). Annual Report of the Proceedings of the University for the year ended 31st December, 1988. In *University of Melbourne calendar 1989*. Parkville, Australia: Melbourne University Press.
University of Melbourne. (1989b). *University of Melbourne calendar 1989*. Parkville, Australia: Melbourne University Press.
University of Melbourne. (1991a). In University of Melbourne (Ed.), *A commitment to quality: University of Melbourne strategic plan*. Parkville, Australia.
University of Melbourne. (1991b). *University of Melbourne calendar 1991*. Parkville, Australia: Melbourne University Press.
University of Melbourne. (1992a). Joint committee on policy, meeting 9/92, Appendix A to Minutes, pp. 704–725.
University of Melbourne. (1992b). Joint committee on policy, minutes of meeting 9/92, Item 1, pp. 689–695.
University of Melbourne. (1992c). Annual Report of the Proceedings of the University for the year ended 31st December, 1991. In *University of Melbourne calendar 1992*. Parkville, Australia: University of Melbourne.
University of Melbourne. (1992d). *Asia in the University of Melbourne*. University of Melbourne Joint Committee on Policy, meeting 9/92, Item 3.1, Appendix A, pp. 838–873.
University of Melbourne. (1993). *Minutes of meeting 2/93 of the selection procedures committee of the Academic Board*. Parkville, Australia: University of Melbourne.

University of Melbourne. (1994). *Building on quality: Strategic plan 1994–1996*. Parkville, Australia: University of Melbourne.
University of Melbourne. (1995). *The University of Melbourne annual report 1994*. Parkville, Australia: University of Melbourne.
University of Melbourne. (1997). *Building esteem: The University of Melbourne Strategic Plan 1997–2001*. Parkville, Australias: University of Melbourne.
University of Melbourne. (1998a). *The University of Melbourne calendar 1998*. Parkville, Australia: Melbourne University Press.
University of Melbourne. (1998b). *The University of Melbourne annual report 1998*. Parkville, Australia: University of Melbourne.
University of Melbourne. (1999a). *The University of Melbourne annual report 1999*. Parkville, Australia: University of Melbourne.
University of Melbourne. (1999b). *The University of Melbourne calendar 1999*. Parkville, Australia: Melbourne University Press.
University of Melbourne. (2006). *Viking studies B: Society & language*. Accessed from http://www.unimelb.edu.au/HB/2006/subjects/126-069.html on 31 Oct 2013.
University of Melbourne. (2013a). *Arabic languages and studies*. Accessed from http://asiainstitute.unimelb.edu.au/study/arabic on 17 Oct 2013.
University of Melbourne. (2013b). *Chinese language and studies*. Accessed from http://asiainstitute.unimelb.edu.au/study/chinese on 17 Oct 2013.
University of Melbourne. (2013c). *Indonesian language and studies*. Accessed from http://asiainstitute.unimelb.edu.au/study/indonesian on 17 Oct 2013.
University of Melbourne. (2013d). *Japanese language and studies* Accessed from http://asiainstitute.unimelb.edu.au/study/japanese on 17 Oct 2013.
University of Melbourne. (2013e). *School of languages and linguistics-French studies*. Accessed from http://languages-linguistics.unimelb.edu.au/areas/french on 17 Oct 2013.
University of Melbourne. (2013f). *School of languages and linguistics-German studies*. Accessed from http://languages-linguistics.unimelb.edu.au/areas/german on 17 Oct 2013.
University of Melbourne. (2013g). *School of languages and linguistics-Italian studies*. Accessed from http://languages-linguistics.unimelb.edu.au/areas/italian on 17 Oct 2013.
University of Melbourne. (2013h). *School of languages and linguistics-Russian studies*. Accessed from http://languages-linguistics.unimelb.edu.au/areas/russian on 17 Oct 2013.
University of Melbourne. (2013i). *School of languages and linguistics-Spanish and Latin American studies*. Accessed from http://languages-linguistics.unimelb.edu.au/areas/Spanish-latin-american on 17 Oct 2013.
University of Melbourne. (2014). *Growing esteem 2014: A discussion paper*. Parkville, Australia: University of Melbourne.
University of Melbourne Archives (UMA). (n.d.).
University of Melbourne Asia Institute. (n.d.). *Endowed chair at Asia Institute*. Accessed from http://asianinstitute.unimelb.edu.au/study/islamic_studies/endowed_chair on 15 Apr 2014.
University of Melbourne Council Minutes. (1992). *Council meeting No.3, Monday 4 May 1992*. Accessed from www.unimelb.edu.au/Council/minutes/may92.html on 20 Nov 2012.
University of Melbourne Council Minutes. (1998). Item 7. *Council meeting No. 1*.
University of Melbourne Executive Committee Minutes. (1997), *Executive committee meeting No. 1*, Item 3.6.3.
University of Melbourne, Faculty of Arts Minutes, Book 5, 1943–1946 (n.d.).
University of Melbourne, Faculty of Arts Minutes, Meeting No. 5/91, 1991, Item 6.
University of Melbourne, Joint Committee of Enquiry. (1913). Report of the joint committee of enquiry submitted to council at its meeting No. 14, Monday 17 November, 1913. Council minutes, 1 November 1913, item 3, pp. 461–475.
University of Melbourne Matriculation results (1902). UMA.
University of New Brunswick. (n.d.). *Classics and ancient history*. Accessed from http://www.unb.ca/fredericton/arts/departments/classics/index.html on 1 Mar 2018.

Bibliography

University of New South Wales. (1991). *Faculty of Arts handbook 1991*. Kensington, Australia: University of New South Wales Press.

University of New South Wales. (1999). *Faculty of Arts handbook 1999*. Kensington, Australia: University of New South Wales Press.

University of New South Wales. (2013). *About languages and language learning*. Accessed from https://hal.arts.unsw.edu.au/disciplines/languages-language-learning/about/ on 20 Sept 2013.

University of Otago. (n.d.). *History and governance*. Accessed from http://www.otago.ac.nz/about/history/ on 8 Mar 2018.

University of Oxford. (1903). *The student's handbook to the university and colleges of Oxford* (16th ed.). Oxford, UK: The Clarendon Press.

University of Queensland. (1990). *The University of Queensland calendar 1991 Volume 2, student handbook metropolitan campuses*. St Lucia, Australia: The University of Queensland.

University of Queensland. (1999). *The University of Queensland undergraduate studies handbook 1999*. St Lucia, Australia: University of Queensland.

University of Queensland. (2013). *School of languages & comparative cultural studies*. Accessed from www.slccs.uq.edu.au/index.html?page=17998 on 17 Oct 2013.

University of Queensland Senate. (1935). In University of Queensland Senate (Ed.), *An account of the University of Queensland during its first 25 years 1910–1935*. Brisbane, Australia.

University of Sydney. (1853). *The Sydney University calendar. 1852–53*. Sydney, Australia: University of Sydney Accessed from http://calendararchive.usyd.edu.au/Calendar/1852/1852-3.pdf on 25 July 2011.

University of Sydney. (1854). *The Sydney University calendar. 1854*. Sydney, Australia: University of Sydney Accessed from http://calendararchive.usyd.edu.au/Calendar/1854/1854.pdf on 25 July 2011.

University of Sydney. (1856). *The Sydney University calendar. 1856*. Sydney, Australia: University of Sydney Accessed from http://calendararchive.usyd.edu.au/Calendar/1856/1856.pdf on 25 July 2011.

University of Sydney. (1867). *The Sydney University calendar. 1867*. Sydney, Australia: University of Sydney Accessed from http://calendararchive.usyd.edu.au/Calendar/1867/1867.pdf on 14 Jan 2014.

University of Sydney. (1868). *The Sydney University calendar. 1868*. Sydney, Australia: University of Sydney Accessed from http://calendararchive.usyd.edu.au/Calendar/1868/1868.pdf on 14 Jan 2014.

University of Sydney. (1870). *The Sydney University calendar. 1870*. Sydney, Australia: University of Sydney Accessed from http://calendararchive.usyd.edu.au/Calendar/1870/1870.pdf on 14 Jan 2014.

University of Sydney. (1919). Report of the Senate of the University of Sydney for the year ended 31 December 1918. In *Calendar of the University of Sydney 1919*. Sydney, Australia: Angus & Robertson.

University of Sydney. (1925). *University of Sydney calendar 1925*. Sydney, Australia: University of Sydney.

University of Sydney. (1931). *University of Sydney calendar 1931*. Accessed from http://calendararchive.usyd.edu.au/Calendar/1931/1931.pdf on 25 June 2014.

University of Sydney. (1952). *University of Sydney calendar 1952*. Sydney, Australia: University of Sydney.

University of Sydney. (1955). *University of Sydney calendar 1995*. Sydney, Australia: University of Sydney.

University of Sydney. (1956). *University of Sydney calendar 1956*. Sydney, Australia: University of Sydney.

University of Sydney. (1957). *University of Sydney calendar 1957*. Sydney, Australia: University of Sydney.

University of Sydney. (1991). *The Sydney University calendar 1991*. Sydney, Australia: University of Sydney Accessed from http://calendararchive.usyd.edu.au/Calendar/1991/1991.pdf on 23 Jan 2014.
University of Sydney. (1996). *The Sydney University calendar 1996*. Sydney, Australia: University of Sydney Accessed from http://calendararchive.usyd.edu.au/Calendar/1996/1996.pdf on 23 Jan 2014.
University of Sydney. (1999). *The Sydney University calendar 1999*. Sydney, Australia: University of Sydney Accessed from http://calendararchive.usyd.edu.au/Calendar/1999/1999.pdf on 23 Jan 2014.
University of Sydney. (2000). *Annual report of the University of Sydney 1999*. Accessed from the University of Sydney Annual Report Archive http://hdl.handle.net/2123/83543 on 24 Sept 2013.
University of Sydney. (2013). *Departments and programs within the school of languages and cultures*. Accessed from http://sydney.edu.au/arts/slc/departments_programs/index.shtml on 18 Apr 2013.
University of Tasmania. (1891). *University of Tasmania calendar 1892*. Hobart, Australia: J. Walch & Sons.
University of Western Australia. (1929). *Calendar for the University of Western Australia for the year 1929*. Perth, Australia: Fred W. M. Simpson, Government Printer.
University of Western Australia. (1990). *Faculty of Arts handbook 1991*. Nedlands, Australia: The University of Western Australia.
University of Western Australia. (1998). *Faculty of Arts handbook 1999*. Nedlands, Australia: The University of Western Australia.
University of Western Australia. (2013a). *Classics and ancient history: School of Humanities* Accessed from www.humanities.uwa.edu.au/home/clah on 20 Sept 2013.
University of Western Australia. (2013b). *European languages and studies: School of Humanities*. Accessed from www.humanities.uwa.edu.au/home/els on 20 Sept 2013.
University of Western Australia. (2013c). *Asian studies: School of Social Sciences*. Accessed from www.sscs.arts.uwa.edu.au/home/asian-studies on 20 Sept 2013.
University of Wollongong. (1980). *Campus News, 6*(2), 1–12.
University of Wollongong. (1982). *Campus News,* November, pp. 1–6.
University of Wollongong in Dubai. (2014a). *Undergraduate programs*. Accessed from http://www.uowdubai.ac.ae/undergraduate-programs on 21 Jan 2014.
University of Wollongong in Dubai. (2014b). *Language training*. Accessed from http://www.uowdubai.ac.ae/language-studies-centre/language-training on 30 Jan 2014.
Victorian Curriculum and Assessment Board (VCAB). (1990). *1990 VCE (HSC) assessment program statistical information*. Melbourne, Australia: VCAB.
Victorian Tertiary Admissions Centre (VTAC). (1986). *A guide to diploma in education courses 1987*. Melbourne, Australia: VTAC.
Victorian Tertiary Admissions Centre. (1987). *A guide to diploma in education courses 1988*. Melbourne, Australia: VTAC.
Victorian Tertiary Admissions Centre. (1988). *A guide to diploma in education courses 1989*. Melbourne, Australia: VTAC.
Victorian Tertiary Admissions Centre. (1989). *The VTAC guide to courses in colleges and universities 1990*. Melbourne, Australia: VTAC.
Victorian Tertiary Admissions Centre. (1990). *The VTAC guide to courses in colleges and universities 1991*. Melbourne, Australia: VTAC.
Victorian Tertiary Admissions Centre. (1991). *The 1992 VTAC guide to tertiary courses*. Melbourne, Australia: VTAC.
Victorian Tertiary Admissions Centre. (1992). *The 1993 VTAC guide to tertiary courses*. Melbourne, Australia: VTAC.
Victorian Tertiary Admissions Centre. (1994). *Postgraduate education courses for 1995*. Melbourne, Australia: VTAC.

Victorian Tertiary Admissions Centre (VTAC) (1995). *Postgraduate education courses for 1996*. Melbourne, Australia: VTAC.
Victorian Universities Admissions Committee (VUAC). (1970). *The Victorian universities guide for prospective 1971 students*. Melbourne, Australia: VUAC.
Victorian Universities Admissions Committee. (1975). *The Victorian universities guide for prospective 1976 students*. Melbourne, Australia: VUAC.
Victorian Universities Admissions Committee. (1979). *The Victorian universities guide for prospective 1980 students*. Melbourne, Australia: VUAC.
Victorian Universities Admissions Committee. (1984). *The Victorian universities guide for prospective 1985 students*. Melbourne, Australia: VUAC.
Victorian Universities Admissions Committee. (1985). *A guide to diploma in education courses 1986*. Melbourne, Australia: VUAC.
Winter, J. (2009). *Collaborative models for the provision of languages in Australian universities*. DASSH Steering Committee: Accessed from http://dassh.edu.au/resources/uploads/publications/project_reports/2009_CASR_Collaborative_Models.pdf on 15 Oct 2013.

Newspapers

A Staff Correspondent. (1953, April 19). How important are Asian languages? *The Sunday Herald, Sydney*, p.2.
A strong Asian narrative but now for the real work. [Editorial]. (2012, October 30). *The Australian*, p. 13.
Armitage, C. (1996, May 25). Vanstone lectures don't impress VCs. *The Australian*, p. 2.
Barrett, R. (2014, December 12). National curriculum changes referred to national authority ACARA after Education Council meeting. *ABC News*. Accessed from http://www.abc.net.au/news/2014-12-12/national-curriculum-changes-on-education-council-agenda/5962092 on 20 Feb 2015.
British Academy. (2013). *Lost for words*. Report shows language skills deficit threatens UK's security and global influence. Accessed from http://www.britac.ac.uk/news/news.cfm/newsid/1019 on 25 Mar 2014.
Callan, L. (2012, December 5). UWS course cuts going ahead. *The Sun (Parramatta, Holroyd)*. Accessed from http://search.proquest.com.eproxy.slv.vic.gov.au/anznews/printviewfile?accountid=13905 on 22 Jan 2014.
Curtin, J. (1941, December 27). The task ahead. *The Melbourne Herald*, p. 10.
Far East is near north to Australia. (1948, November 30). *The Canberra Times*, p. 2.
Govt. will grant extra money for universities. (1951, November 28). *Sydney Morning Herald*, p.3.
Helmore. (2013). Policy needs to change to address the US and UK's language deficits. *The Guardian*. Accessed from http://www.theguardian.com/education/2013/oct11/global-citizens-language-skills on Mar 2014.
Lane, B. (2012a, November 19), Language loss at UWS 'surprising'. *The Australian*. Accessed from http://www.theaustralian.com.au/higher-education/language-loss-at-uws-surprising/story-e6frgcjx-1226518313592 on 23 Jan 2014.
Lane, B. (2012b, August 1). Languages soar as 'breadth' options. *The Australian*. Accessed from http://www.theaustralian.com.au/higher-education/languages-soar-as-breadth-options/story-e6frgcjx-1226439751879# on 10 Mar 2014.
Letters to the Editor. (1956, September 13). *The Melbourne Age*, p.2; (1956, September 15), p.2; (1956, September 19), p.2; (1956, September 20), p.2; (1956, September 22), p.2; (1956, September 24), p.2; (1956, September 25), p. 2.
Lindsey, T. (2012, October 30). Mind your language, *The Age*, p. 7.

Lo Bianco, J., Nettelbeck, C., Hajek, J., Wood, A. (2011, November 22). No quick fix in any language, *The Age*. Accessed from http://www.theage.com.au/federal-politics/society-and-culture/no-quick-fix-in-any-language-20111121-1nquo.html on 18 June 2014.

Macdonald, E. (2013, November 15). ANU gets $1m gift for languages. *The Canberra Times*. Accessed from http://www.canberratimes.com.au/act-news/anu-gets-1m-gift-for-languages-20131114-2xk09.html on 28 Nov 2013.

Preiss, B. (2012, October 29). Languages studies plan backed despite high cost. *The Age*, p. 2.

Purvis, W. (1977, April 22). Campuses face spending axe. *Times Higher Education Supplement*.

Snedden, W. (1969a, July 26). Mixed race society not for us- Snedden. *The Australian*, p.2.

Snedden, W. (1969b, September 19). We are not in Asia, Snedden. *The Age*, p.10.

Spender critical of Professor's China speech. (1951, January 30). *Sydney Morning Herald*, p. 7.

Staff Correspondent. (1953, January 7). Casey pleased Indonesia in Colombo Plan. *Sydney Morning Herald*, p. 2.

Thom, P. in Harvey, C. (1998, March 18). Row over ANU languages cutback plan. *The Australian*, p. 37.

Tovey, J. (2014, January 14), Educators take ministers to task over national curriculum review. *Sydney Morning Herald*. Accessed from http://www.smh.com.au/national/education/educators-take-minister-to-task-over-national-curriculum-review-20140113-30qm4.html on 11 Mar 2014.

Trounson, A. (2014, April 2). Lack of Asian 'no bar to Colombo Plan'. *The Australian Higher Education*. p. 28.

Wentworth, C. (1849, September 7). Foundation of a university. *Sydney Morning Herald*, p. 2.

Theses

Quinn, J. (2005). *Asian studies in Australian education.* (Doctoral dissertation). Accessed from University of Melbourne Research Collections (UMER: www.lib.unimelb.edu.au/eprints) (PID 264393.)

Slaughter, Y. (2007). *The study of Asian languages in two states: Considerations for language-in-education policy and planning.* (Doctoral dissertation). Accessed from University of Melbourne Research Collections (UMER: www.lib.unimelb.edu.au/eprints) (PID 67660.)

Secondary

Books, Articles and Websites

Ab-duhou, I. (1989). The socio-economic significance of teaching Arabic in Australia. *Vox, 2*, 31–41.

Ackroyd, J. (1988). *Sadler, Arthur Lindsay (1882–1970)*. Canberra, Australia: Australian Dictionary of Biography, National Centre of Biography, Australian National University. Accessed from http://adb.anu.edu.au/biography/sadler-arthur-lindsay-8321/text/14597, on 25 Apr 2012.

Akami, T., & Milner, A. (2013). Australia in the Asia-Pacific Region. In A. Bashford & S. Macintyre (Eds.), *The Cambridge history of Australia Volume 2, The Commonwealth of Australia* (pp. 537–560). Port Melbourne, Australia: Cambridge University Press.

Alexander, F. (1963). *Campus at Crawley*. Melbourne, Australia: F. W. Cheshire for the University of Western Australia Press.

Bibliography

Anderson, B. (1983). *Imagined communities*. Thetford, UK: The Thetford Press.

Andrews, E. (1985). *Australia and China: The ambiguous relationship*. Carlton, Australia: Melbourne University Press.

Andrews, E. M. (1988). *A history of Australian foreign policy* (2nd ed.). South Melbourne, Australia: Longman Cheshire.

Ang, I., Hawkins, G., & Dabboussy, L. (2008). *The SBS story: The challenge of cultural diversity*. Sydney, Australia: UNSW Press.

Armstrong, D. (1979). The community college in the Australian context: The experience of Prahran CAE. In J. Anwyl (Ed.), *Australian community colleges* (pp. 29–49). Parkville, Australia: CSHE, University of Melbourne.

Armstrong, J. (1996). *The Christesen romance*. Carlton South, Australia: Melbourne University Press.

Auchmuty, J. in collaboration with Jeffares, A. (1959). Australian Universities: The historical background. In A. Grenfell Price (Ed.), *The humanities in Australia: A survey with special reference to the Universities* (pp. 14–33). Sydney: Angus & Robertson for the Australian Humanities Research Council.

Australasian Universities Modern Languages Association (AUMLA). (1950). *Proceedings of the first congress Melbourne, 14–19 August 1950*. Melbourne, Australia: AUMLA.

Australian Academy of Science. (n.d.). *Biographical Memoirs-Herbert Cole-Coombs*. Accessed from http://www.science.org.au/fellows/memoirs/coombs.html on 8 Sept 2011.

Australian Centre for Italian Studies (ACIS). (n.d.). *Cassamarca positions*. Accessed from http://acis.org.au/cassamarca-positions/ on 15 Apr 2014.

Baldassar, L. (2004). Italians in Western Australia: From 'dirty ding' to multicultural mate. In R. Wilding & F. Tilbury (Eds.), *A changing people: Diverse contributions to the state of Western Australia* (pp. 252–265). Perth, Australia: Department of the Premier and Cabinet, Office of Multicultural Interests.

Baldauf, R., Jr., & Djité, P. (2000). An Australian perspective: Second language teaching and learning in the university. In J. Rosenthal (Ed.), *Handbook of undergraduate second language education* (pp. 231–252). Mahwah, NJ: Lawrence Erlbaum Associates.

Baldauf, R., Jr., & White, P. (2010). Participation and collaboration in tertiary language education in Australia. In A. Liddicoat & A. Scarino (Eds.), *Languages in Australian education: Problems, prospects and future directions* (pp. 41–70). Newcastle upon Tyne, UK: Cambridge Scholars Publishing.

Baldwin, J. (2018). The place of Arabic language teaching in Australian universities. *The History of Education Review, 47*(1), 77–86. https://doi.org/10.1108/HER-05-2016-002111.

Ball, W. (1969). *Australia and Japan*. Melbourne, Australia: Thomas Nelson Australia.

Barcan, A. (1980). *A history of Australian education*. Melbourne, Australia: Oxford University Press.

Barcan, A. (1993). Latin and Greek in Australian schools. *History of Education Review, 22*(1), 32–46.

Barclay, G. (1977). Australia and the Cold War. In J. Siracusa & G. Barclay (Eds.), *The impact of the Cold War: Reconsiderations* (pp. 3–25). Port Washington, NY: Kennikat Press.

Barko, I. (1994). *Languages at the University – Tensions, past and present. Farewell lecture by the Head, School of Languages, Wednesday 1 June 1994*. Parkville, Australia: University of Melbourne.

Barko, I. (1996). A history of language education in universities: The background (1853–1965). *Australian Language Matters, 4*(1), 6–7.

Barnard, M. (1962). *A history of Australia*. Sydney, Australia: Angus & Robertson.

Barratt, G. (1988). *The Russians and Australia, Russia and the South Pacific, 1696–1840, Volume I*. Vancouver, Canada: University of British Columbia Press.

Beaglehole, A. (n.d.). Immigration regulation. *Te Ara – The encyclopedia of New Zealand*. Accessed from https://teara.govt.nz/en/immigration-regulation/ on 9 Mar 2018.

Beaumont, J. (2003). Creating an elite? The diplomatic cadet scheme, 1943–56. In J. Beaumont, C. Waters, D. Lowe, & G. Woodard (Eds.), *Ministers, mandarins and diplomats: Australian foreign policy making, 1941–1969* (pp. 19–44). Carlton, Australia: Melbourne University Press.

Bell, P. (2010). *Our place in the sun*. Townsville, Australia: James Cook University.

Bettoni, C., & Leal, B. (1994). Multiculturalism and modern languages in Australian universities. *Language Problems and Language Planning, 18*(1), 19–37.

Bielenstein, H. (1962). News of the profession. *The Journal of Asian Studies, 21*(2), 257–261.

Birrell, R. (1978). The future of migrant services: A further assessment of the Galbally report. *Ekstasis, (the newsletter of the Centre for Urban Research and Action), 21*(August), 27–29.

Blackton, C. (1951). The Colombo Plan. *Far Eastern Survey, 20*(3), 27–31.

Blackwood, R. (1968). *Monash University: The first ten years*. Melbourne, Australia: Hampden Hall.

Blainey, G. (1957). *A centenary history of the University of Melbourne*. Melbourne, Australia: Melbourne University Press.

Bolton, G. (1985). *It had better be a good one: The first ten years of Murdoch University*. Perth, Australia: Murdoch University.

Bongiorno, F. (2013). Search for a solution, 1923–39. In A. Bashford & S. Macintyre (Eds.), *The Cambridge history of Australia, Volume 2, the Commonwealth of Australia* (pp. 64–87). Port Melbourne, Australia: Cambridge University Press.

Bonyhady, A. (1965). Languages taught to matriculation level in Australia. *Babel, 1*(3), 32–33.

Bowman, A., & Bowman, S. (2006). *Obituary: The Rev John Bowman*. Accessed from http://www.guardian.co.uk/news/2006/sep/08/obituaries.readersobituaries/print on 5 Sept 2011.

Bowman, J. (1976). *Middle Eastern studies in Australia since 1958*. Sydney, Australia: Sydney University Press for the Australian Academy of the Humanities.

Bradshaw, J., Deumart, A., & Burridge, K. (2008). *Victoria's languages – Gateway to the world*. Melbourne, Australia: VITA Language Link.

Breen, W. (Ed.). (1989). *Building La Trobe University*. Melbourne, Australia: La Trobe University Press.

Brennan, N. (Ed.). (1974). *The migrant worker: Proceedings and papers of the migrant workers' conference, October 1973*. Melbourne, Australia: The Migrant Worker Conference Committee and the Good Neighbour Council of Victoria.

Brett, J. (2013). The Menzies era, 1950–66. In A. Bashford & S. Macintyre (Eds.), *The Cambridge history of Australia, Volume 2, the Commonwealth of Australia* (pp. 112–134). Port Melbourne, Australia: Cambridge University Press.

Brock, M., & Curthoys (Eds.). (1997). *The history of the University of Oxford: Volume VI nineteenth-century Oxford, part I*. Oxford, UK: Clarendon Press.

Broinowski, A. (1996). *The yellow lady: Australian impressions of Asia* (2nd ed.). South Melbourne, Australia: Oxford University Press.

Brooke, C. (1993). *A history of the University of Cambridge, Volume IV, 1870–1990*. Cambridge, MA: Cambridge University Press.

Browne, G. (1967). Trends in foreign language teaching in Queensland. *Babel, 3*(1), 16–19.

Bunting, J. (1988). *R. G. Menzies, a portrait*. North Sydney, Australia: Allen & Unwin.

Burnaby, B. (1996). Language policies in Canada. In M. Herriman & B. Burnaby (Eds.), *Language policies in English-dominant countries* (pp. 159–219). Clevedon, UK: Multilingual Matters.

Burnaby, B. (2008). *Language policy and education in Canada*. Accessed from https://www.researchgate.net/publication/227194713_Language_Policy_and_Education_in_Canada on 1 Mar 2018.

Burton, H. (1953). The Canberra University College. *Education News, IV*(3), 3–5.

Buzo, A., Dalton, B., Kimberley, J., & Wood, C. (1995). *Unlocking Australia's language potential: Profiles of languages in Australia: Volume 2- Korean*. Canberra, Australia: The National Languages & Literacy Institute of Australia.

Calvert, A. (2003). *The evolving international environment and Australia's national interest.* Accessed from http://www.dfat.gov.au/media/speeches/department/031126_lowy_institute.html on 15 Nov 2013.

Calwell, A. (1945). *How many Australians tomorrow?* Melbourne, Australia: Reed & Harris.

Calwell, A. (1948). Population-Australia's biggest deficit. *Twentieth Century: An Australian Quarterly Review, III*(1), 10–17.

Campbell, C., & Proctor, H. (2014). *A history of Australian schooling.* Crows Nest, Australia: Allen & Unwin.

Campbell, S., Dyson, B., Karim, S., & Rabie, B. (1993). *Unlocking Australia's language potential: Profiles of 9 key languages in Australia: Volume 1: Arabic.* Canberra, Australia: Commonwealth of Australia and the National Languages & Literacy Institute of Australia.

Canadian Museum of Immigration at Pier 21. (n.d.). *Canadian Multiculturalism Policy, 1971.* Accessed from https://www.pier21.ca/research/immigration-history/canadian-multiculturalism-policy-1971 on 9 Mar 2018.

Cannon, M. (1993). *Melbourne after the gold rush.* Main Ridge, Australia: Loch Haven Books.

Cannon, M. (2002). *Slater, William (Bill) (1890–1960).* Canberra, Australia: Australian Dictionary of Biography, Australian National University. Accessed from http://adb.edua.u/biography/slater-william-bill-11709/text20929 on 21 Nov 2012. Main Ridge, Vic.

Caro, D., Martin, R., & Oliphant, M. (1987). Leslie Harold Martin. 21 December 1900–1 February 1983. *Biographical Memoirs of Fellows of the Royal Society, 33*(Dec.), 388–409.

Castle, J. (1991). *University of Wollongong, an illustrated history 1951–1991.* Wollongong, Australia: University of Wollongong.

Castles, S., Cope, B., Kalantzis, M., & Morrissey, M. (1992). *Mistaken identity: Multiculturalism and the demise of nationalism in Australia* (3rd ed.). Leichhardt, Australia: Pluto Press Australia.

Cater, N. (Ed.). (2006). *The Howard factor: A decade that changed the nation.* Carlton, Australia: Melbourne University Press.

Challinger, M. (2010). *Anzacs in Arkhangel: The untold story of Australia and the invasion of Russia 1918–19.* Prahran, Australia: Hardie Grant Books.

Chisholm, A. (1957). We are still waiting for Italian. *Babel, 6,* 8–10.

Chisholm, A. (1958). *Men were my milestones: Australian contacts and sketches.* Melbourne, Australia: Melbourne University Press.

Chisholm, A., & Hunt, H. (1940). The study of Japanese in Australia. *The Australian Quarterly, 12*(1), 73–78.

Christa, B. (2001). Russians. In J. Jupp (Ed.), *The Australian people: An encyclopaedia of the nation, its people and their origins* (pp. 636–642). Cambridge, UK: Cambridge University Press.

Christesen, N. (1982). A Russian migrant. In P. Grimshaw & L. Strahan (Eds.), *The half-open door* (pp. 56–77). Sydney, Australia: Hale & Iremonger.

Christesen, N. (1996). *Goldman, Maurice David (1898–1957).* Canberra, Australia: Australian Dictionary of Biography, National Centre of Biography, Australian National University. Accessed from http://adb.edu.au/biography/goldman-maurice-david-10319/text18263 on 5 Sept 2011.

Clark, M. (1969). *Bromby, John Edward (1809–1889).* Canberra, Australia: Australian Dictionary of Biography, National Centre of Biography, Australian National University. Accessed from http://adb.anu.edu.au/biography/bromby-john-edward-3063/text4517 on 26 Sept 2013.

Clarke, E. (1987). *Assessment in Queensland secondary schools: Two decades of change 1964–1983.* Brisbane, Australia: Policy and Information Services Branch, Division of Planning and Special Programs, Department of Education, Queensland.

Clyne, M. (1964). Migrant languages in schools. *Babel, 27,* 11–13.

Clyne, M. (1982). *Multilingual Australia.* Melbourne, Australia: River Seine Publications.

Clyne, M. (1988). Bilingual education – What can we learn from the past? Australian Journal of Education, 32(1), 95–114.

Clyne, M. (1991). *Community languages – The Australian experience*. Cambridge, UK: Cambridge University Press.
Clyne, M. (1997). Language policy in Australia – Achievements, disappointments, prospects. *Journal of Intercultural Studies, 18*(1), 63–71.
Clyne, M. (2003). *Dynamics of language contact*. Cambridge, UK: Cambridge University Press.
Clyne, M. (2005). *Australia's language potential*. Sydney, Australia: University of New South Wales Press.
Clyne, M., & Kipp, S. (1999). *Pluricentric languages in an immigrant context: Spanish, Arabic and Chinese*. Berlin, Germany: Mouton de Gruyter.
Clyne, M., & Kipp, S. (2006). Australia's community languages. *The International Journal of the Sociology of Language, 180*, 7–21.
Clyne, F., Marginson, S., & Woock, R. (2001). International education in Australian universities: Concepts and definitions. *Melbourne Studies in Education, 42*(1), 111–127.
Coady, T. (Ed.). (2000). *Why universities matter: A conversation about values, means and directions*. St Leonards, Australia, Allen & Unwin.
Committee for Economic Development of Australia (CEDA). (1969). *Immigration and Australia's future*. Melbourne, Australia: Committee for Economic Development of Australia.
Connell, W., Sherington, G., Fletcher, B., Turney, C., & Bygott, U. (1995). *Australia's first – A history of the University of Sydney, Volume 2, 1940–1990*. Sydney, Australia: The University of Sydney in association with Hale & Iremonger.
Copland, D. (1948). Concept of a national university. *Education News, 1*(7), 16–17.
Coppel, C. (forthcoming). Roller-coaster: The University of Melbourne experience. In P. Thomas (Ed.). *Talking North: History literacy and policy in Australia's first Asian language*. Melbourne, Australia: Monash Publishing.
Cotton, J. (1997). Australia and the four Asian dragons. In J. Cotton & J. Ravenhill (Eds.), *Seeking Asian engagement: Australia in world affairs 1991–95* (pp. 191–206). South Melbourne, Australia: Oxford University Press.
Cotton, J. (2010). *International relations in Australia: Michael Lindsay, Martin Wight and the first department at the Australian National University* (Working Paper 2010/2). Canberra: Department of International Relations, School of International, Political and Strategic Studies, ANU College of Asia and the Pacific, Australian National University. Accessed from www.ips.cap.anu.edu.au/ir/pubs/work_papers/10-2.pdf on 18 Apr 2013.
Coulmas, F. (1989). The surge of Japanese. *International Journal of the Sociology of Language, 80*, 115–131.
Croft, K., & Macpherson, R. (1991). The evolution of languages administrative policies in New South Wales: 1962/1979. *Australian Review of Applied Linguistics, 14*(1), 35–58.
Curran, J., & Ward, S. (2010). *The unknown nation: Australia after empire*. Carlton, Australia: Melbourne University Press.
Dalrymple, R. (2003). *Continental drift: Australia's search for a regional identity*. Aldershot, UK: Ashgate Publishing.
Darian-Smith, K. (2013). World War 2 and post-war reconstruction, 1939–49. In A. Bashford & S. Macintyre (Eds.), *The Cambridge history of Australia, Volume 2, the Commonwealth of Australia* (pp. 88–111). Port Melbourne, Australia: Cambridge University Press.
Davis, R. (1990). *Open to talent: The centenary history of the University of Tasmania 1890–1990*. Hobart, Australia: University of Tasmania.
Davison, G., & Murphy, K. (2012). *University unlimited: The Monash story*. Sydney, Australia: Allen & Unwin.
de Garis, B. (Ed.). (1988). *Campus in the community: The University of Western Australia 1963–1987*. Perth, Australia: University of Western Australia Press.
Dessaix, R. (1997). Russia: The end of an affair. *Australian Humanities Review*, June, 1–6.
Dines, E. (1994). The public face of linguistics. In P. Mühlhäusler (Ed.), *The public face of linguistics* (pp. 12–15). Adelaide, Australia: Centre for Language, Teaching and Research, University of Adelaide.

Dixon, R. (1980). *The languages of Australia*. Cambridge, UK: Cambridge University Press.
Djité, P. (2011). Language policy in Australia: What goes up must come down? In C. Norrby & J. Hajek (Eds.), *Uniformity and diversity in language policy: Global perspectives* (pp. 53–67). Bristol, UK: Multilingual Matters.
Doran, M. (2012). History of an education leader. *The Soldiers' Newspaper, Army*, July (1286), 19.
Duncan, W., & Leonard, R. (1973). *The University of Adelaide 1894–1974*. Adelaide, Australia: Rigby.
Dutton, D. (2001). A British outpost in the Pacific. In D. Goldsworthy (Ed.), *Facing north: A century of Australian engagement with Asia, Volume 1:1901 to the 1970s* (pp. 21–60). Carlton South, Australia: Melbourne University Press. Canberra: Department of Foreign Affairs and Trade.
Edgeloe, V. (1990). *French and German in the University of Adelaide during the university's first hundred years of teaching 1876–1975: A brief account*. Adelaide, Australia: Victor Edgeloe Publications.
Edgeloe, V. (2003). *Annals of the University of Adelaide*. Adelaide, Australia: Barr Smith Press.
Edwards, P. (1983). *Prime ministers and diplomats*. Melbourne, Australia: Oxford University Press in association with The Australian Institute of International Affairs.
Ethnic Communities Council (ECC). (1978). Summary appraisal of the Galbally report. *Ekstasis, (the newsletter of the Centre for Urban Research and Action), 21*(August), 18–20.
Evans, B. (2001). *Out in the cold: Australia's involvement in the Korean war 1950–1953* (Rev. ed.). Canberra, Australia: Department of Veterans' Affairs.
Faulkner, A. (1978). The Galbally report: An invitation to change. *Ekstasis, (the newsletter of the Centre for Urban Research and Action), 21*(August), 12–18.
Fennessy, K. (2007). *A people learning: Colonial Victorians and their public museums, 1860–1880*. Melbourne, Australia: Australian Scholarly Publishing.
Fewster, A. (2009). *Trusty and well beloved: Biography of Keith Officer*. Carlton, Australia: The Miegunyah Press.
Firdaus. (2013). Indonesian language education in Australia: Politics, policies and responses. *Asian Studies Review, 37*(1), 24–41.
Firth, C. (1929). *Modern languages at Oxford 1724–1929*. London: Oxford University Press.
Fitzgerald, S. [Shirley]. (1997). *Red tape, gold scissors – The story of Sydney's Chinese*. Sydney, Australia: State Library of New South Wales Press.
Fitzgerald, S. [Stephen]. (2002). *Australia's China reassessed: The management of expectations on the 30th anniversary of diplomatic relations*. (The 2002 Australia in Asia series). Conducted at the Mitchell Galleries, The State Library of NSW, Sydney, Australia.
Fitzhardinge, L. (1983). *Hughes, William Morris (Billy) (1862–1952)*. Canberra, Australia: Australian Dictionary of Biography, National Centre of Biography, Australian National University. Accessed from http://adb.anu.edu.au/biography/hughes-william-morris-billy-6761 on 9 Nov 2014.
Foot, R. (2017). *Immigration policy in Canada* (rev. ed.). Accessed from http://www.thecanadianencyclopedia.ca/en/article/immigration-policy/ on 9 Mar 2018.
Ford, A. (1953). Australian university development in the post-war period. *The Australian Quarterly, 25*(2), 53–59.
Fornasiero, J., & West-Sooby, J. (2003). *Adelaide's outreach programme: Who's responsible?* Unpublished conference, *Marking Our Difference* Conference, Melbourne.
Fornasiero, J., & West-Sooby, J. (2012). A tale of resilience: The history of modern European languages at the University of Adelaide. In N. Harvey, J. Fornasiero, G. McCarthy, C. Macintyre, & C. Crossin (Eds.), *A history of the Faculty of Arts at the University of Adelaide, 1876–2012* (pp. 133–180). Adelaide, Australia: University of Adelaide Press.
Forsyth, H. (2014). *A history of the modern Australian university*. Sydney, Australia: NewSouth Publishing.
Fort Street Boys' High School. (1918). *Fortian*- Round the school, para. 12.

Foster, L., & Stockley, D. (1984). *Multiculturalism: The changing Australian paradigm*. Clevedon, UK: Multilingual Matters.

Foster, S., & Varghese, M. (1996). *The making of the Australian National University 1946–1996*. St Leonards, Australia: Allen & Unwin.

Frankel, J. (1970). *National interest*. London: Pall Mall Press.

Frei, H. (1984). Japan discovers Australia. The emergence of Australia in the Japanese world-view, 1540s–1900. *Monumenta Nipponica, 39*(1), 55–81.

French, E. (1959). The humanities in secondary education. In A. Grenfell Price (Ed.), *The humanities in Australia: A survey with special reference to the universities* (pp. 34–55). Sydney, Australia: Angus & Robertson for the Australian Humanities Research Council.

Fricke, G. (1990). *Profiles of power: The prime ministers of Australia*. Knoxfield, Australia: Houghton Miflin Australia.

Funch, C. (2003). *Linguists in uniform: The Japanese experience*. Clayton, Australia: Japanese Studies Centre, Monash University.

Galbally, A. (1995). *Redmond Barry: An Anglo-Irish Australian*. Melbourne, Australia: Melbourne University Press.

Gallagher, H. (2003). *We got a fair go: A history of the commonwealth reconstruction training scheme 1945–1952*. Kew, Australia: Hector Gallagher.

Garton, S., & Stanley, P. (2013). The great war and its aftermath, 1914–22. In A. Bashford & S. Macintyre (Eds.), *The Cambridge history of Australia, Volume 2, the Commonwealth of Australia* (pp. 39–63). Port Melbourne, Australia: Cambridge University Press.

Gerster, R. (2008). *Travels in atomic sunshine: Australia and the occupation of Japan*. Carlton North, Australia: Scribe Publications.

Gifford, P. (2001). The Cold War across Asia. In D. Goldsworthy (Ed.), *Facing north: A century of Australian engagement with Asia. Volume 1, 1901 to the 1970s* (pp. 171–219). Carlton South, Australia: Melbourne University Press Canberra: Department of Foreign Affairs and Trade.

Gill, G. (2007). Australia and the USSR: From Cold War to Perestroika. In A. Massov, J. McNair, & T. Poole (Eds.), *Encounters under the Southern Cross: Two centuries of Russian-Australian relations 1807–2007* (pp. 232–252). Belair, Australia: Crawford House Publishing Australia.

Glenn, J. (1989). The planning phase. In W. Breen (Ed.), *Building La Trobe University* (pp. 21–30). Melbourne, Australia: La Trobe University Press.

Goldsworthy, D. (2001). Appendix III, Australian diplomatic and consular post appointments in Asia, 1901–2001. In *Facing north: A century of Australian engagement with Asia, Volume 1, 1901 to the 1970s* (pp. 387–402). Carlton South, Australia: Melbourne University Press. Canberra: Department of Foreign Affairs and Trade.

Goldsworthy, D. (2003). Regional relations. In P. Edwards & D. Goldsworthy (Eds.), *Facing north: A century of Australian engagement with Asia, Volume 2, 1970s to 2001* (pp. 130–177). Carlton South, Australia: Melbourne University Press Canberra: Department of Foreign Affairs and Trade.

Goldsworthy, D., Dutton, D., Gifford, P., & Pitty, R. (2001). Reorientation. In D. Goldsworthy (Ed.), *Facing north: A century of Australian engagement with Asia. Volume 1, 1901 to the 1970s* (pp. 310–371). Carlton South, Australia: Melbourne University Press Canberra: Department of Foreign Affairs and Trade.

Gordijew, I. (1986). The Ukrainian Studies Foundation in Australia: A brief survey. In M. Pavlyshyn (Ed.), *Ukrainian settlement in Australia* (pp. 141–148). Clayton, Australia: Department of Slavic Languages, Monash University.

Gothard, J. (2013). *Colombo II: Send students to Asia but don't ignore the Asian students at home*. Accessed from http://theconversation.com/colombo-ii-send-students-to-asia-but-dont-ignore-the-asian-students-at-home-18156 on 13 Nov 2013.

Govor, E. (2001). Russian-Australian relations. In G. Davison, J. Hirst, & S. Macintyre (Eds.), *The Oxford companion to Australian history* (Rev ed., pp. 572–573). South Melbourne, Australia: Oxford University Press.

Grant, B. (1964). *Indonesia*. Parkville: Australia: University Press.

Gregory, J. (2013). Introduction. In J. Gregory (Ed.), *Seeking wisdom: A centenary history of the University of Western Australia* (pp. 1–14). Crawley, Australia: UWA Publishing.

Griffin, J. (1988). Schiassi, Omero (1877–1956). Canberra, Australia: Australian Dictionary of Biography, National Centre of Biography, Australian National University. Accessed from http://adb.anu.edu.au/biography/sciassi-omero-8357/text14677 on 10 Oct 2011.

Groenewegen, P. (1986). *Mills, Richard Charles (1886–1952)*. Canberra, Australia: Australian Dictionary of Biography, National Centre of Biography, Australian National University. Accessed from http://adb.anu.edu.au/biography/mills-richard-charles-7593/text13261 on 30 July 2013.

Gungwu, W. (1993). In memoriam: Professor C. P Fitzgerald 1902–1992. *The Australian Journal of Chinese Affairs, 29*, 161–163.

Gyngell, A., & Wesley, M. (2007). *Making Australian foreign policy* (2nd ed.). Port Melbourne, Australia: Cambridge University Press.

Haebich, A., & Kinnane, S. (2013). Indigenous Australia. In A. Bashford & S. Macintyre (Eds.), *The Cambridge history of Australia, Volume 2, the Commonwealth of Australia* (pp. 332–357). Port Melbourne, Australia: Cambridge University Press.

Hajek, J., & Slaughter, Y. (Eds.). (2015). *Challenging the monolingual mindset*. Bristol, UK: Multilingual Matters.

Hall, H. (1969). *Childers, Hugh Culling Eardley (1827–1896)*. Canberra, Australia: Australian Dictionary of Biography, National Centre for Biography, Australian National University. Accessed from http://adb.anu.edu.au/biography/childers-high-culling-eardley-3202/text4813 on 26 Sept 2013.

Haque, E. (2010). Bilingualism, multiculturalism, and language training. In M. Morris (Ed.), *Canadian language policies in comparative perspective* (pp. 267–296). Montreal, Canada: McGill-Queen's University Press.

Harman, G. (2005). Implementing comprehensive national higher education reforms: The Australian reforms of Education Minister John Dawkins, 1987–90. In A. Gornitzka, M. Kogan, & A. Amaral (Eds.), *Reform & change in higher education: Analysing policy implementation* (pp. 169–185). Dordrecht, The Netherlands: Springer.

Harper, M. (1993). *Copland, Sir Douglas Berry (1894–1971)*. Canberra, Australia: Australian Dictionary of Biography, National Centre of Biography, Australian National University. Accessed from http://adb.anu.edu.au/biography/copland-sir-douglas-berry-247/text17371, on 27 May 2012.

Harris, R. (1976). *A history of higher education in Canada 1663–1960*. Toronto, Canada: University of Toronto Press.

Hart, S. (2014). *Look ever forward: A history of Curtin University 1987–2012*. Perth, Australia: Curtin University.

Harte, N. (1986). *The University of London 1836–1986: An illustrated history*. London: The Athlone Press.

Harvey, S. (2015). Superdiversity, language and policy: Where should the intersections be for Aotearoa/New Zealand? Paper presented at the AKTESOL Expo (Auckland branch of the TESOL Association of Aotearoa New Zealand). Accessed from https://www.researchgate.net/publication/281830847_Superdiversity_language_and_policy_Where_should_the_intersections_be_for_Aotearoa_New_Zealand on 12 Mar 2018.

Hay, R., Lowe, D., & Gibb, D. (2002). *Breaking the mould: Deakin University, the first twenty-five years*. Geelong, Australia: Deakin University.

Henderson, D. (2003). Meeting the national interest through Asia literacy- an overview of the major stages and debates. *Asian Studies Review, 27*(1), 23–53.

Henderson, D. (2007). A strategy cut-short: The NALSAS strategy for Asian languages in Australia. *Electronic Journal of Foreign Language Teaching, 4*(Suppl. 1), 4–22.

Henderson, D. (2008). Politics and policy-making for Asia literacy: The Rudd report and a national strategy in Australian education. *Asian Studies Review, 32*(2), 171–195.

Henderson, D. (2011). Why teaching about Asia matters in higher education. *Asian Currents*, March, 3–5.

Herriman, M. (1996). Language policy in Australia. In M. Herriman & B. Burnaby (Eds.), *Language policies in English-dominant countries: Six case studies* (pp. 35–61). Avon, UK: Multilingual Matters.

Hilliard, D. (1991). *Flinders University: The first 25 years, 1966–1991*. Adelaide, Australia: The Flinders University of South Australia.

Hirst, J. (2010). *Looking for Australia*. Melbourne, Australia: Black Publishing.

Holt, R. (1976). The statistics merry-go-round. *Babel, 12*(3), 27–32.

Horne, J., & Sherington, G. (2012). *Sydney: The making of a public university*. Carlton, Australia: Melbourne University Publishing.

Horne, J., & Sherington, G. (2013a). 'Dominion' legacies: The Australian experience. In D. Schreuder (Ed.), *Universities for a new world: Making a global network in international higher education, 1913–2013* (pp. 285–307). London: The Association of Commonwealth Universities and Sage Publications.

Horne, J., & Sherington, G. (2013b). Education. In A. Bashford & S. Macintyre (Eds.), *The Cambridge history of Australia, Volume 1, the Commonwealth of Australia* (pp. 367–390). Port Melbourne, Australia: Cambridge University Press.

Hudson, W. (1993). *Casey, Richard Gavin Gardiner (1890–1976)*. Canberra, Australia: Australian Dictionary of Biography, National Centre of Biography, Australian National University. Accessed from http://adb.anu.edu.au/biography/casey-richard-gavin-gardiner-9706/text17135, on 5 June 2012.

Hunt, H. (1959). Oriental and Pacific studies. In A. Grenfell Price (Ed.), *The humanities in Australia: A survey with special reference to the universities* (pp. 165–171). Sydney, Australia: Angus & Robertson for the Australian Humanities Research Council.

Inglis, C. (2004). Australia: Educational changes and challenges in response to multiculturalism, globalization and transnationalism. In S. Luchtenberg (Ed.), *Migration, education and change* (pp. 186–205). London: Routledge.

Inglis, K. (1991). Multiculturalism and national identity. In C. Price (Ed.), *Australian national identity* (pp. 13–32). Canberra, Australia: The Academy of the Social Sciences in Australia.

Jackson, R. (1968). In R. Jackson, & E. Horwood. *The place of foreign languages and literatures in Australian universities*. Sydney: Sydney University Press for Australian Humanities Research Council.

Jacobs, M. (1953). Oriental studies in the University of Sydney. *The Australian Quarterly, 25*(2), 82–90.

Japan Foundation. (n.d.). *The Japan foundation*. Accessed from http://www.jpf.org.au/aboutus.html on 23 Apr 2014.

Jenkins, J., & Richards, J. (1989). La Trobe as a teaching university. In W. Breen (Ed.), *Building La Trobe University* (pp. 75–84). Melbourne, Australia: La Trobe University Press.

Jones, G. (2014). An introduction to higher education in Canada. In K. Joshi & S. Paivandi (Eds.), *Higher education across nations* (Vol. 1, pp. 1–38). Delhi, India: B. R. Publishing.

Jones, P., & Oliver, P. (Eds.). (2001). *Changing histories: Australia and Japan*. Clayton, Australia: Monash Asia Institute, Monash University.

Jones, R. (2004). Blended voices: Crafting a narrative from oral history interviews. *The Oral History Review, 31*(1), 23–42.

Jordens, A.-M. (1997). *Alien to citizen: Settling migrants in Australia 1945–75*. St Leonards, Australia: Allen & Unwin in association with the Australian Archives.

Joske, P. (1978). *Sir Robert Menzies 1894–1978*. Sydney, Australia: Angus & Robertson.

Jupp, J. (1966). *Arrivals and departures*. Melbourne, Australia: Cheshire-Lansdowne.

Jupp, J. (Ed.). (1989). *The challenge of diversity: Policy options for a multicultural Australia*. Canberra, Australia: Australian Government Publishing Service.

Jupp, J. (1993). Perspectives on the politics of immigration. In J. Jupp & M. Kabala (Eds.), *The politics of Australian immigration* (pp. 243–255). Canberra, Australia: Commonwealth of Australia.

Jupp, J. (1996). *Understanding Australian multiculturalism*. Canberra, Australia: Commonwealth of Australia.

Jupp, J. (Ed.). (2001). *The Australian people: An encyclopaedia of the nation, its people and their origins*. Cambridge, UK: Cambridge University Press.

Jupp, J. (2011). Politics, public policy and multiculturalism. In J. Jupp & M. Clyne (Eds.), *Multiculturalism and integration: A harmonious relationship* (pp. 41–52). Canberra, Australia: ANU E Press.

Jupp, J., & Clyne, M. (2011). Introduction. In J. Jupp & M. Clyne (Eds.), *Multiculturalism and integration: A harmonious relationship* (pp. xiii–xxiii). Canberra, Australia: ANU E Press.

Kalantzis, M., & Cope, B. (1983). *Multicultural education and the schools commission: Experimentation and social reform*. Stanmore, Australia: Social Literacy Monograph 2.

Karmel, P. (2000). Funding universities. In T. Coady (Ed.), *Why universities matter: A conversation about values, means and directions* (pp. 159–185). St Leonards, Australia: Allen & Unwin.

Kelly, P. (2008). The Howard decade – Separating fact from fiction. *New Critic, 7*, 1–12. Accessed from http://www.ias.uwa.edu.au/new-critic/seven/howarddecade on 26 Sept 2013.

Kerr, E., & Anderson, G. (1970). *The Australian Presbyterian mission in Korea 1889–1941*. Sydney, Australia: Australian Presbyterian Board of Missions.

Kingston, B. (2006). *A history of New South Wales*. Cambridge, UK: Cambridge University Press.

Kinoshita, Y. (2018). Educational impact of replacing on-campus courses with cross-institutional arrangements: A language case study. *The Language Learning Journal*. https://doi.org/10.1080/09571736.2018.1448431.

Kipp, S. (2008). The language ecology of Australia's community languages. In A. Creese, P. Martin, & N. Hornberger (Eds.), *Encyclopedia of language and education* (Ecology of Language, Vol. 9, 2nd ed., pp. 69–83) New York: Springer.

Kipp, S., Clyne, M., & Pauwels, A. (1995). *Immigration and Australia's language resources*. Canberra, Australia: Australian Government Publishing Service.

Klarberg, F. (1996). Italian in Australia: Accreditation as a public examination subject 1920–1935. *ConVivio, 2*(2), 154–163.

Knight, J. (2004). Internationalization remodelled: Definition, approaches, and rationales. *Journal of Studies in International Education, 8*(5), 5–30.

Koscharsky, H., & Pavković, A. (2005). Slavonic studies at Macquarie University 1983–1998: An experiment in migrant language maintenance. *Australian and East European Studies, 19*(1–2), 149–162.

Lack, J., & Templeton, J. (1995). *Bold experiment: A documentary history of Australian immigration since 1945*. Melbourne, Australia: Oxford University Press.

Lee, D. (2001). Indonesia's independence. In D. Goldsworthy (Ed.), *Facing north: A century of Australian engagement with Asia, Volume 1, 1901 to the 1970s* (pp. 134–170). Carlton South, Australia: Melbourne University Press Canberra: Department of Foreign Affairs and Trade.

Lee, S. (2009). *To Korea with love: Australian Presbyterian work in Korea, 1889–1941*. Melbourne, Australia: Presbyterian Church of Victoria.

Legge, J. (1999). *Australian outlook: A history of the Australian institute of international affairs*. St Leonards, Australia: Allen & Unwin in association with the Australian Institute of International Affairs and the Department of International Relations, Research School of Pacific and Asian Studies, Australian National University.

Levi, W. (1958). *Australia's outlook on Asia*. Sydney, Australia: Angus & Robertson.

Lewins, F. (2001). Assimilation and integration. In J. Jupp (Ed.), *The Australian people: An encyclopaedia of the nation, its people and their origins* (pp. 752–755). Cambridge, UK: Cambridge University Press.

Li, L. (2012). Internationalising university curriculum with multilingual knowledge and skills: Power, politics and policy. *Local-Global Journal, 9*, 44–58.

Liddicoat, A., & Scarino, A. (2010). Languages in Australian education: An introduction. In A. Liddicoat & A. Scarino (Eds.), *Languages in Australian education: Problems, prospects and future directions* (pp. 1–8). Newcastle upon Tyne, UK: Cambridge Scholars Publishing.

Lo Bianco, J. (1998). The implications for languages of the emergence of the international university. *Australian Language Matters, 6*(4), 1 8–10.

Lo Bianco, J. (2009). Second languages and Australian schooling. *Australian Education Review, 54*. Melbourne, Australia: Australian Council for Educational Research.

Lo Bianco, J., & Aliani, R. (2013). *Language planning and student experiences: Intention, rhetoric and implementation*. Bristol, UK: Multilingual Matters.

Lone, S., & McCormack, G. (1993). *Korea since 1950*. South Melbourne, Australia: Longman Cheshire.

Lopez, M. (2000). *The origins of multiculturalism in Australian politics 1945–1975*. Carlton South, Australia: Melbourne University Press.

Love, P. (2007). *Practical measures: 100 years at Swinburne*. Hawthorn, Australia: Swinburne University of Technology.

Lowe, D. (2013). Security. In A. Bashford & S. Macintyre (Eds.), *The Cambridge history of Australia, Volume 2, the Commonwealth of Australia* (pp. 494–517). Port Melbourne, Australia: Cambridge University Press.

Macintyre, S. (1986). *Latham, Sir John Grieg (1877–1964)*. Canberra, Australia: Australian Dictionary of Biography, National Centre of Biography, Australian National University. Accessed from http://adb.anu.edu.au/biography/latham-sir-john-greig-7104/text12251, on 10 May 2012.

Macintyre, S., & Marginson, S. (2000). The University and its public. In T. Coady (Ed.), *Why universities matter: A conversation about values, means and directions* (pp. 49–71). St Leonards, Australia: Allen & Unwin.

Macintyre, S., & Selleck, R. (2003). *A short history of the University of Melbourne*. Carlton, Australia: Melbourne University Press.

Mackerras, C. (2006). Speech on the occasion of his admission to the degree of Doctor of Griffith University. Accessed from http://redlandsu3a.pbworks.com/w/page/9724971/Mackerras on 27 May 2012.

Mackey, W. (2010). Language policies in Canada. In M. Morris (Ed.), *Canadian language policies in comparative perspective* (pp. 18–66). Montreal, Canada: McGill-Queen's University Press.

Mackinnon, A., & Proctor, H. (2013). Education. In A. Bashford & S. Macintyre (Eds.), *The Cambridge history of Australia, Volume 2, the commonwealth of Australia* (pp. 429–451). Port Melbourne, Australia: Cambridge University Press.

MacLaurin, E. (1969). *Beg, Wazir (1927–1885)*. Canberra, Australia: Australian Dictionary of Biography, National Centre of Biography, Australian National University. Accessed from http://adb.anu.edu.au/biography/beg-wazir-2964/text4315 on 14 Jan 2014.

Manne, R. (2001). *The barren years: John Howard and Australian political culture*. Melbourne, Australia: Text Publishing.

Mansfield, B., & Hutchinson, M. (1992). *Liberality of opportunity: A history of Macquarie University 1964–1989*. Sydney, Australia: Hale & Iremonger.

Marginson, S. (1997). *Educating Australia: Government, economy and citizen since 1960*. Cambridge, UK: Cambridge University Press.

Marginson, S. (2002). Nation-building universities in a global environment: The case of Australia. *Higher Education, 43*, 409–428.

Marginson, S. (Ed.). (2013). *Tertiary education policy in Australia*. Melbourne, Australia: Centre for the Study of Higher Education, University of Melbourne.

Marriott, H., Neustupný, J., & Spence-Brown, R. (1993). *Unlocking Australia's language potential: Profiles of 9 key languages in Australia: Volume 7: Japanese*. Canberra, Australia: National Languages & Literacy Institute of Australia.

Martin, A. (2007). *The 'Whig' view of Australian history and other essays*. Carlton, Australia: Melbourne University Press.

Martin, J. I. (1978). *The migrant presence: Australian responses 1947–1977.* Sydney, Australia: George Allen & Unwin.

Martin, J. S. (1967). Swedish at Melbourne University. *Babel, 3*(2), 32–33.

Martin, J. S. (2007). *Augustin Lodewyckx (1876–1964) teacher and scholar.* Parkville, Australia: The University of Melbourne, The History of the University Unit, Working Paper No. 7.

Martin, M. (2005). Permanent crisis, tenuous persistence: Foreign languages in Australian universities. *Arts and Humanities in Higher Education, 4*(1), 53–75.

Mascitelli, B., & Merlino, F. (2012). By accident or design? The origins of the Victorian School of Languages. *Babel, 46*(2/3), 40–47.

Matheson, L. (1980). *Still learning.* South Melbourne, Australia: Macmillan.

Mayne, A. (1997). *Reluctant Italians? One hundred years of the Dante Alighieri Society in Melbourne 1896–1996.* Melbourne, Australia: Dante Alighieri Society.

McDougall, D. (1998). *Australian foreign relations – Contemporary perspectives.* South Melbourne, Australia: Longman.

McDowell, R., & Webb, D. (1982). *Trinity College Dublin, 1592–1952: An academic history.* Cambridge, UK: Cambridge University Press.

McLauchlan, G. (2004). *A short history of New Zealand.* Auckland, New Zealand: Penguin Books (NZ).

McLure, M. (2011). Thirty years of economics: UWA and the WA branch of the economics society from 1963 to 1992. *History of Economics Review, 54,* 70–91.

Meaney, N. (1985). *Australia and the world.* Melbourne, Australia: Longman Cheshire.

Meaney, N. (1988). *Piesse, Edmund Leolin (1880–1947).* Canberra, Australia: Australian Dictionary of Biography, National Centre of Biography, Australian National University. Accessed from http://adb.anu.edu.au/biography/piesse-edmund-leolin-8046/text14033 on 10 May 2012.

Meaney, N., Matthews, T., & Encel, S. (1988). *The Japanese connection.* South Melbourne, Australia: Longman Cheshire.

Mein Smith, P. (2005). *A concise history of New Zealand.* Cambridge, UK: Cambridge University Press.

Melleuish, G. (1998). *The packaging of Australia: Politics and culture wars.* Sydney, Australia: University of New South Wales Press.

Menzies, R. (1961). The challenge to education. In The Australian College of Education (Ed.), *The challenge to Australian education* (pp. 1–12). Melbourne, Australia: F. W. Cheshire for the Australian College of Education.

Michaelides, J. (2000). *Laurantus, sir Nicholas (Nick). (1890–1980).* Canberra, Australia: Australian Dictionary of Biography, National Centre of Biography, Australian National University. Accessed from http://adb.anu.edu.au/biography/laurantus-sir-nicholas-nick-10789/text19135 on 18 Oct 2013.

Millar, T. (1991). *Australia in peace and war: External relations since 1788* (2nd ed.). Sydney, Australia: Australian National University Press – A division of Maxwell Macmillan Publishing Australia.

Milne, F. (2001). The Australian universities: A study in public policy failure. *Queen's Economic Department Working Paper No. 1080.* Accessed from http://www.qed.queensu.ca/working_papers/papers/qed_wp_1080.pdf on 21 Mar 2013.

Mitchell, A. (1959). The university faculties. In A. Grenfell Price (Ed.), *The humanities in Australia: A survey with special reference to the universities* (pp. 56–98). Sydney, Australia: Angus & Robertson for the Australian Humanities Research Council.

Molony, J. (2000). Australian universities today. In T. Coady (Ed.), *Why universities matter: A conversation about values, means and directions* (pp. 72–84). St Leonards, Australia: Allen & Unwin.

Moore, D. (2001). *Duntroon: A history of the Royal Military College of Australia 1911–2001.* Canberra, Australia: Royal Military College of Australia.

Morris, M. (Ed.). (2010). *Canadian language policies in comparative perspective*. Montreal, Canada: McGill-Queen's University Press.

Moses, I. (2004). *Unified national system or uniform national system? The Australian experience.* Accessed from http://www.innovation.gov.au/HigherEducation/StudentSupport/NationalProtocolsForHigherEducationApprovalProcesses/Documents/NationaProtocolsforHEApprovalProcesses/uni_new_england_info_pdf.pdf on 14 Aug 2013.

Mulvaney, J. (2003). Foreword. In H. Gallagher (Ed.), *We got a fair go: A history of the commonwealth reconstruction training scheme 1945–1952* (pp. iii–iiv). Kew, Australia: Hector Gallagher.

Mulvaney, J. (2011). *Digging up a past*. Sydney, Australia: University of New South Wales Press.

Murray, J. (2004). *Watching the sun rise: Australian reporting of Japan 1931 to the fall of Singapore*. Lanham, MD: Lexington Books.

Murray, D. (2013). Internationalisation: Where to from here? In S. Marginson (Ed.), *Tertiary education policy in Australia* (pp. 113–122). Melbourne, Australia: CSHE, University of Melbourne.

Murray-Smith, S., & Dare, A. (1987). *The tech: A centenary history of the Royal Melbourne Institute of Technology*. South Yarra, Australia: Hyland House.

Myers, D. (1989). The first decade. In W. Breen (Ed.), *Building La Trobe University* (pp. 31–38). Melbourne, Australia: La Trobe University Press.

Nadel, G. (1957). *Australia's colonial culture: Ideas, men and institutions in mid-nineteenth century Eastern Australia*. Melbourne, Australia: F.W. Cheshire.

Nagata, Y. (1996). *Unwanted aliens: Japanese internment in Australia*. St Lucia, Australia: University of Queensland Press.

Nelles, H. (2004). *A little history of Canada*. Don Mills, Canada: Oxford University Press.

Norrick, N. (2005). Talking about remembering and forgetfulness in oral history interviews. *The Oral History Review, 32*(2), 1–20.

Norton, A. (2013). *Mapping Australian higher education 2013 version*. Carlton, Australia: Grattan Institute Accessed from http://grattan.edu.au/publications/reports/post/mapping-australian-higher-education-2013 on 1 Mar 2014.

O'Farrell, P. (1999). *UNSW: A portrait*. Sydney, Australia: University of New South Wales Press.

Oliver, P. (2001a). Japanese immigrant merchants and the Japanese trading company network in Sydney, 1880s to 1941. In P. Jones & P. Oliver (Eds.), *Changing histories: Australia and Japan* (pp. 1–23). Clayton, Australia: Monash Asia Institute, Monash University.

Oliver, P. (2001b). The work of D C S Sissons. In P. Jones & P. Oliver (Eds.), *Changing histories: Australia and Japan* (pp. 119–133). Clayton, Australia: Monash Asia Institute, Monash University.

Osborne, M. (1967). *Thomson, Sir Edward Deas (1800–1879)*. Canberra, Australia: Australian Dictionary of Biography, National Centre of Biography, Australian National University. Accessed from http://adb.anu.edu.au/biography/thomson-sir-edward-deas-2732/text3855 on 11 Feb 2014.

Osmond, W. (1981). *Eggleston, Sir Frederic William (1875–1954)*. Canberra, Australia: Australian Dictionary of Biography, National Centre of Biography, Australian National University. Accessed from http://adb.anu.edu.au/biography/eggleston-sir-frederic-william-344/text10409, on 27 May 2012.

Ozolins, U. (1991). National language policy and planning: Migrant languages. In S. Romaine (Ed.), *Language in Australia* (pp. 330–348). Cambridge, UK: Cambridge University Press.

Ozolins, U. (1993). *The politics of language in Australia*. Cambridge, UK: Cambridge University Press.

Pascoe, J. (1901). *History of Adelaide and vicinity*. Adelaide, Australia: Hussey & Gillingham.

Pavlyshyn, M. (Ed.). (1986). *Ukrainian settlement in Australia*. Clayton, Australia: Department of Slavic Languages, Monash University.

Bibliography

Pavlyshyn, M. (1998). How much do we know about Ukrainians in Australia? In H. Koscharsky (Ed.), *First wave emigrants: The first fifty years of Ukrainian settlement in Australia* (pp. 7–17). Huntington, NY: Nova Science Publishers.

Penington, D. (1993). Excellence, not competence, why competency-based training is inappropriate for higher education. *IPA Review, 46*(1), 26–30.

Penington, D. (2010). *Making waves: Medicine, public health, universities and beyond*. Carlton, Australia: The Miegunyah Press.

Persse, M. (1967). *Wentworth, William Charles (1790–1872)*. Canberra, Australia: Australian Dictionary of Biography, National Centre of Biography, Australian National University. Accessed from http://adb.anu.edu.au/biography/wentworth-william-charles-2782/text3961, on 11 Feb 2014.

Petrikovskaya, A. (2007). Russian and Australia: Cultural links. In A. Massov, J. McNair, & T. Poole (Eds.), *Encounters under the southern cross: Two centuries of Russian Australian relations 1807–2007* (pp. 278–304). Belair, Australia: Crawford House Publishing Australia.

Pfennigwerth, I. (2006). *A man of intelligence: The life of captain Eric nave, Australian codebreaker extraordinary*. Dural, Australia: Rosenberg Publishing.

Phillips, J. (n.d.). History of immigration, *Te Ara – The Encyclopedia of New Zealand*. Accessed from https://teara.govt.nz/en/history-of-immigration/print on 23 Feb 2018.

Phillips, A., Akbarzadeh, S., & Mathew, R. (1995). *Unlocking Australia's language potential: Profiles of languages in Australia: Volume 1 – Russian*. Canberra, Australia: The National Languages & Literacy Institute of Australia.

Piesse, E. (1926). Japan and Australia. *Foreign Affairs, 4*(3), 475–488.

Pietsch, T. (2013). *Empire of scholars: Universities, networks, and the British academic world, 1850–1939*. Manchester, UK: Manchester University Press.

Poole, T. (1992). The establishment of the first Australian diplomatic mission in the USSR: Outstanding landmark or great embarrassment? In J. McNair & T. Poole (Eds.), *Russia and the fifth continent: Aspects of Russian-Australian relations* (pp. 172–209). St Lucia, Australia: University of Queensland Press.

Poole, T. (2007). Comrades-in-arms during world war II. In A. Massov, J. McNair, & T. Poole (Eds.), *Encounters under the southern cross: Two centuries of Russian Australian relations 1807–2007* (pp. 204–230). Belair, Australia: Crawford House Publishing Australia.

Poynter, J. (2012). *Paton, Sir George Whitecross (1902–1985)*. Canberra, Australia: Australian Dictionary of Biography, National Centre of Biography, Australian National University. Accessed from http://adb.anu.edu.au/biography/paton-sir-george-whitecross-15033/text26230 on 31 Jan 2013.

Poynter, J., & Rasmussen, C. (1996). *A place apart: The University of Melbourne: Decades of challenge*. Parkville, Australia: Melbourne University Press.

Prest, J. (Ed.). (1993). *The illustrated history of Oxford University*. Oxford: Oxford University Press.

Price, C. (Ed.). (1991). *Australian national identity*. Canberra, Australia: The Academy of the Social Sciences in Australia.

Protopopov, M. (2006). *A Russian presence, a history of the Russian orthodox church in Australia*. Piscataway, NJ: Gorgias Press.

Quirke, N. (1996). *Preparing for the future – A history of Griffith University 1971–1996*. Brisbane, Australia: Boolarong Press with Griffith University.

Research Data Australia. (n.d.). *Victorian institute of secondary education*. Accessed from http://researchdata.ands.org.au/victorian-institute-of-secondary-education/145945 on 10 Oct 2014.

Rich, R. (1993). Recognition of states: The collapse of Yugoslavia and the Soviet Union. *European Journal of International Law, 4*(1), 36–65.

Rickard, J. (1996). *Australia, a cultural history* (2nd ed.). Harlow, UK: Addison Wesley Longman.

Rigby, T. (1992). Russian and soviet studies in Australian universities. In J. McNair & T. Poole (Eds.), *Russia and the fifth continent: Aspects of Russian-Australian relations* (pp. 264–292). St Lucia, Australia: University of Queensland Press.

Rix, A. (Ed.). (1988). *Intermittent diplomat: The Japan and Batavia diaries of W. Macmahon Ball*. Carlton, Australia: University Press.

Rizvi, F., & Walsh, L. (1998). Difference, globalisation and internationalisation of curriculum. *Australian Universities Review, 2*, 7–11.

Robertson, B. (2010). *The people's university: 100 years of the University of Queensland*. St Lucia, QLD: University of Queensland Press.

Rolls, E. (1992). *Sojourners: Flowers and the wide sea*. St Lucia, Australia: University of Queensland Press.

Romaine, S. (1991). Introduction. In S. Romaine (Ed.), *Language in Australia*. Cambridge, UK: Cambridge University Press.

Ryan, P. (1990). *William Macmahon ball, a memoir*. Carlton, Australia: Melbourne University Press.

Ryan, S., & Bramston, T. (2003). *The Hawke government: A critical retrospective*. North Melbourne, Australia: Pluto Press Australia.

Sagona, A. (2006). Obituary-John Bowman. *Ancient Near Eastern Studies, XLIII*, 3–6.

Samuel, R. (1959). Modern European languages. In A. Grenfell Price (Ed.), *The humanities in Australia: A survey with special reference to the universities* (pp. 139–143). Sydney, Australia: Angus & Robertson for the Australian Humanities Research Council.

Schedvin, B. (2008). *Emissaries of trade: A history of the Australian trade commissioner service*. Canberra, Australia: Austrade, Department of Foreign Affairs and Trade.

Scott, E. (1936). *A history of the University of Melbourne*. Melbourne, Australia: Melbourne University Press.

Scott, J. (1989). The open door. In W. Breen (Ed.), *Building La Trobe University* (pp. 177–184). Melbourne, Australia: La Trobe University Press.

Selleck, R. (2003). *The shop – The University of Melbourne 1850–1939*. Melbourne, Australia: Melbourne University Press.

Seneta, E. (1986). Ukrainians in Australia's censuses. In M. Pavlyshyn (Ed.), *Ukrainian settlement in Australia* (pp. 15–27). Clayton, Australia: Department of Slavic Languages, Monash University.

Shapley, M. (2008). *Korean missionaries – Bessie, Belle Menzies & Agnes Brown*. Accessed from http://womenshistory.net.au/2008/02/05/korean-missionaries-bessie-moore-belle-menzies-and-agnes-brown/ on 10 Sept 2012.

Shiel, T. (2013). *What next for universities under Abbott?* Accessed from http://theconversation.com/what-next-for-universities-under-abbott-17950 8 Nov 2013.

Singleton, G. (Ed.). (2000). *The Howard government*. Sydney, Australia: University of New South Wales Press.

Sissons, D. (1986). *Murdoch, James (1856–1921)*. Canberra, Australia: Australian Dictionary of Biography, National Centre of Biography, Australian National University. Accessed from http://adb.anu.edua.u/biography/murdoch-james-7690/text13461, on 24 Apr 2012.

Slaughter, Y. (2011). Bringing Asia to the home front: The Australian experience of Asian language education through national policy. In C. Norrby & J. Hajek (Eds.), *Uniformity and diversity in language policy: Global perspectives* (pp. 157–173). Bristol, UK: Multilingual Matters.

Smith, S. (2001). Towards diplomatic representation. In D. Goldsworthy (Ed.), *Facing north: A century of Australian engagement with Asia, Volume 1, 1901 to the 1970s* (pp. 21–60). Carlton South, Australia: Melbourne University Press Canberra: Department of Foreign Affairs and Trade.

Sneddon, J. (2003). *The Indonesian language: Its history and role in modern society*. Sydney, Australia: University of New South Wales Press.

Stefanowska, A. (1984). In memoriam: A. R. Davis 1924–1983. *Japanese Studies, 4*(1), 17–18.

Storey, W. (2004). *Writing history: A guide for students* (2nd ed.). New York: Oxford University Press.

Tavan, G. (1997). 'Good neighbours': Community organisations, migrant assimilation and Australian society and culture, 1950–1961. *Australian Historical Studies, 27*(109), 77–89.

Tavan, G. (2005). *The long slow death of White Australia*. Carlton North, Australia: Scribe Publications.
Thomis, M. (1985). *A place of light & learning – The University of Queensland's first seventy-five years*. St Lucia, Australia: University of Queensland Press.
Thomis, M. (1986). *Melbourne, Alexander Clifford Vernon (1888–1943)*. Canberra, Australia: Australian Dictionary of Biography, National Centre of Biography, Australian National University. Accessed from http://adb.anu.edu.au/biography/melbourne-alexander-clifford-vernon-7552 on 26 Aug 2011.
Tisdell, M. (1998). Socio-economic aspect of languages policies: An Australian perspective. *International Journal of Social Economics, 25*(2/3/4), 134–145.
Torney-Parlicki, P. (2001). Selling goodwill: Peter Russo and the promotion of Australia-Japan relations, 1935–1941. *Australian Journal of Politics and History, 47*(3), 349–365.
Travers, M. (1971). The first twenty-five years. *Melbourne Slavonic Studies, 5–6*, 223–231.
Travers, M. (1977). *Slavonic languages in Australia since 1958*. Sydney, Australia: Sydney University Press.
Turner, B. (1983). Outhouses of excellence: The development of the RAAF School of Languages. *Defence Force Journal*, No. 38, January/February.
Turney, C., Bygott, U., & Chippendale, P. (1991). *Australia's first. A history of the University of Sydney, Volume 1, 1850–1939*. Sydney, Australia: Hale & Iremonger.
Tweedie, S. (1994). *Trading partners: Australian and Asia 1790–1993*. Sydney, Australia: University of New South Wales Press.
UN at Glance. (n.d.). *UN official languages*. Accessed from http:www.un.org/en/aboutun/languages.shtml on 22 Jan 2013.
Universities Alliance. (n.d.). *The case for targeted supported for modern foreign language study in higher education: enhancing the economic competitiveness of the UK; maintain the strength and diversity in HE*. Accessed from http://www.unialliance.ac.uk/wp-content/uploads/2013/02/UA_Proposal_Targeted-Support-for-MFL.pdf on 22 Mar 2014.
Vamplew, W. (1987). *Australians: Historical statistics*. Broadway, Australia: Fairfax, Syme & Weldon Associates.
Victorian Arabic Social Services. (n.d.). Mission. Accessed from www.vass.org.au/about/mission/ on 5 Mar 2013.
Vinson, J. (1962). The Imperial conference of 1921 and the Anglo-Japanese alliance. *Pacific Historical Review, 31*(3), 257–266.
Wächter, B. (2003). An introduction: Internationalisation at home in context. *Journal of Studies in International Education, 7*(5), 5–11.
Walker, D. (2009). *Anxious nation* (2nd ed.). New Delhi, India: SSS Publications.
Walker, J. (1896). *Can we afford it? The Tasmanian university – Its cost and work*. Hobart, Australia: William Grahame.
Waller, L. (1995). In comparative contexts: Australia. In M. Davis (Ed.), *Teaching Jewish civilization: A global approach to higher education* (pp. 72–74). New York: New York University Press.
Walsh, M. (1993). Languages and their status in Aboriginal Australia. In M. Walsh & C. Yallop (Eds.), *Language and culture in Aboriginal Australia* (pp. 1–14). Canberra, Australia: Aboriginal Studies Press.
Waters, C. (2001). War, decolonisation and post-war security. In D. Goldsworthy (Ed.), *Facing north: A century of Australian engagement with Asia, Volume 1, 1901 to the 1970s* (pp. 97–133). Carlton South, Australia: Melbourne University Press Canberra: Department of Foreign Affairs and Trade.
Watt, A. (1967). *The evolution of Australian foreign policy 1938–1965*. Cambridge, UK: Cambridge University Press.
Wettenhall, J. (2000). Reshaping the commonwealth public sector. In G. Singleton (Ed.), *The Howard government* (pp. 65–95). Sydney, Australia: University of New South Wales Press.

White, M. (1996). *WAIT to Curtin: A history of the Western Australian institute of technology*. Bentley, Australia: Paradigm Books.

White, R. (1981). *Inventing Australia: Images and identity 1688–1980*. North Sydney, Australia: George Allen & Unwin Australia.

Wigmore, L. (1963). *The long view – A history of Canberra, Australia's national capital*. Melbourne, Australia: F. W. Cheshire.

Williams, R. (2013). System funding and institutional allocation. In G. Croucher, S. Marginson, A. Norton, & J. Wells (Eds.), *The Dawkins revolution: 25 years on* (pp. 91–107). Carlton, Australia: Melbourne University Press.

Willis, A. (1983). *The University of New South Wales: The Baxter years*. Kensington, Australia: New South Wales University Press.

Wilton, J., & Bosworth, R. (1984). *Old worlds and new Australia: The post-war migrant experience*. Ringwood, Australia: Penguin Books Australia.

Windle, K. (1998). Kevin Windle responds to Robert Dessaix and Paul Thom, *Australian Humanities Review*. Accessed from www.australianhumantiesreview.org/emuse/russian/windle.html on 15 Oct 2013.

Woodburn, S. (1983). *The founding of a university: The first decade*. (Prepared from original records in the University Archives). Adelaide, Australia: University of Adelaide.

Woolcott, R. (2003). *The hot seat: Reflections on diplomacy from Stalin's death to the Bali bombings*. Sydney, Australia: HarperCollins Publishers.

Worsley, P. (1994). *Unlocking Australia's language potential. Profiles of 9 key languages in Australia. Volume 5: Indonesian/Malay*. Canberra, Australia: The National Languages & Literacy Institute of Australia, Department of Employment, Education and Training.

Wright, D. (1992). (assisted by R. Geale). *Looking back: A history of the University of Newcastle*. Callaghan, Australia: The University of Newcastle.

Zainu'ddin, A. (1968). *A short history of Indonesia*. North Melbourne, Australia: Cassell Australia.

Zainu'ddin, A. (1988). The teaching of Japanese at Melbourne University 1919–1941. *History of Education Review, 17*(2), 46–62.

Zajda, J. (1976). Russian studies in Australia. *Babel, 12*(1), 30–32.

Zubrzycki, J. (1968). *The questing years*. Canberra, Australia: ANU Press.

Zubrzycki, J. (1991). The evolution of multiculturalism. In C. Price (Ed.), *Australian national identity* (pp. 117–138). Canberra, Australia: The Academy of the Social Sciences in Australia.

Zubrzycki, J. (1995). *The evolution of the policy of multiculturalism in Australia 1968–95*. Accessed from www.immi.gov.au/media/publications/multicultural/confer/06/speech29a.htm on 20 Mar 2012.

Printed in the United States
By Bookmasters